Decolonizing Feminism

Decolonizing Feminism

Transnational Feminism and Globalization

Edited by Margaret A. McLaren

ROWMAN &
LITTLEFIELD
INTERNATIONAL
London • New York

Published by Rowman & Littlefield International Ltd
Unit A, Whitacre Mews, 26–34 Stannary Street, London SE11 4AB
www.rowmaninternational.com
Rowman & Littlefield International Ltd. is an affiliate of Rowman & Littlefield
4501 Forbes Boulevard, Suite 200, Lanham, Maryland 20706, USA
With additional offices in Boulder, New York, Toronto (Canada), and Plymouth (UK)
www.rowman.com

British Library Cataloguing in Publication Data

A catalogue record for this book is available from the British Library

ISBN: HB 978-1-7866-0258-9
PB: 978-1-7866-0259-6

Library of Congress Cataloging-in-Publication Data Available

ISBN: 978-1-78660-258-9 (cloth : alk. paper)
ISBN: 978-1-78660-259-6 (pbk. : alk. paper)
ISBN: 978-1-78660-260-2 (electronic)

∞™ The paper used in this publication meets the minimum requirements of American National Standard for Information Sciences—Permanence of Paper for Printed Library Materials, ANSI/NISO Z39.48–1992.

Printed in the United States of America

Contents

Preface

Toward a Decolonial Feminism for the 99 Percent

Chandra Talpade Mohanty

As I write this, our understandings of feminism, decolonization, and transnationalism are in flux, contested in social movements, state policy, and social and political theory. In 2010, Jacqui Alexander and I wrote about the use of the transnational as a normativizing gesture in neoliberal times.[1] We asked then what a radical, counterhegemonic, transnational/decolonial feminism might look like. My questions are not substantially different seven years later, although the explicit exercise of power is more visible at this historical moment. In 2017, the transnational necessitates acknowledging explicitly carceral regimes; geopolitical climate destruction; militarized national borders; massive displacement of peoples (war, climate, and economic refugees); proliferation of corporatist, racist, misogynist cultures; lean-in and glass ceiling (liberal) feminisms; the decimation of labor movements, and the rise of right-wing, proto-fascist governments around the world (Modi in India, Erdovan in Turkey, Trump in the United States).

An important moment then for a book on *Decolonizing Feminism*, especially one that offers original, nuanced, and visionary feminist analysis that crosses epistemological and disciplinary borders and provides conceptual tools to decolonize hegemonic feminisms and fracture the transnational as a normativizing gesture. Organized around the central question of what it would mean to "decolonize transnational feminism" in the age of neoliberalism, feminist philosophers, and social theorists take up core transnational feminist concerns in deeply thoughtful and provocative analyses of human rights, citizenship and immigration, and dialogue/solidarities in the quest for justice and freedom. The volume consists of ten smart and provocative chapters organized around four central themes: Decolonizing Epistemologies, Methods, and Knowledges; Rethinking Rights; Citizenship and Immigration: The Space-Between; and Decolonizing Dialogue, Solidarity, and Freedom.

Margaret A. McLaren in her *Introduction* to the volume describes the questions at the core of the project: "What does it mean to decolonize feminism? How do the frameworks/approaches of decoloniality and feminism inform, enhance, contradict, and mutually influence one another? How can decolonial approaches to feminism help to navigate twenty-first-century concerns of the increasing influence of global capital and transnational corporations, repressive state forces, nationalism, xenophobia, the forced displacement of peoples and immigration, the increasing gap between the wealthy and the poor within nations, the increasing global wealth gap between nations of the global North and the global South, and the looming environmental crisis?"

These are urgent and important political and intellectual questions at this time when the rhetoric of "transnational" has been co-opted on a large scale in neoliberal university settings. Administrators are "transnational" since they travel across the globe in search of profitable partnerships with universities in other countries, and for "international" students who can pay for higher education that is no longer available to working-class and poor students in the United States. Academic curricula are also "transnational" since "study abroad" programs now buttress a normative curriculum that supposedly prepares students to compete in a global market. In the U.S. academy "transnational" often becomes a placeholder for business as usual, marked as "progressive" in the face of a conservative, xenophobic backlash. Globalization and transnational knowledge production becomes the new managerial mantra in neoliberal universities.

In addition, the larger geopolitical landscape poses urgent and significant challenges to those of us committed to an anti-capitalist, anti-imperialist, decolonial feminist praxis. While the old/new, constantly shifting political terrain of Trump and company suggests the consolidation of a white supremacist, ableist, heteropatriarchal, carceral regime with billionaire state managers, the multiple, visible, and persistent uprisings of communities in resistance is truly extraordinary. Since the inauguration of Donald Trump (less than two months ago), there have been over 150 documented demonstrations, rallies, boycotts, and strikes across the country, in small and large cities and towns. New solidarities have been forged, and feminists of all stripes and colors continue to be in leadership in most of these mobilizations. What lies ahead is the hard work of deepening and consolidating the nascent solidarities that have emerged through these mobilizations, to imagine a decolonized public polity anchored in a horizontal feminist solidarity across borders and divides. Recently (March 8, 2017), the organizers of the International Women's Strike called for a "feminism for the 99 percent," a grassroots, anti-capitalist, anti-imperialist feminism where the "idea is to mobilize women, including trans women, and all who support them in an international day of struggle—a day of striking, marching, blocking roads, bridges, and squares, abstaining from domestic, care, and sex work, boycotting, calling out misogynistic politicians and companies, and striking in educational institutions. These actions are aimed at making visible the needs and aspirations of those whom lean-in feminism ignored: women in the formal labor market, women working in the sphere of social reproduction and care, and unemployed and precarious working women."[2]

The challenge now, post–March 8, 2017, is how to connect this vision of feminism for the 99 percent to the material praxis of the diverse, gendered, and racialized communities of women (cis and trans) across the spectrum of class, sexuality, ability, and citizenship status. Operationalizing such a vision requires deep and innovative thinking and praxis around questions of decoloniality, transnational feminism, and solidarity, and it is just this kind of thinking that is evident in the pages of this volume. *Decolonizing Feminism* offers deeply thoughtful analyses on questions of justice and freedom—theoretical and methodological constructs that can help us envision and consolidate a decolonial feminism for the 99 percent! Thus, for instance, unlike the superficial debates on the left around "identity politics," Linda Martín Alcoff analyzes how "categories of social identity are effects of history and refer back to the narrativized experiences of group-related events such as migrations, enslavement, conquest, and war," and thus, changing identities "requires changing the world." And Gaile Pohlhaus Jr. encourages us to undertake a project of "epistemic gathering" so that we can decolonize our inherited privileges and struggle collectively "on the ground" with marginalized, nondominant communities of women shifting the dominant questions of Euro-American feminist philosophy: "Who knows/whose knowledge?" to questions like "with whom am I knowing?" and "how does my knowing make possible or undermine the practice of solidarity with other women?" Epistemic gathering then can become a methodology for horizontal dialogue and solidarity in the context of unequal power relations among communities of women.

Similarly, Barbara Fultner extends our understandings of cross-cultural dialogue and solidarity by examining the conditions for the realization of a meaningful transnational feminist dialogue. Fultner draws on Gadamer's notion of horizon wherein one's location or standpoint determines visibility that is both limited *and* changeable to theorize cultures as expansive, hence suggesting the possibility of transnational dialogue across cultures as sources of new forms of solidarity. Kelly Oliver's exploration of the "plight of women refugees" offers an original and nuanced analysis of the contradictions of the material realities of migrants, refugees, and asylum seekers who unsettle the Indigenous/settler opposition that anchors studies of settler colonialism. Arguing that refugee women are neither Indigenous nor settlers (since they cannot be defined in terms of national group identity), Oliver challenges us to rethink the notion of national sovereignty that underlies the construct of "transnational," arguing that the militarized carceral humanitarianism and rescue politics that frame our thinking about women refugees is profoundly problematic. Oliver suggests that "national borders and international conventions governing asylum seekers create the refugee. Moreover they create her as destitute, criminal, and mentally ill." Refugees, Oliver demonstrates, are put in an impossible conundrum since they must "prove both their radical victimization and their own sovereignty." Thus, neither the carceral model nor the charity model is an adequate framework in acknowledging the agency and material realities of refugee women at this time. Allison Weir's chapter adds another dimension to the volume's unsettling of normative analytic categories (hence decolonizing feminism), drawing on Indigenous feminisms to challenge the secularity of mainstream feminism. Weir examines the centrality of land and constructs of freedom as anchored in a profoundly relational understanding of the self for Indigenous feminists. Thus, she argues, taking Indigenous feminist understandings of freedom as relational (connected to land, sovereignty, and spirituality) directly challenges "western secular ontologies, epistemologies, and understandings of freedom." Arguing that "indigenous philosophy offers a conception of freedom that includes heterogeneity and change while maintaining rootedness in relation to land," Weir calls on feminists to reframe questions of "individual freedom and politics of sovereignty within a theory and politics of relationality."

Alcoff's materialist notion of identity as historically and contextually specific, coupled with a notion of changeability (changing identity requires changing the world), Pohlhaus's notion of "epistemic gathering" as a way of shifting focus from the "I" to the "we," in asking questions about knowing, Fultner's call for creating the conditions for meaningful dialogue by understanding standpoints as horizons rather than schema, Oliver's challenge to rethink the transnational outside the bounds of the nation by centering the epistemological location of women refugees, and Weir's practice of deep listening as a settler feminist to Indigenous feminist understandings of freedom as profoundly relational, linked to questions of land, sovereignty, and spirituality are just a few of the analytic gems to be mined in this volume.

Taken together, these ten chapters demonstrate decolonizing feminism at its best. Here are theoretical and methodological innovations that can be mobilized to imagine what it would mean to theorize a feminism for the 99 percent—a feminism that is inclusive, dialogic, decolonial, and capable of envisioning expansive horizons of solidarity across gender, class, sexuality, nation, ability, race, and citizenship status. This is a book that belongs on the bookshelves of all feminists and social justice scholar/activists working to confront power and domination in all its incarnations, especially those of us who think a new world is possible, and are committed to an ethical praxis of solidarity across borders.

NOTES

1. Chandra Talpade Mohanty and M. Jacqui Alexander, "Cartographies of Knowledge and Power: Transnational Feminism as Racial Praxis," in *Critical Transnational Feminist Praxis* (Albany: SUNY Press, 2010).

2. https://www.theguardian.com/commentisfree/2017/feb/21/womens-day-strike-march-8-donald-trump.

Introduction

Decolonizing Feminism

Margaret A. McLaren

What does it mean to decolonize transnational feminist theory in the context of globalization? As a project concerned with multiple power structures, feminist theory must address the historical legacies of colonialism, postcolonialism, and more recently, decoloniality. This book offers chapters organized around a coherent set of research questions about how to conceptualize an inclusive feminist politics. This has been, and continues to be, a central project in feminist theory, particularly in light of neoliberal globalization.[1]

Chandra Talpade Mohanty has called for an inclusive feminist politics that would be decolonizing and anti-capitalist and would allow for solidarity. In a time of globalization, what would this entail? Focusing on the issue of decolonizing feminism, this volume takes up a range of important questions: Which methodologies promote a decolonized transnational feminism? How is decolonization enacted in specific locations and projects? Are the visions of a global feminism and transnational feminism compatible? Is the human rights approach the best way for feminists to improve women's well-being in the twenty-first century? How do social locations/positionalities/identities influence proposed strategies for achieving global gender justice? What are some possible interfaces between the local and the global? What strategies of resistance work against the force of neoliberal globalization? How do we (feminists) create networks of solidarity transnationally?

The authors in this volume engage with these questions in a variety of ways from a range of perspectives, traditions, and disciplinary backgrounds. Our hope is to contribute to the ongoing project of advocating a decolonizing feminist approach to pressing social issues. We offer original analyses and some methodological suggestions, while opening up space for creative and innovative ways to address gender and social justice issues. This book is divided into four parts, with each part focusing on a main theme:

Part One: Decolonizing Epistemologies, Methods, and Knowledges: Feminist philosophy engages in the project of attempting to elaborate general and abstract conceptions of gender and identity, but this theoretical articulation often obscures important differences among local, cultural understandings of these ideas. In response, what is called for is a decolonizing feminist philosophy. Among other things, such a philosophy requires taking into account intersectionality as part of its methodology in a way that leaves open both the meaning and value of gender. A decolonizing feminist philosophy also calls for further rethinking of our concept of knowledge in a way that challenges the assumed individualism of knowledge, but, instead, allows for "knowing across borders" and includes the ways that knowledge is constructed, including its basis in material labor and bodily practices.

Part Two: Rethinking Rights: Similarly, the framework of human rights as a tool and strategy for feminists needs to be rethought, both in terms of whether and how it has benefited feminists engaged in struggles for global justice, including Indigenous women activists, and in terms of the theoretical roots of universal human rights discourse. Again, the individualist presuppositions of the human rights framework are critically examined in relation to the struggles of collective social movements. Additionally, this priority of the individual obscures the background situation that these collective social movements are struggling against: the nexus of neoliberal states and powerful corporate interests. Thus the discourse of human rights functions ambivalently: it is both an important liberatory strategy and a possible impediment to new, innovative ways of conceptualizing women's issues and social justice struggles.

Part Three: Citizenship and Immigration: The Space Between: Prominent liberal, democratic conceptions of citizenship, including feminist ones, such as Benhabib's, remain Western and Eurocentric and stand in need of decolonizing. By focusing on the experiences of (im)migrant women—be they immigrant women providing essential care to Europeans, Filipina-American immigrants (re)constructing (notions of) home, or increasingly and disproportionately vulnerable women refugees—it is possible to develop decolonizing models of citizenship, belonging, and of, "in-between" spaces. From such multivalent places, practices of belonging and solidarity can emerge.

Part Four: Decolonizing Dialogue, Solidarity, and Freedom: In order to build a decolonized transnational feminist solidarity, feminists continue to wrestle with questions such as the following. How to engage in dialogue? How to act in solidarity with one another across difference? And what constitutes freedom? Decolonizing dialogue is bound to be sensitive to how concepts cross borders and it needs to be transformative. These processes are exemplified by a number of transnational feminist networks, including Indigenous ones. Finally, Indigenous women's knowledges contribute to and transform conceptions of freedom from traditional Western notions of freedom as, "freedom to act without constraint," into decolonized notions of freedom as, "acting in harmony with creation."

DECOLONIZING FEMINISM

These essays emerge out of a specific historical moment and context in the world, and in feminist theoretical and activist work. While earlier feminist scholarship explored the meaning of global feminism and transnational feminism, this collection centers on the questions and issues surrounding feminism and decoloniality. What does it mean to decolonize feminism? How do the frameworks/approaches of decoloniality and feminism inform, enhance, contradict, and mutually influence one another? How can decolonial approaches to feminism help to navigate twenty-first century concerns of the increasing influence of global capital and transnational corporations, repressive state forces, nationalism, xenophobia, the forced displacement of peoples and immigration, the increasing gap between the wealthy and the poor within nations, the increasing global wealth gap between nations of the global North and the global South, and the looming environmental crisis?

Decoloniality, like transnational feminism, has multiple meanings and sources.[2] Some scholars associate the term with Latin American scholar Anibal Quijano, who argues that the coloniality of power is intimately linked to the creation of races and the racialization of labor under global capitalism; his account focuses on the colonial conquest of the Americas. Quijano argues that the coloniality of power has to do with global capitalism and the creation of race/racial dominance that attended the colonization of the "new world"/ Americas. Moreover, he claims that race and the division of labor are structurally linked and mutually reinforcing.[3] While Quijano's analysis breaks new ground, he pays little attention to gender. María Lugones criticizes his lack of attention to gender and extends the idea of coloniality of power to include gender relations as well as race relations and capitalism, and their intersection.[4] Indigenous theorists and settler-colonial scholars associate decoloniality primarily with the challenges by Indigenous peoples to white settler colonialism.[5] Rita Dhamoon's incisive article, "A Feminist Approach to Decolonizing Anti-racism: Rethinking Transnationalism, Intersectionality, and Settler Colonialism," provides an excellent analysis of some of the issues that arise when feminist approaches are not attentive to the unique and specific impacts of settler colonialism and Indigenous dispossession. A third touchpoint for decolonizing approaches has been the work of feminists of color, specifically Chandra Talpade Mohanty, who in *Feminism without Borders: Decolonizing Theory, Practicing Solidarity* calls on feminists to adopt a decolonizing approach, which is also anti-racist, and anti-capitalist.[6] Mohanty articulates a positive feminist vision of a "world that is pro-sex and [pro]-women, a world where women and men are free to lead creative lives, in security and with bodily health and integrity, where they are free to choose who they love, and whom they set up house with, and whether they want to have or not have children . . . a vision in which economic stability, ecological sustainability, racial equality, and the redistribution of wealth form the basis of peoples well-being."[7] In order to achieve this vision, "everyday feminist, antiracist, anticapitalist practices are as important as larger, organized political movements."[8]

Common threads running through all three of these articulations of decoloniality/decolonizing are attention to both micro- and macro-political structures; a sense of historical consciousness and specificity; a commitment to liberatory practices and values; and an awareness of the effects of colonization not only as political, historical, and economic forces but also as effects on consciousness, theories, research practices, epistemological frameworks, and ways of knowing. Each thread contributes to the overall understanding of decolonization. In what follows, I briefly explore these different sources and approaches to decoloniality: Latin American, Indigenous feminist, and non-Indigenous feminist of color.

In "Coloniality of Power, Eurocentrism, and Latin America," Anibal Quijano discusses the interconnections among capitalism, colonialism, and racial domination. His account shows the intimate linkages between expansionist capitalism, colonization, and the creation of racial dominance. Significantly, this account demonstrates the historical contingency of racial dominance through the creation of races as justification for exploitative labor practices. Quijano articulates the structural connections and interdependence among capitalism, colonization, and the creation of racial divisions and domination, which produced a source of cheap labor. As he notes, "a new technology of domination/exploitation, in this case race/labor, was articulated in such a way that the two seemed naturally associated."[9] With the expansion of global capitalism through colonization, unpaid labor was assigned to, and subsequently associated with, the colonial races, that is, those who were dominated through colonization. This "new world order" creates a "new geography of power."[10] Quijano traces the historical emergence of global capitalism as it arose through colonization; his analysis highlights the inseparability of racial categories and the division of labor necessary for global capitalism. It is worth noting that U.S. feminist of color Audre Lorde also observes that Western European history constructs differences as simplistic oppositions, and as hierarchical. In an interesting parallel to Quijano's articulation of global capital as founded upon a racial division of labor, Lorde states, "In a society where the good is defined in terms of profit rather than in terms of human need, there must always be some group of people who, through systematized oppression, can be made to feel surplus, to occupy the place of the dehumanized inferior."[11] Note that Lorde's formulation leaves open an analysis that looks at both gendered and racialized divisions of labor.

Quijano claims that the modern world system enforced three elements that affected the everyday lives of individuals in societies across the globe: the coloniality of power, capitalism, and Eurocentrism. Moreover, these elements of power are expressed through social institutions that have become dominant since Modernity: the nation-state, the bourgeoisie family, the capitalist corporation, and Eurocentric rationality.[12] For Quijano, the expansionist imperialism of Europe during colonization also promoted a specific worldview: Eurocentrism. Eurocentric rationality results in a Eurocentrism that is a specific rationality or perspective of knowledge that was made globally hegemonic, colonizing, and overcoming other previous or different formations and their respective concrete knowledges; this includes a secularization of knowledge and the centralization of European colonial power. The process and perspective of Eurocentrism is not only about the imposition of Western, European, Enlightenment capitalism on the colonized world but also happens within Europe when hegemonic, dominant rationality and perspectives supplant minority, Indigenous, and socially marginalized peoples and perspectives. Eurocentrism also homogenized and homogenizes differences among distinct groups. For example, the Aztecs, and Mayans, became Indians, and the distinct African tribes of the Yoruba, Azande, and so on became Africans, and then Blacks.[13]

Quijano's analysis provides important resources for a decolonizing perspective, namely the coloniality of power and a clear articulation of Eurocentrism. As María Lugones points out, however, his theory lacks a gender analysis and a feminist perspective. Lugones draws upon and extends Quijano's work to develop what she calls the "colonial/modern gender system."[14] She challenges Quijano's uncritical acceptance of the hegemonic understanding of gender; she says this understanding is too narrow; it is patriarchal and heterosexist/heteronormative. Lugones points out that gender (at least the hegemonic conception that Quijano employs), like race, has its origins in modernity. She notes that

> "coloniality" does not just refer to "racial" classification. It is an encompassing phenomenon, since it is one of the axes of the system of power and as such it permeates all control of sexual access, collective authority, labor, subjectivity/inter-subjectivity and the production of knowledge from within these inter-subjective relations. Or, alternatively, all control over sex, subjectivity, authority and labor are articulated around it.[15]

In this way, Lugones complicates Quijano's analysis by questioning what he sees as a "basic area of existence" (sex, its resources, and its products). She convincingly argues that Quijano leaves unproblematized conventional, modern notions of gender and concepts such as sexual dimorphism, heterosexuality, and the patriarchal distribution of power. Lugones points out that even the patriarchal distribution of power cannot be taken for granted in a feminist analysis. She uses Oyeronke Oyewumi's example that patriarchy should not be thought of as a valid transcultural category because gender was not an organizing principle in Yoruba society prior to colonization by the West. Lugones's challenge to Quijano's uncritical deployment of a hegemonic conception of gender adds an important element to his rich and detailed historical analysis of the emergence of global capitalism and its structural connection with the creation of racial categories that ensured that global capital had access to exploitable labor. This analysis of the colonization of the Americas includes discussions of the impact on Indigenous peoples but does not make this central to the analysis. For this, we need to look at Indigenous philosophies.

Many Indigenous theorists and settler-colonial theorists associate decoloniality primarily with the challenges by Indigenous peoples to white settler colonialism. Indigenous knowledges have long been suppressed, devalued, neglected, and dismissed by white, European, non-Indigenous peoples. Along with the occupation and conquest of their land by white settlers, Indigenous peoples have endured and continue to endure, disproportionate levels of violence, both physical and epistemic.

Indigenous political theorists, including Taiaike Alfred, Glen Coulthard, Leanne Simpson, Aileen Moreton-Robinson, Audra Simpson, and Andrea Smith, theorize resistance to the continuing colonization of Indigenous peoples within settler states and challenge the legitimacy of those states. Many argue for a politics of Indigenous "resurgence," drawing on Indigenous relationships to land and revaluing Indigenous traditions and knowledges as sources of resistance and transformation. While they are critical of state sovereignty, many argue for alternative forms of sovereignty grounded in Indigenous law. Here they draw on the work of Indigenous philosophers including Vine Deloria and Viola Cordova, who have critiqued Western philosophy and policy from Indigenous perspectives and who have argued for the specificity of Indigenous philosophy and knowledges.[16]

Other Indigenous theorists focus on methodological and epistemic violence. In her book, *Decolonizing Methodologies: Research and Indigenous Peoples*, Linda Tuhiwai Smith discusses the history of imperialism and the ways that imperialism, and its asymmetrical power relations, carries over into research, theorizing, and epistemology. She criticizes the methodologies of anthropologists who have treated Indigenous peoples as objects of knowledge and outlines research methodologies that draw on Indigenous knowledges.

Drawing from the work of Indigenous theorists, settler-colonial theorists including Patrick Wolfe, Lorenzo Verancini, and Nira Yuval-Davis distinguish colonial from settler-colonial domination, arguing that while colonialism aims at the permanent domination of the colonized Other, settler colonialism aims at erasure, effectively repressing, co-opting, and extinguishing Indigenous alterities, through policies of genocide and assimilation.

Indigenous feminist approaches interrupt some of the dominant notions in feminist theory, rethinking the essentialist–anti-essentialist divide and retheorizing feminist politics in relation to struggles for Indigenous resurgence and sovereignty.

The decolonial turn in feminism can be traced back to early anthologies such as *Third World Women and the Politics of Feminism* and *Decentering the Center: Philosophy for a Multicultural, Postcolonial, and Feminist World* that challenged not only the identity politics of feminism as a white, liberal enterprise but also the epistemological frameworks employed by feminists, and the representation of the "Other" in feminist work.[17] One of the earliest significant challenges to feminist conceptualizing of the Other was raised by Chandra Talpade Mohanty in her now classic essay, "Under Western Eyes: Feminist Scholarship and Colonial Discourses."

Aiming to "discover and articulate a critique of 'Western feminist' scholarship on Third World women via the discursive colonization of Third World women's lives and struggles," Mohanty revealed how the power structures in research and writing within academia often replicated the asymmetrical and dominating power structures in the larger sociopolitical context.[18] It has now been more than three decades since "Under Western Eyes" was published, and it has been taken up in a variety of ways and contexts, both critically and productively. According to Mohanty: "The uses and translations of my work as it is embodied in particular sites, communities, and feminist projects illustrates both the productive adaptations of decolonizing antiracist feminist thought and the pitfalls of the convergence of postmodernist feminism and neoliberal logics in the academy. . . . The circulation of ["Under Western Eyes" and "Under Western Eyes Revisited"] in various geopolitical locales reveals feminist complicity in imperial and capitalist/neoliberal projects and points to the limitations of knowledge-making projects in academia."[19]

One significant misreading of Mohanty's work is to label it postmodernist, and, further to equate a postmodern perspective with relativism.[20] Although she points out the pervasiveness of power in a Foucauldian sense, pervasive power and the recognition of limited and partial perspectives and approaches do not necessarily lapse into relativism. In fact, Mohanty is quite clear that feminist liberatory struggles require normative commitments, specifically, an anti-racist, anti-capitalist, decolonizing approach. As Quijano argues, racism and global capitalism are interdependent and are linked to colonization of knowledges as well. Decolonial approaches are grounded in historical, material conditions; they must attend to the complexity and richness of diversity of experiences and identities without decontextualizing those identities from the processes of domination and subordination and exploitation that create and maintain identities as social locations in a matrix of unequal power relations. And, finally decolonial approaches reveal the power relations implicit in knowledge making and theorizing.

Decoloniality or a decolonizing approach challenges mainstream, hegemonic, dominant theories of knowledge, language, power, and politics. It differs from postcolonialism because it unsettles the concept of colonialism in the first place; whereas postcolonialism is the "after" of colonization, decoloniality is the liberation from colonial structures, including values, methods, and knowledges. But decolonizing does not remain, nor indeed is it primarily at the theoretical and epistemological level. It is an active, ongoing struggle for social justice in every sense—economic, political, cultural, racial, gender, and so forth—at every level in every arena. Decolonization offers the possibility of new, creative, and innovative approaches to contemporary problems. As Kanchana Mahadevan says, "Decolonization is not just a withdrawal from Empire, but an active grassroots movement at the social, economic, cultural and political levels initiating alternate cultures and solidarities" (this volume).

CHAPTER SUMMARIES

Part One, "Decolonizing Epistemologies, Methods, and Knowledges," sets the context for the subsequent parts of the book. In this section, the authors ask us to rethink the very means and methods by which we approach feminist philosophy and ways of knowing. In chapter 1, "Decolonizing Feminist Philosophy," Linda Martín Alcoff suggests that the polarized views of deconstructionists and those who present gender as a singular category unmediated by race, ethnicity, nationality, religion, class status, culture, ability, and sexuality share a mistaken commitment to universalism. Alcoff argues that one strand of U.S. feminist philosophy has followed de Beauvoir in asserting that one is not born, but rather becomes a woman. These feminist philosophers who view gender as a socially constructed category, such as Judith Butler and Sally Haslanger, see gender as an effect of oppression and believe that liberation then involves resisting the identitarian logic of gender classification. Feminists who advocate social construction of gender attempt to propose an alternative to the false universalism of conceiving women as a unitary category, by stressing the fluidity, variance, and fictive nature of gender categories themselves. However, Alcoff counters that social constructionist feminists err in a similar way to those who purport a generalized, universalizing view of women, and the category woman. Both those who abstract from material, social, political, historical differences among women by using the category "women" as a universal and those who seek to trouble the category of gender by showing its roots in oppressive forces, and highlighting the damage that an abstract, universal category of women can do, ultimately make the same mistake: false universalization. As Alcoff says, "The deconstruction of gender is not made as a contextually specific argument that accounts for specific historical and cultural contexts where concepts of difference emerge, but as an argument that ranges over all contexts, synchronically and diachronically, encompassing all of humanity." Alcoff makes a persuasive argument that countering a universalist conception of gender with a deconstructionist view employs a similar methodology and does little to decolonize feminist philosophy. She proposes a new approach: in her words, "Decolonizing feminist philosophy requires being prepared to do philosophy differently. I have argued this involves challenging universalist deconstructionist agendas, but also universal conceptualizations of gender and gender related forms of oppression" (this volume).

Continuing the theme of challenging universalist methods, practices, and ways of knowing, in chapter 2, Gaile Pohlhaus Jr. discusses knowing without borders. She provides an insightful reading of Mohanty's *Feminism without Borders*, drawing out and making explicit what the work of knowing without borders means and how it can be implemented. To this end, she proposes a decolonizing and democratic process of knowledge making, knowledge production, which she calls "the work of epistemic gathering." Significantly, the work of epistemic gathering accounts for the materiality of bodies and their being in the world. She draws on Sara Ahmed's work to show how the materiality of the body orients us to the world in specific ways, depending on the particular features of our material embodiment. Importantly, as Pohlhaus points out, knowledge and knowledge production have effects in the world. Thus, we are responsible for the ways that our methods of knowledge production may exclude others or render their resistance to oppression and domination unintelligible. Feminists concerned with decolonizing and democratizing knowledge must realize that knowledge production is not individual but collective, not isolated but occurs in specific contexts, and not abstract but embodied and material. Pohlhaus concludes by suggesting a shift in the types of questions that we ask:

> Rather than asking: "who knows?" or "whose knowledge?" (which have been galvanizing questions within Euro-American philosophical feminism) we might begin to ask instead "with whom am I knowing?" "at whose expense might this

> knowing be made possible?" "what does my knowing here at this time and in this place do?" and finally "how does my knowing make possible or undermine the practicing of solidarity with other women?" (this volume)

Shifting from methodological and epistemological to political concerns, Part Two, "Rethinking Rights" examines how and if human rights can further the project of decolonizing feminist theory and practice. Human rights have been the dominant paradigm for transnational politics (including feminist transnational political work) in the twentieth century. The popular slogan, "Women's rights are human rights," attests to the widespread endorsement of mobilizing the discourse of human rights to promote women's equality and inclusion globally. Human rights have been promoted as the most efficacious and practical manner of achieving gender equity transnationally. Here, however, the concept and efficacy of universal human rights come under scrutiny. The chapters in this section raise challenges to simply accepting the prevalence and dominance of human rights as the best method for feminist transnational solidarity and activism.

In chapter 4, Margaret A. McLaren provides a brief overview of the women's rights as human rights movement, assessing both its accomplishments and its drawbacks. She notes the ways in which rights discourse functions ambivalently, opening up new possibilities while shutting down others. The limits to rights discourse, she argues, are both practical and theoretical. In a practical sense, the history of the way that rights has been taken up in international bodies and much of Western transnational feminism focuses on legal and political rights, and splits these off from economic and social rights. She then takes up the question: Can the discourse and practice of rights be expanded to include, and even prioritize, economic and social rights? While broadening rights in this way may address some of the pragmatic considerations of the ways that rights discourse has been used to promote women's equality, it does not fully address the theoretical limitations of such discourses.

Focusing on both the strengths of rights theory and its weaknesses, McLaren points out that the specific history of rights discourse as it has been utilized in transnational contexts to promote women's equality has its roots in the Western, European, Enlightenment tradition, and is thus deeply implicated in colonialism. Considering claims by those who advocate and those who challenge the dominant paradigm of rights discourse and practice, McLaren explores questions such as, Must rights be abandoned? Or can they be reformulated to provide an integrated approach to social justice that would include the material conditions of social and economic justice that are necessary to exercise one's political and legal rights? Does an integrated approach to rights overcome the theoretical limitations of exclusion, inclusion, and integration? Does the framework of rights carry too much conceptual baggage, not only from the Western, European, Enlightenment tradition but also the correlative concepts of property, individualism, and "negative freedom"? These questions resonate with issues raised in other chapters. For example, in chapter 5, Mahadevan discusses the processes of inclusion, exclusion, and citizenship in European democracies by looking at the ways that democratic theory functions to both assimilate and marginalize women migrants by denying them citizenship while depending on their care work. And in chapter 10, Weir shows how Indigenous concepts of relationality, community, and land produce new conceptions of freedom as relational, rather than the freedom from interference by others, which is the dominant conception in Western political theory.

In chapter 3, Pascha Bueno-Hansen and Sylvanna M. Falcón discuss the limits of human rights awards. Looking at the lives and experiences of two different Indigenous/campesina women leaders and activists from Latin America, Berta Cáceres, a Lenca woman from Honduras, and Máxima Acuña Chaupe, a Quechua-speaking campesina woman from Peru, they argue that human rights awards must be understood against the background and context of neoliberalism and transnational corporate interests. In their chapter, Bueno-Hansen and Falcón raise the issue of how to practice transnational feminist solidarity, particularly when situated in the global North. They offer this important guideline for actors from or located in the global North: "In situations where global North actors initiate solidarity, we emphasize accountability to historical and systemic geopolitical power dynamics." The stories of Cáceres and Acuña help to illuminate some of the complex dynamics of practicing feminist solidarity across national borders, specifically solidarity with Indigenous leaders, struggles, and communities working "to defend their land, water, communities and lifeways" against global corporate interests, foreign investment, and megaprojects, such as large dams and extractive mining. From a close engagement with the lives, stories, and struggles of Cáceres and Acuña, authors Bueno-Hansen and Falcón draw three significant lessons for practicing transnational feminist solidarity: First, honor the spirit and pluralism of activists' consciousness; for Indigenous activists such as Cáceres and Acuña, this will mean respecting their "cosmovision—a philosophical vision of and consciousness about the world that embraces a loving and non-hierarchical coexistence with all beings." The second lesson illuminates some of the complexities of transnational feminist solidarity; they note that human rights prize-giving practices highlight individuals rather than the collective movement and that there are complex power dynamics involved in these prize-giving practices. The third lesson involves using Chandra Talpade Mohanty's "cartographies of struggle" as a methodology to map the struggles of Indigenous communities in Latin America against the background of neoliberal containment "against what Cáceres refers to as 'rapacious capitalism' and what Acuña refers to as corporate greed." Using Mohanty's cartographies of struggle brings to the foreground the power dynamics of the neoliberal state combined with global corporate interests that form the systemic inequalities of the terrain on which these struggles are waged.

In Part Three, "Citizenship and Immigration: The Space Between," the authors explore the limits of rights further in their discussions of citizenship, migration, and immigration and the special plight of women refugees. In chapter 5, Kanchana Mahadevan uses critical theory (Habermas and Benhabib) to examine issues of citizenship and inclusion. Drawing on Habermas's model of full democratic inclusion as "constitutional patriotism," for which he uses the European Union (EU) as the paradigmatic case, Mahadevan notes a lacuna in his theory because of his inattention to women and gender. Turning to Benhabib (who does include a gender analysis) Mahadevan finds that her proposal for full democratic inclusion is also lacking. Mahadevan argues that although Benhabib discusses women's particular position in a multicultural deliberative democracy, her cosmopolitan conception of citizenship remains Eurocentric. Mahadevan proposes to redress this by focusing on a crucial phenomenon in contemporary global capitalism: women migrants' position in the global care chain. Mahadevan points out that we must look at the specific position of women immigrants in the EU, and she aptly notes that many of these women immigrants perform care work, such as childcare, elder care, household cleaning, cooking, and other domestic duties. Thus, the ideal model of full democratic inclusion in a deliberative democracy such as the EU is, in fact, parasitic on the work of migrant women's care labor. Although immigrant women are necessary to the smooth functioning of Europe's welfare systems, social programs, and social democracies, they themselves do not have the status of citizens. Mahadevan shows the importance of not only looking at women's position within deliberative democracies but also connecting global care chains with processes of democratic inclusion and exclusion.

Celia T. Bardwell-Jones explores another facet of the issue of women and migration in chapter 6. Working with Espiritu's notion of "home-making" and María Lugones's idea of "world-traveling," Bardwell-Jones maps out what she calls the "space-between" in transnational feminist thought. She discusses feminist views of "home," for feminists' home has very different meanings, some are suspicious of the concept of home and associate it with a false sense of safety and security, while others see home as a place of comfort and belonging.[21] Focusing on Filipina migrants—who often carry a dual sense of home, both their country of origin and their new place of residence—Bardwell-Jones incorporates the ideas of world-traveling with home-making and shows how it is possible to have a dual sense of home that draws upon multiple meanings and spans cultures, identities, and practices. Rather than seeing this new sense of home as liminal or decentered, she argues that it creates a new space of possibility—the "space-between." From this "space-between," new possibilities for productive transnational dialogue and feminist solidarity emerge.

In chapter 7, Kelly Oliver examines "the special plight of women refugees." Her chapter looks specifically at issues of violence against women, to which female refugees are particularly vulnerable. Women suffer disproportionately during times of crisis or emergency; they are more vulnerable to violence, particularly sexual violence. For women refugees this vulnerability to violence of all sorts is exacerbated by their precarious status: they lack citizenship status and they are held in camps that inhibit their freedom of mobility. Moreover, these refugee camps often subject them to substandard living conditions. This lack of basic necessities such as food, clean water, adequate shelter, and access to health resources affects women disproportionately because they are usually responsible for caring for the children and meeting the family's daily basic needs. Additionally, the lack of adequate health care has specific effects on women because they need specialized ob-gyn care, especially during and immediately after pregnancy. Oliver points out that global forced displacement is at an all-time high and around 50 percent of those forcibly displaced are female. Moreover, of this large number of refugees that are female, 51 percent are eighteen years old or under. These younger women are particularly vulnerable to sexual violence, abuse, and exploitation. In the recent wave of forced migration from Syria, 70,000 women were pregnant when they fled, meaning they will likely give birth while living in refugee camps. Refugee camps have very high infant and maternal mortality rates. And, depending on the laws in the nation they are born in, these children may remain "stateless." Oliver decries what she calls, "carceral humanitarianism and rescue politics," and she urges us to rethink how the categories of human, humanitarianism, and human rights are used. Along with Hannah Arendt, Giorgio Agamben, and Jacques Derrida, she challenges the abstract concepts of "humans" and "humanity," noting, with them, that the abstraction involved in these concepts can even be an alibi for genocide. Ultimately Oliver agrees with Arendt that "the right to have rights" is primary in order for women refugees to have access to resources, protection from violence, including gender-based and sexual violence, and to enforce fair and equal treatment.

The final part, Part Four, "Decolonizing Dialogue, Solidarity, and Freedom," develops accounts of decolonized feminist dialogue, solidarity, and freedom. In chapter 8, "The Dynamics of Transnational Feminist Dialogue," Barbara Fultner draws on Gadamer's idea of open horizons to demonstrate that culturalistic explanations are mistaken about the very nature of culture and often foreclose rather than invite dialogue and engagement with difference. Cultural relativists tend to see culture as bounded, isolated, and static, whereas in reality cultures are porous, dynamic, overlapping, and interpenetrating. Fultner convincingly argues that culture as a system of meaning can still have a place in philosophical accounts without lapsing into relativism, subjectivism, or determinism. Rather than engaging in the large-scale and sometimes pernicious philosophical debates around relativism, she focuses specifically on transcultural, transnational feminist dialogue. As transformative practice, such dialogue does not require complete agreement among interlocutors. Rather, it transforms them and their differences and thus can be a dynamic means for bringing about political change. At the same time, Fultner's model of transnational feminist dialogue foregrounds the notion of accountability. Elaborating Habermas's formal-pragmatic account, she argues that accountability needs to be articulated not merely in reference to truth, normative legitimacy, and sincerity or authenticity. Rather, its parameters need to be expanded to include epistemic responsibility, vulnerability, power and privilege, embodiment, and solidarity. With this expansion of the theory of communicative action, transnational feminist dialogue can emerge as a tool of decolonization. As many feminists have noted, including Chandra Talpade Mohanty, transnational feminism is not served well by relativism because feminism itself involves normative commitments. (However, just which set of normative commitments is continually open for debate.) By acknowledging the importance of culture, but viewing it as porous, not bounded, Fultner carves out a middle ground between approaches that overemphasize culture and those that ignore it. By doing so, she establishes that productive dialogue among feminists need not overlook or ignore cultural, or other, differences while we address the range of issues that affect all of us, including large-scale economic institutions. This bodes well for the possibilities of a decolonizing feminist transcultural, transnational dialogue.

Indeed, decolonizing feminist transcultural and transnational dialogues is an important aspect of "Building Transnational Feminist Solidarity Networks," which Sergio A. Gallegos takes up in chapter 9. Gallegos identifies two major trends in the scholarship around feminist transnational solidarity and activist networks. One trend maintains that transnational feminist solidarity is akin to social movements, such as peace and justice movements, or the environmental movement. This group of scholars holds that transnational feminist solidarity is goal based, like social movements. The other trend in feminist scholarship that Gallegos identifies claims that feminist solidarity relies on a shared social location, a politics of location that may be shared more or less among women from specific contexts; feminist scholars who articulate this position hold an identity-based, rather than goal-based model of solidarity. Gallegos articulates both of these approaches and ultimately argues that these two approaches to transnational feminist solidarity—

goal-based versus identity-based—are, in fact, complementary and mutually reinforcing. He illustrates this by looking at two organizations that have successfully developed transnational feminist networks: *Frente Indígena de Organizaciones Binacionales*, created by Indigenous Mexican women, and the *Red Latinoamericana de Mujeres transformando la Economia* (REMTE), a Latin American transnational feminist network. Building on Nira Yuval Davis's conception of "transversal politics," Gallegos shows how these transnational networks can form new alliances to one another around both issues and identities. For example, REMTE developed a collective identity as "anti-capitalist Latin American feminists," and this understanding of themselves allowed them to forge connections with the LGBT organization South-South dialogue. Transnational feminist solidarity, Gallegos argues, requires a commitment to transversal politics, which enables feminists to work together from a variety of identities and perspectives against oppressive structures and toward a decolonized feminist solidarity.

Once we have developed new understandings of dialogue and solidarity, other central philosophical concepts, such as freedom, must also be reexamined with an eye to decolonization. In chapter 10, Allison Weir argues that decolonizing feminist theory would require foregrounding Indigenous resistance to settler colonization. This would require expanding our models of intersectionality to include relationships to land and to sovereignty and questioning the sovereignty of settler states. Weir notes that Indigenous relations to land are grounded in Indigenous relational ontology and epistemology, and she argues that this philosophy grounds a specific relational theory of freedom. Indigenous relationality also challenges the secularity of mainstream feminism: Indigenous women and feminists argue that their relational philosophies are rooted in spiritual traditions and in a valuation of the sacred. Falcón and Bueno-Hansen also note this grounding of relations to land in sacred and spiritual traditions in their chapter: for the Indigenous peoples of Peru and Honduras, water has a spiritual essence. As Weir holds, the spirituality that pervades relations to land, water, and nonhuman others in Indigenous philosophies challenges the secular ontologies and epistemologies, and the conceptions of freedom, of Western feminism, including the assumption of unlimited skeptical critique. Decolonizing feminism, Weir writes, requires challenging binaries of secular/religious, as well as colonizer/colonized and essentialism/anti-essentialism. The arguments of Indigenous feminists and queer theorists require us to rethink critiques of essentialism, which often deploy an opposition between the post-modern fluid, hybrid subject, and the premodern fixed and landlocked native. Against this binary, Weir articulates an Indigenous conception of self that is both rooted in place *and* heterogeneous and in process. Weir concludes by arguing that Indigenous relational individual freedom is deeply connected to struggles for sovereignty. Thus Indigenous feminist struggles, such as the intervention of the Native Women's Association of Canada into the drafting of the Canadian constitution, require us to rethink connections between individual rights and freedoms, and the collective freedom of Indigenous peoples.

These ten original chapters by feminist philosophers and social theorists will shape the direction of future conversations about feminism because of their careful engagement with the challenges of theorizing, and the imperative of continuing the work of building coalitions and solidarity among feminists across borders.

NOTES

1. My deep appreciation to Barbara Fultner for her helpful comments and edits on this "Introduction." And, many thanks are due to Allison Weir for contributing her expertise to add to the section on Indigenous and settler-colonial philosophies. Special thanks are due to Veronica Leary (Rollins College, Master's of Liberal Studies, 2017) for her meticulous preparation of the index for this book.

2. See Chandra Talpade Mohanty and M. Jacqui Alexander, "Cartographies of Knowledge and Power: Transnational Feminism as Racial Praxis," in *Critical Transnational Feminist Praxis* (Albany: SUNY Press, 2010), for an excellent analysis of the varieties of ways that transnational feminisms have been used. And, see Linda E. Carty and Chandra Talpade Mohanty, "Mapping Transnational Feminist Engagements: Neoliberalism and the Politics of Solidarity," in *The Oxford Handbook of Transnational Feminist Movements*, eds. Rawwida Baksh and Wendy Harcourt (New York: Oxford University Press, 2015), 82–115.

3. Anibal Quijano, "Coloniality of Power, Eurocentrism, and Latin America," *Nepantla: Views from South*, 1 (3) (2000): 533–80. Durham: Duke University Press.

4. Lugones, María, "The Coloniality of Gender," *Worlds & Knowledge Otherwise* (Spring 2008): 1–17.

5. Rita Dhamoon, "A Feminist Approach to Decolonizing Anti-Racism: Rethinking Transnationalism, Intersectionality, and Settler Colonialism," *Feral Feminisms* 4 (Summer 2013): 20–37.

6. Chandra Talpade Mohanty, *Feminism without Borders: Decolonizing Theory, Practicing Solidarity* (Durham: Duke University Press, 2003).

7. Ibid., 3.

8. Mohanty, *Feminism without Borders*, 4.

9. Anibal Quijano, "Coloniality of Power, Eurocentrism, and Latin America," 537.

10. Quijano, "Coloniality of Power," 544.

11. Audre Lorde, "Age, Race, Class and Sex: Women Redefining Difference," in *Sister/Outsider* (New York: Crossing Press, 1984), 114–23.

12. Quijano, "Coloniality of Power," 545.

13. Quijano, "Coloniality of Power," 549–52.

14. Lugones, "The Coloniality of Gender," 1.

15. Ibid., 3.

16. Thanks are due to Allison Weir for contributing this overview of Indigenous philosophies.

17. *Third World Women and the Politics of Feminism*, eds. Chandra Talpade Mohanty, Ann Russo, and Lourdes Torres (Bloomington, IN: Indiana University Press, 1991); *Decentering the Center: Philosophy for a Multicultural, Postcolonial, and Feminist World*, eds. Uma Narayan and Sandra Harding (Bloomington, IN: Indiana University Press, 2000).

18. Mohanty, *Feminism without Borders*, 222.

19. Chandra Talpade Mohanty, "Transnational Feminist Crossings: On Neoliberalism and Radical Critique," *Signs* 38 (4) (2013): 972.

20. These are two separate but related points. Mohanty distinguishes her work from both postmodernism and relativism, as do other feminists, such as Linda Alcoff. Often it is assumed that a postmodern approach entails a commitment to relativism. I make an extended argument against this in my book, *Feminism, Foucault and Embodied Subjectivity* (Albany: SUNY Press, 2002).

21. Allison Weir, in *Identities and Freedom: Feminist Theory between Power and Connection* (Oxford: Oxford University Press, 2013), challenges this dichotomous view and argues that home can be (and should be) a place of both belonging and risk.

BIBLIOGRAPHY

Carty, Linda E., and Chandra Talpade Mohanty. "Mapping Transnational Feminist Engagements: Neoliberalism and the Politics of Solidarity." In *The Oxford Handbook of Transnational Feminist Movements*. Eds. Rawwida Baksh and Wendy Harcourt. New York: Oxford University Press, 2015.

Dhamoon, Rita. "A Feminist Approach to Decolonizing Anti-Racism: Re-thinking Transnationalism, Intersectionality, and Settler Colonialism." *feral feminisms* 4 (Summer 2013): 20–37.

Lorde, Audre. "Age, Race, Class and Sex: Women Redefining Difference." In *Sister/Outsider*. New York: Crossing Press, 1984.

Lugones, María. "The Coloniality of Gender." *Worlds & Knowledge Otherwise* (Spring 2008): 1–17.

McLaren, Margaret A. *Feminism, Foucault and Embodied Subjectivity*. Albany: SUNY Press, 2002.

Mohanty, Chandra Talpade. *Feminism without Borders: Decolonizing Theory, Practicing Solidarity*. Durham: Duke University Press, 2003.

———. "Transnational Feminist Crossings: On Neoliberalism and Radical Critique." *Signs* 38 (4) (2013): 972.

Mohanty, Chandra Talpade, and M. Jacqui Alexander. "Cartographies of Knowledge and Power: Transnational Feminism as Racial Praxis." In *Critical Transnational Feminist Praxis*. Albany: SUNY Press, 2010.

Mohanty, Chandra Talpade, Ann Russo, and Lourdes Torres, eds. *Third World Women and the Politics of Feminism*. Bloomington, IN: Indiana University Press, 1991.

Narayan, Uma, and Sandra Harding, eds. *Decentering the Center: Philosophy for a Multicultural, Postcolonial, and Feminist World*. Bloomington, IN: Indiana University Press, 2000.

Quijano, Anibal. "Coloniality of Power, Eurocentrism, and Latin America." *Nepantla: Views from South* 1 (3) (2000): 533–80. Durham: Duke University Press.

Weir, Allison. *Identities and Freedom: Feminist Theory between Power and Connection*. Oxford: Oxford University Press, 2013.

Part 1

DECOLONIZING EPISTEMOLOGIES, METHODS, AND KNOWLEDGES

Chapter 1

Decolonizing Feminist Philosophy

Linda Martín Alcoff

Feminist philosophy is a project analogous in many respects to the project of decolonizing philosophy. The decolonization of philosophy requires the contextualization of master discourses in order to be able to discern and understand the persistent colonial content that may be operating in our most cherished ideas and arguments. This pits it in opposition to a liberalism that separates ideas from their genealogy or location, such as process-oriented or formal approaches, or a postmodernism that, in the guise of an anti-foundationalism about meaning, would reject the determinate effect of material contexts. Much of feminist philosophy has been working to put context back into philosophy, to understand male-embodied experience as working behind common ideas about the self, for example, and to highlight the social location and identity of knowers as part of how real-world justification and judgment occurs.

Yet, feminist philosophy's relationship to decolonial projects is fraught with specific challenges, as this chapter will discuss. The current trend toward decolonizing is not simply an add-on of the colonial difference or an extension of intersectionality to include another form of difference but an attempt at shifting standard paradigms and methodologies about the way we understand our problematics in regard to gender. Inevitably, the decolonial challenge has generated new questions about how to articulate a transnational feminist agenda based on the imagined collectivity of women.

Imagining a global collectivity of women poses daunting challenges, as Simone de Beauvoir noted many decades ago, since women are dispersed across every community rather than collected together in any region or any specific social layer of society.[1] As Chandra Talpade Mohanty has argued, there is no way to achieve unity based on a shared unified experience, or on common treatment, or even on similar ideational representation across our diverse contexts.[2] There are too many differences of kind in each of these categories, far beyond differences of degree. If we were to try to fashion a collectivity based on female identity that did not deny or cover over these substantive differences, it would end up being too abstract and minimal to do effective political work.

Beauvoir herself is most productively read as offering an analysis of the situation of a certain cultural and class grouping. In this restricted sense, her account has much to teach and can inspire useful questions we might put to diverse contexts in which women are "made." She inspires us, for example, to ask about how the specific bodily aspects of women's experiences—such as menstruation, pregnancy, heterosexual coitus—are affected by our social context. In this way, we can draw a catalog of helpful questions from Beauvoir without taking her diagnosis of the oppression of women, based as it is on middle-class French women, to be universally applicable.

Some decades after *Le Deuxìeme Sexe* was published, however, theorists took up Beauvoir's assertion that women are made and not born in new directions to argue that the category "woman" itself is so universally problematic and even dangerous that it has lost its utility for a collective social praxis.[3] Gender identity, some argued, is *necessarily* a prison house of coercive performances, rigid boundaries, and identitarian logics.[4] Sometimes this claim is based on the formal characteristics of language to suggest that concepts and categories inevitably produce exclusions and marginalization, but sometimes it is based on social histories of the way in which gender categories came about. Haslanger, for example, defines gender (as well as race) as the effect of social oppression and calls for their elimination.[5] She and others such as Butler also argue that the concept of gender is unable to accommodate the empirical facts about the actual bodily variation among human beings, and as a result, this variation is systematically suppressed. There are many real and material dissimilarities among those designated female that encompasses physical and biological features as well as psychological and social ones. And it is also the case that what we mean by gender changes through history and across cultures. Yet all this variation is of course a challenge to the naturalistic ways in which male supremacy is justified based on invariant gender characteristics. Hence, some today hold that the very category of gender itself exists only for the purposes of oppression.

As a result, primarily in the global North, both feminist political practice and feminist theory have been defined in increasingly generic and oppositional terms of critique and resistance to identity itself, or the negative or critical project of undoing gender, dismantling identities, and escaping cultural scripts. Just as some have argued that racism creates race, some feminists argue that sexism creates gender; some even argue it creates sex. In the case of racism, such arguments rely primarily on the history of global political economy, but in the case of sexism, the primary arguments, as I've suggested, hinge on making a case for the disconnect between bodily variance and the necessarily binary nature of gender categories. As a result, the deconstruction of gender is not made as a contextually specific argument that accounts for specific historical and cultural contexts where concepts of difference emerge but as an argument that ranges over all contexts, synchronically and diachronically, encompassing all of humanity.

Thus, in the guise of producing an orientation to feminism that will avoid exclusions and recognize difference, this generalized stance of resistance to gender identity has become a new universal with little attempt at either intersectional or decolonial theorization. The argument of this chapter is that a uniform take on gender deconstruction needs a decolonial critique. If gender identities are in every case mediated by other vectors of identity categories and communities—changing their form and their degree of intensity—then we need to think through what the intersectional mediations of gender mean for our universal deconstructive politics.

Discerning the grounds of gender identities, after all, is not merely elusive because of the elusiveness of substances, or because we have mistakenly taken a social kind to be a natural kind, but because there is actual *material* diversity across contexts of gender meanings and gender formation. Whether our perceived gender identity is taken to place us on a pedestal or rendered us as the mule of the world, or, alternatively, whether gender is a more positive and livable form of life in a given community depends on mediations of intersecting systems of meaning and practice. Acknowledging such differences of kind may seem to destabilize gender and make it a fitting subject for just the sort of deconstruction I have described. But putting gender under erasure, in Heidegger or Derrida's sense, is distinct from pluralizing it and circumscribing its explanatory scope. To deconstruct gender is to argue that the concept can never be adequate to its referent and that it can never be modified or contextualized.

Against this view, I want to insist on the open-ended nature of the question decolonial theory is putting on the table: what would it mean to decolonize our approach to questions about the nature and the politics of gender, including the meaning of gender itself?

The intersectional approaches to questions of gender oppression have too often focused on race/ethnicity, class, and sexuality without attending equally to nationality, religion, geographical region, disability, and political status (i.e., citizenship). Intersectional feminism has usefully underscored the differences in our lives and families and histories that generate different priorities and interests. But this can yield a picture of a pluralist feminism with compatible, though distinct, orientations. Decolonizing feminism may push us toward a paradigm shift of a different order in which founding categories and concepts, of "women" and "oppression," are more radically contested. We must be prepared to understand that when gender is mediated by these varied forms of identity—such as sexual, ethnic, racial, national, and religious—there may be varied political effects and meanings. It is not just that the content of the identity scripts may vary across cultural contexts, but the manner of identity formation or subject formation may also vary as well as the political effects of gender-based social organization. It is a piece of colonial hubris to assume without investigation that any gender-based division of labor will be oppressive: this is to assume that gender will always operationalize in the same way, as I will explore in what follows.

If gender cannot stand alone because its form is always the product of mediated processes, then we should reconsider whether we can theorize a universal response to gender, or a resistance to gender, or a solution to gender, while ignoring the hybrid nature of gender. Taking intersectionality seriously means that we cannot separate gender off from other social identities as having its own unique identitarian logic. Taking up the decolonial challenge means a willingness to acknowledge coloniality within the framing assumptions used in feminist theory itself.

IDENTITY

It is useful in this context to begin with the case of Anders Behring Breivik, whose attack on his fellow Norwegians in the summer of 2011 aimed at instigating a race-based civil war that could conceivably bring down the multiculturalist, pluralist policies of his government. By specifically targeting Norwegians, Breivik hoped to bring the cost of multiculturalism home, in effect. His murders targeted the liberal Labour Party youth who he feared would chart the way for an even more pluralist future for Norway. His understanding of this pluralist future had everything to do with his understanding of feminism's effect on Norway. And the connection he drew between rising immigration and feminism holds lessons that are useful for other areas of the world where a xenophobic, sexist right is on the rise. It is certainly relevant to the misogynist form of xenophobic nationalism the Trump presidency represents. Breivik's ideology is now operating very much inside rather than outside the United States.

Like other European countries, Norway has moved from a nearly homogeneous ethnic society to a relatively harmonious multiethnic one in just a few decades. The firebombings and hate crimes that beset Germany and Denmark, as their immigrant populations increased, were rare in Norway, and social democratic policies ensured that immigrant workers would share in the famed social safety net and high standard of living the nation enjoys.

Norway's famed oil revenues ensured a good standard of living for all, even with high taxes, so the racist extremist reaction that has recently developed cannot be reasonably blamed on worsening economic conditions. Rather, it was simply the policies of inclusion that besotted Breivik and other racist extremists. It is important to remember that Breivik was not a lone madman but someone who held a more extreme version of views that many others in Norway and across Scandinavia persist in holding. One Swedish politician commented shortly after the 2011 attacks that if Norway had remained a "Norwegian Norway" this would never have happened.

Social identities—ethnic, racial, national, and religious—increasingly animate national and international politics, policy debates, and electoral party formations. Racist extremists like Breivik overplay the importance of these identities; misconstrue the political meanings of identity; collapse national and ethnic identities as if they were identical; and target specific identities as posing insurmountable obstacles to security, harmony, and national prosperity. In response to these sorts of reductive and essentialist approaches to identity, minimalism about identity can begin to look pretty attractive. Yet it's clearly insufficient to approach the issue of identity simply in terms of its political effects, even its political dangers, or through the misconstrued ideas of maniacs. We need first to consider the issue of the actual social ontology of identity and identity formations before we can understand our political options in relation to them.

Let me return to Breivik. On the day of the attacks, Breivik distributed a manifesto of more than 1,500 pages titled "2083—A European Declaration of Independence." In it he targeted a number of groups classified into two categories: first, non-Norwegians, especially Muslims; second, various Norwegians, such as liberals, supporters of the European Union (EU), and feminists, who were open to immigration. Feminists were especially targeted because he saw them as weakening Norway's resolve to maintain closed borders, and thus opening Norway to the advances of non-Norwegians. The category of non-Norwegian that he targeted is of course an interesting one. We might first wonder, does it include the Indigenous Saami people? Perhaps it could, as long as the Saami don't demand curricular inclusion or quotas in Parliament.[6]

But what is most interesting in Breivik's formulations of identity categories is their slide from self-consciously political identities to social identities in a more physical form. In other words, Breivik does not explicitly target women but does target feminism, and does not target non-Norwegian Europeans but does target pro-EU Europeans, and only targets non-Norwegian non-Europeans who are trying to enter Norway or espousing a "political Islam." One might think he has moved to chosen identities or self-consciously political identities and away from the racialist, determinist logic of another era. And this helps Breivik present himself as a rationally enlightened white nationalist, the kind who simply believes in a clash of cultures rather than an indefeasible race-based inferiority. But this distinction does not actually hold up in the manifesto. Feminists are identified by their opposition to traditions of Norwegian protective masculinity that might guard the country against external enemies, and the external enemies of Norway are identified by their ethnic, religious, and even racialized identity as Arabs and/or Muslims. And so what might look to be political categories determined by individual agency and chosen allegiances devolve into determined categories of social identity once again. In other words, Breivik closes the assimilation option along with the cultural amalgamation option. Non-Norwegian non-European immigrants can never be accommodated because they will never change, and Norwegians *should* never change: a change inside Norway can only be attributed to mongrelization, or racialized devolution.

Moreover, Breivik's aim is, as the Swedish politician put it, a Norwegian Norway, not in the sense of a Norway with Norwegian traditions but in the sense of a Norway made up of people with Norwegian ethnic heritage. Thus, identity is still operating here in terms of older ideas of heritable, and thus biological, race, or something like it. One has an identity forever and passes it down to one's children, and in this way the identity group remains a closed set with clearly defined borders. Just as Spain decided in the sixteenth century that *conversos* were not to be trusted, launching the Inquisition, Breivik and his compatriots believe that assimilation is unreliable.

The importance of gender in this analysis is one that is terribly familiar: women's role is to maintain the purity of the racial reproductive line. White men may procreate with others as they like, but it is crucial that white women procreate exclusively with white men in order to reproduce a Norwegian line. The centrality of gender identity for Breivik, and hence his concern with feminism, is in its capacity to undermine the continuation of a racial genealogy for this ethnicized (or racialized) configuration of Norway as a nation.

Can one imagine, within this ideology, a feminism or a progress for LGBTQ communities within a Norway that is for Norwegians? Can there be a gender progress, so to speak, within the construct of a Norway for Norwegians? The answer must be no, not simply because there is an identitarian logic operating for gender categories, but because there is a very pragmatic need to maintain certain gender roles in order to *maintain the race* (a term I am using very purposefully here). The policing of gender has a source or motivation, then, outside of or beyond gender itself. In this instance, *it is only in the mediations of a particular gender in a particular place that we can find its logic*. It is only in gender's mediations with race that we can trace the source of gender-based roles and restrictions.

Breivik's main explicitly articulated target is multiculturalism. Like other racial nationalists, he wants his own national identity to be an unmuddied, uncomplicated collectivity. He resists the idea that a nation can be constituted by difference, and again, this is a powerfully influential idea motivating policy in many countries, from the anti-immigrant practices in the United States to the ethnic and racial uniformity demanded by the Janjaweed to the concerns within EU states about the extent of the religious and political differences the EU can tolerate. Multiculturalism is not the target merely of violent extremists but elicits widespread concern for its ostensibly deleterious effects on national unity and civic life. There are different forms and definitions of multiculturalism, it is clear, but the kind that concerns many is the kind that challenges the glowing national narratives that assert unity around a single, optimal form of communal life. Hence, multiculturalism has both backward- and forward-looking aspects. The multiplicity of narratives about the historical founding of a nation necessarily brings with it a contestation, a kind of earthquake affecting the whole with new ideas about the future. Multiculturalism is not merely the threat of inclusion or of sharing one's space but of having one's own narrative identity challenged and contested. If the problem was merely sharing space, quotas could limit access, but when the problem is competing narratives and contrasting futures, no quotas are small enough. Hence, Breivik.

INTERSECTIONALITY

Intersectionality, as it was developed primarily by women of color theorists in the nineteenth and twentieth centuries, is the thesis that gender is constituted by difference all the way down, that there is no core of gender untouched by the co-constituting effects of multiple vectors of oppression and identity formation.[7] Though the idea has blossomed and developed in a rich ongoing discussion in North American feminism, there remains a recalcitrance in taking up its most important implication: that we really cannot theorize gender or gender progress without taking up its mediating elements.

The intersectional nature of ethnic, racial, and gendered identity was also articulated, somewhat unwittingly, in an analysis of ethnicity developed by Max Weber nearly a century ago. Weber's account, I will suggest, helpfully explains both Breivik's antipathy to feminism and Western feminism's own tendency to deflect the implications of an intersectional approach.

In 1922, Max Weber developed an argument about the formation of ethnic identities that interestingly prefigures more contemporary deconstructive approaches to identity (e.g., Appiah, Gilroy, Fraser).[8] Weber views social identities of numerous types as founded in wrong beliefs, as a kind of false consciousness produced by elite manipulation.[9] He holds that ethnic identities in particular are founded in false historical beliefs that he called "artificial origin" stories. These artificial origin stories cover over "the original motives and reasons for the inceptions of different habits of life."[10] Like Ivan in *The Brothers Karamazov*, who believed that morality required a false belief in religion, Weber thinks ethnicities require a false belief about group origins. The messy reality of group origins can never justify the exaggerated claims about the unanimity of group interests or the inviolability of cultural traditions; hence, we must be made to "forget" these origins so that we fall into line. This forgetting works to naturalize group formations, according to Weber, circumventing possibilities of critique and change. But forgetting also facilitates the creation of the conditions for the *actual heritability* of ethnic "qualities and traits" in the following way.

Weber asserts that the *belief* in group commonalities "often delimits social circles" to create practices tending toward "monopolistic closure."[11] In other words, false beliefs form ethnic groups by creating a reproductive community with delimited boundaries that eventually yields shared physical features. Notice that by this argument, the distinction between race (as biology) and ethnicity (as cultural practice) all but disappears: on Weber's account, ethnicity in the form of ethnic-related beliefs and practices creates racially defined groups with visible features marked as racial. Thus, the existence of visible physical commonalities and shared kinship networks does not prove that group identities are natural, according to Weber, but just the reverse: that their boundaries were created by shared acceptance of artificial origin stories.

Weber acknowledges that processes of group formation can enhance survival, increasing the ability of individuals to flourish in hostile climates by creating networks of solidarity and material support. Thus, even if origin stories are on some level, or to some degree, false, he allows that they are not necessarily irrational or without real utility. Yet Weber shares the general view of his contemporary ethnicity theorists that most of the effects of ethnicity are negative, in particular, the trend toward "monopolistic closure." This is believed to produce, on balance, more social and political problems than it solves, because it promotes in-group interaction over a wider social intercourse, because it exacerbates hostilities with others, and because it generates "special interest" approaches to public reasoning in which identity considerations preempt discussions of the common good. Nathan Glazer and Daniel Patrick Moynihan's influential characterization of ethnicity in the 1960s expresses this most forthrightly: in their view, strongly felt ethnic identities are an *a priori* problem requiring political policies that would enhance their dissolution and irrelevance.[12] Importantly, Glazer and Moynihan's analysis centered on the persistent poverty patterns in the United States of African

Americans and Puerto Ricans, contrasting these groups with southern European white ethnics, leaving the dominant northern European ethnic identity untheorized. In brief, Glazer and Moynihan blamed black and Latino poverty on unassimilated minority enclaves with distinct practices and allowed the social and economic success of white ethnics to be attributed to merit and wider spheres of social interaction.[13] Thus, in their view, race and ethnicity explained poverty but did not explain success. These views remain influential today and presage the widespread trend that articulates a progressive future as one where ethnic and racial identities all but disappear.

There are certain parallels with the views about gender deconstruction I described earlier. For Weber, ethnicity no less than race is a form of group identity with coercive effects based on false beliefs, just as gender deconstructionists argue is true of gender. And both ethnicity and race are said to be maintained through pretensions to naturalism, like gender is said to be. Further, Weber thinks that once we give up on naturalistic explanations for the existence of race and ethnicity and turn to explore the social causes, we will mainly find nefarious forces at work. Following this sort of argument, more recent theorists have argued that self-interested strategic manipulations of history are not simply the work of states or those with power but also promoted by the internal leaders of oppressed minority groups that claim to speak for the group. The influential liberal theorist Arthur Schlesinger suggests this idea in his diagnosis of the "cult of ethnicity," which he blamed for derailing the United States' move toward a genuine melting pot, an argument that is perpetually used today to explain Trump's election. According to Schlesinger, the "cult of ethnicity" was not a product of the grassroots or of social movements against identity-based forms of social oppression but of elites who were wrangling to become the "ethnic spokesmen."[14] Schlesinger claims that these intellectuals were "moved by real concern for distinctive ethnic values [but] also by real if unconscious vested interest in the preservation of ethnic constituencies."[15]

Yet whether identity is thought of as something produced from outside or inside communities, from the state or from nefarious elites, the resulting analysis presents a coherent picture. From Weber through Schlesinger to today's opponents of "identity politics," the claim is that identity almost always involves a bad faith about the contingency of social construction, that the belief in identity naturalizes group categories with coercive effects on individual freedom and social interaction. Here we find a view completely in sync with the project of undoing gender.

In fact, the critique of ethnic and racial identities produces a new argument for deconstructing gender: if gender scripts are required for enacting monopolistic closure, then gender must be undone in order to undo other problematic forms of identity.

No intersectional analysis is required to complicate the claim that all identities are political disasters.

DECOLONIZING IDENTITIES

There are three problems we can identify here that present obstacles to decolonizing feminist theory. First, there is a resonating concordance between these influential but overly generalized approaches to understanding what identities are and how they are formed, conferring an excessive plausibility on such approaches. This excuses theorists who neglect the particulars of geohistorical factors involved in identity formation, as well as specific social movements that address identity-based forms of oppression. All identity beliefs and identity-based movements can be criticized in one metalevel move, without historical, political, or sociological analysis of actual events or organizations or discourses. Second, there is a hubris of universalism, taking a theory of the construction of a specific identity, such as Beauvoir's middle-class French women, as the basis of a generic approach to gender formation. And third, the thesis of social construction is developed in such a way that it all happens at the top, by states or leaders, without a sense of multiple causes contributing to a dominant construction, including causes instigated by the experiences and resistance of non elites.

The legacy of Weber offers little space for those identified by ethnic and racial categories to inhabit these with agency. There is no Foucauldian insistence on the ever-present agency and resistance from below, such as Michael Omi and Howard Winant build into their theory of racial formations and racial projects. For Omi and Winant, the meaning of race is a product of multiple historical forces, subject to constant change, renegotiation, and revision. Effective historical forces, in their view, are not merely those orchestrated by elites but can also be those animated by social movements of oppressed groups and coalitions as well as by creative engagements of cultural agents and the sometimes radically new forms of practice invented by "regular" folks. Theorists should not read the political languages taken up by social movements as mere echoes of elite discourse but as strategic interventions that can transform meanings as well as invent new terminologies. Transforming the meanings of our identities—their scope and boundaries and criteria and reference points—does not emerge only from high art gallery spaces or state policies or the mainstream media; in fact, the latter must often be responsive to group demands and desires, and we can watch attempts at recuperation and management of the languages and meanings generated from below. The gender diversity becoming more visible around the world outside its binary system is emerging from below. Restrictive laws and policies, such as new bathroom legislation, are responses, not evocations. Racial and ethnic and religious and disabled identities are undergoing a similar proliferation insistently visible in the public sphere.

Hence, the Weberian legacy of theorizing identity is not only wrong in its substance as I've argued in more detail elsewhere,[16] but it is also wrong in its method of analysis by collapsing distinctions in the historical formations of identities and by ignoring the creative agency, and influence, of non elites. Decolonizing feminist philosophy will require a retreat from metalevel universal analyses that attempt to establish the criteria by which to identify oppression, harm, constraint, and injustice. Only if one thinks identity formation occurs in the same way everywhere with similar or even identical political effects can a unified account of resistance be justifiable. But how can this be known before undertaking the dialogical work of understanding across differences of context? This would be to once again set a priori terms from the metropole about the criteria for a theoretically adequate and politically defensible position.

Categories of social identity are effects of history and refer back to the narrativized experiences of group-related historical events such as migrations, enslavement, conquest, and war. Macro events of history underdetermine our political responses and interpretations of them, without doubt, but they cannot be summarily ignored by those whose present-day life is continually impacted by them. One way to understand the role of history in relation to identity is to make use of Gadamer's concept of the hermeneutic horizon that operates as a backdrop of historical experiences and an orienting perspective from which individuals make sense of new events. The horizon is a substantival location from which we look out at the world, but it also denotes a perspective that is open and dynamic. This concept helps us to capture the background, framing assumptions we bring with us to perception and to the effort of understanding. *Some* of the content of our horizons will be group related, shared by those who share a social identity, such as the trauma of dislocation, slavery, racist representations, and collective violence.

Group-related historical experience creates a substantive content to our identities beyond the dominant narratives imposed by the state. This also suggests the limits on the elasticity of discursive constructions of identities, and limits on the efficacy of elite manipulation. Discursive constructions and state-based categories must work within the limits of these dimensions of identity, and they cannot foist on us monikers that have no explanatory value or material purchase on our lived reality, although states can certainly create the conditions in which identity categories come to have overarching material reality. Yet there is a limit to what states can do: they may counsel us to become color-blind, for example, by removing categories from all state forms, but if color continues to operate to organize our shared social world, then color will continue to be an important aspect of our material practices and will continue to have explanatory value in understanding our lives. Discourses, whether based in state practices or otherwise, are not simply reflective but also constructive of experience and can produce meanings and reliable explanations through producing experience, such as the experience of sanctioned discrimination or of social invisibility. There is a feedback loop, in other words, in which states or other forces may produce the identities of which they speak, to paraphrase Foucault. Yet the point remains that the feedback loop only works to the extent it actually produces an alteration of the visible registry, or the macro historical experiences that contribute content to our horizons, or the communal meanings by which we organize shared practices. Identities are part of the real world, and changing identities requires changing that world, not simply changing our self-ascriptions.

If ethnic identities are as substantive as this account suggests, they will indeed come into conflict in the ways that the critics of multiculturalism claim. And the conflicts will, moreover, be difficult to manage as long as they are allowed to stand apart as a nonintersecting set. Recognizing the interconnection between identities is the best solution to false origin stories, the best way to correct deficient and distorted historical narratives. Turning away from our differences by attempting to eliminate identities simply leaves in place the implicit background layer of meanings we inevitably operate with as we struggle to understand new experiences and encounters.

Collectivity is reached through the serious engagement of conflicting narratives of meaning and history and practice. Preemptive attempts to dissolve the need to do this work via a kind of metaphysical policy paper against identity terms does nothing to change social reality and in fact disables the process of discursive negotiations through which new meanings and practices might actually emerge. My argument is that we need to work through our social identities rather than pretending they are unreal fictions, and in fact, that this working through will enhance their fluidity and possibly transform the way we understand their meaning. I have given a rough sketch of a way to approach ethnic and ethno-racial identities, of which religious and national identities are more often than not intimately tethered. But what of gender?

Gender cannot be approached theoretically apart from its mediations. The process of forming gender identities, the content and strictness of scripts, and the bodily practices around the sexually specific aspects of human reproduction and physiology vary across contexts. It is not simply the intensity with which gender is lived, or enforced, that changes across contexts but also its meaning and manner of formation. As it intersects with other ways of being, gender changes not merely in degree but in kind.

For example, there are contrasting affective ties to gender identities across contexts. But to see why this is so, we have to understand gender in its mediations within a neocolonial world. Some groups may be more ready to deconstruct gender than others, not simply because of their understandings or experiences of gender but also because of their experience of their ethnic or racial identity. Whites who long to escape their ties to painful histories may be more than ready to try out a nonidentity. These painful relationships to one's identity can certainly motivate a desire for escape. On the other hand, if gender expression is part of the way I am connected to a culture, a history, a genealogy that I value, that I in fact want to help survive into the future, then my attitude may be quite different. If gender is the means to produce group identities such as ethnicity, then undoing gender, on such a view, will be the means to undo ethnicity, to some people's delight and others' consternation. My attachment to my gender identity cannot be disambiguated from other aspects of my social identities. This does not spell doom for change but affects the terms in which change can more realistically be planned out.

CONCLUSION

I have tried to develop a contrasting view to the idea of the prison house of gender, where gender's relation to ethnic, racial, religious, or national identities can only be construed, along the lines both Breivik and deconstructionists would construe them, as the coerced means for reproducing identities through reproductive closure. In reality, social identities are never closed and stable but movable horizons that connect and overlap in multiple ways. The idea of walling off outside influences and shutting down change is unrealistic, and yet the aspiration to assist group survival does not need to be interpreted as an attempt to circumvent all change or transformation.

Decolonizing feminist philosophy requires contextualizing feminism itself in order to be able to discern the particular, context-based ways in which gender is understood, and progress is imagined, from any given location. It also requires developing a reflexively attuned skepticism toward the hubris of universal analysis and projects of liberation. The idea that all those who share a designated gender share a set of understandings or interests or forms of oppression is no more feasible than Beauvoir noted: the mediations of gender make our differences quite real. Solidarity can only be achieved, then, through piecemeal or partial coalitions, best pursued on the basis of concrete issues, rather than on the articulation of a thin or artificial collectivity organized around ideas about freedom from gender. And piecemeal coalitions will require a kind of multicultural negotiation in which contested narratives will have to be brought into some measure of alignment. A relevant example here would be the multinational efforts to address sex trafficking, in which some global North approaches render analyses that place questions of the global political economy off the frame, as if evil coyotes are the ultimate cause of the problem rather than cruel transnational markets that destroy other ways of making livelihoods at the same time as they demand female flesh. A coalition to address coercive sex work will require negotiations that work through contrasting narrative explanations about the problems and the solutions.

Decolonizing feminist philosophy requires being prepared to do philosophy differently. I have argued that this involves challenging not only universalist deconstructionist agendas but also universal conceptualizations of gender and gender-related forms of oppression.

NOTES

1. Simone de Beauvoir, *The Second Sex*, trans. Constance Borde and Shelia Malovany-Chevallier (New York: Vintage Books, 2011).

2. Chandra Talpade Mohanty, *Feminism without Borders: Decolonizing Theory, Practicing Solidarity* (Durham, NC: Duke University Press, 2003).

3. For Beauvoir, the distinction between sex and gender was intentionally collapsed within her treatment of what she called "the body in situation." The body, on her view, cannot be disentangled from the cultural, historical situation in which it finds itself, but her lengthy discussion of material embodied experiences such as menstruation and coitus indicates, as many commentators have noted, that for her, the body is not an inert or substantively vacuous repositories of meaning created elsewhere. See Sara Heinamaa, *Toward a Phenomenology of Sexual Difference: Husserl, Merleau-Ponty, Beauvoir* (Lanham, MD: Rowman and Littlefield, 2003). This means that the body is a player, so to speak, in the production of meaning. But the meaning of any given aspect of our lives—for example, pregnancy, menstruation—is always best understood as "the body in situation," such that both our materiality and our cultural context are involved.

4. Judith Butler, *Undoing Gender* (New York: Routledge, 2004); Sally Haslanger, *Resisting Reality: Social Construction and Social Critique* (New York: Oxford University Press, 2012).

5. Haslanger, *Resisting Reality*.

6. See Niillas Holmberg and Jenni Laiti, "The Saami Manifesto 15: Reconnecting Through Resistance," IdleNoMore, March 23, 2015, which outlines what the Saami people do want. www.idlenomore.ca/the_saami_manifesto_15_reconnecting_through_resistance.

7. Valerie Smith, *Not Just Race, Not Just Gender: Black Feminist Readings* (New York: Routledge, 1998); Kimberlé Crenshaw, *On Intersectionality: Essential Writings* (New York: The New Press, Forthcoming).

8. Anthony Appiah, *In My Father's House: Africa in the Philosophy of Culture* (New York: Oxford University Press, 1992); Nancy Fraser, *Justice Interruptus: Critical Reflections on the "Postsocialist" Condition* (New York: Routledge, 1997); Paul Gilroy, *Against Race: Imagining Political Culture beyond the Color Line* (Cambridge, MA: Belknap Press, 1992); Max Weber, "Ethnic Groups," in *Theories*

of Ethnicity: A Reader, ed. Werner Sollors (New York: New York University Press, 1996). The arguments in this section are developed further in my *Visible Identities* (2006).

9. In some cases, the account is not based on elite manipulation so much as categories recognized by the state and various expert discourses that operate as if such categories of identity are natural. Such a form of analysis would be more Foucauldian, for example, with less of an emphasis on the agency of elites and more on the *historical a priori* or framing effects of a discursive practice.

10. Weber, "Ethnic Groups," 55.

11. Weber, "Ethnic Groups," 55–57.

12. Nathan Glazer and Daniel Patrick Moynihan, *Beyond the Melting Pot: The Negroes, Puerto Ricans, Jews, Italian, and Irish of New York City*, 2nd ed. (Cambridge, MA: MIT Press, 1970).

13. See Tommie Shelby, *Dark Ghettos: Injustice, Dissent and Reform* (Cambridge, MA: Harvard University Press, 2016), for an effective anecdote.

14. Arthur M. Schlesinger, *The Disuniting of America: Reflections on a Multicultural Society* (New York: W.W. Norton, 1992), 34.

15. Ibid.

16. Linda Martín Alcoff, *Visible Identities: Race, Gender, and the Self* (New York: Oxford University Press, 2006).

BIBLIOGRAPHY

Alcoff, Linda Martín. 2006. *Visible Identities: Race, Gender, and the Self.* New York: Oxford University Press.

Beauvoir, Simone de. 2011. *The Second Sex*. Translated by Constance Borde and Shelia Malovany-Chevallier. New York: Vintage Books.

Breivik, Anders Behring. 2011. "2083: A European Declaration of Independence." https://publicintelligence.net/anders-behring-breiviks-complete-manifesto-2083-a-european-declaration-of-independence/

Brown, Wendy. 1997. "The Impossibility of Women's Studies." *Differences: A Journal of Feminist Cultural Studies* 9 (3): 79–101.

Butler, Judith. 2004. *Undoing Gender*. New York: Routledge.

Crenshaw, Kimberlé. Forthcoming in 2018. *On Intersectionality: Essential Writings*. New York: The New Press.

Foucault, Michel. 1980. *Power/Knowledge: Selected Interviews and Other Writings 1972–1977*. Edited by Colin Gordon, translated by Colin Gordon, Leo Marshall, John Mepham, Kate Soper. New York: Pantheon.

Haslanger, Sally. 2012. *Resisting Reality: Social Construction and Social Critique*. New York: Oxford University Press.

Heinamaa, Sara. 2003. *Toward a Phenomenology of Sexual Difference: Husserl, Merleau-Ponty, Beauvoir*. Lanham, MD: Rowman and Littlefield.

Mohanty, Chandra Talpade. 2003. *Feminism without Borders: Decolonizing Theory, Practicing Solidarity*. Durham, NC: Duke University Press.

Omi, Michael, and Howard Winant. 1986. *Racial Formations in the United States: From the 1960s to the 1980s*. New York: Routledge.

Schlesinger Jr., Arthur M. 1992. *The Disuniting of America: Reflections on a Multicultural Society*. New York: W. W. Norton.

Shelby, Tommie. 2016. *Dark Ghettos: Injustice, Dissent and Reform*. Cambridge, MA: Harvard University Press.

Smith, Valerie. 1998. *Not Just Race, Not Just Gender: Black Feminist Readings*. New York: Routledge.

Weber, Max. 1996. "Ethnic Groups." In *Theories of Ethnicity: A Reader*. Edited by Werner Sollors. New York: New York University Press.

Chapter 2

Knowing without Borders and the Work of Epistemic Gathering

Gaile Pohlhaus Jr.

In her now classic essay, "Under Western Eyes,"[1] originally published in 1984, Chandra Talpade Mohanty criticizes a set of writers for the ways in which they seek to know women across borders. In analyzing feminist knowledge production, Mohanty is deeply concerned about the ways in which women's experiences can be colonized, even by those claiming to do so in the name of feminism.[2] At the same time, in other places in her work and in the reflections on "Under Western Eyes" that appear in the final chapter of her 2003 book *Feminism without Borders* in which "Under Western Eyes" is reprinted as the first chapter, Mohanty points to the harms of a pluralist approach that does not engage with and across differences among women but simply promotes the proliferation of isolated communities of women who are similarly situated.[3] Her criticisms that appear in the first chapter, therefore, are not made in the spirit of placing borders on what epistemic agents can know or ought to try to know based on their social position. Rather, they are made in an effort to caution dominantly positioned feminists about the effects of their knowing and to call on feminists to know more responsibly. Importantly, Mohanty's critique is one which insists that feminists *can* and *ought* to know better.

In light of this call, I examine some of the epistemic implications of *Feminism without Borders* to develop the idea of "knowing without borders" as a set of epistemic practices to accompany Mohanty's "feminism without borders." Guided by the twin imperatives identified above (i.e., to avoid colonizing knowledges *and* to know better), I emphasize attention to the effects of knowing rather than stipulating the conditions of knowing. In other words, I argue that social position matters, not because one's identity determines what one can know, but rather because inattention to social position, particularly by those who are dominantly socially positioned, can have harmful epistemic effects. Utilizing this emphasis, I develop the idea of "knowing without borders" as a set of practices that includes investigating the contingent and current borders that enable and disable knowing in particular instances, recognizing that the epistemic borders we animate have effects on others, considering what kinds of things would need to shift in order to work across or reshape epistemic borders, and working collectively to enable such shifts. I argue that "knowing without borders" as a set of decolonial feminist practices is suggested not only by what Mohanty *says* in *Feminism without Borders* but also by what she *does* throughout the book. In contrast to colonialist and capitalist models of knowledge that stress production, distribution, and ownership, the pictures of knowing that animate Mohanty's text call attention to relations of responsiveness and responsibility, materiality, and interdependence.

Refocusing attention to knowing as an embodied practice with others, I bring Mohanty's work into conversation with the work of Sara Ahmed, particularly in those places where Ahmed attends to the material and collective conditions that sustain philosophical thinking. Considering Mohanty and Ahmed together, I develop the idea of "epistemic gathering," a collective practice that works to make claims that resist dominance and oppression intelligible. Epistemic gathering is one way of describing how the material and collective aspects of knowing are crucial to "knowing without borders."

"KNOWING WITHOUT BORDERS" AS DECOLONIAL EPISTEMIC PRACTICE

In her introduction to *Feminism without Borders*, Mohanty insists that feminist work must be "deeply collective"[4] and that this deep collectivity calls for struggle "through, with, and over . . . borders in our everyday lives."[5] I am interested in the epistemic implications of this call, particularly in light of Mohanty's concern with the ways in which women's experiences can be discursively colonized. Some hints and precautions concerning what Mohanty might (and might not) mean here can be found in what she says about the title of her book, which she notes deliberately evokes the international humanitarian aid group "doctors without borders," who are known for their deployment of medical services within precarious regions of the world.[6] Given this fashioning, one thing that might be helpful to bear in mind with my use of "knowing without borders" to describe a set of epistemic practices is that these practices might be risky or even dangerous. Part of that danger involves not only working in conditions that are contested and unjust but also working from contexts that structure knowers multiply in relations of dominance and oppression to one another. Consequently, "knowing without borders," like the feminism Mohanty advocates, cannot ignore borders. As Mohanty notes:

> Feminism without borders is not the same as "border-less" feminism. It acknowledges the fault lines, conflicts, differences, fears, and containment that borders represent. It acknowledges that there is no one sense of a border, that the lines between and through nations, races, classes, sexualities, religions, and disabilities, are real—and that a feminism without borders must envision change and social justice work across these lines of demarcation and division.[7]

Acknowledging that there is no one sense of a border might seem at first to pose an epistemological problem: if there is no *one* sense of a border, how do we know where the borders are and how do we attend to them? Mohanty's work, however, suggests we attend to what she says here in a different fashion, not because there is no danger of failing to acknowledge differences and conflicts, but because the assumptions that lend intelligibility to the epistemological problem as stated before are ones that Mohanty's decolonial knowledge making actively resists. These include the idea that if we are to acknowledge conflicts and differences they must have an established or predetermined sense and the idea that responsible knowing requires feminists to determine how we attend to the world in advance of our engagements with others within it. The first assumption suggests that responsibility requires an unchanging sense of what we mean by differences and that "difference" be a firmly bounded concept. The second assumption suggests that if knowers are to work responsibly together, the relations among them must be established and predictable. Both assumptions construe responsibility in terms of securing borders, an epistemic move that runs directly counter to how Mohanty herself treats concepts and to the type of relations among knowers that she recommends for decolonizing knowledge and working across borders.[8]

For example, in the second chapter of *Feminism without Borders*, when situating her own concepts for constructing a positive account of Third World[9] women's relations to feminism, Mohanty notes that the definitions, methodologies, and contexts upon which she draws to construct her account must necessarily be "noncomprehensive" so that as inquiry develops, "our very conceptual maps are redrawn and transformed."[10] Recognizing that her own perspective and entry points make salient some aspects of the world and not others, she emphasizes that her own conceptual maps are "partial." This partiality, however, is not a failing. It is only a failing if we assume that the aim of epistemic practices is to establish an unchanging relation to the world, for then the partiality of definitions, methodologies, and contexts would indeed be limiting. In contrast, if the aim of epistemic practices is to call our attention to the world in ways that help us to respond more justly (both epistemically and practically) to that world and the people who inhabit it with us, then the partiality of the map is not a problem; it is simply a place from where we respond at a given moment in time. With this understanding, the conceptual maps that provide a starting point for attending to the world "will of necessity have to be redrawn as our analytic and conceptual skills and knowledge develop and transform the way we understand questions of history, consciousness, and agency."[11] Consequently, "knowing without borders" as a decolonial epistemic practice resists the enforcement of conceptual borders simply for the sake of having them, seeking instead nondominating ways of being responsive to a world that is not static. Moreover, "knowing without borders" endeavors to respond *from* knowers' situatedness that is likewise not static but capable of being transformed through knowers' interactions in the world. This way of regarding the concepts we use in our epistemic relations is consonant with Mohanty's reflections on her own work in the last chapter of *Feminism without Borders* where she insists, "My own language in 1986 needs to be open to refinement and inquiry—but not institutionalization."[12]

If we consider what Mohanty says about the practicing of solidarity, it is clear that the borders that exist between knowers must also be regarded as contingent. In contrast to a solidarity secured in advance that is the basis for struggle, Mohanty recommends struggle as the basis for solidarity. In other words, some models of solidarity envision commonality in identity as a starting position for politics, where common identity is thought to guarantee common interest and common knowledge. This understanding of solidarity is, for example, akin to a mistaken understanding of standpoint epistemology that sees the epistemic privileging of certain social positions as the privileging of particular knowers who automatically know well owing to social position.[13] In contrast, Mohanty's notion of solidarity is much more akin to the standpoint epistemology developed by Patricia Hill Collins,[14] whereby knowledge is not assumed but achieved among knowers struggling together in relation and through their resistance to common structures of dominance and oppression. Similarly, for Mohanty, feminist solidarity is achieved in interaction, the result of "active struggle."[15] Consequently, "knowing without borders" must attend to where knowers are currently located in relation to one another, but these relations neither secure nor preclude the work of knowing together. Instead it is what knowers *do* in light of these relations that constitutes whether they are able to know well together or not.

Paying attention to the way epistemic borders operate in our thinking is particularly important for understanding Mohanty's critical intervention in "Under Western Eyes" in conjunction with her reflections on that essay in "Under Western Eyes Revisited." In the former, Mohanty critiques what she calls the "discursive colonization" of Third World women by particular texts while simultaneously offering an example of a cross-cultural text that does not colonize women. In the latter, she calls on feminist educators to teach students to "democratize rather than colonize" differently situated women's experiences. I further develop the notion of "knowing without borders" by analyzing what Mohanty means by "discursive colonization" and her call to "democratize rather than colonize" women's experiences. In my analysis, I bring Mohanty's work into dialogue with Sara Ahmed's concept of "orientating," in order to emphasize the materiality and sociality of knowing implicit in Mohanty's use of "colonizing" and "democratizing" to describe epistemic relations toward the experiences of others.

KNOWING AS AN ACTIVITY WITH MATERIAL EFFECTS

To understand what Mohanty means when she critiques authors for colonizing Third World women's experience and when she recommends instead that knowers learn to democratize experiences, we need to develop and use a language that calls attention to knowing as an activity that has material effects. When considering the idea that knowing is an activity that does something in and to the world, one might at first contend that knowing itself does not do anything, but rather people do things. In other words, one might argue, the world may certainly be altered by people acting on account of what they know or even just on what they think they know, but this does not entail that knowledge or knowing itself does something. While the world is no doubt affected by what people do on account of their beliefs, Mohanty's concern with knowledge production includes scrutiny of the ways in which producing knowledge can structure and reinforce hierarchies among groups of persons. The harms she highlights are not adequately described as being the results of what a person or even group of people might do on account of what they believe to be true. Indeed, if the problems Mohanty describes were simply a matter of false beliefs, she could resolve them by identifying the incorrect beliefs, furnishing true beliefs with which the false ones need to be replaced, and providing justification for those true beliefs. However, the problems and difficulties she describes are not this straightforward.

For example, in "Under Western Eyes," Mohanty criticizes several feminist cross-cultural texts for the analytic tools they use to establish knowledge of Third World women and in particular of Third World women's oppression. Mohanty does not simply point out cases of false or unjustified beliefs; instead, she attends to assumptions and analytic tools that structure and guide the theorists' attention (and lack of attention) to the world. These same assumptions and analytic tools structure the intelligibility of their written work, which in turn encourages readers to participate and maintain habits of attention Mohanty seeks to disrupt. Specifically Mohanty is concerned with habits of attention that fail to engage and even obscure the subjectivities of the Third World women who are discussed in the works she criticizes. For example, the theorists she criticizes regard large and diverse groups of women together, do not engage with the ways in which the women studied understand themselves, do not acknowledge that contextual information might matter in order to understand the various details concerning the women studied, and do not consider the material and discursive effects of how they frame the details they relay in the work they produce. These sorts of epistemic moves, Mohanty argues, lead to an assemblage of "facts" that fails to recognize the agency of Third World women,[16] thereby contributing to a picture of the world whereby women of the "Western" world[17] are more advanced than the rest. Mohanty characterizes this type of knowing as "colonizing": in these cases, theorists organize multiple aspects of the lives of the women they seek to know in a way that takes dominantly situated subjectivity and interests as a referent for organizing. In other words, by attending to the details of Third World women's lives through the use of conceptual tools calibrated to the lived experiences and material interests of dominantly situated women, this type of knowing establishes dominantly situated women as the standard by which the world is to be made intelligible, and it does so in these instances precisely by mining (or extracting from) the lives of Third World women. For this reason it is rightly characterized as "colonizing."

To be clear on the manner in which knowing here does something, we cannot simply think of knowing as holding a belief that has certain characteristics (e.g., being true and justified). Instead, we first need to observe that knowing itself is an act, one that could be described as an action of the knower who is herself a material being. The actions of the knower include the ways she comports herself toward the world and how she attends to the world. The language of "orientation" developed by Sara Ahmed in her book *Queer Phenomenology* is particularly helpful for calling attention to these aspects of knowing. One of the ways in which Ahmed uses "orientation" is to mean how we inhabit space such that our bodies are directed toward and moved by some objects in the world and not others. This kind of directedness is influenced by a great many things. Directedness repeated over time, for Ahmed, leads to habits of attention: "repetition of action takes us in certain directions: we are orientating ourselves toward some objects more than others, including not only physical objects but also objects of thought, feeling, and judgment."[18] The directedness of others can also orientate us, as when an entire crowd looks up at the sky, one is inclined to do so as well, or when walking amongst a large group of pedestrians it is easier to walk with the flow of traffic rather than against it.[19] Importantly, however, acts of attention are simultaneously acts of inattention.[20] The background or context against and within which what is foregrounded is made intelligible can be "produced by acts of relegation: some things are relegated to the background in order *to sustain* a certain direction; in other words, in order to keep attention on what is faced."[21] Moreover, "the world is shaped by the directions taken by some bodies more than others."[22] Using this language, we can say knowing is made possible by orientating oneself and being orientated in the world such that one is able to give attention to various aspects of the world and respond to it. At the same time as the knower is orientated and orientates herself toward the world, she contributes to the world by which others are orientated. In comporting oneself toward the world, the knower contributes to the shape of the world itself, given that knowers are part of the world.

These considerations, however, can be obscured by a picture of knowledge as something that is simply held in the mind, written in a book, or stored in cyberspace. Picturing knowledge as a thing held in the mind makes it seem as though knowledge is something that could be unproblematically transferred from one individual to another. We might call this picture the "transactional" model of knowing. According to such a view, knowing (or knowing about) others would simply be a matter of relaying reliable information, where reliability is tied up in questions of authority, authenticity, and trust. The transactional model of knowing, however, encourages us to forget things that are important for knowing well along the lines suggested by Mohanty: first, that knowers are always material beings, themselves part of the world; second, that knowing requires the material beings that knowers are to be directed toward, to attend to, respond to, and interact with other material parts of the world; and third, that the directedness, attention, responses, responsiveness, and nonresponsiveness of the material world (including the material beings that knowers are) contribute to the contexts within which the directedness, attention, responses, and interactions of other knowers make sense (or fail to make sense). In other words, how knowers are simultaneously orientated toward the world contributes to a world in which some things are more easily known and others less so.

Indeed, part of the project of feminism is to question patterns of interaction and the institutions supporting those patterns, so as to intervene when those patterns structure possibilities for meaningful action inequitably or when those patterns make knowing some parts of the world difficult, less likely, or even impossible. This critical approach involves not only investigating the meanings by which we structure our lives (asking questions such as: how does this practice or institution shape possibilities for action? for whom? and on account of whom?) but also working to change them (asking: how might we restructure our interactions so as to open new possibilities for action? with whom, for whom, and on account of whom are these new possibilities made?). In Mohanty's words, feminist thought is "a mode of intervention into particular hegemonic discourses" and thus feminist practices "are inscribed in relations of power—relations that they counter, resist, or perhaps implicitly support."[23] Engaging in knowledge practices directs one's body, one's attention, affect, and comportments in the world. We can describe these bodily comportments and habits of mind as changes in and to the world. And yet, as knowers, we are not always fully aware of the conditions that make our knowing possible. Consequently, as Mohanty points out, knowing practices may "counter, resist, or perhaps implicitly support" particular ways of being in the world.

Even as feminists attempt to resist oppressive patterns of meaning, it is within the backdrop of our coordinated interactions in the world, the enacting of what Alexis Shotwell has termed *implicit understandings*,[24] that we come to regard and respond to the world knowingly, including the ways of responding to and knowing the world that we engage as feminists. The ways in which we coordinate our bodily attention, our somatic and affective responses, to the world, form the ground within which beliefs that are candidates for knowledge as traditionally conceived can be formulated, investigated, and known. It follows that, when we know the world, whether as feminists or not, we are participating in implicit acts of understanding that help to make what we know knowable, but that may also make other aspects of the world obscure, illegible, or less knowable to ourselves *and* to others. In this way, knowing *does* something: it contributes to the conditions that make knowing certain things possible and others less possible or even impossible. Moreover, given the fact that certain actions and ways of being in the world require a kind of recognition or uptake from others, knowing can also contribute to the conditions that make certain ways of being and acting possible or impossible. For these reasons, to know is to move through the world in ways that affect the world.

Returning to Mohanty's criticism of the ways in which certain modes of feminist scholarship close down lines of knowing in relation to the very women these scholars were attempting to know, I think it is important to note that in "Under Western Eyes" Mohanty offered the work of María Mies as an example of Western feminist scholarship that does not colonize. As I will discuss in the next section, this example reminds readers that there is more than one way to move through the world knowingly and invites feminists of the overdeveloped world to know otherwise. Equally significant, however, is the fact that this very example was missed by many readers of Mohanty's original essay. Writing nearly two decades after its initial publication, in her reflections on the reception of "Under Western Eyes," Mohanty notes that some readers took her to be offering "a testament to the impossibility of egalitarian and noncolonizing cross-cultural scholarship" and showing "no possibility of solidarity between Western and Third World Women."[25] In other words, while Mohanty's essay received wide circulation, her invitation to feminists to know otherwise received little uptake among many of the feminist academics who circulated it. Here, we might say, is an example of one of the ways in which "recognition can entail avoidance."[26] In analyzing the ways in which intersectional scholarship has been frequently misunderstood, Vivian May notes that often those who misinterpret intersectional texts fail to approach these texts guided by the "both/and" logic within which they were forged, leading precisely to a kind of recognition of intersectional scholarship that misunderstands and/or avoids its political implications. In other words, knowers who are orientated by an "either/or" binary such as "either structural or local analyses reflect the world as it is" can fail to understand that both sorts of analyses are operative in a text. This kind of failure appears to animate readings of Mohanty's essay that neglect her treatment of María Mies's work in favor of misunderstanding the essay as forwarding the claim that cross-cultural knowing is always colonizing.

In the face of this sort of misunderstanding of her essay, I think it is also important to pay close attention to how Mohanty reflects upon her essay "Under Western Eyes" in the last chapter of the book for which "Under Western Eyes" is reprinted as the first. Mohanty indicates that this last chapter is written "to take fuller responsibility for my ideas and perhaps explain what influence they have had in debates in feminist theory."[27] In framing her reflections this way and comporting herself toward her earlier work in this manner, Mohanty is doing something important that cannot be fully appreciated under the "transactional" model of knowing. A transactional model would suggest that one is responsible only for forwarding ideas one can reasonably believe to be true. In other words, according to a transactional model, the epistemic responsibilities of one who communicates knowledge are to do so sincerely and competently. But responsibility ends there; what people do with the knowledge shared is their epistemic responsibility, not the responsibility of the one who has shared it. In contrast, the model of "knowing without borders" I am developing from Mohanty's work calls attention to the orientations and implicit understandings that knowers ask or invite others to participate in when they communicate or share knowledge. Knowers are not always aware of these orientations, indeed much of Western philosophy and the colonialist forms of life, with which it is intertwined, encourages us to forget them. In addition, readers and receivers of knowledge are not always aware of the orientations they bring to their understanding of the knowledge communicated. These orientations and implicit understandings shape the intelligibility, saliences, and urgencies of what is communicated. For this reason, claims made in one context may resonate differently in others, giving them a different sense, or at the very least, different emphases and saliences. In some cases, receiving and interpreting claims with a different orientation than the one from which the claims were made leads to misreading and misinterpreting, which is how I understand the propensity of some readers to have completely missed (or ignored) Mohanty's use of María Mies's work as an example of cross-cultural scholarship that does not colonize. In light of the notion of "knowing without borders," I understand the "responsibility" with which Mohanty begins chapter 9 as a mode of *responding* to not only a text that she has made but also one that "has enjoyed a remarkable life" of its own.[28]

In responding to her earlier essay, Mohanty notes that she is writing from a different position than the one from which she originally wrote the essay upon which she reflects. The communities within which she was situated when she wrote the original essay have shifted as the world has shifted and her position vis-à-vis the academy has changed as well. These are things that matter when considering the factors that influence her to write and that give intelligibility, salience, and urgency to the knowledge she creates. Importantly also, however, her relationship to her prior work is neither one of possession nor one of indifference. By placing "the apparent and continuing life of 'Under Western Eyes'" side by side with her "own travels through transnational feminist scholarship and networks,"[29] Mohanty suggests a number of things about readers, writers, and texts. First, she suggests that texts themselves are not inert, but rather continue to have lives as they travel among different constituencies of readership and understanding. Second, because of this the different constituencies of readership contribute to the life of a text by situating and responding to it. This, in turn, leads to a third point: to take responsibility for a text, the writer, too, must consider how the writing she produced was a way of responding to a particular set of situations within which the text was written and to consider the context from which she now approaches her own text in responding to it. Within the model of "knowing without borders" as I am developing it, to take responsibility for one's own writing is not to take responsibility for something one owns but to be justly responsive to something one has created. To be justly responsive at any given moment, one needs to consider the place from which one is responding now. The situations and history of the writer between the time of writing and the time of reflection may now require a different way of responding to the text. For example, the "from where" one responds may require reformulating claims so that those claims can continue to do liberatory work in the world in which the writer now finds herself. This way of regarding epistemic responsibility is completely lost if we think of the knowledge we produce as inert in the manner that the transactional model encourages us to do. Instead, we have an ongoing and complicated relationship to the knowledge we produce that requires a more robust understanding of epistemic responsibility such as the one I am recommending here. This sense of epistemic responsibility, as responsiveness to that which one has created, is suggested by Mohanty when she writes that "[p]erhaps mapping the intellectual and institutional context in which I wrote back then and the shifts that have affected its reading since would clarify the intentions and claims of the essay,"[30] and when she endeavors to make her "own political choices and decisions transparent," and to provide "readers with a productive and provocative space to think and act creatively for feminist struggle."[31] These motivations make sense within a framework that recognizes that commitments provide an anchoring from which to regard the world, and that this anchoring is animated by our engagements with one another. The commitments we embody and animate through our engagements with one another provide the borders within which knowers make various aspects of the world intelligible and salient. "Knowing without borders" insists that the space from which we know is creative and dynamic so that we can continue to know responsibly. To know in ways that do not colonize, knowers must take care to be aware of what anchors their responsiveness to the world. In particular, knowers must avoid (and be vigilant about relapsing into) anchoring their responses to the world in ways that posit dominantly situated lives as the standard by which the world is to be judged and through the use of concepts that are designed to serve dominantly situated interests. Part of the work of epistemic responsibility and responsiveness must therefore entail allowing the subjectivities of those in relation to whom a knower is dominantly situated to make significant impressions upon that knower, so that the knower's approach to the world, the patterns she picks up on, the connections she makes, and the inferences she draws from them change. This is not merely a mental exercise but requires physical labor that takes time (e.g., to produce better habits of attention). It also necessitates building commitments toward and working with others who are nondominantly situated in relation to the knower.[32] This way of thinking about epistemic responsibility entails that we understand situatedness not as something static or decided once and for all but as capable of evolving in response to the changes we make in the world and in ourselves in resistance to dominance. By this I do not mean that knowers can simply decide upon how they are situated, but rather that when we work upon the world and change it, our situation changes. While this can include dismantling and chipping away at various forms of dominance and oppression, given that dominance and oppression, too, are not static, it also means that knowers who wish to resist dominance and oppression will need to identify and respond to the ways in which dominance reasserts itself in new forms.

EPISTEMIC GATHERING, OR KNOWING OTHERWISE

Given the materiality of knowing (given that any knower is an embodied knower) and given the sociality of knowing (given that knowing is a practice that exceeds the individual embodied knower), what might it mean for feminists to acknowledge epistemic borders without abandoning the work of knowing otherwise? Typically, European and Euro-American philosophers posit knowing in a way that makes it seem like a borderless activity or even an activity designed to eliminate borders between mind and reality. When philosophers have spoken about borders and knowing they have typically meant something like a limit "where no man can know," and then they have concerned themselves with whether it is possible to "make sense" of such limits in ways that would define the boundaries of what it is we can and cannot know. However, it seems to me that this kind of "making sense" is unhelpful and even harmful insofar as it seeks to define in advance that which is possible, leading us to disregard systematically any experience or any one that does not fit.

Ahmed's work can again be helpful for thinking about what is at stake here and for considering what it would mean to treat epistemic borders differently. When analyzing the ways in which the world "appears" to the phenomenologist, Ahmed draws attention to the manner in which the world presses itself upon people differently, depending upon a person's habitual relation to the world as well as the habitual relations to the world of others around us. For example, in considering the work of various European philosophers, she turns to the manner in which the writing table is often used as a paradigmatic "simple" object appearing before the phenomenal consciousness of the philosopher. In her analysis, Ahmed denaturalizes this phenomenal appearance by noting that the material relations that make it possible for there to be writing tables do not figure into these accounts. Moreover, she asks how those bodies that build and clean writing tables might face and experience writing tables differently than those bodies which simply sit before them to write. Using some of the conceptual tools of phenomenology to reflect on bringing different bodies into focus, Ahmed notes:

> When bodies take up spaces that they were not intended to inhabit, something other than the reproduction of the facts of the matter happens. The hope that reproduction fails is the hope for new impressions, for new lines to emerge, new objects, or even new bodies, which gather, in gathering around this table. The new would not involve the loss of background. Indeed, for bodies to arrive in spaces where they are not already at home, where they are not "in place" involves hard work; indeed it involves painstaking labor for bodies to inhabit spaces that do not extend their shape. . . . Yes, women philosophers do gather and have gathered creating their impressions. Our task is to recall their histories of their arrival, and how this history opens up spaces for others that have yet to be cleared.[33]

In other words, spaces are formed and form the bodies that inhabit them in ways that not only make certain kinds of movement possible but also encourage certain movements and not others. Architects study this phenomenon and it has been an important issue in the disability rights movement insofar as some spaces are more or less accessible to people with different sorts of bodies. By bringing Ahmed's phenomenological reflection to the epistemic context, and specifically to the question of how to regard epistemic borders, I highlight three things that are crucial to the work of knowing without borders. First, as I have already stressed, it is critical that we keep in mind that knowers are embodied creatures who, in part, comprise the world we know (and do not know). Second, decolonizing knowing requires a good deal of work, painstaking labor, since knowing that challenges colonial epistemic moves and institutions disrupts that which is "in place." In light of the difficulties facing those who are, and those who think in ways that are, "out of place" in resistance to dominant institutions, it is critical that knowers attend to the collectivities we inhabit and form coordinated embodied habits that sustain resistant thought and practice. In order to effectively disrupt the habits of attention that Western feminists have inherited from our colonialist pasts, we must therefore "gather," epistemically speaking. In other words, we need to struggle collectively in ways that organize and respond to the world in less coercive ways, and specifically, in ways that allow the subjectivities and the material realities of nondominantly situated women to press upon us. With the idea of "epistemic gathering," therefore, I mean the sustained on-the-ground work with women who are not similarly situated, which disrupts ingrained habits of attention and develops new ways of acting in concert.[34] This sort of work changes the material beings that we are, allowing the world to press upon knowers and enabling knowers to respond to the world in new ways. This work does not happen in an instant, but rather takes time and requires practice, commitment, and struggle. It is not just the work of changing individual knowers' habits of attention and comportments toward the world (although it is certainly that) but includes also the work of creating communities within which what could not previously have been thought can now be thought. It is, in short, the work of making intelligible through our embodied epistemic practices that which dominant epistemic institutions continually and relentlessly render unintelligible in their own commitments to serve dominant interests.

If we take seriously what Mohanty says about borders and couple it with what Ahmed says about orientations and the importance of "gathering," we might come to think of epistemic borders (or borders to our knowing) differently. In her analysis of Mies's scholarship on the women lace workers in Narsapur, India, Mohanty asks her readers to consider not only what Mies notices in her work with these women (including various practices, institutions, and processes) but also how Mies "generates theoretical categories from within the situation and context being analyzed."[35] Rather than bringing epistemic tools to organize her sense of the women with whom she comes into contact and the significance of the work they do, Mohanty argues that Mies allowed her habits of attending to the world to be reoriented by the ways in which the lace makers understood themselves, their work, and other women. In doing so, Mies allowed the subjectivities and the agency of the women lace makers of Narsapur to (in Ahmed's language) reorientate her. This is not to say that Mies passively received information relayed to her (as a transactional model would suggest), but rather that Mies allowed lived experiences and interests beyond her own to impact her ways of attending to the world. Starting from these ways of attending to the world as her guiding referent, Mies therefore generated knowledge *with* the women she worked. Following this example, if feminist knowing is to resist colonizing moves, it must be *guided and shaped by* experiences of those whose lives extend beyond the dominant social imaginary. Making sense *from* and *with* (rather than just *of*) these experiences is to allow such experiences to make an impression that moves us, epistemically speaking. This, then, is a way of understanding what Mohanty means when she says we ought to democratize rather than colonize experiences. In contrast to discursively colonizing experiences, understood as organizing the details of another's experience through epistemic tools calibrated to dominant interests, democratizing allows the experiences of nondominantly situated women to orientate one's attention to the world, to move one, epistemically speaking. This movement contributes to the ongoing material and discursive commitments we engage in order to know and live well together.

CONCLUSION

If we think of the set of implicit understandings within which we know as a set of commitments enacted in our epistemic practices, our habits of mind, as well as our interactive and affective bodily comportments, making our knowing not only possible but also capable of shifting and being shifted, the thought of crossing epistemic borders takes on new meaning. Following this sense, "knowing without borders" would require an ability to shift (and to continue to shift when necessary) the commitments that anchor us as knowers. These shifts must be embodied in our material and somatic practices. And they involve more than the individual knower and her individual will. Epistemic gathering is the kind of work that must be engaged with other knowers with whom a knower can come to know. This kind of knowing with others and its implications do not make sense when we are guided by a transactional model of knowing, for it is not the sort of knowing that extracts information, but rather it is the sort of knowing that engages intersubjectively so that the world can press upon the knower and upon knowers generally. Epistemic gathering attends to (and enables) women's agency in ways that are more equitable, democratizing (rather than colonizing) experiences.

How does this way of thinking about knowing redirect our attention with regard to feminist knowledge projects? For one, I hope it highlights that knowing is not something we do on our own, nor is "knowledge" something that moves seamlessly from one knower to the next. Indeed, I hope it makes clear that attempts to "simply" know run the serious risk of enacting epistemic violence, particularly if we are in the habit of forgetting that we ourselves are part of the material conditions within which the world is known and unknown. In addition, it shifts the kinds of questions we might ask of ourselves and others when attempting to make sense of situations. Rather than asking: "who knows?" or "whose knowledge?" (which have been galvanizing questions within Euro-American philosophical feminism) we might begin to ask instead "with whom am I knowing?," "at whose expense might this knowing be made possible?," "what does my knowing here at this time and in this place do?," and finally, "how does my knowing make possible or undermine the practice of solidarity with other women?"

NOTES

1. Chandra Talpade Mohanty, "Under Western Eyes: Feminist Scholarship and Colonial Discourse," *Boundary 2* 12, no. 2 (1984): 333–58. Reprinted as the first chapter of Chandra Talpade Mohanty, *Feminism without Borders: Decolonizing Theory, Practicing Solidarity* (Durham: Duke University Press, 2003).
2. Mohanty, *Feminism without Borders*, 17–42.
3. Jacqui Alexander and Chandra Talpade Mohanty, "Introduction: Genealogies, Legacies, Movements," in *Feminist Genealogies, Colonial Legacies, Democratic Futures*, ed. Jacqui Alexander and Chandra Talpade Mohanty (New York: Routledge, 1997), xvii; Chandra Talpade Mohanty, "Transnational Feminist Crossings: On Neoliberalism and Radical Critique," *Signs* 38, no. 4 (Summer 2013): 967–91; Mohanty, *Feminism without Borders*, 192–97.
4. Mohanty, *Feminism without Borders*, 5.
5. Ibid., 2.
6. Ibid., 1.
7. Ibid., 2.
8. Ibid., 7.
9. Here and throughout I follow Mohanty's use of the term *Third World women* to refer to women who are nondominantly situated with regard to global location. As Mohanty notes in "Under Western Eyes Revisited" this locution is not without problems even as it retains political and explanatory value.
10. Mohanty, *Feminism without Borders*, 45.
11. Ibid.
12. Ibid., 226.
13. See for example, Bat-Ami Bar On's "Marginality and Epistemic Privilege" for this sort of mistaken reading of standpoint epistemology. Uma Narayan, *Dislocating Cultures*, and Emmalon Davis, "Typecasts, Tokens, and Spokespersons"

call attention to the dangerous effects of viewing nondominantly situated persons as having "automatic" knowledge. Both Patricia Hill Collins, *Black Feminist Thought*, and Sandra Harding, *Whose Science? Whose Knowledge*, develop more nuanced standpoint epistemologies that emphasize knowing as a practice that requires work as opposed to knowledge "states" that are automatic.

14. Collins, *Black Feminist Thought* (New York: Routledge, 2001).

15. Mohanty, *Feminism without Borders*, 7.

16. Ibid., 22.

17. Again, I follow Mohanty's usage here. Nonetheless, it is important to note that "the West" and the "Western world" are colonial discursive constructions. One difficulty that the account I develop in this chapter raises is how to refer to such locutions in order to analyze their workings without participating in and contributing to the epistemic systems that maintain their sense. This is not simply a matter of "finding the correct word" but of decolonizing epistemic attention, deconstructing colonial epistemic practices, and attending to the world anew.

18. Sara Ahmed, *Queer Phenomenology: Orientations, Objects, Others* (Durham: Duke University Press, 2006), 56.

19. Ibid., 119–20.

20. Shannon Sullivan, "White Ignorance and Colonial Oppression," makes a similar point when she notes that acts of knowing can be simultaneously acts of ignoring.

21. Ahmed, *Queer Phenomenology*, 31.

22. Ibid., 159.

23. Mohanty, *Feminism without Borders*, 19.

24. Alexis Shotwell, *Knowing Otherwise: Race, Gender, and Implicit Understanding* (College Park: Penn State University Press, 2011).

25. Mohanty, *Feminism without Borders*, 224.

26. Vivian May, "'Speaking into the Void'?: Intersectionality Critiques and Epistemic Backlash," *Hypatia* 29, no. 1 (2014): 94.

27. Mohanty, *Feminism without Borders*, 221.

28. Mohanty, *Feminism without Borders*, 270, endnote 1.

29. Ibid., 222.

30. Ibid., 224.

31. Ibid., 223.

32. By this I do not mean to imply that nondominantly situated knowers are obligated to help dominantly situated knowers with this task, since this would once again structure relations along lines that attend to dominant interests. Instead, dominantly situated knowers need to avail themselves of opportunities to shift the comportments and expectations that guide their epistemic activity when they arise and to work toward changing structural conditions so that more equitable and reciprocal relations among wider and wider groups of knowers become possible. In some case, this may mean acknowledging that one does not know some things one might wish to know and acknowledging one's epistemic dependence on others who have no obligation to respond or attend to that dependence.

33. Ahmed, *Queer Phenomenology*, 62–63.

34. I take what I say here about the notion of epistemic gathering to be consonant with Barbara Fultner's notion of solidarity as joint action or movement within

a shared horizon in "The Dynamics of Transnational Feminist Dialogue," 20. My own emphasis highlights that bodies acting in concert can literally create (or close down) horizons within which certain things can be known (or prevented from being known), thereby generating epistemic responsibilities with regard to the effects of our epistemic practices. Fultner's emphasis highlights that those who inhabit shared horizons may notice different things and be affected by what is known from within those horizons in very different ways, thereby making space for differences within solidarity. Both points are crucial for decolonizing feminist thought.

35. Mohanty, *Feminism without Borders*, 32.

BIBLIOGRAPHY

Ahmed, Sara. *Queer Phenomenology: Orientations, Objects, Others*. Durham: Duke University Press, 2006.

Alexander, M. Jacqui, and Chandra Talpade Mohanty. "Introduction: Genealogies, Legacies, Movements." In *Feminist Genealogies, Colonial Legacies, Democratic Futures*, edited by M. Jacqui Alexander and Chandra Talpade Mohanty. New York: Routledge, 1997.

Bar On, Bat-Ami. "Marginality and Epistemic Privilege." In *Feminist Epistemologies*, edited by Linda Alcoff and Elizabeth Potter, 83–100. New York: Routledge, 1993.

Collins, Patricia Hill. *Black Feminist Thought: Knowledge, Consciousness, and the Politics of Empowerment*. New York: Routledge, 2011.

Davis, Emmalon. "Typecasts, Tokens, and Spokespersons: A Case for Credibility Excess as Testimonial Injustice." *Hypatia* 31, no. 3 (2016): 485–501.

Fultner, Barbara. "The Dynamics of Transnational Feminist Dialogues." In *Decolonizing Feminism: Transnational Feminism and Globalization*, edited by Margaret McLaren. New York: Rowman and Littlefield, 2017.

Harding, Sandra. *Whose Science? Whose Knowledge?: Thinking from Women's Lives*. Ithaca: Cornell University Press, 1991.

May, Vivian. "'Speaking into the Void'? Intersectionality Critiques and Epistemic Backlash." *Hypatia* 29, no 1 (2014): 94–112.

Mohanty, Chandra Talpade. "Under Western Eyes: Feminist Scholarship and Colonialist Discourse." *Boundary 2* 12, no. 3 (1984): 333–58.

Mohanty, Chandra Talpade. *Feminism without Borders: Decolonizing Theory, Practicing Solidarity*. Durham: Duke University Press, 2003.

Mohanty, Chandra Talpade. "Transnational Feminist Crossings: On Neoliberalism and Radical Critique," *Signs* 38, no. 4 (Summer 2013): 967–91.

Narayan, Uma. *Dislocating Cultures: Identities, Traditions, and Third World Feminism*. New York: Routledge, 2013.

Shotwell, Alexis. *Knowing Otherwise: Race, Gender, and Implicit Understanding*. College Park: Penn State Press, 2011.

Sullivan, Shannon. "White Ignorance and Colonial Oppression or Why I Know So Little about Puerto Rico." In *Race and Epistemologies of Ignorance*, edited by Shannon Sullivan and Nancy Tuana. Albany, NY: SUNY Press, 2007.

Part 2

RETHINKING RIGHTS

Chapter 3

Indigenous/Campesina Embodied Knowledge, Human Rights Awards, and Lessons for Transnational Feminist Solidarity

Pascha Bueno-Hansen and Sylvanna M. Falcón

When Indigenous/campesina[1] movement leaders receive international human rights awards, both their individual activist contributions and their broader movements gain political visibility and access to new avenues of funding primarily from the global North. While these benefits are noteworthy, we are deeply unsettled by the enormous insecurity experienced by many award recipients, in particular throughout the Americas. This chapter focuses on the lives of two Indigenous/campesina women who have won the prestigious Goldman Environmental Prize (GEP), Berta Cáceres and Máxima Acuña Chaupe. Cáceres, assassinated in her home in 2016 soon after receiving the GEP, led the struggle of the Lenca peoples against displacement and the destruction of their environment by megaprojects in southwestern Honduras. Acuña, still among the living, is at the forefront of the struggle of Quechua-speaking peasant communities against extractivist mining in the Andean highlands of Peru. We contend in this chapter that the activism of Cáceres and Acuña reveals the perils of Western-centric knowledge production that divides human reasoning from the natural world.[2]

"Divergent histories and social locations," as Chandra T. Mohanty argues, are "woven together by the political threads of opposition to forms of domination that are not only pervasive but also systematic."[3] We envision our engagement with transnational feminist solidarity as a contribution to these political threads of opposition. By prioritizing accountability to historical and systemic dynamics of geopolitical power, we wish to enact what Papaschase Cree scholar Dwayne Donald calls *ethical relationality*, "to understand more deeply how our different histories and experiences position us in relation to each other."[4] Therefore, transnational feminist solidarity must read relations in their multidirectional and contextual complexity rather than as unidirectional from north to south. In addition, the fact that transnational acts of solidarity do not by default involve global North actors reminds us of the need for epistemic humility. This chapter merges divergent histories, multiple social locations, and ethical relationality to present three lessons for transnational feminists situated in the global North.

The first lesson honors the spirit and pluralism of activists' consciousness. We foreground their cosmovision—a philosophical vision of and consciousness about the world that embraces a loving and nonhierarchical coexistence with all beings. The second lesson confronts the inherent contradictions of human recognition in human rights prize-giving practices. This lesson emphasizes the collective aspects of struggle and the multidirectionality of the exchange. The third lesson utilizes Mohanty's methodology to map "the cartographies of struggle," specifically under the auspices of neoliberal containment. This mapping exercise mandates forceful declarations and transnational feminist organizing against what Cáceres refers to as "rapacious capitalism" and what Acuña refers to as "corporate greed."

Building from Mohanty's insights, analyzing prize-giving requires "a more finely honed" and "context specific feminist method."[5] While the human rights awards process accentuates the dangers activists face every day, this chapter illuminates the repressive forces of the neoliberal state-corporate nexus that undergirds this intense insecurity. Cáceres received the Goldman Environmental Prize (GEP) just a few months prior to being assassinated, suggesting at first glance that perhaps the award somehow contributed to an insecurity increase, precipitating her killing. However, the political climate and activist insecurity in Latin America have been ongoing for the past couple of decades, where threats against environmental and human rights activists are drastically increasing every year, especially in Honduras and Peru. In other words, we do not contend that there is a link between Cáceres receiving the GEP and her being killed. In fact, her receipt of the award garnered her access to the GEP security grants that may very well have extended her life. We maintain, however, that the consolidation of this nexus of transnational corporations and neoliberal states in Latin America means avenues of accountability have been blurred, producing a situation in which growing threats against grassroots activists go increasingly unchecked. Award-granting agencies must confront these harsh and brutal realities.

Cáceres and Acuña are engaged in similar struggles related to the environment in countries that heavily favor neoliberal megaprojects and intense foreign investment. Both Honduras and Peru were largely exempt from the Latin American Pink Tide in which the regions experienced a surge in left and left-leaning governance.[6] Honduras and Peru are among the top four most dangerous countries in the world for environmental activists or land defenders, along with Brazil and the Philippines.[7] These precarious conditions raise critical questions of *how* to practice transnational feminist solidarity, in particular when situated in the global North, without exacerbating an already intense situation. We first turn to the story of Cáceres and her community struggle to address the praxis question.

BERTA CÁCERES, THE LENCA STRUGGLE, AND COPINH

> We must shake our consciousness free of the rapacious capitalism, racism, and patriarchy that will only ensure our own self-destruction.
>
> —Berta Cáceres's acceptance speech, 2015 GEP ceremony

The Lenca peoples are one of largest and most organized of the Indigenous groups in Honduras.[8] They live in the central department of La Paz, and the western departments of Lempira, Ocotepeque, and Intibucá, as well as in some smaller communities in the northern part of the country. Berta Cáceres was a leader in the struggle of the Lenca peoples against displacement and the destruction of their environment by megaprojects in southwestern Honduras and was one of the most outspoken critics of the 2009 coup against President Manuel Zelaya.[9]

Cáceres's story is inextricably tied to The Council of Honduran Popular and Indigenous Organizations/Consejo Cívico de Organizaciones Populares e Indígenes de Honduras (COPINH), an organization she cofounded on March 27, 1993, to stop logging projects resulting in deforestation and to begin consolidating popular social movements. Its organizational structure contains sixteen members with equal representation of eight men and eight women endorsed by statute; these members are charged with leading various coordination efforts. COPINH identifies itself as "an Indigenous and popular organization, anti-patriarchal, anti-imperialist, anti-neoliberal, sensitive to the problems, needs and rights of Indigenous, rural and urban communities of the Honduran people and the world."[10] The organization offers what anthropologist Mark Anderson contends is "biting critiques of neoliberalism as neocolonialism, linking the structural crisis facing Indigenous peoples not just to histories of oppression but to contemporary global politics." Not only has COPINH "link[ed] Indigenous rights mobilization to an anti-neoliberal stance,"[11] the organization strongly believes in gender equality: "COPINH believes that to increase participation and decision making, from the Indigenous perspective, it is essential to support gender equality and denounce any abuse against women."[12]

Global Witness reports that over 100 land and environmental activists have been killed in Honduras alone between 2010 and 2015,[13] a stunning increase from 10 recorded killings between 2002 and 2009.[14] Cáceres, as well as other community leaders who worked alongside her, joins this death list after being assassinated in her home in La Esperanza, Intibucá, on March 3, 2016, soon after she received the GEP for her work defending the Gualcarque River against the Agua Zarca hydropower project,[15] which involves several key players, including a private national company, Desarrollos Energéticos, SA (DESA);[16] several international banks;[17] and a Chinese company, SinoHydra.[18]

The Gualcarque River is sacred to the Lenca community, which is why they are so fiercely and bravely determined to protect it. The river is used "for drinking, bathing and for spiritual reasons, and [the Lenca peoples] argue that the dam will jeopardize their access to it."[19] The Agua Zarca project represents an ongoing struggle over water, land rights, and spiritual well-being for the Lenca peoples. The result of the Agua Zarca hydroelectric dam project "would [be to] create a 300-meter long reservoir and divert 3 kilometers of the river," destroying their livelihood.[20]

Gustavo Castro Soto, a Mexican environmental activist, was with Cáceres for several days prior to her killing because she had been receiving more consistent and aggressive threats. Her daughter Laura "heard that her mother had been receiving threats from state and corporate agents."[21] Castro's accompaniment was an effort to protect Cáceres and, ideally, deter the violence. However, he was shot twice and then detained at the time of her assassination. Amnesty International issued an urgent alert for his release, which stressed that he was in grave danger as having witnessed her murder.[22] He was held for one month without cause and then released on April 1, 2016, eventually returning to Mexico and telling *Radio Progreso* [Progress Radio] that "what we are confronting are forces very powerful, obscure forces, filled with ambition, and these forces are what the movements are fighting."[23] These obscure forces of "rapacious capitalism" are the underside of the neoliberal state–corporate nexus.

While Honduras is the most dangerous place to live in as an environmental activist in Latin America, particularly in relation to hydropower megaprojects, Peru is the most volatile place to challenge the mining industry. Mining in Peru has a long history that traces back to Spanish colonialism starting in 1550 and has continued through Peruvian independence in 1824. Peru currently has thirty-eight social conflicts related to mining projects, the highest number of mining-related social conflicts in Latin America.[24] The Peruvian Ombudsman stated in February 2015 that out of every ten social conflicts, on average, seven are due to mining activity.

MÁXIMA ACUÑA CHAUPE, HER FAMILY, AND THE BLUE LAKE

Because I defend my lakes, they want to take my life . . . .
I defend the land and water because it is life.
I am not afraid of corporate power. I will continue the struggle.

—Máxima Acuña Chaupe's acceptance speech, 2016 GEP ceremony[25]

The intensification of mining in the 1990s contextualizes the current social conflict in the northern Andean department of Cajamarca. One of the most well-known and controversial mining projects is Yanacocha's Conga project. Yanacocha is a corporation established in 1992 and comprised of the following groups: Newmont Mining Corporation (51.35%) based in the United States; Compania de Minas Buenaventura (43.65%) based in Peru; and International Finance Corporation (5%), an investment arm of the World Bank. Conflicts surrounding Yanacocha consortium's mining in Cajamarca initiated in 1993, shortly after they established their presence there.[26] Yanacocha's Conga project, engulfed in social conflict since its inception in 2009, would be the largest gold mining project in Peruvian history with a $4.8 billion price tag.

The struggle of Andean Quechua-speaking peasant Máxima Acuña Chaupe and her family in defense of their land and water against the Conga project is emblematic of the many peasant and Indigenous struggles across the country. Acuña, a forty-six-year-old married woman with four children, has become the global symbol of resistance against extractivist projects, such as the mining industry. Acuña has been fighting Yanacocha since 2011. In 1994, she bought the land she and her family live on, called Tragadero Grande, from a family member, Yanacocha claims to have bought the land from the community of Sorochuco in 1996 and 1997 for the Conga project.[27]

The Acuña family purchased *Tragadero Grande* with the goal of building a life based on farming and maintaining livestock. The proposed gold mining project would need to drain four lakes, one of which, the Blue Lake/*la laguna azul*, is located beside Acuña's land. For her defense of the land, the lake, and the water, she has gained the nickname, *la dama de la laguna azul*, the lady of the blue lake. The proposed open-pit gold mine would use the Blue Lake as a depository for excess earth with chemical and heavy metal residue from the project. To extract the gold, cyanide, a lethal and toxic substance, is mixed with the soil. While Yanacocha promises to respect the highest environmental standards, it has a history of repeated spills and contaminations.[28]

Acuña's resistance is grounded in the defense of her way of life. Independent from formal education and literacy, her claims are built upon an ancestral knowledge of how to coexist with the land. Fully cognizant that she and her family are up against a determined transnational corporate consortium, Acuña refuses to acquiesce to neoliberal state-corporate power. The isolated location of Acuña's land makes her struggle seem quite solitary, and yet she's been able to build a network of support.

There is a constellation of organizations and groups that create the broader context for Acuña's struggle. Acuña's advocacy efforts are supported and defended by her attorney, Mirtha Vásquez, who is also the executive director of GRUFIDES, a nongovernmental organization in Cajamarca. Catholic priest Marco Arrana founded GRUFIDES in 2001 to defend the environment and human rights, with an emphasis on collective well-being through ecological sustainability, the right to water, economic solidarity, gender equity, and intergenerational dialogue. Milton Sanchez Cubas, General Secretary of the Inter-Institutional Platform of Celedín, is another notable local activist close to Acuña.[29] Those involved in the antimining protest include peasant farmers, unions, nongovernmental organizations, students, church groups, and urban professionals.[30]

The individual stories of Cáceres and Acuña should be viewed as part of a collective narrative, highlighting what happens when neoliberal state-corporate power is threatened: lethal and nonlethal violence against the perceived leaders of movements. In defense of their communities' rights to land and water against corporate greed and state efforts to pursue megaprojects, these women, through their communities' struggles, have illustrated a relationship to the environment that puts them at risk because "rapacious capitalism" does not value these relationships or Indigenous knowledge. We link their stories because their complementary environmental struggles are occurring in a region that is being violently remade through attacking and killing activists to undermine social movements.

In an act of south-south solidarity, Acuña invoked Cáceres in her own struggle when at a recent Peruvian protest. She held a sign that read *Berta Vive La Lucha Sigue* ("Berta Lives the Struggle Continues").[31] As shown in this display of solidarity, the global North does not figure at all. This sign challenges the conceptual reduction of transnational feminist solidarity to being about unidirectional north to south gestures.

ELITE PHILANTHROPY MEETS HUMAN RIGHTS REALITIES: LESSONS FOR TRANSNATIONAL FEMINIST SOLIDARITY EFFORTS

The GEP has become one of the most recognizable and prestigious awards in grassroots enviornmental activism, with an incredible access to world leaders, its invite-only grand ceremonies in San Francisco and Washington, DC, and its professionally and beautifully filmed profiles of award winners. Cofounders Richard N. Goldman (1920–2010) and his wife Rhoda H. Goldman (1924–1996) established the GEP in 1989 "to demonstrate the international nature of environmental problems, draw public attention to global issues of critical importance, reward ordinary individuals for outstanding grassroots environmental achievement, and inspire others to emulate the examples set by the Prize recipients."[32] The prize comes with a cash award of $175,000 for each of the six annual winners.[33]

In situations where global North actors initiate solidarity, we emphasize accountability to historical and asymmetrical geopolitical power dynamics. How do we respond to the consolidation of neoliberal regimes in Latin America, under the current right turn in Honduras and Peru specifically, and to the increased repression of Indigenous/campesina struggles to defend their land, water, communities, and lifeways? Breny Mendoza questions the viability and effectiveness of transnational feminist solidarity at the practical level;[34] the lived realities of activists in Latin America, especially women, complicate the terrain of transnational feminist solidarity because the tremendous divide—geographic, linguistic, political, and spiritual—can feel insurmountable or irreconcilable. Yet this divide can offer a new point of departure in which to envision networks of transnational solidarity that first and foremost honor the embodied knowledge of those on the forefront of the struggles and at the same time reckons with the real shortcomings of our solidarity (see chapter 9 of this book). We offer three lessons in the following section to fortify the meaning of transnational feminist solidarity.

Lesson 1: Honoring the Spirit and Pluralism of Women's Consciousness

The plural and collective consciousness of Cáceres and Acuña—which emerges from a combination of their social position, cosmovision, and direct activism—situates their struggles beyond individualism and secularization. In this cosmovision, a profound reverence exists for water as source of life,[35] as well as the living spiritual connection with bodies of water such as lakes and rivers. This profound reverence shatters assumptions of individualism and secularization based on the coloniality of knowledge and the ontological separation of human reasoning and the natural world. Contextualizing this ontological separation further, Dwayne Donald defines colonialism as simply "an extended process of denying relationship whether it be with the places where we live, or our head and our heart, or people who look different from us."[36] This decontextualized and disembodied way of knowing facilitates the claim of objectivity and universality,[37] and renders irrelevant Indigenous/campesina embodied knowledges, cosmovisions, and struggles.

Latin American decolonial theorist Edgardo Lander explains that modernity is the colonial and imperial frame that subsumes time, space, and peoples into its ordering of the world. Modernity determines social organization and the doings of "normal" human members of society.[38]

In sharp contrast to the assumptions about normal human socialization based on the ontological separation of human reason from the natural world, Cáceres and Acuña live relationally and in coexistence with bodies of water. For Cáceres and the Lenca peoples, the Gualcarque River is "inhabited by a female spirit" and has ancestral and spiritual importance. The Lenca peoples are taught that girls are the custodians of the river and that the river signifies life; the medicinal plants along the river are also a part of this relational ecology. When Cáceres would immerse herself in the water, she would have a dialogue with the river. She was always confident that her people would beat the Agua Zarca dam project from coming to fruition because she said, "the river told me." Western-informed methodologies or epistemologies based on the coloniality of knowledge[39] deny the relational ecology, or "the webs of relationships," in which Cáceres's spiritual and personal connections to the river are enmeshed.[40]

Similarly, the Lady of the Blue Lake, Máxima Acuña, understands her life as inextricably tied to her family, her livestock, the land, and the water. This "web of relationships" spans the human and nonhuman realm. The regional movements that prioritize the defense of natural resources such as water, which is fundamental to the maintenance of their agriculture and livestock, utilize the discourse of defending resources for future generations as well as fulfilling the ancestral responsibility given to them by the water itself. Anthropologist Fabiana Li explains that water can be understood as "a web of relations among humans and other-than-human beings that are sustained through everyday relations."[41] Therefore, the struggle for water, life, and future generations contests "the state's assertion that the country's economic development depended on resource extraction."[42]

Many activists against the Conga mining project frame their struggle in relation to the earth and its living beings, both human and nonhuman. They offer a much deeper analysis of their environmental struggle, viewing themselves as born with the responsibility to protect water, and they treat bodies of water as blessed relations and gifts rather than natural resources from which to extract profit. As Ryan Mack, program officer of the GEP, explains, the struggle of Acuña and her family for their land is emblematic of the struggle of local communities and local people against the Peruvian state's historic complicity with companies dedicated to natural resource extraction at the cost of their lives.[43] The struggles of the present are coconstituted with the struggles of the past and of the future.[44]

The 2016 GEP ceremony honored Acuña and included a stunning tribute to Cáceres by poets Leslie Valencia, Terisa Siagatonu, and Erika Vivianna Céspedes in an act of Indigenous and women of color transnational solidarity and love. The following is an excerpt of a poem they performed during the ceremony that beautifully weaves their honoring of Cáceres's embodied knowledge with the pain of what the world lost when she was killed:

> Berta, as Indigenous women, we know that death is just the Earth's way of reminding us of who we belong to: the land. Tonight, we summon you as courage, as mother, as teacher, as patience, as joy, as activist with a contagious smile who cut her teeth on revolution for the love of the people and the land of Honduras. Last year on this very stage you said, 'We come from the land, water, and corn.' *Somos seres surgidos de la tierra, el agua y el maíz.* You were carrying the power of clenched fists and sacred rivers in your speech, the Rio Blanco and the Rio Gualcarque, sources of life and medicine for the Lenca people. It is why you were so fearless against the threats. The river had already warned you that your victory would be difficult, but you stood brave. And tonight the river runs throughout this room, a living vein connecting all of us to this planet, a call to protect Mother Earth just as lovingly and fiercely as you did Berta.[45]

In this exquisite reading, the poets collectively reaffirm and make a call for ontological continuity between human reasoning and the natural world through our connection to the river. The poem echoes the river as other-than-human or as a living earthbeing.[46] This profoundly decolonizing message celebrates our interdependent web of relations and stands in strong rebuke of the coloniality of knowledge. It is impossible to deny the emotional impact of Cáceres's life and the knowledge she clearly passed on to not only the Lenca people but other Indigenous peoples as well. Hence, the poem affirms Cáceres's embodied knowledge and COPINH's collective radical feminist praxis against racism, imperialism, neoliberalism, and patriarchy.

In another artistic tradition at the same event, Acuña delivered her acceptance speech in song, a key part of Andean oral tradition and arguably an assertion of "oppositional consciousness and agency" on her own terms.[47] Communicating outside of the rational and linear, her song related the story of her struggle. Acuña closed her acceptance speech with the following statement, "I defend the land and the water because it is life. I do not fear the corporations and I will continue the struggle . . . for those killed in Celendín and Bambamarca and all those in the struggle."[48] Though she does not identify her struggle as a feminist political project, Acuña's embodied knowledge and struggle reflects transnational feminist views on anti-racism, anti-imperialism, and anti-corporatism. Moreover, the state-sanctioned violence that she faces on a daily basis (and that took Cáceres's life) is part of a lengthy regional history of systematic and gender-based violence against women.[49]

Human rights awards run the risk of secularizing and individualizing the plurality and collectivity of Indigenous/campesina collective struggles. Human rights discourse takes the individual as the unquestioned unit of analysis and the right to property assumes an exploitative relationship to the land and nature rooted in the ontological separation of human reasoning from the natural world. Land and water in these terms are reduced to nonliving, nonhuman entities with no spirit or relation. Through ethical relationality, transnational feminist activism must attend to the renewal and repair of the web of relations upon which all our lives depend.[50]

Lesson 2: Acknowledging the Inherent Contradictions of Human Recognition and Support

In a gesture of transnational solidarity as well as philanthropy, the GEP celebrates grassroots activists who are suffering the very real violent repression of the neoliberal state-corporate nexus. The GEP's annual honoring of grassroots environmental activists and their concerted efforts to protect the environment merits further assessment, especially now that an award recipient's life has been taken. Following the assassination of Cáceres, the GEP has the difficult work of evaluating the entanglement between good intentions and deadly outcomes. Based on our interview with Mack, it is clear that the first ever killing of a GEP award winner has been devastating for the organization.

These grand efforts to support and recognize the brave activism of individual leaders hold inherent contradictions. As previously mentioned, recognizing individual leaders spotlights one activist while the collective nature of the struggle ends up as a backdrop to the narrative. Even though creating a joyful experience for the winner and introducing their struggles to a broader audience are commendable, an erasure occurs of the holistic community struggle. The significant prize money also reinforces individualism and can potentially foment conflict in the community. Lastly, the delicate negotiation of and decision-making regarding reference points and needs between the prize-giver and prizewinner can be overdetermined by historical and global power asymmetries.

The GEP recognized Cáceres for her efforts in protecting the Gualcarque River, yet Cáceres had a much larger vision and purpose that cannot be separated from COPINH's goals of gender equality, anti-imperialism, and anti-neoliberalism. Hence, a tangible limitation of a human rights award is discursive containment wherein an individual winner's select actions are privileged over the totality of the collective struggle. The benevolent effort to recognize their environmentally based struggles by granting them an award must be infused with acknowledging the entirety of their lives, including their communities and full relational ecology. A decolonial project, at its core, embodies all of these elements—and the accompanying joy, pain, confusion, messiness, rage, love, and grief—often in a contradictory manner.

The extremely generous prize money reinforces individualism and has the potential of creating jealousy and distrust back home. Though we find it commendable that the GEP has no expectations on how the winners spend their prize money, providing individuals monetary awards renders invisible the efforts and contributions of many other important activists in these very concerted efforts against environmental destruction. Even though we do not believe this is the GEP's intention—to create problems for the award winner—the situation remains that providing a large sum of money to a specific individual in an increasingly violent context may have that outcome.

The GEP staff plays the critical role of "supportive interlocutor" between a prestigious award process and the social position of the award winners.[51] During our interview with Mack, he became a supportive interlocutor and noted the complexities inherent in this role. For example, he admitted that the ten-day award tour in the United States can be awkward for some award winners. During his trips to Honduras and Peru with a film crew to create biographical video clips for the awards ceremonies, he discussed with Cáceres and Acuña *their* expectations of the ten-day award tour. He understood that the GEP, because of its reputation and network, has the ability to facilitate critical connections for these winners that might make a tangible difference in their communities' struggles. In answering Mack's question regarding expectations for the tour, Acuña's family conveyed a real need for downtime because the situation had become so volatile. Mack responded by prioritizing the needs of Acuña over the GEP's agenda for the visit by scheduling in protected time for her to rest. This effort minimized, to some degree, the rigors of the GEP tour agenda given the needs of the winner. It can be exhausting to talk at length about the injustices in one's life, especially to a foreign audience, and therefore, respecting activists' needs of rest and self-care may result in making decisions that require compromising initial agendas.[52]

The GEP is an extremely well-funded organization that aims to genuinely take care of their winners when they arrive to the United States. In San Francisco, winners stay at the renowned Fairmont Hotel (hotel rooms average $500 per night). Based on one's social position though, the Fairmont Hotel may not feel like a pleasurable experience. Thus, what may seem like a grand gesture from one social position to luxuriate in a highly refined environment can feel heavy, awkward, and even oppressive to another person because different reference points inform pleasure and beauty, as well as value. For example, Acuña questions the fascination and the value placed on gold. Besides her metal pots and a capped tooth, she does not own any metal articles. Human life does not depend on metal. Yet, gold is valued more than water, on which life does depend. For this reason, the Blue Lake and surrounding lakes hold immeasurable value, at the headwaters of five watersheds, as well as beauty.[53] Human recognition and support must consider multiple reference points when it comes to pleasure and value, as well as beauty. Creating this moment of seeming celebration, pause, and relaxation can inadvertently produce a situation in which winners have to exert extreme emotional and psychic labor. Addressing and bridging cultural and material gaps is critical for transnational feminist solidarity.

North-south transnational solidarity produces at least dual, if not multidirectional, dynamics. The intercultural exchange that emerges from the GEP prize award process reveals a dual directionality between the staff and the winner and echoes dynamics that unfold when transnational feminists engage in a transformative decolonizing experience. When we listen, and genuinely feel for and with each other, we are ultimately transformed through the repair and renewal of relations.[54] Affective sensibility and connection is, after all, life-changing and life-giving. It is important to emphasize and honor this aspect of any genuine *intercambio* or exchange that can go unnoticed given the assumed directionality of a philanthropic celebration. Not only is epistemic humility required from the global North counterpart but also an openness and vulnerability are required for any shared experience with our global South comrade.

Mack had a transformational lesson through a very intense personal experience when he traveled to personally meet Cáceres in western Honduras. The national police came looking for her in a car with Mack and other members of the film crew, who were stopped at a roadblock. For an unknown reason, the police did not recognize Cáceres and left them to continue on their way. Though he was shaken by the police's fervent search for Cáceres, in sharing that critical moment, he better understood her, and COPINH's daily struggle. Mack expressed his deepest care and respect for Cáceres. Having experienced such a deeply life-giving connection, her killing affected him profoundly.

Acknowledging the inherent contradictions of human recognition and support means that not only is activist accompaniment and witnessing instrumental but also that networks of support often have to be mobilized in unanticipated ways for protection. During the roadblock with Cáceres, Mack called his San Francisco office and the U.S. embassy for protection and assistance. He was there to film a touching story about Cáceres for a primarily U.S. audience but ended up having to mobilize his network for security to protect Cáceres as well as himself and the others in the car. His response to this situation demonstrates the utter importance of strengthening local and international networks. In this situation, their lives literally depended on it. His access to a network for security was not something readily available to Cáceres, a striking contrast given the frequency in which her life was threatened compared to his.

In our interview with Mack, it is clear that the GEP has ongoing, and confidential, discussions regarding security threats for award recipients. In the evaluation of prize nominees, security is a consideration rather than a priority. Cáceres herself discussed with the GEP staff that the threats to her life were so frequent and intense that she feared she would not be alive for the GEP ceremony. Upon learning of her situation, and witnessing firsthand the daily violence and threats in her life when the recording crew went to film her profile, the GEP offered some assistance through a programmatic initiative of threat assessment to provide her with security. This support typically comes in the form of "letters of support from the foundation, action alerts promoted through earned and social media, pro bono legal assistance, and urgent defense grants."[55] Given the current level of threats and killings, the security of prizewinners from Honduras, Peru, Brazil, and the Philippines demands priority attention, as opposed to consideration, and requires carefully designed security plans.

The lesson here for transnational feminists situated in the global North is to acknowledge how global power asymmetries can result in inherent contradictions when engaged in solidarity. We must never lose sight of the precarious conditions in which communities live and that even our best intentions to engage in solidarity can have the unintended outcome of insecurity for the very movements and activists we aim to support. We must mobilize through ethical relationality to build networks across the region with an understanding that attacks against individual leaders are part of a strategy to undermine community struggles. May our humble efforts to repair and renew relations[56] mitigate the life-taking obscure forces of "rapacious capitalism."

Lesson 3: Mapping "Cartographies of Struggle" under Neoliberal Containment

Current social protests against hydropower projects in Honduras and mining projects in Peru reveal a neoliberal state-corporate nexus with profound disregard for all forms of life to secure enormous profit. Neoliberal states in partnership with transnational corporations aggressively attempt to contain social movements by using lethal and nonlethal methods to stifle, minimize, homogenize, and control them, as well as individual activists. As Linda Carty and Chandra Talpade Mohanty write, "movements anchored in anticapitalist, anticolonial struggles for 'freedom' from patriarchal practices and gender-based violence and Indigenous sovereignty and freedom (not equal rights) pose a fundamental challenge that cannot be easily contained by neoliberal states."[57] The underlying purpose of neoliberal containment is to protect the interests of a neoliberal state-corporate nexus, a consolidation of power through the proliferation of resource extraction, hydropower, and other megaprojects. The process of neoliberal containment mobilizes an arsenal of tools, including repression by police, military, and private security forces, leveraging the legal system to criminalize communities and their claims to the land and water, cutting off modes of communication (such as radio), and framing Indigenous/campesina struggles as obstacles to national development and prosperity. Further, neoliberal containment violently secularizes Indigenous/campesina activism in the service of capitalist projects.

Lessons for transnational feminist solidarity, given these cartographies of struggle under neoliberal containment, are twofold. First, immediate and effective responses to threats must be based upon a thorough understanding of the social actors involved both on the side of the repression and the local networks of support including activists accompanying and witnessing the person(s) under threat. Second, transnational corporate power requires the support of government policy to thrive, indicating that transnational feminist solidarity mandates an anticapitalist commitment, especially from the north. To engage in what José Medina calls an act of "epistemic resistance, that is [using] our epistemic resources and abilities to undermine and change oppressive normative structures and the complacent cognitive-affective functioning that sustains those structures," would require challenging "rapacious capitalism," as Cáceres called it.[58] Transnational feminist solidarity from the north with Indigenous/campesinas from the south must expose and denounce the corruption underlying the nexus between the state, military, police, judiciary, and corporations.

Honduras has experienced major political upheaval since the 2009 coup of democratically elected and left-leaning president Manuel Zelaya, especially once the U.S. government maintained that the coup was legal.[59] The anti-Zelaya coalition was formidable, and it became impossible to reinstate him.[60] Conservative rancher Porfirio "Pepe" Lobo Sosa became the next elected president in November 2009. He enacted extensive business-friendly propositions typified by an economic conference in May 2011 entitled "Honduras is Open for Business." Legal and human rights scholar Lauren Carasik described the Lobo state policy as containing "an ambitious and far-reaching legislative agenda that gives primacy to corporate rights."[61] The goal, as supported by a law passed in 2013, was to privatize biodiverse Honduras for the benefit of the military and neoliberal elites. Under this law, all of the country's resources could be exploited, undermining the established international protections to consult with Indigenous communities. Cáceres denounced the very obscure forces of the Honduran neoliberal state-corporate nexus:[62] "There are rarely more than a few degrees of separation between politicians, military leaders, business elites, and traffickers," signaling out Miguel Facussé specifically—as coup plotter, business tycoon, the uncle of a former president, and a key architect of "Honduras is Open for Business."[63]

Cáceres pointed out many times in her life that corporate companies work alongside and are endorsed by the Honduran security regime.[64] The fact that DESA, the private company behind the Agua Zarca project, has its own private security force demonstrates the collusion between private neoliberal interests and security. COPINH charges DESA with Cáceres's murder and faults the *Ministerio Publico* (Public Ministry) for failing to do a thorough investigation and of keeping COPINH in the dark. COPINH documented the forcible removal by police of about fifty Lenca families in February 2016, and the *Los Angeles Times* reported that "Cáceres and other leaders feared the Honduran government was trying to revive the dam project" of 2013.[65]

In addition to hydropower megaprojects, extractivist projects, whether mining, logging, gas, or oil, have been crucial for economic growth throughout Latin America no matter the political leanings of those in power. In the case of Peru, a neoliberal state facilitates corporate interests and foreign investment to maximize the possibilities of extractivist mining. The Yanacocha consortium arrived to Cajamarca in response to former Peruvian president Alberto Fujimori's neoliberal reforms in the early 1990s that attracted foreign investment in resource extraction.[66] In Peru, laws facilitated corporate contracts with the Peruvian National Police for private security to protect neoliberal megaprojects from social protest. Extractivist projects are the core of the neoliberal promise of prosperity, and the state has put laws into place to protect them and facilitate their growth.[67] Moreover, the state deploys police and military to quell mobilizations and social unrest against mining corporations. Unfortunately, the passage of Peruvian Law 30151 in 2014 grants the police and armed forces complete impunity, expanding the reach of the repressive arm of the state.[68]

Private security, provided by both the transnational security company Securitas[69] and police, constantly stages coordinated attacks on Acuña, her family, livestock, agriculture, and house. The isolated location of their land makes the family vulnerable to attack, and they are under constant threat and surveillance. In 2011, the security forces and police burned down their house and destroyed all their belongings in an attempt to dispossess them of their land. The security forces came back for several days to destroy anything they had, and the family was forced to sleep outside in freezing temperatures with only hay to cover them. Yanacocha has successfully cut communication and movement by constructing a fence around the Acuña family property with checkpoints that control any contact with others. Yanacocha also does not allow public transportation service to Acuña.

The legal system is largely an ambivalent realm that primarily benefits the powerful with multiple avenues to attack those who oppose resource extraction projects. In 2012, for example, Yanacocha took the family to court for aggravated usurpation of their land. Yanacocha won two trials in the provincial court in Celedín. The family however appealed the case in the superior court of the region of Cajamarca. In December 2014, Yanacocha lost and the Acuña family was absolved. Nevertheless, Yanacocha has registered six more legal complaints against Acuña.[70] In Honduras, activists experience constant threats and surveillance, as well as false charges and imprisonment, to a greater extent than in Peru. In the case of Cáceres, for instance, she was falsely imprisoned in May 2013 on claims by police "in vehicles owned by DESA/SINOHYDRO" of having "an unregistered handgun." After being subsequently charged for allegedly having this weapon, the court "conditionally dismissed" the charge the following month with an understanding that the prosecutors could continue to gather evidence for up to five years; an appeals court later overturned the dismissal, and Cáceres had to register with the courts every week.[71] She also received numerous rape and sexual assault threats. The Honduran press even reported that Lisa Kubiske, the U.S. Ambassador to Honduras, supported "the prosecution of those who engage in land occupations and human rights defense."[72]

Quick and effective responses to the increase in violent repression against Indigenous/campesina activists depend upon tracking the murky terrain of insecurity and threats by the neoliberal state-corporate nexus. Mechanisms of containment are the multiple and fluid structures of domination that locate Cáceres and Acuña (and us!) differently, given each of our contexts. Against these mechanisms of containment, we insist on their/our oppositional agency and ethical relationality. According to Mohanty, "Oppositional political relation to sexist, racist, and imperialist structures constitutes our potential commonality. Thus it is the common context of struggles against specific exploitative structures and systems that determines our potential political alliances."[73] Exposing the mechanisms of neoliberal containment through mapping the cartographies of struggle facilitates transnational alliance-building across multiple differences and asymmetric power relations, thereby renewing and repairing our relations.[74] The exercise of mapping cartographies of struggle in Honduras and Peru features the overlapping and escalating repression by police, military, and corporate security forces, and the mobilization of the judicial system and the law to serve state and corporate interests.

CONCLUSION

We sense the undeniable urgency to address the increased threats and insecurity of Latin American prizewinners who are being recognized for their activism during this growth and consolidation of neoliberal regimes under right-leaning governance in the region. We also honor the depth of emotional investment and political commitment of people working in the prize-giving industry and the complicated terrain of transnational solidarity within a sociopolitical context of historic global power asymmetries. The affective connection to the prize-winners and their struggles evidence a sustained and genuine gesture from the heart and the life-giving connections they forge with their counterparts. While not quantifiable, this feeling is impossible to ignore and opens a space for meeting the Indigenous/campesina activists on their own terms.

Transnational feminists must contend with a complicated terrain of solidarity within and across national borders in order to address entrenched inequalities, widespread violence, and intense insecurities perpetuated by the neoliberal state-corporate nexus. By recognizing the embodied knowledge produced by women like Cáceres and Acuña, and their respective communities and families in struggle, we can better inform our solidarity interventions in a way that never loses sight of the stakes involved for Indigenous/campesina communities.

The taking of Cáceres's life in March 2016 marks an ever-present absence and punctuates the urgency behind the concerns for protecting Acuña's life. We value the ways in which Indigenous/campesina activists continually assert the holistic integrity of their struggles and use their new platform to communicate the resistance of their people. Their challenge to Western-centric knowledge production that divides human reasoning from the natural world is anchored in the web of relations upon which all of our lives depend. Their safety and security should be of paramount concern to everyone, including human rights awards organizations that have the capacity, resources, and networks to take action.

NOTES

1. *Indigenous/campesina* is a term used for people of the Américas that have living relations with the land, practice their traditional culture, and/or speak their Indigenous language. While some self-identify as Indigenous, others may self-identify as campesina (peasant).

2. The 2016 historic Indigenous-led uprising against the Dakota Access Pipeline at the Standing Rock Sioux Reservation in North Dakota echoes hemispheric struggles, including the Indigenous/campesina struggles to protect water in Peru and Honduras discussed in this chapter. We dedicate this chapter to Standing Rock and all our water protectors of the Américas.

3. Chandra T. Mohanty, *Feminism without Borders: Decolonizing Theory, Practicing Solidarity* (Durham: Duke University Press, 2003), 47.

4. Dwayne Donald, "On What Terms Can We Speak?" Lecture presentation at the University of Lethbridge, Alberta, Canada, 2010, accessed December 21, 2016, www.vimeo.com/15264558.

5. Mohanty, *Feminism without Borders*, 84.

6. Steven Levitsky and Kenneth M. Roberts, eds., *The Resurgence of the Latin American Left* (Baltimore: Johns Hopkins University Press, 2011); Gustavo A. Flores-Macias, *After Neoliberalism? The Left and Economic Reforms in Latin America* (New York: Oxford University Press, 2012); Rosario Queirolo, *The Success of the Left in Latin America: Untainted Parties, Market Reforms, and Voting Behavior* (Notre Dame: University of Notre Dame Press, 2013); Steve Ellner, ed., *Latin America's Radical Left: Challenges and Complexities of Political Power in the Twenty-First Century* (Lanham: Rowman and Littlefield, 2014).

7. Global Witness, "Deadly Environment," April 15, 2014, accessed August 30, 2016, https://www.globalwitness.org/en/campaigns/environmental-activists/deadly-environment/.

8. Mark Anderson, "When Afro Becomes (like) Indigenous: Garifuna and Afro-Indigenous Politics in Honduras," *Journal of Latin American and Caribbean Anthropology* 12 (2007): 389.

9. The Associated Press stated that at the time of the coup, Zelaya was "pushing a constitutional amendment that would have allowed him to run for re-election." Associated Press, "Clinton Says U.S. Aid to Resume to Honduras," *NBC News*, March 4, 2010, accessed August 29, 2016, http://www.nbcnews.com/id/35714555/ns/world_news-americas/t/clinton-says-us-aid-resume-honduras/#.V65JuI5Ye9Y.

10. Consejo Cívico de Organizaciones Populares e Indígenas de Honduras COPINH, "Que es COPINH," December 10, 2008, accessed August 29, 2016, https://www.copinh.org/article/que-es-copinh/.

11. Anderson, "When Afro Becomes (Like) Indigenous," 402.

12. COPINH, "Que es COPINH."

13. Global Witness, "New Data on the Murder Rate of Environmental and Land Activists in Honduras, the Highest in the World," press release, March 4, 2016, https://www.globalwitness.org/en/press-releases/global-witness-releases-new-data-murder-rate-environmental-and-land-activists-honduras-highest-world/.

14. Global Witness, "Deadly Environment."

15. The Goldman Environmental Prize, "Berta Cáceres," accessed August 29, 2016, http://www.goldmanprize.org/recipient/berta-caceres/.

16. As reported in the *Intercept*, "DESA is partially controlled by the controversial Honduran Atala family, whose members are involved in a variety of business ventures and suspected by many of having backed the 2009 coup. Best known among them is billionaire Camilo Atala, president of Banco Fichosa, a regional bank that in 2014 acquired most of Citibank's assets in the region, making it the largest bank in Honduras." See Danielle Marie Mackey, "Drugs, Dams, and Power: The Murder of Honduran Activist Berta Cáceres," *The Intercept*, March 12, 2016, accessed August 29, 2016, https://theintercept.com/2016/03/11/drugs-dams-and-power-the-murder-of-honduran-activist-berta-caceres/; and Blake Schmidt, "Central American Billionaires Discovered amid Citi Asset Sales," *Bloomberg*, April 21, 2015, accessed August 29, 2016, http://www.bloomberg.com/news/articles/2015-04-21/central-american-billionaires-discovered-amid-citi-asset-sales.

17. Three banks have been funding the project: BCIE (Banco Centroamericano de Integración Economical); El Banco de Desarrollo Holandes (the Dutch Development Bank—FMO); and El Banco de Desarrollo Finlandes FinnFund (the Finnish Development Bank FinnFund). The European banks pulled out after the assassination of Cáceres.

18. A Chinese company that has been charged with building the dam in the Rio Blanco area as well as other parts of the country (specifically in non-Lenca territory, which is displacing the Garifuna community).

19. Yessenia Funes, "In the Wake of Her Mom's Assassination, Laura Cáceres Hits the DNC with Fervor," *Colorlines*, July 28, 2016, accessed August 29, 2016, http://www.colorlines.com/articles/4-months-after-her-moms-death-laura-caceres-hits-presidential-conventions-fervor-and-smile.

20. Elisabeth Malkin and Alberto Arce, "Berta Cáceres, Indigenous Activist, Is Killed in Honduras," *New York Times*, March 3, 2016, accessed August 29, 2016, http://www.nytimes.com/2016/03/04/world/americas/berta-caceres-indigenous-activist-is-killed-in-honduras.html?_r=0.

21. Funes, "In the Wake of Her Mom's Assassination."

22. Amnesty International, "Urgent Action: Witness to Defender's Murder at Risk," accessed August 31, 2016, https://www.amnestyusa.org/sites/default/files/uaa05016_0.pdf.

23. *Democracy Now!*, "Gustavo Castro Soto, Witness to Berta Cáceres' Murder, Finally Freed," accessed August 31, 2016, http://www.democracynow.org/2016/4/4/headlines/gustavo_castro_soto_witness_to_berta_caceres_murder_finally_freed.

24. "Mapa de conflictos mineros, proyectos y empresas mineras en América Latina," Observatorio de Conflictos Mineros de América Latina, accessed August 29, 2016, http://mapa.conflictosmineros.net/ocmal_db/.

25. The Goldman Environmental Prize. "Máxima Acuña Acceptance Speech, 2016 Goldman Prize Ceremony," April 21, 2016, accessed August 29, 2016. https://www.youtube.com/watch?v=orxv3jPsOgM.

26. Yanacocha, "Quiénes Somos," accessed August 30, 2016, http://www.yanacocha.com/quienes-somos/.

27. BBC, "Máxima Acuña, la campesina peruana 'heredera' de la activista asesinada Berta Cáceres," *BBC Mundo*, April 18, 2016, accessed August 30, 2016, http://www.bbc.com/mundo/noticias/2016/04/160418_peru_campesina_maxima_acuna_gana_premio_goldman_heredera_berta_caceres_lv.

28. OjoPúblico, "Máxima Acuña: la dama de la laguna ahora es intocable," accessed August 31, 2016, http://ojo-publico.com/204/maxima-acuna-la-dama-de-la-laguna-ahora-es-intocable.

29. Cubas testified before the U.S. Congress in 2015 about Conga and called for halting the World Bank's support for, and private investment through the International Financial Corporation to, the project due to the social and environmental threats it poses. See Inter-Institutional Platform of Celendin and Columbia Law School Human Rights Clinic, "Gold Mine Risks 'Irreparable' Damage to the Environment in Violation of World Bank Standards, Peruvian Human Rights Leader Tells U.S.

Congress," press release, accessed August 30, 2016, http://www.conganova.com/news/2015/9/29/press-release-title.

30. Fabiana Li, *Unearthing Conflict: Corporate Mining, Activism, and Expertise in Peru* (Durham: Duke University Press, 2015), 6.

31. To view the picture of Acuña holding sign, see Rick Kearns, "Bertha [*sic*] Cáceres among Those on Honduran Military Hit List, *Indian Country Today Media Network.com*, June 27, 2016, accessed August 25, 2016, http://indiancountrytodaymedianetwork.com/2016/06/27/bertha-caceres-among-those-honduran-military-hit-list-164930.

32. The Goldman Environmental Prize, "Prize History," accessed August 1, 2016, http://www.goldmanprize.org/history/.

33. Kurtis Alexander, "Goldman Prize Winners Honored in SF for Environmentalism," *San Francisco Gate*, April 17, 2016, accessed August 1, 2016, http://www.sfgate.com/bayarea/article/Goldman-prize-winners-honored-in-SF-for-7254042.php#photo-9810274.

34. Breny Mendoza, "Transnational Feminisms in Question," *Feminist Theory* 3 (2002): 295–314.

35. See Fabiana Li, "In Defense of Water: Modern Mining, Grassroots Movements, and Corporate Strategies in Peru," *The Journal of Latin American and Caribbean Anthropology* 21 (2016): 109–29.

36. Donald, "On What Terms Can We Speak?"

37. Edgardo Lander, "Ciencias Sociales: Saberes Colonials y Eurocéntricos," in *La colonialidad del saber: eurocentrismo y ciencias sociales: persepctivas latinoamericanas*, ed. Edgardo Lander (Caracas, Venezuela: La Facultad de Ciencias Económicas y Sociales, el Instituto International de la UNESCO para la Educación Superior en América Latina y Caribe, 2000), 17.

38. Lander, "Ciencias Sociales," 31.

39. Smith, Linda Tuhiwai, *Decolonizing Methodologies: Research and Indigenous Peoples*. Second edition (New York, NY: Zed Books).

40. Donald, "On What Terms Can We Speak?"

41. Li, *Unearthing Conflict*, 219.

42. Li, *Unearthing Conflict*, 2.

43. Mack, Ryan. Interviewed by authors. Personal interview. San Francisco, CA, July 12, 2016.

44. For a discussion of temporality and Indigenous/campesina struggles, see Pascha Bueno-Hansen, *Feminist and Human Rights Struggles in Peru: Decolonizing Transitional Justice* (Urbana: University of Illinois Press, 2015).

45. "Tribute to Berta Cáceres at the 2016 Goldman Environmental Prize Ceremony," April 21, 2016, Goldman Environmental Prize, accessed August 1, 2016, https://www.youtube.com/watch?v=yMybBm6RT5g.

46. Marisol de la Cadena, *Earth Beings: Ecologies of Practice across Andean Worlds* (Durham: Duke University Press, 2015).

47. Mohanty, *Feminism without Borders*, 84.

48. In July 2012, President Humala declared a state of emergency, and police and military killed five people in Celedín and Bambamarca.

49. See Rosa-Linda Fregoso and Cynthia Bejarano, eds., *Terrorizing Women: Feminicide in the Americas* (Durham: Duke University Press, 2010).

50. Donald, "On What Terms Can We Speak?"

51. Manisha Desai, "The Possibilities and Perils for Scholar-Activists and Activist-Scholars: Reflections on the Feminist Dialogues," in *Insurgent Encounters: Transnational Activism, Ethnography, and the Political*, eds. Jeffrey S. Juris and Alex Khasnabish (Durham, NC: Duke University Press, 2013), 106.

52. See Sylvanna M. Falcón, "Transnational Feminism as a Paradigm for Decolonizing the Practice of Research: Identifying Feminist Principles and Methodology Criteria for US-Based Scholars," *Frontiers: A Journal of Women Studies* 37 (2016): 184–86.

53. Li, *Unearthing Conflict*, 219.

54. Donald, "On What Terms Can We Speak?"

55. The Goldman Environmental Prize, "Beyond the Prize," accessed August 1, 2016, http://www.goldmanprize.org/beyond-the-prize/.

56. Donald, "On What Terms Can We Speak?"

57. Linda Carty and Chandra Talpade Mohanty, "Mapping Transnational Feminist Engagements: Neoliberalism and the Politics of Solidarity," in *The Oxford Handbook of Transnational Feminist Movements*, eds. Rawwida Baksh and Wendy Harcourt (New York City: Oxford University Press, 2015), 103.

58. José Medina, *The Epistemology of Resistance: Gender and Racial Oppression, Epistemic Injustice, and Resistant Imaginations* (New York City: Oxford University Press, 2013), 3.

59. Tracy Wilkinson, "Clinton Insists She Hasn't Changed Her Position on 2009 Honduras Coup," *Los Angeles Times*, May 1, 2016, accessed August 5, 2016, http://www.latimes.com/world/la-fg-clinton-honduras-coup-20160501-story.html.

60. Scholars have noted that the "traditional elite" were the source of problems and conflict in Honduras and specifically identified the "nation's capitalist 'oligarchy,' consisting of a few dozen powerful families, as the cause of most of Honduras's miseries." See J. Mark Ruhl, "Honduras Unravels," *Journal of Democracy* 21 (2010): 99; and Andy Baker and Kenneth F. Green, "The Latin American Left's Mandate Free-Market Policies and Issue Voting in New Democracies," *World Politics* 63 (2011): 43, doi: 10.1017/S0043887110000286.

61. Lauren Carasik, "Honduras: Where the Blood Flows and the Rivers Are Dammed," *Al Jazeera English*, August 6, 2013, accessed August 10, 2016, http://www.aljazeera.com/indepth/opinion/2013/08/201385102953341 59.html.

62. K. McSweeney and Z. Pearson, "Prying Native People from Native Lands: Narco Business in Honduras," *NACLA Report on the Americas* 46 (2013): 8, accessed August 11, 2016, doi: 10.1080/10714839.2013.11721883.

63. McSweeney and Pearson, "Prying Native People," 11.

64. Carasik, "Honduras: Where the Blood Flows."

65. Chris Kraul, "Honduran Environmental Leader and Rights Activist Berta Caceres Slain by Assailants," *Los Angeles Times*, March 3, 2016, accessed August 10, 2016, http://www.latimes.com/world/la-fg-honduras-caceres-slain-20160303-story.html.

66. Li, *Unearthing Conflict*.

67. For example, a 1999 law allows the national police to contract with private companies in the provision of security services, using police uniforms, equipment, and vehicles in the delivery of services. See Lynn Holland, "The House on the Mountain: How Mining Corrodes Democracy in Peru," *Council on Hemispheric Affairs*, July 30, 2014, accessed August 1, 2016, http://www.coha.org/the-house-on-the-mountain-how-mining-corrodes-democracy-in-peru/.

68. "According to the new wording of the provision, which has been widely criticized by civil society organizations as well as Peru's Ombudsman, any 'personnel of the Armed Forces or National Police of Peru who cause injury or death in the performance of their duties and through the use of their weapons or other means of defense,' would be exempt from liability to criminal prosecution." See "IACHR Troubled by Entry into Force of Law 30151 in Peru," press release, January 23, 2014, *Organization of American States*, accessed August 1, 2016, http://www.oas.org/en/iachr/media_center/PReleases/2014/004.asp.

69. Roxana Olivera, "Peruvian Anti-Mining Activist Máxima Acuña to Newmont Mining Corporation: 'I Will Never Give Up My Land,'" *Toward Freedom*, August 5, 2016, accessed August 30, 2016, http://towardfreedom.com/32-archives/environment/4311-peruvian-anti-mining-activist-maxima-acuna-i-will-never-give-up-my-land.

70. OjoPúblico, "Máxima Acuña: la dama de la laguna."

71. McSweeney and Pearson, "Prying Native People," 7.

72. Lauren Carasik, "US Ambassador to Honduras Offers Tacit Support of Brutal Crackdown," *Al Jazeera America*, January 7, 2014, accessed August 1, 2016, http://america.aljazeera.com/opinions/2014/1/u-s-ambassador-humanrightsviolationshonduras.html; Annie Bird, "The Agua Zarca Dam and Lenca Communities in Honduras: Transnational Investment Leads to Violence against and Criminalization of Indigenous Communities," *Rights Action*, October 3, 2013, 14, accessed August 20, 2016. http://rightsaction.org/sites/default/files/Rpt_131001_RioBlanco_Final.pdf.

73. Mohanty, *Feminism without Borders*, 49.

74. Donald, "On What Terms Can We Speak?"

BIBLIOGRAPHY

Alexander, Kurtis. "Goldman Prize Winners Honored in SF for Environmentalism." *San Francisco Gate*, April 17, 2016. Accessed August 1, 2016. http://www.sfgate.com/bayarea/article/Goldman-prize-winners-honored-in-SF-for-7254042.php#photo-9810274.

Amnesty International. "Urgent Action: Witness to Defender's Murder at Risk." Accessed August 31, 2016. https://www.amnestyusa.org/sites/default/files/uaa05016_0.pdf.

Anderson, Mark. "When Afro Becomes (Like) Indigenous: Garifuna and Afro-Indigenous Politics in Honduras." *Journal of Latin American and Caribbean Anthropology* 12 (2007): 384–413.

Associated Press. “Clinton Says U.S. Aid to Resume to Honduras,” *NBC News*, March 4, 2010. Accessed August 29, 2016. http://www.nbcnews.com/id/35714555/ns/world_news-americas/t/clinton-says-us-aid-resume-honduras/#.V65JuI5Ye9Y.

Baker, Andy, and Kenneth F. Green. “The Latin American Left’s Mandate: Free-Market Policies and Issue Voting in New Democracies.” *World Politics* 63 (2011): 43–77. Accessed August 5, 2016. doi: 10.1017/S0043887110000286.

BBC. “Máxima Acuña, la campesina peruana ‘heredera’ de la activista asesinada Berta Cáceres.” *BBC Mundo*, April 18, 2016. Accessed August 30, 2016. http://www.bbc.com/mundo/noticias/2016/04/160418_peru_campesina_maxima_acuna_gana_premio_goldman_heredera_berta_caceres_lv.

Bird, Annie. “The Agua Zarca Dam and Lenca Communities in Honduras: Transnational Investment Leads to Violence against and Criminalization of Indigenous Communities.” *Rights Action*, October 3, 2013. Accessed August 20, 2016. http://rightsaction.org/sites/default/files/Rpt_131001_RioBlanco_Final.pdf.

Bueno-Hansen, Pascha. *Feminist and Human Rights Struggles in Peru: Decolonizing Transitional Justice*. Urbana: University of Illinois Press, 2015.

Carasik, Lauren. “Honduras: Where the Blood Flows and the Rivers Are Dammed.” *Aljazeera English*, August 6, 2013. Accessed August 10, 2016. http://www.aljazeera.com/indepth/opinion/2013/08/20138510295334159.html.

———. “US Ambassador to Honduras Offers Tacit Support of Brutal Crackdown.” *Al Jazeera America*, January 7, 2014. Accessed August 1, 2016. http://america.aljazeera.com/opinions/2014/1/u-s-ambassador-humanrightsviolationshonduras.html.

Carty, Linda, and Chandra Talpade Mohanty. “Mapping Transnational Feminist Engagements: Neoliberalism and the Politics of Solidarity.” In *The Oxford Handbook of Transnational Feminist Movements*, edited by Rawwida Baksh and Wendy Harcourt, 82–115. New York: Oxford University Press, 2015.

Consejo Cívico de Organizaciones Populares e Indígenas de Honduras COPINH. “Que es COPINH.” Accessed August 29, 2016. https://www.copinh.org/article/que-es-copinh/.

de la Cadena, Marisol. *Earth Beings: Ecologies of Practice across Andean Worlds*. Durham: Duke University Press, 2015.

Democracy Now! “Gustavo Castro Soto, Witness to Berta Cáceres’ Murder, Finally Freed.” Accessed August 31, 2016. http://www.democracynow.org/2016/4/4/headlines/gustavo_castro_soto_witness_to_berta_caceres_murder_finally_freed.

Desai, Manisha. “The Possibilities and Perils for Scholar-Activists and Activist Scholars: Reflections on the Feminist Dialogues.” In *Insurgent Encounters: Transnational Activism, Ethnography, and the Political*, edited by Jeffrey S. Juris and Alex Khasnabish, 89–107. Durham: Duke University Press, 2013.

Donald, Dwayne. “On What Terms Can We Speak?” Paper presented at the University of Lethbridge, Lethbridge, Alberta, Canada, 2010. Accessed December 21, 2016. www.vimeo.com/15264558.

Ellner, Steve, ed. *Latin America’s Radical Left: Challenges and Complexities of Political Power in the Twenty-First Century*. Lanham, MD: Rowman and Littlefield, 2014.

Falcón, Sylvanna M. "Transnational Feminism as a Paradigm for Decolonizing the Practice of Research: Identifying Feminist Principles and Methodology Criteria for US-Based Scholars." *Frontiers: A Journal of Women Studies* 37 (2016): 174–94.

Flores-Macias, Gustavo A. *After Neoliberalism? The Left and Economic Reforms in Latin America*. New York: Oxford University Press, 2012.

Fregoso, Rosa-Linda, and Cynthia Bejarano, eds. *Terrorizing Women: Feminicide in the Americas*. Durham: Duke University Press, 2010.

Funes, Yessenia. "In the Wake of Her Mom's Assassination, Laura Cáceres Hits the DNC with Fervor." *Colorlines*, July 28, 2016. Accessed August 29, 2016. http://www.colorlines.com/articles/4-months-after-her-moms-death-laura-caceres-hits-presidential-conventions-fervor-and-smile.

Global Witness. "Deadly Environment." London: Global Witness Limited. April 15, 2014. Accessed August 30, 2016. https://www.globalwitness.org/en/campaigns/environmental-activists/deadly-environment/.

———. "New Data on the Murder Rate of Environmental and Land Activists in Honduras, the Highest in the World." Press release, March 4, 2016. Accessed August 30, 2016. https://www.globalwitness.org/en/press-releases/global-witness-releases-new-data-murder-rate-environmental-and-land-activists-honduras-highest-world/.

The Goldman Environmental Prize. "Berta Cáceres." Last modified August 29, 2016a. http://www.goldmanprize.org/recipient/berta-caceres/.

———. "Beyond the Prize." Last modified August 1, 2016b. http://www.goldmanprize.org/beyond-the-prize/.

———. "Máxima Acuña Acceptance Speech, 2016 Goldman Prize Ceremony." April 21, 2016c. Accessed August 29, 2016. https://www.youtube.com/watch?v=orxv3jPsOgM.

———. "Prize History." Last modified August 1, 2016d. http://www.goldmanprize.org/history/.

———. "Tribute to Berta Cáceres at the 2016 Goldman Environmental Prize Ceremony." April 21, 2016e. Accessed August 1, 2016. https://www.youtube.com/watch?v=yMybBm6RT5g.

Holland, Lynn. "The House on the Mountain: How Mining Corrodes Democracy in Peru." *Council on Hemispheric Affairs*, July 30, 2014. Accessed August 1, 2016. http://www.coha.org/the-house-on-the-mountain-how-mining-corrodes-democracy-in-peru/.

Inter-Institutional Platform of Celendín and Columbia Law School Human Rights Clinic. "Gold Mine Risks 'Irreparable' Damage to the Environment in Violation of World Bank Standards, Peruvian Human Rights Leader Tells U.S. Congress." Press release. Accessed August 30, 2016. http://www.conganova.com/news/2015/9/29/press-release-title.

Kearns, Rick. "Bertha [sic] Cáceres among Those on Honduran Military Hit List." *Indian Country Today Media Network.com*, June 27, 2016. Accessed August 25, 2016. http://indiancountrytodaymedianetwork.com/2016/06/27/bertha-caceres-among-those-honduran-military-hit-list-164930.

Kraul, Chris. "Honduran Environmental Leader and Rights Activist Berta Caceres Slain by Assailants." *Los Angeles Times*, March 3, 2016. Accessed August 10, 2016. http://www.latimes.com/world/la-fg-honduras-caceres-slain-20160303-story.html.

Lander, Edgardo. “Ciencias sociales: saberes colonials y eurocéntricos.” In *La colonialidad del saber: eurocentrismo y ciencias sociales: persepctivas latinoamericanas*, edited by Edgardo Lander. Caracas, Venezuela: la Facultad de Ciencias Económicas y Sociales, el Instituto International de la UNESCO para la Educación Superior en América Latina y Caribe, 2000.

Levitsky, Steven, and Kenneth M. Roberts, eds. *The Resurgence of the Latin American Left*. Baltimore: Johns Hopkins University Press, 2011.

Li, Fabiana. “In Defense of Water: Modern Mining, Grassroots Movements, and Corporate Strategies in Peru.” *The Journal of Latin American and Caribbean Anthropology* 21 (2016): 109–29.

———. *Unearthing Conflict: Corporate Mining, Activism, and Expertise in Peru.* Durham: Duke University Press, 2015.

Mackey, Danielle Marie. “Drugs, Dams, and Power: The Murder of Honduran Activist Berta Cáceres.” *The Intercept*, March 11, 2016. Accessed August 29, 2016. https://theintercept.com/2016/03/11/drugs-dams-and-power-the-murder-of-honduran-activist-berta-caceres/.

Malkin, Elisabeth, and Alberto Arce. “Berta Cáceres, Indigenous Activist, Is Killed in Honduras.” *New York Times*, March 3, 2016. Accessed August 29, 2016. http://www.nytimes.com/2016/03/04/world/americas/berta-caceres-indigenous-activist-is-killed-in-honduras.html.

“Mapa de conflictos mineros, proyectos y empresas mineras en América Latina.” *Observatorio de Conflictos Mineros de América Latina*. Accessed August 29, 2016. http://mapa.conflictosmineros.net/ocmal_db/.

“Máxima Acuña: la dama de la laguna ahora es intocable.” *OjoPúblico*. Accessed August 31, 2016. http://ojo-publico.com/204/maxima-acuna-la-dama-de-la-laguna-ahora-es-intocable.

McSweeney, K., and Z. Pearson. “Prying Native People from Native Lands: Narco Business in Honduras.” *NACLA Report on the Americas* 46 (2013): 7–12. Accessed August 11, 2016. doi: 10.1080/10714839.2013.11721883.

Medina, José. *The Epistemology of Resistance: Gender and Racial Oppression, Epistemic Injustice, and Resistant Imaginations*. New York City: Oxford University Press, 2013.

Mendoza, Breny. “Transnational Feminisms in Question.” *Feminist Theory* 3 (2002): 295–314.

Mohanty, Chandra Talpade. *Feminism without Borders: Decolonizing Theory, Practicing Solidarity*. Durham: Duke University Press, 2003.

Olivera, Roxana. “Peruvian Anti-Mining Activist Máxima Acuña to Newmont Mining Corporation: ‘I Will Never Give Up My Land.’” *Toward Freedom*, August 5, 2016. Accessed August 30, 2016. http://towardfreedom.com/32-archives/environment/4311-peruvian-anti-mining-activist-maxima-acuna-i-will-never-give-up-my-land.

Organization of American States. “IACHR Troubled by Entry into Force of Law 30151 in Peru.” Press release, January 23, 2014. Accessed August 1, 2016. http://www.oas.org/en/iachr/media_center/PReleases/2014/004.asp.

Queirolo, Rosario. *The Success of the Left in Latin America: Untainted Parties, Market Reforms, and Voting Behavior*. Notre Dame: University of Notre Dame Press, 2013.

Ruhl, J. Mark. “Honduras Unravels.” *Journal of Democracy* 21 (2010): 93–107.

Schmidt, Blake. “Central American Billionaires Discovered amid Citi Asset Sales.” *Bloomberg*, April 21, 2015. Accessed August 29, 2016. http://www.bloomberg.com/news/articles/2015-04-21/central-american-billionaires-discovered-amid-citi-asset-sales.

Smith, Linda Tuhiwai. 2012. *Decolonizing Methodologies: Research and Indigenous Peoples*. Second edition. New York, NY: Zed Books.

Wilkinson, Tracy. “Clinton Insists She Hasn’t Changed Her Position on 2009 Honduras Coup.” *Los Angeles Times*, May 1, 2016. Accessed August 5, 2016. http://www.latimes.com/world/la-fg-clinton-honduras-coup-20160501-story.html.

Yanacocha. “Quiénes Somos.” Last modified August 30, 2016. http://www.yanacocha.com/quienes-somos/.

Chapter 4

Decolonizing Rights: Transnational Feminism and "Women's Rights as Human Rights"

Margaret A. McLaren

Feminists contend that "women's rights are human rights" and have mobilized the discourse of human rights transnationally.[1] But are human rights the best vehicle for achieving the goals of feminism transnationally? Human rights discourse operates within political strategies, social movements, and ideologies. Many critics claim that human rights discourse is limited in its ability to promote radical social change. One strand of criticism holds that rights emerged within the traditional political theoretical framework of liberalism during the Enlightenment. Another strand of criticism points out the emphasis on legal and political rights in the contemporary implementation of human rights; ignoring economic and social rights reinscribes, rather than undermines, systemic material inequalities. Both of these strands of criticism point us toward (albeit in different ways) the colonial legacies and histories, and the neocolonial implementations of dominant "rights" discourses.[2]

Here I pay particular attention to criticisms of human rights discourse made by women from the global South. Such criticisms reveal a "fault line" between the dominant feminist discourse in the global North and the dominant discourse in the global South. Feminists from the global North have focused on advancing women's political and legal rights in the international arena, allowing scant attention to economic concerns, which are fundamental for many women in the global South. This difference in priorities between feminists from the global South and feminists from the global North reinforces a divide between legal and political concerns, on the one hand, and from social, economic, and cultural concerns, on the other. This divide between feminists from the global South and North replicates a division in the larger discussion of human rights theory and practice. Some feminists from the global South, as well as postcolonial feminists, criticize the use of human rights as the primary vehicle for feminist transnational activism on both practical and theoretical levels; I examine both levels of criticisms. On the practical level, I suggest that following a strategy that foregrounds economic and social rights addresses the concerns raised by many feminist activists from the global South. On the theoretical level, I argue that postcolonial feminist concerns about universal human rights can be addressed by acknowledging the ambivalence of human rights; human rights discourse both opens up and shuts down possibilities for liberatory action and social change. Recognizing this ambivalence, I argue, is an important step in the project of decolonizing rights. I suggest that transnational feminism would be better served by a social justice framework/approach that includes rights, while recognizing that they function ambivalently. Moreover, unlike the framework of human rights, the social justice approach questions background conditions and addresses structural inequalities.

The structure of the chapter is as follows. First, I draw a contrast between an intersectional approach and what I call a "gender-first" approach. Next, I provide background about the women's rights movement as a human rights movement, noting the ways that it has expanded and the ways it has redefined traditional human rights practices. Then, I discuss some feminist criticisms of the women's rights as human rights approach, particularly its emphasis on legal and political rights at the expense of economic and social rights. I demonstrate the importance of economic and social rights, and the ways that these rights have been marginalized in human rights discourse. On the practical level, this inattention to economic and social rights could be remedied with a more integrated approach to rights and, indeed, some feminists argue for the indivisibility of rights. However, even when one uses an "indivisibility of rights" approach, rights discourse itself limits what can be said, questioned, and critiqued. Rights discourse is grounded in Eurocentric notions such as individualism, private property, and freedom as lack of constraint. Because of this, some critics argue that rights discourse is a Western, imperialist concept. In contrast, I argue that rights can both undermine hegemonic conceptions and reinforce them; rights discourse functions ambivalently. On the one hand, it can be a useful strategy within a broader social justice framework. On the other hand, rights discourse often occludes structural injustice, power asymmetries, and the operations of colonialism and imperialism. I conclude that in order to decolonize rights, we need to broaden our understandings of rights to include emphasis on economic, social, and cultural rights, as well as question the theoretical origins of rights and their contemporary applications. Challenging these aspects of universal human rights need not entail their wholesale rejection; critically engaging with human rights may be one element of liberatory political struggles. It is not, however, the only element. I suggest that feminists ambivalently embrace human rights as one transnational strategy within a broader social justice framework.

WOMEN'S RIGHTS AS HUMAN RIGHTS

Many feminists see the transnational advocacy of human rights as the most promising strategy for feminists committed to global gender justice advocating a "women's rights as human rights" position.[3] The "women's rights as human rights" position rose to prominence in the 1990s as the predominant transnational feminist strategy for securing gender justice. One of the primary aims of this strategy was to include women's rights in United Nations documents and covenants. The "women's rights as human rights" position arose as the culmination of a series of international United Nations conferences that focused on women, beginning in 1975 with the United Nations conference and NGO Forum in Mexico City kicking off the UN Decade of Women. The UN Decade of Women concluded in 1985, this time marked by a UN conference and NGO Forum on Women in Nairobi, Kenya. Ten years later, in Beijing, China (in 1995), the Beijing Platform for Action was adopted, which included a specific focus on women's and girls' equality and well-being. The "women's rights as human rights" position seeks not only to include women under the purview of traditional human rights protections, such as right to due process, protection from torture, the right to vote and to hold political office, but it also seeks to broaden the traditional concept of human rights by including gender-based violence such as rape, domestic abuse, and gender-specific practices, such as female genital mutilation (FGM), as human rights violations.

While the traditional conception of human rights serves to protect women from state-sanctioned violence and abuse, it does not generally address the private sphere where most violations of women's rights take place. As Julie Peters and Andrea Wolper note in their introduction to *Women's Rights, Human Rights: International Feminist Perspectives*:

> Traditional human rights standards categorize violations in ways that exclude women, eliding critical issues. While men may care about reproductive freedom, their lives are not actually threatened by its absence; for women in areas of high maternal mortality, full reproductive freedom may mean the difference between life and death. Likewise, while asylum law protects those with a "well-founded fear of being persecuted for reasons of race, religion, nationality, membership in a particular social group or political opinion," it rarely protects those persecuted for reasons of gender. . . . And while men may be the victims of private violence, such violence is not part of a pattern of gender-based abuse.[4]

Thus, promoting human rights for women means not only granting and protecting women's political and legal rights on par with those of men but it also means addressing issues that differentially affect women, such as rape as a form of torture and as a weapon of war, domestic violence, sexual slavery and exploitation, honor killing, dowry murder, and reproductive issues, including sex-selective abortion. Violence against women, broadly construed, characterizes many of the ways that women's human rights are violated. As we'll see, however, protecting women from violence is only one aspect of the feminist struggle for social justice and gender equity.

The power of the "women's rights as human rights" movement stems, in part, from its reliance on the already existing framework of international human rights. Yet the recognition of sex-specific violence broadens the definition of human rights. As a result of feminist activism, major international human rights groups have recognized women's human rights as a distinct category within human rights. For example, Human Rights Watch began their Women's Human Rights Project in 1990.[5] This is certainly one of the successes of the "women's rights as human rights" movement.

The inclusion of women's rights in mainstream human rights organizations is an important step in feminist activism and organizing. Feminists were wise to mobilize the discourse of human rights in the 1990s; "because human rights is a language that has legitimacy among many individuals and governments, the appeal to human rights agreements and international norms can fortify women's organizing."[6] The "women's rights as human rights" strategy has achieved important goals, notably the inclusion of women as equally protected in terms of legal and political rights which were already widely accepted, such as the right to liberty, due process under the law, and property. And it significantly broadened human rights to include freedom from sexual and gender violence, which often occurs in the family and home.

This broadening of rights to recognize violations of human rights in the private sphere challenges the long-standing division between public and private that undergirds the thinking of traditional liberal political theory. Challenging the division between public and private shows how the strategic use of human rights discourse can challenge political and legal norms, and correlatively, broaden the conceptual underpinning of human rights theory. Historically, human rights theory and activism have been concerned with state violations of individuals' rights in the public sphere. Including gender-based violence, such as domestic violence, rape, and FGM, changes this focus in three ways by including violations in the private sphere, violations by individuals, and violations endorsed and supported by cultural and social norms. Yet this challenge to the public/private dichotomy still leaves in place the ideologies of individualism, private property, the notion of freedom as "freedom from constraint," and equality as based upon similarity, which are legacies of the European Enlightenment tradition and liberal political theory.

Because of their emphasis on the individual, rather than on structures and systems, human rights approaches grounded in liberal political theory fail to challenge fundamental systemic inequality and oppressive social, economic, and political structures. In short, a human rights approach seeks to make changes within the existing system, rather than changing the system. And, it fails to challenge deeply embedded theoretical and conceptual assumptions, including the legacies of colonialism, which privilege individuals and abstract them from social systems and political and economic systems.

These legacies of colonialism reappear in the project of neocolonialism now implemented through neoliberal economic policies; women in the global South living in conditions of poverty are more vulnerable to the negative impacts of global neoliberal economic policies, so ignoring social and economic rights contributes to the ongoing structural injustice they endure. Many feminist organizations from the global South focus on poverty, inequality, and basic needs, while the majority of feminist organizations from the global North are primarily concerned with extending women's civil and political rights. For example, the Self-Employed Women's Association (SEWA) in India aims to organize women for self-reliance and full employment. Its eleven-point program includes: employment, income, nutritious food, health care, childcare, housing, asset [*sic*], organized strength, leadership, self-reliance, and education. SEWA's primary mission is organizing women workers in the informal labor sector so they can earn a living wage. By contrast, the most visible and mainstream women's organization in the United States is the National Organization for Women, whose focus has been on women's political and legal rights and equality. The focus on political and civil rights championed by liberal Western feminists reinforces a Western, global North perspective on rights that reflects its dominant position through normalizing a postindustrial, wealthy perspective emphasizing civil and political rights, while virtually ignoring social and economic rights.[7] This difference in emphasis not only underscores a difference in priorities but also introduces the systematic domination of the global South by the global North through processes of colonialism and neocolonialism. These processes have systematically underdeveloped the resource-rich global South, both through enslaving people and shipping them to the colonizing country, and through expropriating nonhuman resources. For women, who globally are among the poorest, this perspective that devalues economic and social rights is especially harmful.

FEMINIST CRITICISMS OF THE WOMEN'S RIGHTS AS HUMAN RIGHTS APPROACH

On the face of it, it may seem odd for feminists to criticize human rights. After all, human rights have long been the mark of progress, equality, and liberatory social movements. But for many critics of rights, it is their association with these Enlightenment ideals of liberation, equality, and progress that poses obstacles to rights being embraced as a transnational strategy. For some, an uncritical advocacy of the universal human rights agenda simply reinscribes hegemonic Eurocentrism. For instance, Muslim feminists, such as Lila Abu-Lughod and Saba Mahmood, challenge the secularism of Western feminism. Western feminists should not assume that justice and equality must be the primary values of women everywhere. In her well-known essay, "Do Muslim Women Really Need Saving?," Abu-Lughod raises the question: are emancipation, equality, and rights part of some universal discourse of justice to which we must all subscribe? On the contrary, she suggests that there may be other values, such as closeness with family and cultivation of piety, to which women in different parts of the world may give greater priority. She reminds feminists engaged in transnational work: "We may want justice for women, but can we accept that there might be different ideas about justice and that different women might want, or choose, different futures from what we envision as best? We must consider that they might be called to personhood, so to speak, in a different language."[8] Abu-Lughod cautions that assuming that ideas of individual freedom, individual rights, and an abstract equality as universal simply ascribes dominant Western liberal values to other cultures. Universalizing particular conceptions of freedom, equality, and rights does not serve feminists well in working toward transnational solidarity. Saba Mahmood explicitly makes the connection between liberal thought and the devaluing of a nonsecular perspective. During her study of the piety movement in Egypt, she explored the pietists' notion of subordination to God as freedom. As she notes, "The account I have presented of the mosque movement shows that the distinction between the subject's real desires and obligatory social conventions—a distinction at the center of liberal, and sometimes, progressive thought—cannot be assumed, precisely because socially prescribed forms of behavior constitute the emergence of the self as such and are integral to its realization."[9]

Likewise, Indigenous feminists, such as Linda Tuhiwai Smith and Winona LaDuke, challenge the secularism of Western feminism.[10] In contrast to Western secularism, many Indigenous philosophies hold that land, water, and animals have spiritual essences, and are sacred. Pascha Bueno-Hansen and Sylvanna Falcón describe the Indigenous worldview, which has a profound reverence for all beings and nature, and a sense of interconnectedness, as "cosmovision." Cosmovision respects all beings and the interdependent web of creation; it recognizes the spiritual in all things. As Bueno-Hansen and Falcón note, "Human rights discourse takes the individual as the unquestioned unit of analysis and the right to property assumes an exploitative relationship to the land and nature rooted in the ontological separation of human reasoning from the natural world."[11]

For other feminists, it is the ways that human rights have been promoted and implemented that poses problems for their wholesale acceptance by feminists as the main international strategy. For instance, Celina Romany claims that the process of securing international human rights for women privileges Northern/Western agendas and organizations. She notes that greater "financial and informational resources of northern NGOs determined their leadership role in feminist reconceptualization of human rights." Additionally, she criticizes the Vienna Declaration and Programme of Action for failing "to address the intersection of gender, class and ethnic subordination in its definition of discrimination."[12] Another compelling criticism about the differing priorities of feminists from the global North and the global South comes from Amrita Basu: "Even when they agree on the importance of an issue such as human rights, women from various world regions frame it differently. While Western women traditionally have based their human rights struggles on issues of equality, non-discrimination, and civil and political rights, African, Asian and Latin American women have focused their struggles on economic, social and cultural rights."[13] Given inequalities of wealth among and within countries, and the stark inequality of wealth between industrialized countries in the global North and poorer countries in the global South, this difference of priorities is understandable. Each of these criticisms focuses on the way in which human rights discourse has been implemented in United Nations conferences and documents, rather than on the conceptual limitations of human rights discourse.

Feminists from the global North and feminists from the global South have different perspectives as well as different priorities. Esther Ngan-ling Chow's statement, written as part of a report on the 1995 United Nations Women's Conference and NGO Forum in Beijing, shows that the difference in approaches between feminists from the global North and feminists from the global South go beyond simply prioritizing rights differently. As Chow notes, "While sharing some common ground, women from the North were primarily concerned with equality and a better quality of life, and women from the South with issues of basic rights and needs, poverty, development, and human security. In the latter case, the struggle of women from the developing [*sic*] South *should also be understood in the context of each country's experience under the domination of imperialism, colonialism and neocolonialism and against 'a background of nationalist struggles aimed at achieving political independence, asserting a national identity, and modernizing society.'* "[14] Chow mentions not only the difference in emphasis between feminists from the global North and feminists from the global South—equality versus meeting basic needs and ameliorating poverty—but she also notes the differences in historical, political, and social context, as well as power differences such as the continuing domination from the global North through the legacies of colonialism.

Simplistically, the fault lines between these feminist positions could be drawn as a North/South divide, or a Western/non-Western divide, or a white women/women of color divide, or a liberal/socialist divide, or a middle and upper middle class/poor and working class divide, or finally as a universalist/culturalist divide. Along this divide, the Northern, Western, white, liberal, middle and upper middle class, universalist perspective privileges gender and advocates universal human rights as the best strategy for feminists, whereas the Southern, non-Western, women of color, socialist, poor and working class, culturalist approach challenges the idea of women's common experience; holds an intersectional view of social structures and identities; and sees economic, social, and cultural rights as equally important to political and legal rights. I'll call the former approach the "gender-first" approach and the latter an "intersectional" approach; these two approaches are analogous to global feminism and transnational feminism. But, of course, the divisions among feminist perspectives and approaches do not line up so neatly. Next, I discuss the reasons why feminists did and do promote universal human rights and women's rights as human rights as a transnational feminist strategy, highlighting the benefits and successes of the rights strategy.

THE INDIVISIBILITY OF RIGHTS

Legal and political rights alone cannot fully address the many interconnected ways that women are disadvantaged and marginalized. They are only one part of a larger strategy that must include socioeconomic change, and changes in cultural institutions, practices, and attitudes. Moreover, women's rights to food, shelter, and work depend on changes in social institutions that are not simply transformed by new laws that allow women to vote or protect women from employment discrimination. Protection from employment discrimination is meaningless if there is a lack of decent work in your village or city, or if you are prevented from pursuing the education or training that would qualify you for available work. Legal and political rights provide a formal structure for women to challenge gender inequality, but more is needed in order to address women's needs, especially if they also suffer material deprivation, are working class, or poor. Some feminists recognize that legal, political, economic, social, and cultural rights cannot be separated; they hold that these different types of human rights are indivisible.

In spite of the differences in focus attributed to feminists from the global North and the global South, some feminists have argued for the indivisibility of rights. For instance, in her essay, "Transforming Human Rights from a Feminist Perspective," Charlotte Bunch notes the importance of social and economic rights, as well as their connection to civil and political rights:

"Much of the abuse of women is a part of the larger socio-economic and cultural web that entraps women, making them vulnerable to abuses that cannot be delineated as exclusively political or solely caused by states. *The indivisibility of rights and the inclusion of the so-called second generation (or socio-economic) human rights to food, shelter and work (clearly delineated in the Universal Declaration of Human Rights) is therefore vital to addressing women's concerns fully*."[15] Interestingly, Bunch has been instrumental in the "women's rights as human rights" movement, which has promoted women's political and legal rights. The gap between Bunch's recognition of the indivisibility of rights, and the practice and implementation of pressing for women's rights transnationally may reflect limitations in current international organizations, structures, and institutions, rather than a lack of commitment on (Western) feminists' part to work for economic and social rights.

Feminist political theorist Rosalind Petchetsky makes a compelling argument for the indivisibility of rights with respect to reproductive rights. She claims that the women's movement has become issue driven, working on such issues as violence, reproductive rights, sexuality, women in development, and women and work; this results in a type of fragmentation that impedes promoting the indivisibility of human rights and the interconnectedness of the issues driving the women's movement. The United Nations Declaration of Universal Human Rights includes social and economic rights, the rights to self-determination and self-development (cultural rights), as well as political and civil rights. Often, however, as we have seen, international organizations focus mainly on legal and political rights. Theorists of human rights classify the UN human rights in terms of generations: legal and political rights are first-generation rights, social and economic rights are second-generation rights, and cultural rights are third-generation rights. Although this classification is falling out of favor, the language reflects a particular perspective and mirrors the ways in which these sets of rights have been given priority in international discourse and policy. Petchetsky believes that without the so-called second- and third-generation rights, first-generation rights cannot be exercised. For example, she says, "[P]ractically speaking, it [the indivisibility of rights] has to do with the real-life fact that a woman cannot avail herself of her 'right to decide freely and responsibly the number, spacing, and timing of her children'" (ICDP Programme of Action, 7.3) if she lacks the financial resources to pay for reproductive health services or the transport to reach them; if she cannot read package inserts or clinic wall posters; if her workplace is contaminated with pesticides or pollutants that have an adverse effect on pregnancy; or if she is harassed by a husband or in-laws who will scorn her or beat her up if she uses birth control."[16] In this example, we see very clearly the relationship among all rights specified in the UN Declaration of Universal Human Rights: political and civil, social and economic, and self-determination and self-development (cultural) rights; we also see why they are indivisible. One cannot exercise the right to family planning without economic resources, a level of education that results in literacy, environmental protections, and changes in society and culture that still allow the harassment of female family members. Moreover, the ability to access health care also often depends on larger social and economic issues such as having an adequate infrastructure, including public transportation and roads to get to clinics and hospitals from rural areas.

In order for the right to health to be realized, social and economic rights would need to be recognized, and institutions, policies, and practices changed so that everyone, regardless of their class or personal resources, had access to free health care. But a comprehensive framework for social justice goes beyond even the recognition that social and economic rights are inseparable from legal and political rights; it includes attention to context, material circumstances and oppression, and structural inequality. Many of Petchetsky's examples are from outside the United States. But the indivisibility of rights highlights the ways that rights discourse has too often left out economic and social concerns in the United States as well.

Women of color in the United States founded the *reproductive justice* movement; they make a powerful argument that a *reproductive rights* framework is individualist and does not account for structural inequality, oppression, and social and economic inequalities.[17] They clearly articulate the limitations of the (reproductive) rights framework and argue for a model founded on a more comprehensive view of social justice, advocating a reproductive justice model. "Reproductive liberty must encompass more than the protection of an individual woman's choice to end her pregnancy. It must encompass the full range of procreative activities, including the ability to bear a child, and it must acknowledge that we make reproductive decisions within a social context, including inequalities of wealth and power. *Reproductive freedom is a matter of social justice, not individual choice*."[18] The reproductive justice framework shifts concerns from freedom and choice associated with negative freedom to concerns with a larger context that supports reproductive health, such as prenatal and maternal health care, adequate nutrition, and an environment free from violence. This shift to adequate material conditions and a context that supports the choice to have and raise a healthy child necessarily includes a shift to the so-called positive rights: social and economic rights. The insights from the reproductive justice movement can inform a broader criticism of abstracting freedom, choice, and rights from their social context and material circumstances.

For feminists interested in abolishing gender discrimination against women globally, the rights framework can provide important structures of accountability at the state level and transnationally. But without corresponding attention to social and economic inequalities, women will remain in a vulnerable position. Moreover, the rights approach is targeted toward changing formal structures, such as laws. But even when the laws are implemented and enforced (which is not always the case), these legal changes do not address the informal institutions and cultural systems that hold social norms and gender norms in place. The persistence of gender discrimination worldwide has a variety of elements: political, economic, legal, religious, and sociocultural. We need to recognize the interconnection of these various elements in order to effectively promote change. However, recognizing the indivisibility of rights is not enough. The discourse and strategy of human rights remain within the liberal political framework, which does not account for power differences, structural oppression, and systemic exploitation.

ECONOMIC RIGHTS AND NEOLIBERAL GLOBALIZATION

As noted earlier in this chapter, there has been a North/South divide between feminists regarding the ways in which "women's rights" have been argued, articulated, and struggled for within the context of international forums, such as United Nations conferences. Feminists from wealthy countries in the global North more often press for legal and political rights for women. Admittedly, a major success of the women's rights as human rights approach was the inclusion of gender-based violence, and the liability of individuals, not only states, in redressing violence against women, such as domestic violence, rape, sexual harassment, sexual exploitation, and sex trafficking. But for the majority of the world's women who live in poverty, economic issues are paramount.

Increasingly, the effect on the global South by the wealthier countries of the global North exacerbates poverty in the global South, especially for women and children. As we consider which frameworks best address justice and equity for women, we must consider economic issues and access to material resources to be among the primary concerns, as there are clear gender discrepancies in terms of inequalities of wealth and power. Yet gender is not the only salient axis of inequality: "We cannot speak about global injustice without speaking about inequality between countries, inequality between classes in each country, and inequalities between the sexes."[19] In many countries, race and ethnicity correlate with class because of the historical consequences of exploitation and oppression. For instance, in the United States there is a wealth gap as well as an income gap between African Americans and white, Anglo-Americans.[20]

Economist Amartya Sen notes that "deprived groups in the 'First World' live, in many ways, in the 'Third.' For example, African Americans in some of the most prosperous U.S. cities (such as New York, Washington, or San Francisco) have a lower life expectancy at birth than do most people in immensely poorer China or even India."[21] Women and children make up the largest and fastest growing population living under poverty level all over the world. Where poverty is particularly acute, women's situation is especially dire. Feminists must continue to struggle for economic and social rights as well as political and legal rights in order to improve women's status and quality of life worldwide. The World Bank estimated that over one billion people were living in absolute poverty in 2011. Of the 1.2 billion people in the world who are recognized as the "absolute poor" (living on less than $1.25 a day), over 900 million are women. These figures mean that 75 percent of the world's absolute poor are women. In the United States, one in three American women (i.e., 42 million women) plus 28 million children either live in poverty or are right on the brink of it.[22] The feminization of poverty, where women rank among the poorest members of society, continues to increase despite the fact that the number of women entering the paid workforce has increased overall in the past ten years. As feminist scholars note, one effect of economic globalization is the global feminization of poverty.[23] The neoliberal economic policies characteristic of contemporary globalization exacerbate the feminization of poverty in a number of ways.

Neoliberalism, like liberalism, purports to increase freedom and opportunities by deregulating, individualizing, and privatizing. Neoliberal economic policies benefit transnational corporations and the wealthy, while widening the gap between rich and poor and further disenfranchising the poor. In addition to policies imposed by the International Monetary Fund, the World Bank, and the World Trade Organization, economic change also results from the creation of free trade zones (FTZs) and export processing zones (EPZs) and the relocation of transnational corporations to the global South in search of cheap and outsourced labor. These economic changes have complex effects. For laborers in the global North the outsourcing of jobs to the global South means fewer jobs and less money in local economies. But the increase of jobs in the global South, especially those in FTZs and EPZs, is not an unmitigated good. The new jobs are often low-paying factory jobs with long hours, no benefits, and little in the way of safety and health protection. Women make up the majority of workers recruited for these low-paying jobs in substandard conditions. Moreover, the outsourcing of production from the global North often undermines local economies in the global South.

Globalization's effects are gendered; women are differentially affected by globalization in a variety of ways. Globalization causes environmental degradation and increased immigration (both within and between countries). Environmental degradation often affects women more negatively, as gathering water and fuel in rural areas for cooking is usually women's work.

Environmental degradation impacts poor communities both in the global South and the global North, whether rural or urban. And within those communities, women, who are primarily responsible for childcare, meeting the family's daily needs, and social reproduction in general, are more negatively impacted. For example, the high levels of lead in the drinking water in Flint, Michigan, in the United States caused health, cognitive, and behavioral problems in children, and their mothers bear the burden of responsibility for caretaking. Immigration, too, has a disproportionate impact on women; often families are separated when one of the adult members of the household migrates to find work. Because women still do the majority of domestic work, including childcare, cooking, cleaning, and taking care of elders, the separation of the family unit increases their burden as they often must juggle paid work with unpaid domestic labor.

In the majority of countries in the global South, the informal economy plays a large role: the informal economy includes home-based work, food vendors or vendors of manufactured products, day laborers engaged in all sorts of work, and much domestic labor. In the informal economy, there is no minimum wage, benefits, or job security. It is tempting to think that new job opportunities in factories open up opportunities for women, because they usually increase the number of women working in the formal economy. However, these jobs in the formal economy often pay subpar wages, lack benefits, and are in unsafe working conditions. Moreover, the expansion of the formal economy may simultaneously undermine the informal economy by promoting policies and structures that do not recognize informal labor. Because women are overrepresented in informal labor (for instance, 94 percent of women in India who are engaged in paid labor work in the informal labor sector), this has a more pronounced negative effect on women. In addition to women's overrepresentation in the informal sector, women still do the majority of unpaid care work worldwide, such as childcare, elder care, and caring for sick family members.[24] The privatization required by various structural adjustment programs, including cuts in public support of education, health care, and other public services, increases women's burden of unpaid labor. With respect to paid labor, globalization also differentially affects women. Because economic globalization includes policies that lower trade barriers and tariffs, it is easier for transnational corporations to relocate to countries where they can pay a lower wage; thus more factories have opened up in the global South, and more jobs are available for women in the formal labor market. However, along with this increased number of jobs in the formal labor market, there has been a feminization of the global labor force in the formal sector. In other words, there are more women in the formal labor sector, but they continue being recruited into low paying jobs in factories or in the service sector. So, while globalization has increased the number of women working in the formal labor market, these jobs lack security, benefits, decent wages, and may have deleterious impacts on women's health. This increase in the formal labor market has spurred a corresponding increase in the informal labor market, which was already dominated by women.[25]

Viewing women's labor in the context of globalization allows us to see the connections among global economic policies and inequalities and the ways they differentially impact women, particularly in and from the global South. It is not surprising that globalization has a differential effect on women since gender stratification pervades most cultures and societies, although, of course, the specifics of gender stratification vary from society to society, and within societies. A social justice approach grounded in an intersectional understanding of identity, and that accounts for structural oppression, recognizes that rights are only one aspect of a more comprehensive framework for social change. Gender stratification and women's oppression result from a variety of interlocking factors, not all of which can be addressed through legal and political remedies.

In my conclusion, I suggest that the project of decolonizing rights will entail opening up space for a plurality of different liberatory strategies and practices. One such strategy could be a social justice approach that may include rights as one aspect of a comprehensive strategy for challenging oppression, domination, and economic injustice; including rights within a comprehensive social justice strategy could help to ameliorate its individualism and its lack of emphasis on economic and social rights. To the extent that rights discourse originates in and perpetuates Eurocentrism, if feminists embrace universal human rights as a useful strategy, it would need to be embraced critically and ambivalently. Taking up the feminist criticisms of individualism in rights discourses, and their emphasis on legal and political rights, I show how each of these ties into its Eurocentric origins.

FEMINIST CRITICISMS OF EUROCENTRISM

Postcolonial feminist criticisms center around the idea that rights are assumed to be a fundamentally Western liberal notion and therefore that the application of rights to other contexts belies a Eurocentric and biased view.[26] One of the features of rights discourse is its claim to universality; it is precisely this claim that is challenged by postcolonial feminists. I have already discussed one of the significant issues with assuming that rights can be applied universally; when human rights is abstracted from its economic and social context, questions of structural oppression, systemic economic and social injustice, and the importance of material conditions fade into the background. By not acknowledging the origin of rights within a particular social and historical context, and thus its specificity as a discourse, theorists who apply rights cross-culturally without attention to context run the risk of Western cultural imperialism. Despite feminism's attention to diversity, Western feminists often reproduce cultural imperialism in our attempts to apply Western standards cross-culturally and when making claims about women as a group. Postcolonial feminists and feminists of color warn white Western feminists to beware of misrepresenting the other by assuming that universal claims can adequately address the range and diversity of specific types of oppression and exploitation that women face in different cultural, political, historical, and economic contexts. Postcolonial and feminists of color[27] also warn theorists to avoid falsely essentializing women by assuming that all women have common interests.[28] They claim that arguing on behalf of women obscures differences of class, caste, race, ethnicity, and religion even among women within the same society. Moreover, white Western feminists who promote women's rights cross-culturally may inadvertently bring their own biases to bear on the situation, including the belief that gender equality and individual rights are more important than cultural tradition or religious identity. This Western liberal bias, the idea that culture, religion, and tradition can easily be left aside in favor of (abstract) individualism, devalues the significance of culture and its impact on identity and agency. This devaluation of culture reinforces the dominance of the hegemonic Western view. As Oyeronke Oyewumi says, "one cannot assume the social organization of one culture (the dominant West included) as universal or the interpretations of the experiences of one culture as explaining another one."[29] Many feminists engaged in cross-border theorizing and activism share her view that categories and concepts cannot simply be extrapolated from one culture to another. If culture provides a set of social meanings through which we make sense of the world and ourselves, then it should be taken into account as we work toward developing approaches for transnational work for gender justice.

Susan Moller Okin's provocative essay, "Is Multiculturalism Bad for Women?" captures well the conflict that arises when one assumes that gender equality and culture conflict. One of the primary reasons for this conflict, according to Okin, is that gender equality relies on a strong sense of individual rights, whereas respecting cultures often means acknowledging group rights. Interestingly, she argues that, in fact, multiculturalism *is* bad for women. She makes a strong argument that most cultures, because they are patriarchal, are antithetical to rights, and thus in order to achieve gender equality, these cultures must be abolished. For instance, Okin states, "[M]ost cultures have as one of their principle aims the control of women by men."[30] The reason for this is that according to Okin, and other feminists such as Charlotte Bunch, patriarchy and culture are inseparable. For instance, Bunch states, "Most cultures as we know them today are patriarchal."[31] Okin even goes so far as to claim that women and girls in minority cultures might be better off if their culture became extinct and they were fully integrated into the majority culture.[32] The distinction between minority and majority culture here is telling. Significantly, her focus and examples of "problematic" cultures are all non-Western cultures. To Okin, and many other Western feminists, the faults of the majority culture are invisible. Majority culture is assumed to be somehow neutral, when in fact it is Western, white, heterosexual, and secular. Moreover, majority culture here is associated with Enlightenment liberal ideas of equality, justice, and progress, and is contrasted with minority cultures, which are characterized as having distinct traditions embedded in a history and belief system specific to its members. Understandably, many feminists respond by defending the ubiquity of and importance of culture both to their own identities and for international feminist discourse and activism.

To be fair, Okin argues against multiculturalism and for liberalism because she believes that multiculturalism—which takes seriously cultural norms and values, and supports the idea of group rights—harms women. She brings up a number of examples, such as honor killing, dowry murder, sati, and female genital mutilation, attributing all of these to culture or religion. Her use of examples of gender violence that she attributes to culture positions liberalism as the bastion of women's protection in postindustrial Western societies and reinforces the view that the liberal rights and equality framework serves to single out violence against women in non-Western countries. She does not discuss the ways in which Western societal norms may contribute to violence against women; for instance, the lack of an extended family structure in the United States isolates women as part of a nuclear family and makes them more vulnerable to domestic violence and economic dependence on their spouse. Additionally, Okin is vehemently secular, noting that three of the major religions—Islam, Christianity, and Judaism—are all patriarchal. Her outright rejection of religion as patriarchal ignores the multiplicity of religious traditions, the many feminist reinterpretations of the major religions she lists, and the fact that secularism is not immune to patriarchy. As discussed previously, in terms of transnational feminism, enforcing secularism ignores the many women globally who have deep religious commitments.[33] She views both culture and religion as monolithic and homogenous and as primarily a vehicle for gender subordination. A more nuanced view of culture reveals the overlap among cultures, the heterogeneity within them, and the ways in which culture can enlarge—and not merely diminish—women's lives and agency.[34]

Okin herself highlights one aspect of the heterogeneity within cultures when she worries that the multiculturalist's support of group or cultural rights may perpetuate existing unequal power relations, specifically privileging voices of males and elders. Heterogeneity and power differences among members of a group are important issues to address while defending group rights; left unaddressed these power differences could easily leave more vulnerable group members, often women and girls, at a disadvantage or open to abuses of power by other group members. Unfortunately, Okin did not extend her analysis of the heterogeneity and power differentials within groups to examine the heterogeneity and power differences among women. Extending the analysis in this way opens up the space for understanding that not only are women differently situated in, for instance, a cultural or religious community or with respect to race and ethnicity, but also our locations in these communities and social groups mean women are situated differently from one another in significant ways.

Many feminists, such as Chandra Talpade Mohanty, Lila Abu-Lughod, and Gayatri Spivak, point out the similarities between the contemporary discourse of equality, freedom, and rights and earlier colonial discourse about Third World women.[35] As Abu-Lughod notes, historically the West has justified its intervention into other cultures by seeking to "protect" women.[36] In her essay, and a recent book of the same name, "Do Muslim Women Really Need Saving?" Lila Abu-Lughod examines the ways that the rhetoric of protecting Muslim women from practices characterized as oppressive by the dominant West, such as veiling, has been used to justify U.S. military intervention in the Middle East. This rhetoric of protecting or saving women of color from men of color is not new; as Gayatri Spivak puts it, history is full of examples of "white men saving brown women from brown men."[37] While Spivak is referring to white men's historical role in colonialism, well-meaning white feminists may inadvertently undermine a woman's cultural or religious identity in the name of gender equality. One contemporary example of feminist disagreement is over the issue of veiling. As Abu-Lughod and others point out, not only does the practice of wearing the veil differ from country to country but also its meaning varies with respect to nation, history, and politics. It is reductive and ethnocentric to view the veil as a sign of women's oppression and to advocate for its abolition. Instead, the practice of veiling (and other cultural and religious practices) must be understood and addressed in their specific historical and cultural context.

Feminist postcolonial critics argue that white Western feminists (or anyone else) should not simply apply notions of equality or rights to other countries and other cultures without recognizing that these concepts have historical roots in the Western liberal tradition. Additionally, concepts like rights and equality impose dominant conceptions, including the superiority of Western values, on non-Western cultures. The criticisms by postcolonial feminists echo some reservations by Asian leaders who voiced their concerns about using the concept of individual rights to frame international guidelines for human rights. They explicitly rejected this imposition of Western norms:

"Singapore's Lee Kuan Yew and Malaysia's Mahatir Mohamad have claimed that the 'Asian values' of collectivism, social duty and economic welfare are inconsistent with Western values of individualism and political rights."[38] Other Asian countries shared this position and joined together to draft the 1993 Bangkok Declaration, which asserts the importance of Asian values and national sovereignty.[39] This joining together of Asian countries to draft a document that specifically criticizes universal human rights as individualistic and focused on political rights, at the expense of social and economic rights, sends a strong message about the underlying assumptions and values of universal human rights. When Western culture is presumed to be neutral, it denies the plurality of cultural values, and it obscures the particularity of its own values. Moreover, privileging Western culture contributes to a reductive view of non-Western cultures; this reductive view assumes that non-Western cultures are static, homogeneous, and isolated.

Ironically, criticizing rights as a "Western" concept itself runs the risk of cultural imperialism. Critics of the Asian values position believe that holding up social duty and collectivism as Asian values, as opposed to Western values of individualism and independence, is a type of cultural reductionism.[40] They argue that by attributing the idea of rights to the European West, without regard for Indigenous struggles for rights in other contexts, critics of universal human rights themselves engage in Orientalism because they exaggerate the difference between Western cultures and non-Western cultures, elide differences among non-Western cultures, and romanticize them.[41]

In spite of this criticism that the Asian values position simplifies and reifies cultural differences, the widespread agreement by leaders and representatives of Asian countries lends the view some credence.[42] The Bangkok Declaration of Asian values underscores the fact that universal human rights, both in its history and in its application, is not neutral and carries a set of values and assumptions as well as a particular history. The universal application of human rights should be viewed in its historical and social context: "The universalization of human rights cannot be dissociated from the complex historical process spreading Western Christian civilization to other regions."[43] Given its association with colonization and the "civilizing mission of white Christianity" we must acknowledge that the universal application of human rights can be, intentionally or unintentionally, a neocolonial imperialist strategy. All too often, the wealthy nations of the global North accuse nations in the global South of rights violations, and not vice versa: "Human rights have become another weapon in the arsenal of western countries in their efforts to bring recalcitrant Third World nations to heel in their 'New World order.' Western nations are increasingly using the very narrow interpretation of human rights as a yardstick with which to judge Third World governments."[44]

To avoid this type of imperialism, Western feminists engaging in international, cross-cultural work need to be reflective about the ways that we include cultural considerations in our work and to recognize our own specific cultural location. Simply applying rights without addressing these concerns may undermine feminist and other causes that rely on different paradigms for political action and social change. Taking cultural difference seriously complicates any attempt to promote a transnational feminism.

As discussed earlier, feminists have made great strides in the past thirty-five years in getting women's rights issues on the international agenda. While including women's rights as human rights represents an important advancement, such advancement should not come at the cost of harming or marginalizing women of the global South. As development theorist Naila Kabeer states, "In listening to the voices raised by women to protest against the unfairness of patriarchal structures as they have experienced them, we do not have to choose between an authentic local voice and an imported Western feminism. These are voices of protest grounded in local experience and articulated in local idioms in societies which are not hermetically sealed off from the rest of the world."[45] Mohanty, Abu-Lughod, and Oyewumi raise significant criticisms of the ethnocentrism and colonialism that can result when feminists adopt the universal human rights framework with regard to women's issues internationally. These criticisms can serve to guide feminists toward a transnational approach that is broader than the human rights approach, is contextually sensitive, is politically and historically grounded, and includes a power analysis that can account for, and challenge, systemic oppression, exploitation, and domination. Moreover, these criticisms help us to see some of the limitations of the human rights approach.

DECOLONIZING RIGHTS

One could argue, following Anibal Quijano, that the idea of universal human rights is too closely tied to the "new geography of power" that characterizes Modernity. This new geography of power includes "three elements: the coloniality of power, capitalism and Eurocentrism. Its hegemonic institutions are: nation-state, the bourgeois family, the capitalist corporation, and Eurocentric rationality."[46] Given this new geography of power, can human rights serve as an effective transnational strategy for feminists in the twenty-first century? The *coloniality of power* refers to the deeply racialized division of labor under global capitalism that resulted from processes of colonization.[47] In her expansion of Quijano's influential conception of the coloniality of power, María Lugones praises him for his contribution to understanding and articulating a framework that analyzes the relations of racialized and gendered labor and its historical formation under colonization. She criticizes his framework, though, for its narrow understanding of gender. Lugones brings together Quijano's work on the coloniality of power, which maintains that "all power is structured in relations of domination, exploitation and conflict" with the work of feminists of color on intersectionality.[48] Intersectional feminist approaches, advocated by Kimberlé Crenshaw and Patricia Hill Collins, as well as many others, point out that gender cannot be separated from culture, race, ethnicity, or religion.[49] An intersectional approach holds that gender oppression takes place within an interlocking set of other systemic oppressions, such as racism, classism, heterosexism, ableism, religious oppression/discrimination, and ethnic oppression. This intersectional approach recognizes that gender cannot be isolated from these other features all of which are formed within a "matrix of domination."[50] A feminist intersectional approach, introduced by Crenshaw and Hill Collins, has been crucial in challenging the hegemony of white, middle-class academic feminism, which historically emphasized gender and sought to find commonality among women's experiences.

Just as the intersectional approach challenges the idea that women share a common experience because they are women (abstracting from the different social locations women occupy and where women are located in the matrix of domination in terms of power and privilege), transnational feminism challenges global feminism's insistence on attempting to base transnational feminist activism on a shared identity as women. There is a parallel and overlap between these approaches: global feminism assumes that women have a shared identity upon which to base our claims and activism, as do feminists who hold that gender is the primary axis of oppression. Both of these approaches put gender first, isolating and abstracting it from other axes of identity and also removing gender from historical, social, political, and economic contexts. Thus, a "gender-first" approach skews feminist discourse and activism toward a hegemonic, dominant view by isolating gender as the primary site of inequality and ignoring the fact that gender is always inflected by other social positions and identities. Feminists who take a "gender-first" approach often see gender as the most salient axis of oppression because in their own lives, it is. In other words, when one holds dominant identities in terms of race, class, and sexuality, but not gender, then gender becomes foregrounded as the most salient issue. Too often the "gender-first" approach invites an identity politics that views women's equality as its primary goal in isolation from ending other types of systemic oppression, such as racism, heterosexism, and class exploitation. In this way, a "gender-first" approach often works within existing systems (political, legal, and economic) rather than challenging systemic inequalities and structural oppression, such as global capitalism.[51] In order to challenge the coloniality of power, we must recognize and challenge the formation of a global capitalist economic system based on racialized and gendered divisions of labor, and the hegemony of power held by the neoliberal state's complicity with transnational corporations.

One step toward decolonizing rights may be to recognize that they function ambivalently. Within the purview of the nation-state, and in associations of nation-states, such as the United Nations, fighting for rights and equality may be the best remedy to achieve political enfranchisement and legal equality and protection for individuals that are discriminated against and for members of socially marginalized groups.[52] Rights provide a minimal formal structure for equality but do not guarantee or provide support for substantive equality; substantive equality involves access to economic and social resources and opportunities. Even when economic and social resources are taken into account, rights rely on a distributive justice framework that looks at a fair process of distribution within the system but does not challenge the system itself. In other words, persistent and systemic inequalities of wealth and power can remain, so long as rights are protected. Without addressing these systemic inequalities, it is likely that they will simply persist. The individualism of rights reinforces the discourse of meritocracy and denies the historical context of resource extraction and labor exploitation. And, although universal human rights is an ideal held as an international standard, rights rely on enforcement by nation-states whose power is eclipsed by transnational corporations and world financial institutions. In the context of globalization, people's day-to-day lives are affected by neoliberal economic policies at the global level.

Because of this, one could argue that the control of people's lives by transnational corporations and global financial institutions calls for a renewal and augmentation of human rights as a protection from economic and corporate policies that violate human rights. Indeed, where the claims for human rights protect individuals and groups from state abuse and violence and from human rights violations, then human rights claims can be strategically useful. Often, however, states and the elite within them benefit from these neoliberal economic policies and so are reluctant to limit the power of transnational corporations. In spite of the limitations I have pointed out, human rights clearly have a role to play in promoting justice within and among states. For example, within the United States, human rights discourse has been useful for securing LGBTQ rights. And, the "women's rights as human rights" campaign helped to ensure that rape committed during wartime can be prosecuted as a human rights violation, and not only as an individual criminal act. Human rights can help marginalized groups to secure equal protection under the law within nation-states. And, a widely shared notion of human rights can help to leverage changes in nation-states to move toward enfranchisement and equality for groups that are socially, economically, and politically marginalized, and discriminated against. But much more is needed. I suggest that a comprehensive social justice framework can further the project of justice for all. Recently, human rights theorists and practitioners are also adopting a social justice framework.[53] Can human rights approaches and social justice approaches work in tandem?

As I have argued, using a social justice model—which views rights as indivisible and within the framework of structural social and economic inequality—can provide a better framework for addressing so many of the pressing issues for feminists engaging in transnational activism and scholarship, and can help to avoid imposing ethnocentric and imperialist frameworks. For instance, the individualistic choice-based framework of traditional liberal theory and much human rights theory ignores social context and material circumstances. The reproductive justice movement recognizes that approaches based on rights and individual choice do not account for oppression, deprivation, and social and economic inequality, so they shift from a rights paradigm to a social justice paradigm. Likewise, I am suggesting that a social justice, rather than a rights, approach would better serve transnational feminists. The social justice model does not simply accommodate but recognizes as integral all of the aspects within the human rights framework. Additionally, a social justice approach recognizes structural inequality, oppression, power differences, and issues of identity and recognition as central, whereas the rights framework does not lend itself easily to accommodating these issues. As we saw in our earlier discussion, it is difficult to address issues of cultural and religious diversity, colonialism, and differences in the power of social groups within the rights framework. Moreover, the social justice approach is compatible with contemporary feminist positions on oppression; intersectionality of identities; structural inequalities; power differences; and the importance of historical, social, and political contexts.

I have demonstrated the need for a new framework that takes these multiple criticisms of human rights seriously. The social justice framework assumes the indivisibility of political, civil, economic, social, and cultural rights, and it is not susceptible to the critiques of rights discussed earlier. A social justice framework includes community and social group membership, and accounts for diverse identities and inequalities of power, and cultural, religious, and social differences. Furthermore, unlike the classic liberal model, which is at odds with theories of oppression and domination, the social justice framework is grounded on the fact of structural violence, and, correspondingly, oppression and exploitation. Without recognition of structural injustice, we cannot develop the tools and strategies to challenge it. Finally, the social justice framework allows for the reflective and culturally sensitive use of human rights discourse to protect and maintain life, bodily integrity, and basic freedoms. In other words, rights are a part of the toolkit of the social justice framework, but they are not the entirety of it. Moreover, the social justice framework is at odds with many of the assumptions of the rights framework, including abstract individualism, difference-blind justice, and the lack of a power analysis. Thus, the social justice framework promotes more radical social transformation and social change.

Feminists engaged in transnational activism and research can adopt a social justice framework without completely rejecting the need for a strategic employment of human rights cross-culturally. For example, the recent inclusion of LGBTQ enfranchisement in the United States with respect to the Marriage Equality Act may at least open up discussion in nations that still criminalize LGBTQ identities and practices.[54] Reframing feminist issues around empowering women to improve the quality of women's and their families' lives rather than the issue of women's liberation or equality may ameliorate some of the negative effects of an uncritical cross-cultural application of human rights. Empowerment has been utilized by women's organizations, NGOs, and has figured centrally in development strategies:

> Because the process [of empowerment]—and its effects and impacts—was so shaped by the interests and contexts of those engaged in it, and hence less predictable in its outcomes, the empowerment approach is not sufficiently "results-oriented," an important priority in current development funding. In such agencies, the "rights-based" approach (as though empowerment is about anything but rights!) finds greater favour, because rights-based interventions—greater access to redress, achievements of the Millennium Development Goals, new legislation—are more readily quantified. *But these [rights-based] approaches often shift agency into the hands of professional intermediaries (lawyers, NGO activists, policy specialists) and away from marginalised women and communities. They also focus on formal structures and equality, rather than on the informal institutions and cultural systems that older empowerment processes attempted to transform (though not always successfully).*[55]

Although the discourse of empowerment itself may have culturally and historically specific origins, it allows women to decide for themselves what they need to improve the quality of their lives. For example, land reform may be more important to poor, rural women than gender equality. This allays the controversial issue of deciding or ranking such things from outside the sociocultural context, especially at the risk of repeating the mistake of a cultural-theoretical imperialism that attempts to universalize. Decolonizing rights may involve starting from local contexts and understandings to see how gender is constructed and defined. Understanding women's various social locations, the ways that they articulate their own intersectional identities within local contexts, and with respect to oppressive and exploitative structures and institutions, such as global capitalism, shifts the focus from gender oppression alone to a complex understanding of the ways that gender oppression is intertwined with other forms of oppression, and the need for collective action to challenge and change structural institutionalized oppression in all its various forms and institutional manifestations. Transnational feminists would be well served by shifting from a rights framework to a social justice framework that can analyze and criticize structural inequality and oppression. A feminist social justice approach includes a focus on women's empowerment, and centers women as agents of change.

CONCLUSION

Decolonizing rights, then, involves a critical questioning of the origins, applications, and uses of human rights discourse. As I have discussed, the "women's rights as human rights" movement made important advances by including violence against women as a human rights violation, and not merely an individual criminal action. Moreover, viewing women's rights as human rights conveys a powerful message that women should enjoy all the same protections and privileges under the law as men. Finally, the "women's rights as human rights" movement blurred the distinction between public and private actions so that violence against women in the home, such as domestic abuse, marital rape, and incest, can be considered human rights violations, even if they are not illegal in the country in which they occurred. However, feminists from the global South, such as Celina Romany, took issue with the way in which the "women's rights as human rights" agenda was promoted and implemented. Her criticism focused on the lack of an intersectional approach and the strong focus on legal and political rights, at the expense of social and economic rights. She attributed this narrow focus to the fact that primarily middle-class white feminists led the "women's rights as human rights" movement from the global North. These criticisms rest mainly on the implementation of human rights discourse at international conferences and United Nations meetings.

Feminist postcolonial theorists raise additional criticisms of human rights that highlight the theoretical limitations of the concept. They challenge the secularity, and individualism of the concept of human rights, as well as its origins in European social contract theory. Some, such as Abu-Lughod and Mahmood, also question the associated view of freedom as liberty, in other words, the negative concept of freedom as lack of constraint and unlimited individual choice. Proponents of the Asian values view also question the strong individualism of human rights, and the focus of human rights discourse which emphasizes legal and political rights, often to the detriment of economic and social rights. For example, in nations where private property and unlimited personal wealth are enshrined in the law, it is more difficult to meet the basic needs of the majority through universal health care. The criticisms of postcolonial theorists, and proponents of the Asian values view, challenge human rights at the theoretical, conceptual level; they suggest that human rights is a particular discourse that privileges some aspects of being human, such as the need for equal respect, and neglects others, such as strong religious identity and a sense of self in relation. Moreover, as Quijano argues, the origin of human rights discourse in the European Enlightenment connects it to a Eurocentric worldview of individualism and domination. So, our use of human rights discourse should be cautious, critical, and strategic.

One way transnational feminists can employ this cautious, critical, and strategic use of human rights discourse would be to view human rights not only as a tool for promoting gender equality (abandoning the "gender-first" feminist approach) but also to see human rights discourse as a tool for particular, interconnected ends. Additionally, we must recognize that human rights discourse is sometimes at odds with promoting specific ends; for example, the individualism of human rights discourse obscures structural oppression and the systemic nature of global capitalist exploitation. Thus, as I have argued, human rights discourse functions ambivalently. In the LGBTQ marriage equality campaign in the United States, some LGBTQ individuals argued that fighting for marriage was not the most progressive stance, because marriage itself is a problematic patriarchal, capitalist, institution. In this example, we can see the ambivalent function of human rights; as human rights includes and enfranchises previously excluded groups, it also makes the newly enfranchised subject to the existing status quo. Moreover, it leaves those who remain unmarried, rejecting the status quo, without benefits. In contrast, a strategy that worked for universal benefits, regardless of marital status, would create social change at a more radical, structural level.

Looking at a specific example may help to clarify the ways that human rights is an important, but not the only, tool that transnational feminists should mobilize in our projects for social justice. A recent *New York Times* article recounts the story of Margarita Caal Caal, an Indigenous woman from Guatemala, who was raped and evicted from her home.[56] She and ten other women from her village, all of whom were gang-raped, have filed a negligence suit against Hudbay Mineral Incorporated in Canada. They took their case to Canada because Mayan villagers have had little legal success in Guatemala. In the past such cases had little chance of being heard in Canadian courts: "Their lawyers have often tried to get cases heard on the basis of violations of human rights or international criminal law. But most were told that Canada had no jurisdiction, and that their claims would be more appropriately heard in the country where the events took place, even if that country's courts were notoriously corrupt or otherwise dysfunctional."[57] Unable to get justice through either their own courts or international courts on the basis of human rights claims, the lawyers turned to the strategy of prosecuting parent multinational companies for the behavior of their subsidiaries overseas. This strategy is remarkably similar to that of the anti-sweatshop movement when they challenged Nike and other large transnational corporations about the working conditions in their overseas factories. In fact, it draws on and builds upon this strategy: "The behavior of multinational companies working in poor countries has come under increasing fire in recent years. Social expectations have changed, experts say, with many citizens of rich countries demanding that corporations be more responsible in the countries where they operate."[58] In this case, there are multiple injustices and violations of human rights: the mining company denies the local population's land rights; they have caused extensive environmental damage, including erosion, sedimentation to ground water, and river contamination; they have beaten, shot, and killed protesters; they have forcibly evicted families from their homes, and then burned the homes down; and they have raped the eleven women named in the lawsuit. One issue in this case that reveals the limitations of human rights as a strategy is human rights violations are difficult to pursue transnationally, and often impossible to pursue in the country where they occurred, especially if the government is complicit in the violations, or benefits from the presence of the multinational corporation in the country. This practical difficulty was remedied by pursuing the human rights violations in a different nation. There are also theoretical limitations to relying on human rights as the sole, or even main, strategy for pursuing social justice; issues as environmental damage, land claims, and the marginalization of the Q'eqchi' people do not all fit easily within the human rights framework. The route of pursuing the claim of negligence by suing the parent corporation in Canada was made possible by the activism of groups like the anti-sweatshop movement and the consequent social pressure by consumers for large multinational corporations to ensure that suppliers do not violate human rights in the making of a product, or in this case, the extracting of a resource. Social justice requires collective action to challenge and change oppressive social structures and exploitative institutions. While some oppressive social institutions are specific to local context, many exploitative institutions, such as global capitalism and the deep and growing economic divide along gendered and racial lines must be met with collective action. Feminists engaged in transnational research and activism would do well to recognize the ambivalence of human rights, employing rights as a specific strategy among others, while working toward social justice.

NOTES

1. My deep appreciation to Shelley Park and Barbara Fultner for their careful reading and edits of this chapter. Thanks are also due to Julia Maskiver and Veronica Leary for their feedback on an earlier draft of this chapter.

2. I owe the formulation of this point to Shelley Park.

3. See, for instance, Julie Peters and Andrea Wolper, *Women's Rights, Human Rights: International Feminist Perspectives* (New York: Routledge, 1995); Rebecca J. Cook, *Human Rights of Women: National and International Perspectives* (Philadelphia: University of Pennsylvania Press, 1994); Niamh Reilly, *Women's Human Rights: Seeking Gender Justice in a Globalizing Age* (Cambridge, UK: Polity Press, 2009); and Charlotte Bunch, "Transforming Human Rights from a Feminist Perspective," in *Women's Rights, Human Rights: International Feminist Perspectives*, eds. Julie Peters and Andrea Wolper (New York: Routledge, 1995), 11–17.

4. Peters and Wolper, *Women's Rights*, 2.

5. Human Rights Watch, *The Human Rights Watch Global Report on Women's Human Rights* (New York: Human Rights Watch, 1995).

6. Charlotte Bunch and Susan Fried. "Beijing 95: Moving Women's Human Rights from Margin to Center," *Signs* 22 (1): 200–204.

7. I characterize this perspective as both "Western" and from the global North, although I recognize that these are not identical. The discourses and policies of the West and those of the global North are both dominant discourses of privileged groups, but they do not divide up the world in precisely the same way. For example, Asian countries such as Japan and China get Orientalized by discourses of Westernization. Yet as a wealthy, postindustrial nation Japan may share with Northern European countries and the United States an economically privileged position similar to that of the global North. In contrast, while Greece shares Western heritage and discourse with the wealthy, postindustrialized nations of Europe and the United States, it is arguably part of the global South because of its economic situation. There isn't one (singular) "dominant" position here. My thanks to Shelley Park for helping me articulate this point.

8. Lila Abu-Lughod, "Do Muslim Women Really Need Saving? Anthropological Reflections on Cultural Relativism and Its Others." *American Anthropologist* 104 (3) (September 2002): 783–90.

9. Saba Mahmood, *The Politics of Piety: The Islamic Revival and the Feminist Subject* (Princeton: Princeton University Press, 2005), 149.

10. See, for instance Linda Tuhiwai Smith, *Decolonizing Methodologies. Research and Indigenous Peoples*, Second Edition (London: Zed Books, 2012); and Winona LaDuke, *All Our Relations: Native Struggles for Land and Life* (Cambridge, MA: South End Press, 1999).

11. Pascha Bueno-Hansen and Sylvanna M. Falcón, "Indigenous/Campesina Embodied Knowledge, Human Rights Awards, and Lessons for Transnational Feminist Solidarity," in *Decolonizing Feminism: Transnational Feminism & Globalization*, ed. Margaret A. McLaren (London: Rowman Littlefield International, 2017—this volume).

12. Celina Romany, "On Surrendering Privilege: Diversity in Feminist Redefinition of Human Rights Law," in *From Basic Needs to Basic Rights: Women's Claim to Human Rights*, ed. Margaret Schuler (Washington, DC: Women, Law and Development, 1995), 543–554.

13. Amrita Basu, "Globalization of the Local/Localization of the Global: Mapping Transnational Women's Movements," in *Feminist Theory Reader: Local and Global*

Perspectives, Third Edition, eds. Carole R. McCann and Seung-kyung Kim (New York: Routledge, 2013), 70.

14. Chow, E.N., "Making Waves, Moving Mountains," *Signs: Journal of Women in Culture and Society* 22 (1996): 185–92. My italics.

15. Bunch, "Transforming Human Rights," 14. My italics.

16. Rosalind F. Petchesky, "Human Rights, Reproductive Health, and Economic Justice: Why They Are Indivisible," in *The Socialist Feminist Project: A Contemporary Reader in Theory and Politics*, ed. Nancy Holmstrom (New York: Monthly Review Press, 2002), 75.

17. Asian Communities for Reproductive Justice, "Reproductive Justice: Vision, Analysis, and Action for a Stronger Movement," in *Women's Lives: Multicultural Perspectives*, eds. G. Kirk and M. Okazawa-Rey (Boston, MA: McGraw-Hill, 2010); Dorothy Roberts, *Killing the Black Body: Race, Reproduction, and the Meaning of Liberty* (New York, NY: Pantheon, 1997); Dorothy Roberts, "Race and the New Reproduction," in *The Reproductive Rights Reader: Law, Medicine, and the Construction of Motherhood*, ed. N. Ehrenreich (New York, NY: New York University Press, 2008).

18. Roberts, *Killing the Black Body*, 6.

19. Nawal El Saadawi, "Women and the Poor: The Challenge of Global Justice," in *Beyond Borders: Thinking Critically about Global Issues*, ed. Paula S. Rothenberg (New York: Worth Publishers, 2006), 400. Reprinted from Nawal El Saadawi, *Nawal El Saadawi Reader* (New York: Zed Books, 1997).

20. Charles Mills, *The Racial Contract* (Ithaca: Cornell University Press, 1997).

21. Amartya Sen, "Foreword," in *Pathologies of Power: Health, Human Rights and the New War on the Poor*, ed. Paul Farmer (Berkeley: University of California Press, 2003), xii.

22. Charlotte Alter, "Eleven Surprising Facts about Women and Poverty." January 13, 2014, accessed July 29, 2015. http://time.com/2026/11-surprising-facts-about-women-and-poverty-from-the-shriver-report/. The Shriver report defines the "brink of poverty" as making $47,000 a year for a family of four.

23. Jan Jindy Pettman, "On the Backs of Women and Children," in *Beyond Borders: Thinking Critically about Global Issues*, ed. Paula S. Rothenberg (New York: Worth Publishers, 2006), 438. Excerpted from Jan Jindy Pettman, *Worlding Women* (New York: Routledge, 1996).

24. Issues of women as caregivers and immigration come together when women migrate to take on care work. For discussions of women's care work and global care chains, see Arlie Hochschild and Barbara Ehrenreich, eds., *Global Woman: Nannies, Maids and Sex Workers in the New Economy* (New York: Metropolitan Books, 2002); Allison Weir, "Global Care Chains: Freedom, Responsibility, and Solidarity," *The Southern Journal of Philosophy* XLVI (2008): 166–75; and Kanchana Mahadevan, this volume.

25. Nancy A. Naples and Manisha Desai, eds. *Women's Activism and Globalization: Linking Local Struggles and Transnational Politics* (New York: Routledge, 2002).

26. A. An-Na'im, "Promises We Should All Keep in Common Cause," in *Is Multiculturalism Bad for Women?* eds. J. Cohen, M. Howard and M. Nussbaum (Princeton: Princeton University Press, 1999), 59–64; Chilla Bulbeck, *Re-Orienting Western*

Feminisms: Women's Diversity in a Postcolonial World (Cambridge: Cambridge University Press, 1998); Chandra Talpade Mohanty, "Cartographies of Struggle: Third World Women and the Politics of Feminism," and "Under Western Eyes: Feminist Scholarship and Colonial Discourses," in *Third World Women and the Politics of Feminism*, eds. C.T. Mohanty, A. Russo, and L. Torres (Bloomington: Indiana University Press, 1991); Chandra Talpade Mohanty, *Feminism without Borders: Decolonizing Theory, Practicing Solidarity* (Durham: Duke University Press, 2003); and Gayatri Chakravorty Spivak, "Righting Wrongs," in *Human Rights, Human Wrongs*, ed. N. Owen (Oxford: Oxford University Press, 2003).

27. Obviously, there is overlap between the group of "postcolonial feminists" and "feminists of color," yet it is not the same set of thinkers. Moreover, there is a range of positions and diversity with these approaches.

28. I use the terms *postcolonial feminists*, *feminists of color*, and *white Western feminists* with some reservations recognizing (along with Mohanty 1991 and many others) that the categories are problematic and may best be thought of as identifying an analytic perspective rather than a social location. Moreover, the categories themselves are not mutually exclusive.

29. Oyeronke Oyewumi, "Visualizing the Body: Western Theories and African Subjects," in *The Feminist Philosophy Reader*, eds. Alison Bailey and Chris Cuomo (New York: McGraw-Hill, 2008), 169.

30. Susan Moller Okin, *Is Multiculturalism Bad for Women?* (New Jersey: Princeton University Press, 1999), 13.

31. Charlotte Bunch, "Prospects for a Global Feminism," in *Feminist Frameworks: Alternative Accounts of the Theoretical Relations between Women and Men*, eds. Alison M. Jaggar and Paula S. Rothenberg (New York: McGraw-Hill, 1993), 251.

32. Okin, *Is Multiculturalism Bad for Women?*

33. See Mahmood, *The Politics of Piety* for a study of the way that religious identity can be constitutive of and inseparable from women's sense of self and identity. See Weir, *Identities and Freedom* for the philosophical implications for identities and freedom when particular identities are acknowledged as constitutive of the self.

34. See Mahmood, *The Politics of Piety*; Naila Kabeer, "Empowerment, Citizenship and Gender Justice: A Contribution to Locally Grounded Theories of Change in Women's Lives," *Ethics and Social Welfare* 6 (3) (2012): 216–32; and Margaret A. McLaren, *Women's Activism and Transnational Feminism: From the Local to the Global*, forthcoming. I owe the formulation of this point to Shelley Park.

35. See Gayatri Chakravorty Spivak, "Can the Subaltern Speak?" in *Marxism and the Interpretation of Culture*, eds. Cary Nelson and Lawrence Grossberg (Chicago: University of Illinois Press, 1988); Lila Abu-Lughod, "Do Muslim Women Really Need Saving? Anthropological Reflections on Cultural Relativism and Its Others," *American Anthropologist* 104 (3) (September 2002): 783–90; and Chandra Talpade Mohanty, *Feminism without Borders: Decolonizing Theory, Practicing Solidarity* (Durham: Duke University Press, 2003).

36. Abu-Lughod, "Do Muslim Women Really Need Saving?"

37. Spivak, "Can the Subaltern Speak?" 296.

38. Daniel Chong, *Freedom from Poverty: NGOs and Human Rights Praxis*. (Philadelphia: University of Pennsylvania Press, 2010), 18.

39. Ibid., 170.

40. Inoue, Tatsuo. "Human Right and Asian Values," in *The Globalization of Human Rights*, eds. Jean-Marc Coicaud, Michael W. Doyle, and Anne-Marie Gardner (Paris: United Nations University Press, 2003), 116–33; and Uma Narayan, *Dislocating Cultures: Identities, Traditions and Third World Feminism* (New York: Routledge, 1997).

41. R.P. Churchill, *Human Rights and Global Diversity* (New Jersey: Pearson Prentice-Hall, 2006), 57; Narayan, *Dislocating Cultures*.

42. The Asian values debate mirrors the liberal/multicultural debate, with liberals defending political and civil rights, and individualism, and defenders of Asian values supporting the priority of economic and social rights, and the importance of community/collectivism. Moreover, defenders of human rights accuse the ASEAN (Association of Southeastern Nations) countries of overlooking (political) human rights violations within their regional association (see Helen M. Stacy, *Human Rights for the 21st Century: Sovereignty, Civil Society, Culture* (Stanford: Stanford University Press, 2009), 12–13, 162–64, and 167–68).

43. James Mouangue Kobila, "Comparative Practice on Human Rights: North-South," in *The Globalization of Human Rights*, eds. Jean-Marc Coicaud, Michael W. Doyle, and Anne-Marie Gardner (Paris: United Nations University Press, 2003), 105.

44. Nikhil Aziz, "The Human Rights Debate in an Era of Globalization: Hegemony of the Discourse," in *Debating Human Rights: Critical Essays from the United States and Asia*, ed. Peter Ness (London: Routledge, 1999).

45. Kabeer, "Empowerment, Citizenship and Gender Justice," 230–31.

46. Anibal Quijano, "Coloniality of Power, Eurocentrism, and Latin America," *Nepantla: Views from South* 1 (3) (2000): 545. Durham: Duke University Press.

47. Quijano, "Coloniality of Power."

48. María Lugones, "The Coloniality of Gender," *Worlds & Knowledges Otherwise* (Spring 2008): 2.

49. The term *intersectionality* was coined by Kimberlé Crenshaw in her now classic article, "Mapping the Margins: Intersectionality, Identity Politics, and Violence against Women of Color," in *Critical Race Theory: The Key Writings that Formed the Movement*, eds. Kimberlé Crenshaw, Neil Gotanda, Gary Peller, and Kendall Thomas (New York: The New Press, 1995), 357–83.

50. Patricia Hill Collins, *Black Feminist Thought: Knowledge, Consciousness, and the Politics of Empowerment* (New York: Routledge Press, 1990).

51. Here I must note that there are two types of "gender-first" approaches that need to be distinguished. Radical feminism (e.g., in the United States in the 1970s) was "gender first," but it also challenged existing systems. Liberal feminism, however, offers another form of "gender first" that doesn't challenge existing (Western) systems. I owe this point to Shelley Park.

52. See, for instance, Narayan, *Dislocating Cultures*.

53. Doutje Lettinga and Lars van Troost, eds., *Can Human Rights Bring Social Justice? Twelve essays* (Amsterdam, Netherlands: Amnesty International, October 2015).

54. I recognize that the Marriage Equality Act is controversial, not only to conservatives who oppose it but also within the LGBTQ community. Some in the LGBTQ community resist marriage altogether as a patriarchal, capitalist institution, and resist

the notion that "marriage equality" is an advance in LGBTQ rights, because marriage itself is an institution that systematically disadvantages women. This is an example of the ambivalent character of human rights, while the expansion of human rights enfranchises and includes, it also constricts.

55. Srilatha Batliwala, "Taking the Power out of Empowerment: An Experiential Account," *Development in Practice* 17 (4/5) (August 2007): 557–65, 563 emphasis added.

56. Suzanne Daley, "Outcry Echoes Up to Canada: Guatemalans Citing Rapes and Other Abuses Put Focus on Companies Conduct Abroad," *New York Times*, April 3, 2016, A1+.

57. Daley, "Outcry Echoes Up to Canada," 11.

58. Daley, "Outcry Echoes Up to Canada," 11.

BIBLIOGRAPHY

Abu-Lughod, Lila. "Do Muslim Women Really Need Saving? Anthropological Reflections on Cultural Relativism and Its Others." *American Anthropologist* 104 (3) (September 2002): 783–90.

Alter, Charlotte, Eleven Surprising Facts about Women and Poverty." January 13, 2014. Accessed July 29, 2015. http://time.com/2026/11-surprising-facts-about-women-and-poverty-from-the-shriver-report/.

An-Na'im, A. "Promises We Should All Keep in Common Cause." In *Is Multiculturalism Bad for Women?* Eds. J. Cohen, M. Howard, and M. Nussbaum. Princeton: Princeton University Press, 1999. 59–64.

Asian Communities for Reproductive Justice. "Reproductive Justice: Vision, Analysis, and Action for a Stronger Movement." In *Women's Lives: Multicultural Perspectives*. Eds. G. Kirk and M. Okazawa-Rey. Boston, MA: McGraw-Hill, 2010. 242–46.

Aziz, Nikhil. "The Human Rights Debate in an Era of Globalization: Hegemony of the Discourse." In *Debating Human Rights: Critical Essays from the United States and Asia*. Ed. Peter Ness. London: Routledge, 1999.

Basu, Amrita. "Globalization of the Local/Localization of the Global: Mapping Transnational Women's Movements." In *Feminist Theory Reader: Local and Global Perspectives*, Third Edition. Eds. Carole R. McCann and Seung-kyung Kim. New York: Routledge, 2013.

Bueno-Hansen, Pascha, and Sylvanna M. Falcón. "Indigenous/Campesina Embodied Knowledge, Human Rights Awards, and Lessons for Transnational Feminist Solidarity." In *Decolonizing Feminism: Transnational Feminism & Globalization*. Ed. Margaret A. McLaren. London: Rowman Littlefield International, 2017.

Bulbeck, Chilla. *Re-Orienting Western Feminisms: Women's Diversity in a Postcolonial World*. Cambridge: Cambridge University Press, 1998.

Bunch, Charlotte. "Prospects for a Global Feminism." In *Feminist Frameworks: Alternative Accounts of the Theoretical Relations between Women and Men*. Eds. Alison M. Jaggar and Paula S. Rothenberg. New York: McGraw-Hill, 1993. 249–52.

———. "Transforming Human Rights from a Feminist Perspective." In *Women's Rights, Human Rights: International Feminist Perspectives*. Eds. Julie Peters and Andrea Wolper. New York: Routledge, 1995.

Bunch, Charlotte, and Susan Fried. "Beijing 95: Moving Women's Human Rights from Margin to Center." *Signs* 22 (1): 200–204.

Chong, Daniel P.L. *Freedom from Poverty: NGOs and Human Rights Praxis*. Philadelphia: University of Pennsylvania Press, 2010.

Chow, E.N. "Making Waves, Moving Mountains." *Signs: Journal of Women in Culture and Society* 22 (1996).

Churchill, R.P. *Human Rights and Global Diversity*. New Jersey: Pearson Prentice-Hall, 2006.

Collins, Patricia Hill. *Black Feminist Thought: Knowledge, Consciousness, and the Politics of Empowerment*. New York: Routledge Press, 1990.

Cook, R.J. *Human Rights of Women: National and International Perspectives*. Philadelphia: University of Pennsylvania Press, 1994.

Crenshaw, Kimberlé William. "Mapping the Margins: Intersectionality, Identity Politics, and Violence against Women of Color." In *Critical Race Theory: The Key Writings that Formed the Movement*. Eds. Kimberlé Crenshaw et al. New York: The New Press, 1995. 357–83.

Daley, Suzanne. "Outcry Echoes Up to Canada: Guatemalans Citing Rapes and Other Abuses Put Focus on Companies Conduct Abroad." *New York Times*, April 3, 2016, A1+.

El Saadawi, Nawal. "Women and the Poor: The Challenge of Global Justice." In *Beyond Borders: Thinking Critically about Global Issues*. Ed. Paula S. Rothenberg. New York: Worth Publishers, 2006. Reprinted from Nawal El Saadawi. *Nawal El Saadawi Reader*. New York: Zed Books, 1997. 400–408.

Hochschild, Arlie. "Love and Gold." In *Global Woman: Nannies, Maids and Sex Workers in the New Economy*. Eds. Barbara Ehrenreich and Arlie Hochschild. New York: Metropolitan Books, 2002.

Human Rights Watch. *The Human Rights Watch Global Report on Women's Human Rights*. New York: Human Rights Watch, 1995.

Inoue, Tatsuo. "Human Right and Asian Values." In *The Globalization of Human Rights*. Eds. Jean-Marc Coicaud, Michael W. Doyle, and Anne-Marie Gardner. Paris: United Nations University Press, 2003. 116–33.

Kabeer, Naila. "Empowerment, Citizenship and Gender Justice: A Contribution to Locally Grounded Theories of Change in Women's Lives." *Ethics and Social Welfare* 6 (3) (2012): 216–32.

Kobila, James Mouangue. "Comparative Practice on Human Rights: North-South." In *The Globalization of Human Rights*. Eds. Jean-Marc Coicaud, Michael W. Doyle, and Anne-Marie Gardner. Paris: United Nations University Press, 2003.

LaDuke, Winona. *All Our Relations: Native Struggles for Land and Life*. Cambridge, MA: South End Press, 1999.

Lettinga, Doutje, and Lars van Troost, eds. *Can Human Rights Bring Social Justice? Twelve Essays*. Amsterdam, Netherlands: Amnesty International, October 2015.

Mahmood, Saba. *The Politics of Piety: The Islamic Revival and the Feminist Subject*. Princeton: Princeton University Press, 2005.

McLaren, Margaret A. *Women's Activism and Transnational Feminism: From the Local to the Global*, forthcoming, 2018.

Mills, Charles. *The Racial Contract*. Ithaca: Cornell University Press, 1997.

Mohanty, Chandra Talpade. "Cartographies of Struggle: Third World Women and the Politics of Feminism." In *Third World Women and the Politics of Feminism*. Eds. C.T. Mohanty, A. Russo, and L. Torres. Bloomington: Indiana University Press, 1991. 1–47.

———. *Feminism without Borders: Decolonizing Theory, Practicing Solidarity*. Durham: Duke University Press, 2003. Print.

Mohanty, Chandra Talpade, Ann Russo, and Lourdes Torres, eds. *Third World Women and the Politics of Feminism*. Bloomington: Indiana University Press, 1991.

Naples, Nancy A., and Manisha Desai, eds. *Women's Activism and Globalization: Linking Local Struggles and Transnational Politics*. New York: Routledge, 2002. Print.

Narayan, Uma. *Dislocating Cultures: Identities, Traditions and Third World Feminism*. New York: Routledge, 1997.

Okin, Susan Moller, ed. *Is Multiculturalism Bad for Women?* New Jersey: Princeton University Press, 1999.

Oyeronke Oyewumi, "Visualizing the Body: Western Theories and African Subjects." In *The Feminist Philosophy Reader*. Eds. Alison Bailey and Chris Cuomo. New York: McGraw-Hill, 2008.

Petchesky, Rosalind, F. "Human Rights, Reproductive Health, and Economic Justice: Why They Are Indivisible." In *The Socialist Feminist Project: A Contemporary Reader in Theory and Politics*. Ed. Nancy Holmstrom. New York: Monthly Review Press, 2002. 74–82.

Peters, Julie, and Andrea Wolper. *Women's Rights, Human Rights: International Feminist Perspectives*. New York: Routledge, 1995.

Pettman, Jan Jindy. "On the Backs of Women and Children." In *Beyond Borders: Thinking Critically about Global Issues*. Ed. Paula S. Rothenberg. New York: Worth. Publishers, 2006. 437–40. Excerpted from Jan Jindy Pettman, *Worlding Women*. New York: Routledge, 1996.

Quijano, Anibal. "Coloniality of Power, Eurocentrism, and Latin America." *Nepantla: Views from South* 1 (3) (2000): 533–80. Durham: Duke University Press.

Reilly, Niamh. *Women's Human Rights: Seeking Gender Justice in a Globalizing Age*. Cambridge, UK: Polity Press, 2009.

Roberts, Dorothy. *Killing the Black Body: Race, Reproduction, and the Meaning of Liberty*. New York, NY: Pantheon, 1997.

———. "Race and the New Reproduction." In *The Reproductive Rights Reader: Law, Medicine, and the Construction of Motherhood*. Ed. Nancy Ehrenreich. New York, NY: New York University Press, 2008. 308–19.

Romany, Celina. "On Surrendering Privilege: Diversity in Feminist Redefinition of Human Rights Law." In *From Basic Needs to Basic Rights: Women's Claim to Human Rights*. Ed. Margaret Schuler. Washington, DC: Women, Law and Development, 1995. 543–54.

Sen, Amartya. "Foreword." In *Pathologies of Power: Health, Human Rights and the New War on the Poor*. Ed. Paul Farmer. Berkeley: University of California Press, 2003. xi–xvii.

Spivak, Gayatri Chakravorty. "Can the Subaltern Speak?" In *Marxism and the Interpretation of Culture*. Eds. Cary Nelson and Lawrence Grossberg. Chicago: University of Illinois Press, 1988.

———. "Righting Wrongs." In *Human Rights, Human Wrongs*. Ed. N. Owen. Oxford: Oxford University Press, 2003.

Stacy, Helen M. *Human Rights for the 21st Century: Sovereignty, Civil Society, Culture*. Stanford: Stanford University Press, 2009.

Tuhiwai Smith, Linda. *Decolonizing Methodologies. Research and Indigenous Peoples*, Second Edition. London: Zed Books, 2012.

Weir, Allison. "Global Care Chains: Freedom, Responsibility, and Solidarity." *The Southern Journal of Philosophy* XLVI (2008): 166–75.

———. *Identities and Freedom: Feminist Theory between Power and Connection*. Oxford: Oxford University Press, 2013.

Part 3

CITIZENSHIP AND IMMIGRATION: THE SPACE BETWEEN

Chapter 5

Constitutional Patriotism and Political Membership: A Feminist Decolonization of Habermas and Benhabib

Kanchana Mahadevan

This chapter contributes to the decolonization of feminism by examining Habermas's proposal for a constitutional patriotism in Europe as an antidote to globalization from the perspective of non-European migrant women.[1] Although the self-professed global validity of his patriotism has been widely critiqued, migration and its gendered dimension have been neglected. Yet, this is a pressing matter given the all-pervasiveness of migration and the impact of legal sanctions on the socially vulnerable. Yet, Habermas's brand of patriotism is driven by the vision of inclusiveness and tolerance. He proposes a reconstruction of Kant's cosmopolitan condition of peace through an international law that proscribes war and guarantees civic freedoms in transnational domains. For Habermas, such a law, at local, national, and transnational levels, is an ongoing project of validation and institutionalization through public deliberation. Public deliberation occurs through transnational mobilization of local/national public spheres by media and nongovernmental organizations. Habermas argues that rather than shared history and culture, such public spheres should be bound through a commitment to law.

Prima facie, Habermas's blueprint is valuable from the perspective of migrant women, whose displacement (both voluntary and involuntary) is linked to political instability, social strife, and lack of resources in the global South. They have to contend with surmounting traditional loyalties of ethnicity, culture, and gender stereotypes in the course of coping with "foreign" (literally) lifeworlds. Hence, their location is best suited for the type of "modern" social integration that Habermas believes would be best achieved through abstract law. Moreover, migrants are not impositions but necessities for European hosts who are increasingly dependent on their labor to sustain welfare institutions due to declining birth rates and an aging population. Needless to add, women who have been traditionally caregivers are at the forefront of a migration that attempts to remedy what Tronto has termed a *care deficit* in modern democracies. However, their elusive relationship to citizenship is precisely what puts migrant women at odds with Habermas's juridical emphasis on constitutionalism—albeit in a postnational form. The displacement of cultures and communities makes women particularly vulnerable, given structural obstacles at the economic, social, and indeed, political levels. Besides, they also often confront overt violence such as xenophobia. Importantly, they become objects of surveillance by the state and the law itself, which endeavor to "reform" their cultures through women-centered assimilative practices. Thus, the social integration that Habermas desires to achieve through the balance of facticity and validity of the law veers toward force for immigrant women, rather than consent; gatekeeping, rather than inclusiveness.

Benhabib, who is critical of his neglect of gender, has extended Habermas's perspective in the feminist direction, which engages with non-Western women's in an inclusive spirit. She nevertheless, upholds Western feminism as a benchmark to which all other cultures have to submit. In this context, then, there is a renewed urgency in Mohanty's call for an inclusive decolonizing feminist, anti-capitalist politics of solidarity. Such a project raises several questions in the context of migrant women: Can care be a critical term in the project of decolonizing feminism? What is the relationship between caregivers and citizens? What is an alternative mode of solidarity to constitutional patriotism?

This chapter explores these questions by critiquing Habermas's constitutional patriotism from a gendered perspective. It begins by analyzing his account of constitutional patriotism and the possibility of a feminist reading of its strengths of decentering administrative and governmental authority. It proceeds to argue that these gains are limited from the feminist point of view. Its rootedness in the law inhibits constitutional patriotism from achieving gender equality for migrant women, for although they are subjects of the law, they are not authors of it. Consequently, Benhabib's feminist appropriation of Habermas, despite its critical distance, tends to encourage colonizing modes of philanthropy toward migrant women. The conclusion explores a decolonized feminist solidarity through the care work by migrant women for the welfare of the aged population in Europe. Both Habermas and Benhabib neglect such sustained institutionalized work, despite theoretically engaging with care.

DEMOCRATIC DEFICIT: CITIZENS AND MIGRANTS

The contemporary period is marked by the largest number of people living in transition outside their home countries. Migrations are not homogeneous.

Those with professional skills voluntarily move across the globe, while some others experience involuntary exodus fueled by wars, poverty, and persecutions. Forced migration leads to refugees and trafficked persons whose services are channeled toward repetitive labor such as factory, domestic, and sex work. It is perceived as a danger by institutions, and despite being encouraged by social needs,[2] the former predominates with concerns about national security acquiring racial, gendered, and classist tones. The International Labor Organization maintains that out of the 52.6 million domestic workers in the world, 83 percent are women; women comprise 50 percent of the world's migrant population.[3] The inevitability of migrant labor in contributing to host and home nations also reveals women to occupy a center stage.[4]

Given their conventional gendered roles as reproducers of community in biological, social, and cultural terms, women's displacement[5] symbolizes the loss of community and political citizenship in an explicit way. The preservation of community identity via customary practice during displacement is dependent on women, who are often targeted during cultural conflict as markers of such identity. However, embodying singular identities becomes difficult in inter- and transnational geographies via "disaggregated citizenship."[6] Migrants adopt multiple identities—even contradictory ones—which they borrow from their homes and hosts. Such uneven negotiations are marked by lack of access to information, ignorance of language, economic insecurity, social discrimination, and political disenfranchisement.[7] Women migrants make visible the precariousness that characterizes migration in general,[8] which, despite being the norm, is construed by the state as an exception—an "emergency"[9]—in the name of safeguarding national safety.[10] National discourses relate citizenship and birthright so that migrants are typically viewed as obstacles to national growth. For instance, migrant children are not citizens and thus do not contribute to national growth. This increases the social vulnerability of women migrants occupying a pivotal position as reproducers of community.

In this context, Habermas's recent theorizations on constitutional patriotism appear relevant from the perspective of working-class migrant women in Western countries. Migration for Habermas is an outcome of the inequalities of neoliberal globalization spurred by deregulated market forces.[11] He is well aware of how the movement of people across national borders and pluralization of cultures have weakened the scope of national institutions. Such a "waning nation-state,"[12] accompanied by new forms of deterritorialized identity, results in a thin line between citizen rights and human rights.[13] Traditional modes of social integration heightening conventional identities of ethnicity and religion express belonging, against the insecurity and unpredictability of market forces.[14] Habermas notes that the "facticity" of authority of traditions, rituals, personalities, practices, institutions, values, and the like—in short, conventional identities—cannot achieve social integration in multicultural contexts.[15] On the contrary, they add to the transnational problem of "democratic deficit"[16] of obstructing people's participation in legal and political institutions. Cultural hybridity and human mobility have led to a paradox, where conventional identity is both affirmed and questioned. Moreover, these problems cannot be resolved through statist international treaties,[17] which are at a disconnect with grassroots interaction and participation.[18] For Habermas, the law alone can integrate in such contexts of "disenchanted internally differentiated and pluralized life-worlds"[19] at the transnational level. Transnationalization of law or constitutional patriotism[20] across European nations appears at first sight to be a sympathetic response to mass migration and its gendered costs.[21] Migrant women who have to face the xenophobic risks of ethnicity and religion can get respite in communities based on transnational law.[22]

In Habermas's view, constitutions are texts about justice based on citizens' commitment to self-legislation, political will, and action.[23] The attempt to realize the welfare state was guided by such a commitment. However, he diagnoses a "democratic deficit,"[24] where the nation-state with increasing insecurity and tyranny of institutions fails to attain equity, welfare, and employment under a capitalist economy.[25] The resultant migration has prevented civil society from forging social bonds due to escalating identity politics. Modern constitutions attempt to exert people's will on the economy, state, and society through political routes has not come close to realization. Unfettered corporatism of a profit economy and a polarized civil society have inhibited the state from taking on expanded welfare responsibilities. There is an erosion of constitutional guarantees on which the public responsibilities of the state, economy, and society depended. In this context, Habermas argues that one needs to turn to the transnational context to fill in the democratic deficit and restore the worth of a constitution as "a self-administering association of free and equal citizens."[26] A common law in the transnational space increases democratic participation by minimizing nationalist and conventional identities. Its grounding in postconventional solidarity accommodates the increasing multiplicity of worldviews caused by migration.[27] Cultural freedom is affirmed by rooting collective freedom, responsibility, and public discourse in transnational law. Constitutional patriotism attempts to "civilize political power,"[28] beyond the borders of the nation with a political constitution for a world society without a world government.[29]

At first glance, Habermas's notion of "constitutional patriotism" can be allied with the concerns of migrant women, as it is specifically directed toward mitigating conflicts and violence of multiple communal allegiances and nationalism, of which women are often at the receiving end. Displaced women on whom identity claims are made by their home communities and the host nations can adopt the postconventionalism of transnational constitution to actively deliberate and negotiate their interests. Indeed, Habermas's position enables women to enter the domain of the political as active participants in deliberations, rather than as passive subjects obeying determinate laws.

Moreover, Habermas's constitutional patriotism also marks an affective relationship to abstract principles of the constitution, to connect to a legal community and a common political ethos. The ambivalence in the latter opens it up to include institutions and practices of associated governance, as well as interpretations of the constitution, national symbols, national history and events, a "cultural inheritance that the *demos* did not choose."[30] There is, consequently, the possibility of contesting particularistic identities underlying xenophobic nationalism that disadvantage women into passivity in polarized social contexts. By redirecting emotions to actively and contextually relate to abstract law, Habermas can be said to concede to feminist claims about women's modes of thinking and moving beyond law's hyperrationalism.

However, as critics argue, the civic constitution as an abstract object of feeling is not necessarily a bulwark against xenophobia.[31] Habermas forsakes his earlier commitment to plural solidarity by turning to the law to bring diverse cultures to equilibrium. The law, which addresses all those who are both its authors and its subjects as citizens, has the potential to transcend the territorial nation-state. Plural cultures have led to dissatisfaction with externally sanctioned authority of traditional beliefs. The normative force that validated these beliefs and practices shifted to the internal sphere of conscience. Justifying the morality of an action by appealing to conscience could have subjective implications. Hence, modern societies integrate society through rules that have the external sanction of positive law; such rules "*exhaust* the normative"[32] and are immune to criticism. Legality brings people together through everyday activities like voting, welfare cards, tickets, and the like; its deliberative processes go beyond the group identity. In an attempt to undermine chauvinistic identities, Habermas adopts the "strategy of redirecting"[33] affect as a way of connecting to the law and formal institutions.

Habermas introduces Europe as a reference point to relate to abstract law. According to him, the diverse nation-states of the European Union (EU) already have a legacy of "achievements" of democratic constitutions[34] like universal civil rights, social welfare, and leisure. Citing the example of easy access to standardized formal schooling, he notes how even language does not obstruct integration. Europe, in Habermas's view, has been assimilating ethnic and cultural diversity at the economic, social, and administrative levels.[35] It, therefore, has the "historical experience of having happily overcome nationalism."[36] Thus, Europe for Habermas is in a position to evolve the context for a constitution across a diversity of nations to thus become the starting point for working toward transnational regimes. He even claims that German federalism "might not be the worst model"[37] for integrating the various nations of Europe under a constitution. Thus, affect is linked to a specific community—namely, the European—which prides itself on possessing a civic or political culture governed by the rule of law.

Habermas's constitutionalism is problematic not so much for its abstraction but for its concreteness of being rooted in Europe.[38] Habermas's "democratic legal domestication"[39] of the constitution as a political/civic process (rather than a statist or a corporate one) grounds citizenship in "an abstract, legally mediated, solidarity between strangers,"[40] rather than an ethnically or religiously homogeneous "European people."[41] Further, the public sphere is a political domain precisely because it is constituted by the points of view of such citizens. It has to be free of coercion, both at the internal and external level; it is the sphere of the formation of public opinion—albeit informal.[42] Such a European particularism attempts to anchor cultural pluralism in the tension between the facticity of particularist identities and norm of universal inclusiveness.[43] The normative core of actualized law supplements the internal conscience of practical reason through threat of external sanctions of prudence.[44] Habermas himself is well aware that a constitution alone is not sufficient to create a cosmopolitan condition, for the latter requires democratic processes, which can only be initiated by such a constitution in which the cosmopolitan condition takes root. He is also aware that a transnational politics cannot merely copy the national politics of Europe, rather such a politics would have to depend upon public will in a global civil society with a divergent logic. The latter is a "polyglot communicative context only if the national school systems see to it that Europeans have a common grounding in foreign languages."[45] However, the problem is that Habermas restricts the "polyglot" to European languages and English to a "second 'first' language."[46]

Although Habermas does engage with the notion of migration in the context of internal mobility within the EU, his stress on legality restricts deliberation to citizens, within the expanded canvas of the EU. As Yuval-Davis notes, European mobility is an instance "of ideological, often racist constructions of boundaries which allow unrestricted immigration to some and block it completely to others."[47] Transnational citizens inhabit "a civil society encompassing interest associations, nongovernmental organizations, citizens' movements etc., and naturally a party system appropriate to a European arena."[48] Habermas's world citizen comes from the ranks of "actors within a European civil society,"[49] whose heritage is "Greek, Roman and Christian."[50] Communication is circulated through a legal, institutionalized process so that European identity is for Habermas "nothing other than unity within national diversity."[51] National and linguistic divisions are maintained by political parties, media, labor unions, and civic groups so that the EU can hardly be regarded as an instance of postnational space.[52] Migration reveals that the social, economic, and political rights necessary for communication are not accessible to "strangers," such as migrant women, who are not always citizens.[53]

Habermas treats migration from the South as a common challenge confronting European nation-states. Thus, "All are in the process of becoming countries of immigration and multicultural societies. All are exposed to an economic and cultural globalization that awakes memories of a shared history of conflict and reconciliation—and of a comparatively low threshold of tolerance towards exclusion."[54] But in this, as commentators note, though Habermas goes beyond the standard East/West dichotomy, he does not take the specificity of local cultures, which are sometimes outside the global economy, into consideration.[55] Despite allowing for hybridity of cultural multiplicity, he does not spell out the nature of such phenomenon. Instead, his abstract universality captures the experiences of Western state and civil society. Such a prominent Western tone reveals a neglect of non-Western perspectives, as it takes the citizen of the EU as its point of departure for a transformative world politics. The role of the non-European people in the creation of a European culture and the possibility of democratic cultures outside Europe are both sidelined.

The European particularism underpinning Habermas's constitutional patriotism overlooks that the debate on citizenship in Western societies centers around the theme of gender and migration to which Yuval-Davis, Hall, and Held have notably contributed. Many "displaced" persons are caught between the impossibility of becoming naturalized citizens in the country where they arrive and the impossibility of returning to the adverse conditions in their home country. On one hand, the Universal Declaration of Rights allows individuals and groups free entry into any territory, but then it also authorizes governments of various nations the right to decide on the fate of such migrants.[56] For example, those who struggle to enter a country and also desire to stay as citizens must pass several assimilation tests, which are often directed toward women. In the case of EU, member nations' second-country citizens have both mobility and welfare, which are not necessarily open or easy for those coming from nonmember as third-country citizens.[57] The latter—particularly women—have to face "double discrimination: gender and immigration status."[58] Gendered migration also opens up a domain that is not governed by law, as trafficking largely targets women for domestic work and sex work. Further, the turn to the law in this context might entail that the women in question lose facilities of health care and income as they and their families could get deported.[59] Even in the case of voluntary migration, one sees how "economic inequalities between nations . . . lead women from poorer countries and regions to seek employment in richer countries and cities."[60] In fact, there is often an increased surveillance over the lives of these women, whereby they resist coming forward to seek the help of state institutions such as when they are victimized by domestic abuse. Often this is because they do not wish their communities to be stereotyped. Habermas does not explore the extent to which migrants—and women in particular—can participate in deliberation on constitutions on their own terms; he links public opinion in Europe with the existing institutional space of civil society and falls into the very trap of discrimination that he wishes to avoid. The law privileges the citizens and yet assumes that institutions can obliterate differences with formal conceptions of equality.[61] Consequently, is Habermas's theorization of "democratic deficit" inadequate in addressing the issues posed by migration and gender? A response demands engagement with Benhabib who attempts to remedy Habermas's limits by extending legal claims to migrant women's cultural assertions through "democratic iterations."

FILLING THE DEFICIT: "DEMOCRATIC ITERATIONS"

The notion of cosmopolitanism, Benhabib suggests, is critical from the point of view of conflicts of migration in the twenty-first century and, one might add, in the light of Habermas's "democratic deficit." Against discussions on migration that focus on "a man travelling alone in search of work,"[62]which echo in Habermas, Benhabib endeavors to engage with women migrants in the West for whom cosmopolitanism is of critical importance.[63] Cosmopolitanism, according to Benhabib, is morally committed to the equality of each individual and to cultural hybridity. From the legal perspective, entangled between the moral and the cultural, each moral person—not just the citizen—is entitled to rights.[64] Hence, cosmopolitanism can reconfigure the law from the perspective of migrant cultural rights. Benhabib appeals to the notion of "democratic iterations" to characterize recurrent deliberations, interpretations, disputes, discussions and conversations that reference the law's universal rights and duties in diverse public contexts.[65] These contexts can be "strong" in the sense of occurring in courts of law. But they can also be "weak" in the sense of informally circulating ideas and words in looser associations such as the civil society. For Benhabib, laws and principles are often transformed and reinvented in the course of such reiterations, with each repetition adding new meaning. Indeed, people are bound by the norms of the law, which is circulated and whose life lies in repetition without an original point.[66]

Benhabib offers a gendered theorization of transnational European law, in keeping with her earlier extensions of Habermas's conceptualizations in a gendered direction. She observes that migration has fragmented the *demos* of constitutional democracy in Europe, which is not united by *ethnos*. Conditions in the South have, in her view, compelled aliens, refugees, and migrants to coinhabit with citizens in Europe. Women undertake the burdens of such displacement by reproducing home cultures in host contexts and meeting cultural expectations of their hosts. Benhabib cites instances from the scarf controversy in France (since 1989 when Algerian students Fatima, Leila, and Samira insisted on wearing their headscarfs to school)[67] and Germany (when Fereshta Ludin, an Afghan-origin elementary schoolteacher, appealed that she be allowed to teach with her scarf on).[68] In both cases, Muslim girls were not permitted to wear headscarves; France considered it to be a violation of the value of secularism, while German courts upheld it to conflict with the equitable right to welfare resources. By engaging with the cultural rights of Muslim women in Europe, Benhabib argues that in both cases, the courts' reasoning for disallowing headscarves lack conviction. In both contexts, she notes that the apprehension regarding the ability of a person with a headscarf to perform secular duties is unjustified. Benhabib observes that the arguments offered by Muslim women in European court are cases of cultural translation through "democratic iterability." Their arguments, in her view, demonstrate that the scarf as a religious symbol is also one of a multicultural European public space; they reveal that citizens have religious freedom, and more importantly, that a symbol from the private sphere is shifted to the public to affirm such freedom.[69] She suggests that courts of law heed such acts of interpretation by migrant women, which in turn results in new forms of solidarity.

Benhabib notes that in transnational contexts, courts may not always argue that the facticity of laws should converse with the deliberations of civil society and institutions in the transnational sphere.[70] In this, the absolutism of single modes of translation and a relativism of several points of view should be avoided. Reasons that are given by courts of law are evaluated by better or worse reasons through public deliberations. In this, the cultural rights of the people are at stake.[71]

Benhabib is, clearly, well aware of the cultural difficulties faced by migrant women in host societies. She argues that their act of wearing scarves be taken into consideration as cultural difference and integrated in citizenship, while being reinterpreted in multicultural contexts. Such entry into citizenship communities is undergirded by communicative freedom, which "enables us both to justify the *human right to membership* and to interdict *loss of membership* or denaturalization."[72] For this the normative commitment that informs the law—the Kantian spirit of a civic-juridical order that comes into existence following the moral law—needs to be recognized: that all human beings have personal autonomy, the right to justify their point of view, and an equal entitlement to respect.[73] This in turn means that freedom can be restricted only through reciprocal and justifiable norms applicable to all. According to Benhabib, all human beings have a right to membership in a nation so that nonnationals can become a part of the rights regimes, not through assimilation but via cultural dialogue. In this process, the voices of the girls in question reveal that the scarf is not just a symbol of religious difference but also a practice of political and cultural resistance.[74] Further, both the state and the religious migrant have to give public reasons for their respective points of view—this contributes to making the religious identity more moderate.

Benhabib's intervention improves over Habermas in directly engaging with the issue of migration and gender. She moves beyond the limit of Europe, taking the cultural perspective of non-European women into consideration. Indeed, Benhabib's interpretation of the right to wear headscarf as cultural can be interpreted as a step toward decolonization. Arguing against "decline of citizenship,"[75] Benhabib notes that the presence of those who do not share the *ethnos* of the *demos* redefine the universality of democracy with difference. In this reinvigoration of democratic practice, women interpret the cultural rights of the community as "reconfigurations of citizenship through democratic iterations."[76] By bringing erstwhile private practices associated with wearing a headscarf into the public sphere, it is gendered.

These advances over Habermas's "legal materialism" notwithstanding, Benhabib's argument has its share of frontiers. Her premise of a multicultural and hospitable Europe emerges from her view that the original statement of the law occurs in Europe, while migrant publics reiterate it. Benhabib introduces iterability as an inclusive principle. However, as a protection against reiteration betraying the original, she also subscribes to a parallel principle of separability.[77] According to the principle of separability, repetition preserves the "moral core" of the constitutional original that is "authoritative,"[78] which implies that the principle of separability is shielded from a possible regressive impact of iteration.[79] It also implies that the original principle is established independently.[80] Thus, as a mode of accommodating the cultural rights of migrant women, it neglects the problem of women's bodies becoming the battleground between secular state assertion and religious-cultural assertion of migrant communities. Cultural and religious affirmation treats citizenship as entitlement—an affirmation of rights—albeit those of the community. Thus, rather than any specifically gendered concept or concern, civic republicanism is prioritized in expanding citizenship to include the cultural canvas of the migrant; but there is a disquiet over the latter's gendered problems such as unemployment, cultural translation, and lack of access to welfare.

If acknowledgement of difference is restricted to cultural rights following Benhabib, it remains within the assimilation paradigm. Contemporary European civic space is not just one of continuous agreement but also of ruptured disagreement or difference.[81] For Benhabib cultural difference introduced by migrants has the onus of translating the *host's* legacy of democracy into contexts of difference. Benhabib assumes—like Habermas—that democracy *belongs to* Europe. Thus, political philosophy is "a monologue coming from the European West."[82] Western political thought follows a "Westphalian narrative" of "well-ordered societies, burdened societies and outlaw states."[83] European liberal theoretical assumptions such as the "deracialized" rights-bearing individual and the capitalist economy are given an absolutist status within which cultural diversity is accommodated. Despite acknowledging non-European cultures, Benhabib does not examine the dimension of "being-in-common"[84] rather than "commonality" entailed by difference in the postcolonial context. Although Benhabib includes a gender analysis, her assimilationist approach overlooks considerations of decolonization. Decolonizing cultural ethnocentrism is essential to gender analyses, and both are integral to migration.

Like Habermas, Benhabib overlooks crises such as poverty and war, prevalent in migrant home societies; these crises triggering migration are often the outcomes of Western policies. The Peace of Westphalia, which gave shape to European nation-states and liberal democracy, also resulted in colonization of the non-European world. The French Revolution in 1789 was followed by the French invasion in 1798 when Napoleon undertook a journey to colonize Egypt so that Europe could be an example for Egypt to follow.[85] Thus, 1798 symbolizes a date when Europe othered Asia and all that was not Europe. With 1798, European political philosophy, which thinks of itself as a unity, has to confront what is outside it; this entails a "postcolonial disruption"[86] of democracy. Democracy has led to a "tyranny" of homogenizing differences and upholding Europe as a beacon. Its "unthinkable" aspect is colonialism, where neither democracy's dependence on colonization nor the agency of the colonized is acknowledged.[87]

Indeed, migration is not necessarily or even majorly "reverse globalization" with those from the South thronging to Europe for livelihood for full membership in communities, as Benhabib believes. Asia, for example, witnessed forced migration during the colonial period, as is instanced in the British sending indentured laborers from India to work on their plantation in other parts of the world, during the nineteenth century. This heightened during the postcolonial period, with the partitioning of India and Pakistan, and the subsequent formation of Bangladesh.[88] In the EU, migrants have mobility within its member states, but the Asian context upholds rigid national borders.[89] The emergence of nation-states in place of erstwhile colonies since the 1940s has triggered off migration flows of "rejected peoples and unwanted migrants"[90] on an unprecedented scale within South Asia.[91] International migration has led to internal migration with major population shifts within Asian national boundaries. Many regions have female-headed households, since most of the men have migrated in search of work. Yet the mainstream retains the "emergency" nationalist view of immigrants prevailing in the West;[92] in the absence of refugee-oriented laws, what has allowed them to settle down is very simply the persistence of humanitarian bonds among people from diverse contexts, despite the overwhelming hostility. The exodus of people within Asia—both internal migration within nation-states and international ones between them—is motivated by a host of factors such as development projects, poverty, religious persecution and conflict, environmental crises, unemployment, and wars to name a few.[93]

It is instructive to examine the position of internal women migrants residing in refugee camps in Afghanistan. They do not struggle for the right to wear veils as their counterparts in Europe do. On the contrary, there is an imposition of the veil with greater restrictions on mobility. Patriarchy reestablished itself in new forms with women in refugee camps in spite of the fact that previously women appeared to be liberated enough to sustain themselves.[94] In the refugee camps, the men—often maimed and unable to get a livelihood—inflicted violence on the women reasserting their patriarchal privilege. Western aid-groups reinforce traditional patriarchies by routing their help through the male authority in refugee camps. Further, it neglected the specific solidarities formed by women, who often headed refugee camps, which in turn were mostly inhabited by single women who were either widows or remained single.

The 1951 convention for refugee protection has not been formally ratified by countries such as India.[95] Nor does India have national legal norms or policies for protection of international refugees. As Samaddar notes, unlike the European context, there is a legal pluralism in South Asian engagement with refugees.[96] For arbitrating matters such as asylum, Indian law courts have invoked international laws. However, large numbers of refugees have inhabited and continue to inhabit India through informal struggles under inhospitable conditions. However as Samaddar observes, this is because of attempts to transcend strict laws and bring in notions of informal humanitarian care for refugees.[97]

Benhabib's legalism is an instance of homogenizing colonization of mainstream Western feminism against which Mohanty cautions;[98] Benhabib tends to regard all non-European women migrants as tradition-bound victims to be salvaged by the democratic institutions of Europe.[99] She overlooks their historical specificities, contexts, and differences. She also sidesteps the role played by Western liberal democracies in dismantling civic structures in Afghanistan, Iraq, and Syria; the collapse of everyday systems in the latter is an outcome of Western intervention's continuities with erstwhile colonial policies of Europe. Colonization functioned as a "disciplinary mechanism of capitalism"[100] by displacing colonized populations through indentured and military labor.[101]

The image of a fleeing "woman usually with small children clinging to her,"[102] reveals that gender is the most visible aspect of displacement. Women constitute almost 80 percent of displaced persons.[103] Yet they occupy a secondary position with respect to rights in discourses on refugees and migrants, for the claim over rights is founded on being recognized as citizens, which is often the male prerogative. Hence, women are often seen as passive and helpless victims in need of aid and care. They are also the battleground for cultural conflict between the state and the community, being the source through which community identity is transmitted.

Migrants are seen as threats to community, if one assumes a static view of community.[104] The expulsion of aliens is the other side of controlling dissent within the nation through imposition of conformism.[105] However, the simple affirmation of cultural rights does not result in taking gender into account while struggling toward nonxenophobic solidarities. The latter is often the outcome of feelings—those such as indignation and anger—at the plight of the undeserved suffering of others.[106] Thus, feelings are the very crux of the matter. The gendered space of migration is also one where decolonization has to be introduced. The phenomenon of gendered migration suggests that Benhabib's feminist lens has to be connected to decolonization. Conversely, discussions on decolonization tend to neglect gender. Intersections between gender, migration, and decolonization occur in what Mills has termed as the heterogeneous space of the "transcontinental,"[107] which reveals Europe's unlikely contacts with the most remote regions. Decolonization[108] is a process that erstwhile colonies of Europe initiated after World War II "to release from being colony."[109] Yet this formal process with the formation of new nation-states was also one of "amnesia" regarding imperialism.[110] Decolonization is not just a withdrawal from empire, but an active grassroots movement at the social, economic, cultural, and political levels, initiating alternate cultures and solidarities.[111] Decolonization encourages thinking beyond assimilating non-European migrant women to a European order that is responsible for their displacement in the first place. This requires dissolving the strong identification of migrants with their traditional lifeworld and that of Europe with democracy, as both Habermas and Benhabib do.

For Habermas—and Benhabib—the transition from submissiveness to traditional practice to a critical postconventional mode marks a shift in thinking about the community from an already existing to a projected one, without "fixed contents."[112] Such an expansive community is anchored in particularisms—such as the supposed democratic legacy of Europe—without identifying with any one of them. Yet the problem is that the Habermas-Benhabib framework does not address how the democratic legacy in Europe has turned into a tyranny. Moreover, they neglect how migrant women work in order to fulfill the needs of Western societies and thereby contribute to their well-being. Thus, it overlooks the intersecting lifeworlds of migrant women and European citizens.

CARE DEFICIT AND MIGRANT WOMEN'S CARE

Benhabib aptly observes with reference to gendered migration that: "we are like travelers navigating a new terrain with the help of old maps."[113] Yet her Habermasian legacy does not allow her to map the "new terrain" of the relationship between the migrant and the citizen, where citizenship depends on the labor of migrants, especially migrant women. For this, she needs to shift focus from assimilating migrant women's cultural habits with the European legal legacy to their contribution to host environments. Migration patterns disclose how women contribute through care work to domestic, medical, and entertainment industries.[114] Special economic zones in Asia, for instance, employ women migrant labor as they are perceived to be pliable and vulnerable to manipulation despite poor economic returns in socially stigmatized jobs. With the exception of nursing, skilled labor does not predominate among them, while informal work without documentation does.[115] Thus, in the instance cited by Benhabib, Ludin, originally from Afghanistan, was contributing to Germany through her care work as a schoolteacher.

The Habermasian problem of "democratic deficit"—to which Benhabib subscribes—does not take migrants into consideration as contributors to host societies.[116] It limits itself to the inability of political and legal institutions to integrate citizen deliberations at the national level for which it recommends the transnational turn. The legalism of the latter requires that migrants become citizens, an option that is not available to all. Benhabib recommends full membership in communities for migrant women, expanding democratic deliberation through reiterations in civil society and courts of law whose contents are migrant cultures. She envisages a rights-oriented focus, albeit in compartmentalized communities. The inability of institutions to deliver welfare cannot be directly addressed by introducing the legal freedom of deliberation over such cultural rights or even welfare needs, following Benhabib, for such a freedom is available only to citizens under the law and is therefore already implicated in the democratic deficit. Further, its assumption of cultural rights fails to engage with the intersecting worlds of the migrant and the citizen as the following instance of a European Court of Justice (ECJ) judgment shows.

The ECJ's intervention in the case of the Spanish-origin migrant Martinez Sala's claim for childcare benefit in Germany as a single mother reveals the limits of the notion of democratic deficit.[117] Welfare benefit is available to German nationals or those with residence permits. Although Sala was a longtime resident of Bavaria, she did not have a residence permit. She held intermittent jobs and was formally unemployed when she applied for welfare. The ECJ expanded the notion of nondiscrimination in the European law to allow welfare benefits to go beyond the economic sphere of an employed worker. It also ruled that any member-state citizen of the EU could be given welfare in Germany, thus, reinforcing European mobility and weakening member-state sovereignty as a criterion for welfare. As a result, Sala did get welfare benefits. However, as Nanz herself notes, the attitude of the court to the care work done by Sala shows that it did not regard this as legal employment.[118]

The ECJ's ruling in favour of mobility over care work is premised upon the treaties signed by the member nations of the EU, rather than the needs or practices of its inhabitants. EU mobility is applicable to its member states, rather than to third nations or the home states of migrants.[119] Migrants have to undergo assimilation tests to acquire citizenship in the member nations of the EU and thus to the EU itself. It does not consider Europe's increasing demand for private domestic service for nurturing the young, the infirm, and the elderly.[120] It neglects the inability of welfare institutions to meet this demand, which migrant labor steps in to fulfill. In short, it overlooks how the democratic deficit has given way to what Tronto terms as the *care deficit*[121] and what Kittay has characterized as the "crisis in care."[122]

Neither Habermas nor Benhabib has engaged with changes within Europe undergirding such care deficit. Demographic patterns, women's changing roles, and a shrinking welfare state have deflated the notion of the European family as a sanctuary. Indeed, the family is sustained through the care work of the unskilled, impoverished non-European woman, a third-country national in Europe, whom citizenship often eludes. Although the state itself, in the German context, offers tax benefits to those who employ such labor, those performing it do not have easy access to citizenship, welfare, or social and political rights.[123] Further, although citizenship might address individual displacement, it does not address the structural problem of care deficit. Hence, even suggestions such as those of Fernández who argue for "foreigners as patriots"[124] in Europe as a model for inclusiveness are restricted by the limitedness of a juridical notion. Although such a model does not refer to the alleged glory of European legacy and has a more futuristic outlook, it confines itself to the law and what is available within the legal framework. It does not engage with the gendered dimension of migrant care work upon which the law depends. The aspiration for an egalitarian Europe—which Habermas and Benhabib express—needs to focus on the phase of transition to membership, rather than claims of full members. The transition is one of reproductive, repetitive, and affective labor—mostly feminized and racialized—with an inextricable relationship to social welfare.

Care has been traditionally neglected in discussions of both national and transnational politics. Both constitutional patriotism (Habermas) and membership in the community of citizens (Benhabib) rehearse this tradition of neglect.[125] Acknowledging the dependence on migrant caregiving—formally in welfare institutions and informally in domestic spaces such as family—opens up the possibility of engaging with migrants as assets, rather than liabilities. Further, care work that was confined to the private sphere becomes a part of the public sphere. For Benhabib this shift is significant in her discussion of Muslim women wearing veils in the public sphere of Europe. However, while translating care work to the public domain, the migrant community does not exercise its entitlements in isolation. Rather, migrants who do care work undertake responsibilities toward vulnerable "others"—nonmigrant communities—to come into contact with them. Care, thus, shifts the burden of displacement from migrants and their home societies to the needs of the European world.

Acknowledging migrant labor—especially women's—introduces care as a critical concept, an alternative to the "tyranny of democracy" and the limitedness of the legal citizen. The European world is not an isolated haven but interlinked to a disparate world whose people are domiciled in Europe. Further, disparities within Europe, such as the inability of the home to fulfill responsibilities of care, have led to care's professionalization, where it is performed in institutions and services peopled largely by migrant women in the public sphere. Thus, the citizen and the displaced migrant woman have an inexorable bond in liberal societies in the context of its "care deficit"; for there is a need for care that "no longer seems to be 'at home.' "[126] There is a need for both its labor and affect (of love), given the scarcity of care. Further, care is not a homogeneous practice but has different modes, contexts, and affects. It performs "the chores required for the daily work of maintaining bodies and things."[127]

Care work, traditionally regarded as "natural," masks the inequalities of its feminization and racialization, and the possibilities of remedying them. An examination of migrant labor indicates that rather than being natural and spontaneous, care work is socially acquired. In the European context, the traditional caregiver, namely the family, or more specifically, the woman of the family, is unable to fulfill its/her role, given its/her increasing participation in the economy. Further, public welfare institutions are unable to deliver care due to shrinking funds. Care as a commodity in the globalized market is out of reach of the financially impoverished. Consequently, "One assigns the responsibilities for caring to non-citizens: women, slaves, 'working-class foreigners.' "[128]

In turning to care as a critical concept, one deconstructs the hierarchical space of relationships between migrants and citizens, one does not valorize exploitation or endorse stereotypes of feminine nurture as its critics allege.[129] Care can be a source of exploitation, as it is in racialized patriarchal societies where class differences also exist. This is, indeed, the experience of unskilled migrant women. However, by acknowledging the human need for care, one also destigmatizes it. There is, as Keller notes, a "double-edged"[130] dimension to the critique of care, for the individualism and the absence of relationships in Western political and moral theory have been critiqued from the care perspective. Benhabib herself was one such critic,[131] although she does not develop it in the context of migrant work. One can discern human vulnerability and need for both caring and being cared in the hierarchical relationships opened up by care. One also realizes that migrant women's care work, which is taken for granted in Western societies, needs to be reconfigured in nonexploitative ways.[132] One such attempt is to treat care as a right (which is closely allied with autonomy) as Kittay does.[133]

The non-European context also reveals the possibility of decolonizing thought by overcoming the limits of Western abstract universalism and non-Western Indigenous particularism by turning to the labor of nondocumented migrant communities. Chatterjee sketches the example of a group of Bangladeshi refugees who settled down without papers in a part of Kolkata on government rail land.[134] Given their lack of legality, the state and nongovernmental agencies did not endorse their legal rights. But then this community adopted the moral claim of livelihood and welfare as a community to continue staying. They were well aware of not being a part of either the civil society or the state, but they argued on grounds of neighborliness and a new political society. One might add to Chatterjee's example that this new community carried out practices of nurture at the informal level, since the men worked in the construction industry and the women as domestic help in middle-class homes. Consequently, it had claims on its host society through labor, in which women also played a significant role. Construction businesses and homes in Kolkata had a need for Bangladeshi migrant work. Hence, caring practices premised on the inevitability of caring and being cared for, since all human beings receive care,[135] can be the basis of decolonizing and gendering the notion of agency from the limited perspectives offered by Western theory.

Caregivers are often made invisible and stigmatized both philosophically and socially; they are not adequately compensated either emotionally or financially. The caregiver's own need for care is not heeded by the family, society, and liberal political institutions that value human independence, rather than interdependence. Care decolonizes feminism because it takes migrant women into consideration on their own terms and from the point of view of what Mohanty has termed as their *everyday lives*.

The plural modes of care are also those of feeling and are anchored in particularistic contexts. However, they are also woven into unequal social relations.

Thus, "if the care needs of a nation can *only* be fulfilled by drawing on a migrant population—as may be the case today given the aging population—then a public ethic of care that is articulated as holding among all those who reside *within* the boundaries of a given society will still fall short."[136] Hence, the rights of the caregiver, as much as the care receiver need to be spelled out. Given the inequalities prevalent in caring practices, there is a need to think through its relationship with freedom through the following questions: How does one care freely and equally? How do caregivers receive care? This mandates raising the bar of democracy from mere formal representation of cultural rights—its *avatar* of "tyranny"—to a more egalitarian and substantive engagement with freedom.[137]

Kittay suggests that the right to care be regarded as a human right. Tronto has enlisted a set of care-based rights, which can be extended to the specific situation of migrant labor.[138] According to them, all human beings have a "right to receive care," whereby it is not imposed on anyone. Moreover, all human beings have a "right to care," including "the right not"[139] to where imposition of the duty to care can be refused. Besides, all human beings have a right to deliberate care, where its heterogeneity is taken into consideration. Tronto cautions against treating care as a commodity to be evenly distributed by the state, as this overlooks its variation and specificity. Instead, according to her, the state's, or one might add the law's, role in hindering or furthering the activities of care should become the subject of debate, so that the linkage between care and freedom is maintained. However, this implies that the freedoms associated with egalitarian care are precarious; they do not have legal guarantees, but are rather excesses that can only be institutionalized partially. Tronto's and Kittay's recommended list of institutional responsibilities include improved pay, immigration rights, and mobility, so that caregivers and receivers are assured of their freedoms. However, if care is inevitably linked to migration, it cannot be exhaustively institutionalized. Tronto would like for democracies to improve themselves through caring practices, and for care to benefit from democracy to become "better practices of care."[140] However, in order to bring about such a balance between democracy and care, she needs to think beyond citizen-centric, institutionalized, liberal democracies.

Alternatively, care has to be related to everyday activities in which citizens and migrants are thrown together outside the space of institutions and exclusive belonging. The right to claim rights, including those of care, is the prerogative of the citizen.[141] The migrant who is not a citizen cannot claim the right to care as a democratic entitlement; such a person embodies "bare life."[142] The nationalist lens severs the interest of the citizen by placing it in conflict with the migrant; further, egalitarian care cannot be achieved through liberal distributive justice measures without repeating its "democratic tyranny" of homogenization. If care practices are also those of migrant women (often undocumented) without institutional support, their bond with the citizen has the potential of ushering in an alternate egalitarianism. As Chatterjee notes, the alternatives of either state or civil society as the basis of agency is challenged by migrant communities such as the one in Kolkata. It undertakes of exercising free agency "not in the classical transaction between state and civil society but in the much less well-defined, legally ambiguous, contextually and strategically demarcated terrain of political society,"[143] where those who have legal claims as citizens come into contact with those who do not, due to the latter's care work.

Care activity leads to a transitional domain that cannot be regulated by institutions, although they can invoke its value. Looking after and being looked after—interdependence—is crucial to human life; it occurs in the space between the public and the private, the personal and the impersonal, the citizen and the migrant. Creating cultures beyond group "membership" care practices leads to intersectional spaces that do not belong to either the migrant or the citizen. Thus, migrant women's struggles are not attempts to seek identification with their communities or attain group membership, as per Habermas or Benhabib; they are rather attempts to create cultures of interdependence through "collective resistance"[144] against individualism and the self-sufficiency of the state and markets. These interdependencies transcend the boundaries of territory, belonging, and entitlement in their attempts to repair, continue, and maintain collectivities.

The transitional space "nested"[145] in caring practices exceeds the letter of the law with its ecological sweep. For care as a "caring with" is never purely logical or singular or juridical; nor is it an exclusively economic commodity.[146] Caregiving is, rather, motivated by emotions, such as the desire to nurture another being and the satisfaction of appreciation that is given in return. It is analogous to family bonds based on affection; caregivers who are not able to either be with their families or look after them, transfer their emotions to people with whom they have commercial bonds. They are motivated by reciprocal responses of their care receivers, rather than economic gains. The bond between the citizen and the migrant is at one level implicated in the hierarchy of power, and as Benhabib notes, brings universalism into conflict with particularism. It is fraught with the risk of the citizen exploiting the migrant. But besides the juridical, there is also an "expressive-collaborative"[147] aspect that brings people together through care practices. Indeed, migrant women's care is given to citizens by going beyond the law. Similarly, displaced migrant women do not necessarily rely upon juridical modes of care, often introduced by powers to mitigate their acts of injury and displacement. Rather, their often-undocumented lives are sustained through tenuous and informal ways of receiving care from other migrants and citizens. Such fragile bonds between migrants and citizens are the precondition for institutionalized democracy but are also at the same time outside the law. Since the bonds of care are outside the law and formal institutions and yet cross-national, class, religious, racial, ethnic, and cultural boundaries, they are the first step toward decolonizing transnational relationships.

NOTES

1. I am obliged to Margaret McLaren, Aakash Singh Rathore, and Barbara Fultner for helpful critiques and suggestions on this chapter. However, all its limitations are entirely mine.

2. See Katie Oliviero, "The Immigration State of Emergency: Racializing and Gendering National Vulnerability in Twenty-First-Century Citizenship and Deportation Regimes," *Feminist Formations* 25 (2013): 1–29.

3. Recent trends reveal that women migrate for work, although in earlier days, marriage led to migration. See Rashmi Sharma, "Gender and International Migration: The Profile of Female Migrants from India," *Social Scientist* 39 (2011): 41.

4. This discussion is derived from Sharma, "Gender and International Migration," 37; and Sara Ortiz Escalante and Elizabeth Sweet, "Migrant Women's Safety: Framing, Policies and Practices," in *Building Inclusive Cities: Women's Safety and the Right to the City*, eds. Carolyn Whitzman, Crystal Legacy, Caroline Andrew, Fran Klodawsky, Margaret Shaw, and Kalpana Viswanath (Routledge Earthscan: London and New York, 2013), 55–56. According to Samaddar, migration is not an exception but a rule. See Ranabir Samaddar, "Forced Migration Situations as Exceptions in History?" *Internal Journal of Migration and Border Studies* 2 (2016a): 99–118. Also see Michael Dummett, *On Immigration and Refugees* (London and New York: Routledge, 2001).

5. See Floya Anthias and Nira Yuval-Davis. "Women and the Nation-State," in *Nationalism*, eds. John Hutchinson and Anthony D. Smith (Oxford: Oxford University Press, 1994), 312–15. Also see Sharma, "Gender and International Migration," for a detailed account.

6. Benhabib, *The Rights of Others*, 174.

7. Sharma, "Gender and International Migration," 45.

8. See Oliviero, "The Immigration State of Emergency," 2, 3, and 16–17. She describes the burden on migrant families of hostile migration policies such as deportation in the context of the United States. Thus, state strategies of surveillance and racial profiling reflect the standard "intersectional logics of foreign peril" (2) in the overlap of race, religion, nationality, and gender (3). Yet the deportation regime causes family emergencies of social, cultural, and economic vulnerability. Migrants without papers have to choose between going back to their home countries or leaving their children behind in the home countries for a better life (16–17). Such fragmentation is neglected by the state.

9. See Oliviero, "The Immigration State of Emergency," 2.

10. See Dummett, *On Immigration*, for an account of hostility toward immigrants and refugees in Britain.

11. See Jürgen Habermas, *Between Naturalism and Religion: Philosophical Essays* (Malden, MA: Polity Press, 2008), 332. Also see Jürgen Habermas, "The European Nation-State and the Pressures of Globalization," *New Left Review* 235 (1999): 46–59, and "Leadership and Leitkultur," *New York Times* (October 28, 2010).

12. Benhabib, *The Rights of Others*, 174.

13. Thus, it is not possible to make "good Germans" out of Turks, when German identity itself is in a state of transition. See Benhabib, *The Rights of Others*, 174.

14. There is a decolonization of world representation with more and more nation states (ex-colonies) having entered the global arena. See Habermas, *Between Naturalism and Religion*, 325.

15. The latter allows "systemic integration of a multicultural world society and . . . civilizing relations of violence within societies." See Habermas, *Between Naturalism and Religion*, 7.

16. Jürgen, Habermas, "Plea for a Constitutionalization of International Law," *Philosophy and Social Criticism* 40 (1) (2014): 7. Also see, Jacques Derrida and Jürgen Habermas. "February 15, or What Binds Europeans Together: A Plea for a Common Foreign Policy, Beginning in the Core of Europe," in *The Derrida-Habermas Reader*, ed. Lasse Thomassen (Edinburgh: Edinburgh University Press, 2006), 270–77.

17. For some of the key treaties on the issues confronting migrants, see Seyla Benhabib, "Transnational Legal Sites and Democracy-Building: Reconfiguring Political Geographies," *Philosophy and Social Criticism* 39 (4–5) (2013): 473–83. Benhabib observes how these have become a part of the national law in Netherlands and South Africa, while other countries adopt a dual approach.

18. Benhabib, "Transnational Legal Sites," 473, 475. Benhabib notes how there are traces of moving beyond the Westphalian Treaty of 1648 in a move to shared transnational area. "Global constitutionalism" debate concerns the possibility of a common jurisdiction emerging from such legal cross-referencing across nations.

19. Habermas, *Contributions to a Discourse Theory of Law and Democracy*, 26. Habermas's perspective on the law's power of arbitration is extended from his work on discourse law to the transnational context. Political culture is liberated from substantive worldviews and practices to be unified "in the multiplicity of subcultures." See Habermas, *The Inclusion of the Other: Studies in Political Theory* (Cambridge: Polity Press, 1998), 117.

20. Habermas ascribes the term *constitutional patriotism* to Dolf Sternberger. See Jürgen Habermas, *The New Conservatism: Cultural Criticism and the Historians' Debate* (Cambridge, MA: MIT Press, 1989), 193; and Patchen Markell, "Making Affect Safe for Democracy? On "Constitutional Patriotism," *Political Theory* 28 (2000): 58.

21. Migration has been the most central phenomenon in Europe in the post–world war context. See Patrizia Nanz, "Mobility, Migrants and Solidarity: Towards an Emerging European Citizenship Regime," in *Migrations and Mobilities: Citizenship, Borders, and Gender*, eds. Seyla Benhabib and Judith Resnik (New York: NYU Press, 2009), 410–14; and Dummett, *On Immigration*, 137–39. After World War II, West Germany received migrants from different parts of the world to build its economy. Prior to the formation of the European Union (EU) in 1992, migration

within Europe was governed by national borders and their norms. However, with the Maatricht Treaty of 1992, the citizens of EU were not restricted in mobility on grounds of their nationality (European). They enjoy the same rights and privileges throughout the EU member states and are not bound by pressures of cultural assimilation. Nationality based on people's unified culture and legality has been dissociated from the EU citizenship. It has created a transnational space for citizens.

22. Habermas argues against Grimm's claim that a constitution requires a homogeneity of people. See Habermas, *The Inclusion of the Other*, 138.

23. Habermas, "The European Nation-State," 47.

24. "Habermas's democratic model is communicative but balances the civic republican emphasis on public discourse with a liberal protection of human rights, especially of minorities or as he names them after Kant with a biblical accent, 'strangers,' for whom, he insists, a theory of justice is primarily needed." See Michael Scrivener, *The Cosmopolitan Ideal in the Age of Revolution and Reaction* (London: Pickering and Chatto, 2007), 25; and Habermas, *Between Naturalism and Religion*, 330–31.

25. Such repression is state-ordered in the name of the law without the backing of its normative force. Breda argues that Habermas's case for constitutional patriotism falls back on a contested account of constitutional history to exclude nationalism. See Vito Breda, "The Incoherence of the Patriotic State: A Critique of 'Constitutional Patriotism,'" *Res Publica* (2004): 261. He also notes that Anthony Smith arrives at the opposite conclusion with reference to the nation.

26. Habermas, *Between Naturalism and Religion*, 332–33. He terms it as "a postnational guise of a constitutionalized world society." For Habermas, this is a matter of empirical grounding and not just a concept of a cosmopolitan society without world government. He views the postnational condition as encouraging a sense of belonging that goes beyond the nation.

27. See Habermas, *The Inclusion of the Other*, 117; and Navid Hassanzadeh, "Post-Nationalism and Western Modernity: Beyond the Limits of the 'European-Wide Public Sphere,'" *Constellations* 22 (3) (2015): 437.

28. Jürgen Habermas, "Plea for a Constitutionalization of International Law," *Philosophy and Social Criticism* 40 (1) (2014): 1. As Fernández notes, constitutional patriotism is an attempt at Kantian universalism, which includes the marginalized. See Christian Fernández, "Patriots in the Making? Migrants, Citizens, and Demos," *International Migration and Integration* 13 (2012): 150, 152. It is not a neatly delineated concept but a "mindset," of including "others" as a response to the horrors of Nazism in the German past. Benhabib notes how the "privileged object domain" ("Transnational Legal Sites," 475) of the discipline of political science is eroded with the porousness of nation-states. Instead, there is an increased emphasis on legal scholarship in transnational contexts.

29. Habermas, "Plea," 7. In his argument for deliberative democracy, Habermas invokes formal proceduralism as a mode of argument. In contrast, he appeals to the irrationalism in nationalism—a substantive argument—endangering republican values, while making a case for constitutional patriotism (Breda, "The Incoherence," 264–65). There is an internal incoherence according to Breda, where the proceduralism restricts the public sphere, which has to be open to enable social integration in a

democratic way. However, this opens Habermas to being "democratically dangerous" (Breda, "The Incoherence," 265).

30. Markell, "Making Affect," 52.

31. Habermas's constitutional patriotism has been critiqued for making abstract principles the object of affect and affirming a civic nationalist identity (Hassanzadeh, "Postnationalism," 438; and Bernard Yack's critique as cited by Hassanzadeh "Postnationalism," 445). This chapter largely focuses on Markell's critique of Habermas's earlier work on constitutional democracy, which is expanded to the latter's transnational constitutionalism. The tension between facticity and validity mandates directing the affect underlying constitutional patriotism to the particularisms of identities, which are prepolitical naturalized identities of ethnicity and religion with their attendant dangers. The tension between facticity and validity mandates directing the affect underlying constitutional patriotism to the particularism of identities; the latter are not ethnic but are prepolitical naturalized identities of ethnicity and religion with their attendant dangers (Markell, "Making Affect," 53).

32. Markell, "Making Affect," 47.

33. Markell, "Making Affect," 39.

34. "The challenge before us is not to *invent* anything but to *conserve* the great democratic achievements of the European nation-state, beyond its own limits." See Jürgen Habermas, *Postnational Constellation: Political Essays* (Cambridge, MA: MIT Press, 2001), 6.

35. Habermas, *Inclusion of the Other*, 161.

36. Ibid.

37. Ibid.

38. Habermas, *The New Conservatism*, 223; Markell, "Making Affect," 53. Gayatri Chakravorty Spivak terms it as an *economic document*, Gayatri Chakravorty Spivak, *Nationalism and the Imagination* (London, New York, and Kolkata: Seagull, 2010), 87. However, this claim overlooks Habermas's privileging of the political. See Jan Werner Müller, *Constitutional Patriotism* (Princeton: Princeton University Press, 2007), for a history of constitutional patriotism.

39. Jürgen Habermas, *The Crisis of the European Union* (Cambridge and Malden, MA: Polity, 2012), 3.

40. Habermas, *Inclusion of the Other*, 159.

41. Ibid., 138.

42. Habermas approvingly cites United States as opposed to the French assimilative paradigm as a country of citizens who are migrants in origin (Habermas, *Inclusion of the Other*, 159).

43. There is an inevitable interdependence between fact and norm (Markell, "Making Affect," 47).

44. This core also assumes a set of factual particularist assumptions such as a body of rights endorsed in a historical legislature, its territorial jurisdiction, its distinction between members and nonmembers, and enforcement by the constitutional state.

45. Habermas, *The New Conservatism*, 58.

46. Habermas, *Post-National Constellation*, 19.

47. Nira Yuval-Davis, "The Citizenship Debate: Women, Ethnic Processes and the State," *Feminist Review* 39 (1991): 61; and "Women, Citizenship and Difference,"

Feminist Review 57 (1997): 4–27. Also see Anthias and Yuval-Davis, "Women and the Nation-state."

48. Habermas, *Inclusion of the Other*, 160.

49. Habermas, *Postnational Constellation*, 19.

50. Ibid., 20.

51. Habermas, *Postnational Constellation*, 161. In this sense, Habermas too seems to suggest that citizenship is a "status bestowed on those who have full membership in a community," although he would clearly reject organic accounts of community and communitarianism.

52. Fernández, "Patriots," 151–52.

53. Habermas believes that national social solidarity should be "widened to embrace all citizens of the Union, so that, for example, Swedes and Portuguese will be ready to *stand by one another*" (Habermas, *Inclusion of the Other*, 57). For Habermas, the juridical route allows for transnational communities that oppose war and support peace.

54. Habermas, *Postnational Constellations*, 22.

55. Hassanzadeh, "Postnationalism," 440, 442. Thus, Chakraborty's notion of *adda* is cited as a mode of conversation in West Bengal India that does not follow the Habermasian paradigm of discourse but is yet democratic. However, such an appreciation of the *adda* overlooks its patriarchal character.

56. Benhabib, "Transnational Legal Sites."

57. Fernández, "Patriots."152–54.

58. Escalante and Sweet, "Migrant Women's safety," 56.

59. Ibid., 57.

60. Ibid., 55.

61. Against Habermas, Western Europe cannot be said to have unique claims over democratic norms, as non-Western societies have their own negotiations with modernity (Hassanzadeh, "Postnationalism," 444). Interestingly, even left thinkers such as Žižek insist that migrants in Europe should follow its supposedly unique culture and legacy! See for instance, his claims in "Non-existence of Norway."

62. See Benhabib and Resnik, "Introduction," 4. Nanz notes how the intra-European migration has largely focused on male wage labor ("Mobility, Migrants," 414).

63. A similar perspective has been articulated previously with reference to Habermas's constitutional patriotism.

64. Benhabib, "Transnational Legal Sites," 473. Benhabib critiques Robert Dahl's difficulties of participation of *demos* or people in decision-making in the international context by pointing to the epistemic, cultural, and procedural deterrents (ibid., 475–77). She argues that this presupposes a homogeneous population with strict national borders, which is no more an absolute reality.

65. Benhabib, *The Rights of Others*, 179.

66. Benhabib evokes this notion from Derrida's and later Wittgenstein's account of language (Benhabib, *The Rights of Others*, 179).

67. Ibid., 185–98.

68. Ibid., 198–202. Also see Joan Wallach Scott, *Politics of the Veil* (Princeton and Oxford: Princeton University Press, 2007). Women wearing headscarves were

discriminated against, rather than assimilated into French society on account of these laws.

69. Benhabib, *The Rights of Others*, 192–97.

70. Benhabib, "Transnational Legal Sites," 482. She terms this as a "transnational conversation of practical reasons" (ibid., 482).

71. Benhabib cites the human rights violation in Turkey as not deterring the possibility of such "democratic iterations" (ibid., 482), which are more valuable in such contexts.

72. Benhabib, *The Rights of Others*, 136.

73. Ibid., 233.

74. Ibid., 191.

75. Ibid., 212. She cites Walzer as an instance.

76. Benhabib, *The Rights of Others*, 212.

77. Thomassen aptly notes that Benhabib's reiteration, unlike Derrida's reiteration attempts to preserve rather than disrupt the gap between the universal original and the particular act of reiteration. See Lasse Thomassen, "The Politics of Iterability: Benhabib, the Hijab, and Democratic Iterations," *Polity* 43 (2011): 141.

78. Thomassen, "The Politics of Iterability," 137.

79. As Thomassen notes, "Benhabib may have introduced the notion of iteration in order to soften the legal, cultural, and other borders that limit the inclusion and equality of agents such as the French Muslim girls, but this only happens within a different set of 'very clear lines' "(Thomassen, "The Politics of Iterability," 137).

80. Thomassen, "The Politics of Iterability," 135–37.

81. Scott's general thesis regarding democracy (*Politics*, 182) is extended to liberal democracy in Europe.

82. Charles W. Mills, "Decolonizing Western Political Philosophy," *Political Science* 37 (2015): 1–24.

83. Ibid., 9.

84. Scott, *Politics*, 183.

85. Feret Güven. *Decolonizing Democracy: Intersections of Philosophy and Postcolonial Theory* (Lanham and Boulder: Lexington Books, 2015), ix–x.

86. Ibid., xi.

87. As Vinay Lal notes, the Haitian Revolution (1791–1803), where the agency of erstwhile slaves overthrew the yoke of the French with 50,000 rebels defeating 1,800 trained French soldiers, never seems to find a place in the annals of intellectual history. See his "Preface: Civilizational Dialogues and the Politics of a Collective," in *India and the Unthinkable: Backwaters Collective on Metaphysics and Politics*, eds. Vinay Lal and Roby Rajan (New Delhi: Oxford University Press, 2016), vii–xxii.

88. For an overview of migration with the South, see "Poor-World Migration, The Beautiful South: The Other Kind of Migration," *Indian Express* (January 2, 2017). In the words of Samaddar, "If the preceding century was a century of partitions, this century may become known as the century of stateless people" ("Forced Migration Situations," 2016a, 102).

89. Myron Weiner, "Rejected Peoples and Unwanted Migrants in South Asia," *Economic and Political Weekly* 28 (1993): 1737.

90. Ibid.

91. Governments in the South context encourage remittances but restrict and control remitters. International migration is accompanied by internal migration, as the case of Kerala reveals. See Sanjay Barbora, Susan Thieme, Karin Astrid Siegmann, Vineetha Menon, and Ganesh Gurung, "Migration Matters in South Asia: Commonalities and Critiques," *Economic and Political Weekly* 43 (24) (2008): 63. In Kerala, the large migration of labor to the Middle East has led to labor forces migrating to Kerala from other states like Bihar and Orissa.

92. For instance, Bangladeshi refugees who come across the borders of West Bengal, Assam, and Arunachal Pradesh in India are often perceived as threats. See, Laxmi Murthy and Mitu Varma, *Garrisoned Minds: Women and Armed Conflict in South Asia* (New Delhi: Speaking Tiger Books, 2016). Also see, Palash Ghosh, "India's 'Mexican' Problem: Illegal Immigration from Bangladesh," *Newsweek* (June 2, 2012), http://www.ibtimes.com/indias-mexican-problem-illegal-immigration-bangladesh-213993. Hostility is directed toward them, since many of them are Muslims. As Ghosh notes, "while Indians are often the target of anti-immigrant rhetoric in many western countries, particularly Britain and the United States, Indians themselves are using the same inflammatory language against unwanted immigrants in their own country."

93. Barbora et al., "Migration Matters," 63. Also see Ranabir Samaddar, "Migrant and the Neo-Liberal City: An Introduction," *Economic and Political Weekly*, no. 26&27 (2016b): 52–54, for an account of migration in neoliberal Indian cities.

94. Rita Manchada, "Gender Conflict and Displacement: Contesting 'Infantilisation' of Forced Migrant Women," 39 (2004): 4184–85.

95. See Dipankar De Sarkar, "Why India Won't Sign Refugee Treaty," *Live Mint*, September 11, 2015, http://www.livemint.com/Opinion/bePZQScFIq1wEWv9Tqt4QO/Why-India-wont-sign-Refugee-Treaty.html?facet=print, accessed on September 12, 2016. Last year, a Citizenship Amendment Bill (2016) was proposed" since the bill was proposed in 2016. It advocates giving citizenship to Hindus, Buddhists, Jains, Parsis, and Christians from Afghanistan, Bangladesh, and Pakistan. See "The Citizenship (Amendment) Bill, 2016, " http://www.prsindia.org/billtrack/the-citizenship-amendment-bill-2016-4348, accessed on December 28, 2016. It is silent on citizenship to Muslims.

96. Samaddar, "Forced Migration," 109.

97. Ibid., 110.

98. Chandra-Talpade Mohanty, "Under Western Eyes: Feminist Scholarship and Colonial Discourses," *Boundary* 2 (12) (1984): 333–58.

99. The veil has been and continues to be a contested practice in countries like Iran. Marjane Satrapi's graphic novel *Persepolis: The Story of a Childhood* (New York: Pantheon Books, 2003) depicts growing up in Iran. The protagonist (who is Satrapi) rues, "I really don't know what to think about the veil. Deep down I was very religious but as a family we were very modern and avant-garde" (6). Her family resisted both the regimes of Shah and Khomeini given their left leanings. Further, migrant women in the West are not necessarily hounded by demands of their tradition. In her second volume, *Persepolis 2: The Story of a Return* (New York:

Pantheon Books, 2004), Satrapi narrates her life in Vienna as an Iranian woman. Rather than negotiating tradition and modernity, her problem is one of loneliness and seeking recognition.

100. Güven, *Decolonizing Democracy*, 67.

101. With formal end of slavery, indentured labor from colonies such as India was used by the British to work on plantations in Mauritius, British Guiana, Trinidad, and Jamaica. See David Northrup, *Indentured Labour in the Age of Imperialism* (Cambridge and New York: Cambridge University Press, 1995). In contrast, the Sikh diaspora's global spread to Europe, North America, and South East Asia occurred with the British recruiting Sikh soldiers to serve in its colonies in the Far East and Malay who then voluntarily migrated to Australia or the Pacific states (Fiji and New Zealand). See Paramjit S. Judge, "Diversity within the Punjabi Diaspora and the Construction of Nationhood," in *Diversities in the Indian Diaspora* (Oxford: Oxford University Press, 2011), 25–48. Also see María Lugones, "The Coloniality of Gender," *Worlds & Knowledges Otherwise* (2008): 1–17, for an account of the relationship between coloniality and gender.

102. Manchada, "Gender Conflict", 4179.

103. Ibid.

104. Benhabib, *The Rights of Others*, 173.

105. "The politics of immigration is closely linked to the politics of conformism of disciplining opposition at home" (Benhabib, *The Rights of Others*, 173).

106. Arne Johan Vetlesen, "Comments on Jürgen Habermas' lecture 'Plea for a Constitutionalization of International Law,'" *Philosophy and Social Criticism* 40 (2014): 23.

107. Mills, "Decolonizing" 13.

108. Moritz Julius Bonn, an economist, introduced this term in the 1930s. See Dietmar Rothermund, *The Routledge Companion to Decolonization* (Oxon and New York: Routledge, 2006), 1.

109. Rothermund, *The Routledge Companion*, 1.

110. Mills, "Decolonizing," 18.

111. As Leopold Senghor noted, "Africans wanted to assimilate and not be assimilated" (Rothmund, *The Routledge Companion*, 2). Also see Rahul Rao, *Third World Protest: Between Home and the World* (Clarendon: Oxford University Press, 2010), for the colonial context of cosmopolitanism.

112. Markell, "Making Affect," 42.

113. Benhabib, "Transnational Legal Sites," 473.

114. Sharma, "Gender and International Migration," 41, 43–44.

115. Women also migrate after marriage, which often puts them in the unskilled labor category.

116. Barbora et al., "Migration Matters," 64.

117. See Nanz, "Mobility, Migrants," 416–17, for details of this case.

118. Nanz notes the problems with neglecting care work, but her lauding of ECJ is problematic (Nanz, "Mobility, Migrants," 417). For instance, it overlooks the need for dual citizenship, which as Dummett notes, makes Turks and other migrants feel disempowered and unconnected to their home (Dummett, *On Immigration*, 143–44).

119. For further details see, Bridget Anderson "Overseas Domestic Workers in the European Union: Invisible Women," in *Gender, Migration and Domestic Service*, ed. Janet Henshall Momsen (London and New York: Routledge, 1999), 113–29.

120. Anderson, "Overseas Domestic Workers in the European Union".

121. Joan Tronto, *Caring Democracy: Markets Equality and Justice* (New York: New York University Press, 2013), 17.

122. See Eva Kittay, "The Global Heart Transplant and Caring across national Boundaries," *The Southern Journal of Philosophy* 46 (2008): 146; and her "The Moral Harm of Migrant Carework: Realizing a Global Right to Care," *Philosophical Topics* 37 (2009): 56.

123. Heide Casteñeda, "Illegal Migration, Gender and Health Care: Perspectives from Germany and the United States," in *Illegal Migration and Gender in a Global and Historical Perspective*, eds. Marlou Schrover, Joanne van der Leun, Leo Lucassen, and Chris Quispel (Amsterdam: Amsterdam University Press, 2008), 171–88.

124. Fernández, "Patriots," 160–61. Fernández is apprehensive about the wide reach of such a pattern.

125. Benhabib's neglect of care in the context of migrant labor is surprising, given her earlier critique of Habermas's similar neglect and appropriation of Gilligan (see Seyla Benhabib, "The Generalized and the Concrete Other: The Kohlberg-Gilligan Controversy and Feminist Theory," *Praxis International* 5 (4) (1986): 402–24. .

126. Tronto, *Caring Democracy*, 1.

127. Ibid., 2.

128. Ibid., 10.

129. For instance, Sandra Lee Bartky in her *Femininity and Domination: Studies in the Phenomenology of Oppression* (New York and London: Routledge, 1990) critiques care as reinforcing stereotypes.

130. Keller, Jean. "Autonomy, Relationality, and Feminist Ethics," *Hypatia* (1995): 128–33.

131. See Benhabib, "Generalized and Concrete Other"

132. The limits of this chapter do not permit exploring the possibility of reconciling migrant women's care with a relational notion of autonomy.

133. See Kittay, "The Moral Harm."

134. Partha Chatterjee, "The Poverty of Western Political Theory: Concluding Remarks on Concepts Like 'Community' East and West," in *Indian Political Thought: A Reader*, eds. Aakash Singh Rathore and Silika Mohapatra (Oxon, New York, and New Delhi: Routledge 2012), 295–97.

135. Ibid., 146.

136. Kittay, "The Global Heart Transplant," 142.

137. The specific type of care compatible with democracy has to be articulated, because Tronto is clear that the caring she refers to is neither feudal nor colonial.

138. For Kittay, see Kittay, "The Global Hear Transplant," 152 and Kittay, "The Moral Harm," 65. For Tronto, see Tronto, *Caring Democracy*, 153–68. Also see López, "Taking the Human Rights of Migrants Seriously."

139. Tronto quotes Finch's expression. See Tronto, *Caring Democracy*, 154.

140. Ibid., 158.

141. Samaddar, "Forced Migration," 112.

142. This expression is borrowed from Agamben by Samaddar (Samaddar, "Forced Migration," 112).

143. Chatterjee, "The Poverty," 298.

144. Talpade-Mohanty, " 'Under Western Eyes' Revisited," 499–535.

145. Tronto, *Caring Democracy*, 21.

146. Kittay, "The Moral Harm," 56.

147. Tronto, *Caring Democracy*, 155.

BIBLIOGRAPHY

Anderson, Bridget. "Overseas Domestic Workers in the European Union: Invisible Women," in *Gender, Migration and Domestic Service*, ed. Janet Henshall Momsen, 113–29. London and New York: Routledge, 1999.

Anthias, Floya, and Nira Yuval-Davis. "Women and the Nation-State," in *Nationalism*, eds. John Hutchinson and Anthony D. Smith, 312–15. Oxford: Oxford University Press, 1994.

Banerjee, Arpita, and Saraswati Raju. "Gendered Mobility: Women Migrants and Work in Urban India." *Economic & Political Weekly* xliv (28) (2009): 115–23.

Barbora, Sanjay, Susan Thieme, Karin Astrid Siegmann, Vineetha Menon, Ganesh Gurung. "Migration Matters in South Asia: Commonalities and Critiques." *Economic and Political Weekly* 43 (24) (2008): 55–65.

Bartky, Sandra Lee. Femininity and Domination: Studies in the Phenomenology of Oppression. New York and London: Routledge, 1990.

Benhabib, Seyla. "The Generalized and the Concrete Other: The Kohlberg-Gilligan Controversy and Feminist Theory." *Praxis International* 5 (4) (1986): 402–24.

———. *The Rights of Others: Aliens, Residents, Citizens*. Cambridge: Cambridge University Press, 2004.

———. *Another Cosmopolitanism*. Oxford and New York: Oxford University Press, 2006.

———. "Claiming Rights across Borders: International Human Rights and Democratic Sovereignty." *The American Political Science Review* 103 (4) (2009): 691–704.

Benhabib, Seyla, and Judith Resnik, eds., *Introduction to Migrations and Mobilities. Citizenship, Borders, and Gender*, 1–44. New York: NYU Press, 2009.

———. "Transnational Legal Sites and Democracy-Building: Reconfiguring Political Geographies." *Philosophy and Social Criticism* 39 (4–5) (2013): 471–86.

Breda, Vito. "The Incoherence of the Patriotic State: A Critique of 'Constitutional Patriotism.' " *Res Publica* (2004): 247–65.

Casteñeda, Heide. "Illegal Migration, Gender and Health Care: Perspectives from Germany and the United States," in *Illegal Migration and Gender in a Global and Historical Perspective*, eds. Marlou Schrover, Joanne van der Leun, Leo Lucassen, and Chris Quispel, 171–88. Amsterdam: Amsterdam University Press, 2008.

Chatterjee, Partha. "The Poverty of Western Political Theory: Concluding Remarks on Concepts Like 'Community' East and West," in *Indian Political Thought: A Reader*, eds. Aakash Singh Rathore and Silika Mohapatra, 287–99. Oxon, New York, and New Delhi: Routledge, 2012 (2010).

"The Citizenship (Amendment) Bill, 2016." *PRS Legislative Research*, accessed on December 28, 2016. http://www.prsindia.org/billtrack/the-citizenship-amendment-bill-2016-4348.

De Sarkar, Dipankar 2015 "Why India Won't Sign Refugee Treaty" *Live Mint*. http://www.livemint.com/Opinion/bePZQScFIq1wEWv9Tqt4QO/Why-India-wont-sign-Refugee-Treaty.html?facet=print, accessed on 12/9/2016

Dempsey, Judith. "A Difficult Choice for Turks in Germany." *New York Times*, April 15, 2013.

Derrida, Jacques, and Jürgen Habermas. "February 15, or What Binds Europeans Together: A Plea for a Common Foreign Policy, Beginning in the Core of Europe," in *The Derrida-Habermas Reader*, ed. Lasse Thomassen, 270–77. Edinburgh: Edinburgh University Press, 2006.

Dummett, Michael. *On Immigration and Refugees*. London and New York: Routledge, 2001.

Escalante, Sara Ortiz, and Elizabeth Sweet. "Migrant Women's Safety: Framing, Policies and Practices," in *Building Inclusive Cities: Women's Safety and the Right to the City*, eds. Carolyn Whitzman, Crystal Legacy, Caroline Andrew, Fran Klodawsky, Margaret Shaw, and Kalpana Viswanath, 53–71. London and New York: Routledge Earthscan, 2013.

Faruqee, Ashrufa. "Conceiving the Coolie Woman: Indentured Labour, Indian Women and Colonial Discourse." *South Asia Research* 16 (1) (1996): 61–76.

Fernández, Christian. "Patriots in the Making? Migrants, Citizens, and Demos." *International Migration and Integration* 13 (2012): 147–63.

Ganis, Richard. *The Politics of Care in Habermas and Derrida: Between Measurability and Immeasurability*. Lanham and Boulder: Lexington Books, 2011.

Ghosh, Palash. "India's 'Mexican' Problem: Illegal Immigration from Bangladesh." *Newsweek*, June 2, 2012. http://www.ibtimes.com/indias-mexican-problem-illegal-immigration-bangladesh-213993.

Gutíerrez-Rodriguéz, Encarnación. *Migration, Domestic Work and Affect: A Decolonial Approach on Value and Feminization of Labor*. New York and Oxon: Routledge, 2010.

Güven, Feret. *Decolonizing Democracy: Intersections of Philosophy and Postcolonial Theory*. Lanham and Boulder: Lexington Books, 2015.

Habermas, Jürgen. *The Philosophical Discourse of Modernity: Twelve Lectures*. Cambridge, MA: MIT Press, 1987.

———. *The New Conservatism: Cultural Criticism and the Historians' Debate*. Cambridge, MA: MIT Press, 1989.

———. *Moral Consciousness and Communicative Action*. Cambridge, MA and London: MIT Press, 1990.

———. *Contributions to a Discourse Theory of Law and Democracy*. Cambridge: Polity Press, 1996.

———. "Kant's Idea of Perpetual Peace, with the Benefit of Two Hundred Years' Hindsight," in *Perpetual Peace: Essays on Kant's Cosmopolitan Ideal*, eds. James Bohman and Mattias Lutz-Bachmann, 113–53. Cambridge, MA: MIT Press, 1997.

———. *The Inclusion of the Other: Studies in Political Theory*. Cambridge: Polity Press, 1998.

———. "The European Nation-State and the Pressures of Globalization." *New Left Review* 235 (1999): 46–59.

———. *Postnational Constellation: Political Essays*. Cambridge, MA: MIT Press, 2001.

———. "Why Europe Needs a Constitution." *New Left Review* 11 (2002): 5–26.

———. *The Divided West*. Malden, MA: Polity Press, 2006.

———. *Between Naturalism and Religion: Philosophical Essays*. Malden, MA: Polity Press, 2008.

———. "Leadership and Leitkultur." *New York Times*, October 28, 2010.

———. *The Crisis of the European Union*. Cambridge and Malden, MA: Polity, 2012.

———. "Plea for a Constitutionalization of International Law." *Philosophy and Social Criticism* 40 (1) (2014): 5–12.

Hassanzadeh, Navid. "Post-Nationalism and Western Modernity: Beyond the Limits of the 'European-Wide Public Sphere.'" *Constellations* 22 (3) (2015): 435–46.

Judge, Paramjit S. "Diversity within the Punjabi Diaspora and the Construction of Nationhood," in *Diversities in the Indian Diaspora*, 25–48. Oxford: Oxford University Press, 2011.

Kant, Immanuel. "To Perpetual Peace: A Philosophical Sketch (1795)," in *Perpetual Peace and Other Essays on Politics, History and Morals*, translated with an introduction by Ted Humphreys, 107–43. Indianapolis: Hackett Publishing Company, 1983.

Keller, Jean. "Autonomy, Relationality, and Feminist Ethics." *Hypatia* (1995): 128–33.

Kittay, Eva. "The Global Heart Transplant and Caring across National Boundaries." *The Southern Journal of Philosophy* 46 (2008): 138–65.

———. "The Moral Harm of Migrant Carework: Realizing a Global Right to Care." *Philosophical Topics* 37 (2009): 53–73.

Lal, Vinay. "Preface: Civilizational Dialogues and the Politics of a Collective," in *India and the Unthinkable: Backwaters Collective on Metaphysics and Politics*, eds. Vinay Lal and Roby Rajan, vii–xxii. New Delhi: Oxford University Press, 2016.

López, Estévez Ariadna. "Taking the Human Rights of Migrants Seriously: Towards a Decolonized Global Justice." *International Journal of Human Rights* 14 (2010): 658–77.

Lugones, María. "The Coloniality of Gender." *Worlds & Knowledges Otherwise* (2008): 1–17.

Manchada, Rita. "Gender Conflict and Displacement: Contesting 'Infantilisation' of Forced Migrant Women." *Economic and Political Weekly* 39 (2004): 4179–86.

Markell, Patchen. "Making Affect Safe for Democracy? On "Constitutional Patriotism." *Political Theory* 28 (2000): 38–63.

Mills, Charles W. "Decolonizing Western Political Philosophy." *Political Science* 37 (2015): 1–24.

Mohanty, Chandra Talpade. "Under Western Eyes: Feminist Scholarship and Colonial Discourses." *Boundary 2* (12) (1984): 333–58.

———. "'Under Western Eyes' Revisited: Feminist Solidarity through Anti-capitalist Struggles." *Signs* 28 (2003): 499–535.

Müller, Jan Werner. *Constitutional Patriotism*. Princeton: Princeton University Press, 2007.

Murthy, Laxmi, and Mitu Varma, eds. *Garrisoned Minds: Women and Armed Conflict in South Asia*. New Delhi: Speaking Tiger Books, 2016.

Nanz, Patrizia. "Mobility, Migrants and Solidarity: Towards an Emerging European Citizenship Regime," in *Migrations and Mobilities: Citizenship, Borders, and Gender*, eds. Seyla Benhabib and Judith Resnik, 410–38. New York: NYU Press, 2009.

Northrup, David. *Indentured Labour in the Age of Imperialism*. Cambridge and New York: Cambridge University Press, 1995.

Oliviero, Katie E. "The Immigration State of Emergency: Racializing and Gendering National Vulnerability in Twenty-First-Century Citizenship and Deportation Regimes." *Feminist Formations* 25 (2013): 1–29.

Rao, Rahul. *Third World Protest: Between Home and the World*. Clarendon: Oxford University Press, 2010.

Rothermund, Dietmar. *The Routledge Companion to Decolonization*. Oxon and New York: Routledge, 2006.

Samaddar, Ranabir. "Forced Migration Situations as Exceptions in History?" *Internal Journal of Migration and Border Studies* 2 (2016a): 99–118.

———. "Migrant and the Neo-Liberal City: An Introduction." *Economic and Political Weekly*, no. 26&27 (2016b): 52–54.

Satrapi, Marjane. *Persepolis: The Story of a Childhood*. New York: Pantheon Books, 2003.

———. *Persepolis 2: The Story of a Return*. New York: Pantheon Books, 2004.

Scott, Joan Wallach. *Politics of the Veil*. Princeton and Oxford: Princeton University Press, 2007.

Scrivener, Michael. *The Cosmopolitan Ideal in the Age of Revolution and Reaction*. London: Pickering and Chatto, 2007.

Sharma, Rashmi. "Gender and International Migration: The Profile of Female Migrants from India." *Social Scientist* 39 (2011): 37–63.

Spivak, Gayatri Chakravorty. *Nationalism and the Imagination*. London, New York, and Kolkata: Seagull, 2010.

Thomassen, Lasse. "The Politics of Iterability: Benhabib, the Hijab, and Democratic. Iterations." *Polity* 43 (2011): 128–49.

Tronto, Joan. *Caring Democracy: Markets Equality and Justice*. New York: New York University Press, 2013.

Vetlesen, Arne Johan. "Comments on Jürgen Habermas' Lecture 'Plea for a Constitutionalization of International Law.'" *Philosophy and Social Criticism* 40 (2014): 19–23.

Weiner, Myron. "Rejected Peoples and Unwanted Migrants in South Asia." *Economic and Political Weekly* 28 (1993): 1737–46.

Yuval-Davis, Nira. "The Citizenship Debate: Women, Ethnic Processes and the State." *Feminist Review*, no. 39 (1991): 58–68.

———. "Women, Citizenship and Difference." *Feminist Review* 57 (1997): 4–27.

Žižek, Slavoj. "The Non-existence of Norway." *London Review of Books*, September 9, 2015, accessed on September 1, 2016. www.lrb.co.uk.

Chapter 6

"Home-Making" and "World-Traveling": Decolonizing the Space-Between in Transnational Feminist Thought

Celia T. Bardwell-Jones

In this chapter, I examine the theoretical space-between in feminist theory through the lens of a metaphysics of belonging framed by notions of travel and home. I examine how travel and home percolate into attempts in feminist theory to cultivate feminist coalitional communities, given the fractured state of feminist politics due to the concerns of difference raised in identity politics. Feminist theory has a history of examining the fundamental nature of the space-between in thinking about categories of "woman" and strategies for coalitional politics. Patricia Hill Collins examines the space-between by observing the "intersecting" nature of oppression and how a "matrix of domination" exists that affects the diverse axes of identity.[1] Intersectionality has become a powerful feminist theoretical framework that exposes the failures of dominant epistemology and reveals the complicated ontological context in which women live out their lives. Feminist theory has been a leading force in the academy and activist activities in realizing the importance of the space-between.

One of the main theoretical contributions in thinking about the space-between is María Lugones's notion of "world-traveling," which addresses the problems of exclusion in feminist coalitional politics. This groundbreaking concept has been cited in numerous fields, including feminist theory, philosophy, and medical ethics.[2] The importance of this work not only exposes the need for a model of understanding relationships between disparate individuals but also highlights the importance of recovering social boundaries as a space of encounter, rather than rendering this space as marginal or merely as marks of separations and distinctions. "World-traveling" is an excellent metaphor that relates to one's lived experience at the social boundaries of what is familiar and what is foreign. I find Lugones's concept of "world-traveling" inspiring and foundational to the project of recovering the space-between in feminist theory.

While fixed and rigid notions of home threaten the liberatory potential of world travel, my aim in this chapter is to show how "world-traveling" is associated with a correlate concept of "home-making" as theorized by Yen Li Espiritu's work surrounding the lives of Filipino Americans. In recovering a sense of home, it is important to recognize that the experience of home may be problematic at two levels. On the one hand, the concept of home may be inhospitable to those who deviate or challenge the norms of the home. On the other hand, the experience of homelessness is apparent for many displaced people. From this perspective, a recovery of home may be seen as a lost cause that leads to a romanticizing nostalgia that inevitably essentializes one's cultural homelands. However, the interpretation I propose in this chapter will reveal how transnational feminist thought, through the work of Chandra Mohanty, revives this notion of home, as a process of belonging for many displaced persons and can provide some nuanced insights in understanding how the framework of world-traveling might contribute toward addressing the state of feminist coalitional politics. Iris Marion Young agrees with the early discussions of the critique of longing for home that emerged from feminist theorists, such as Biddy Martin, Chandra Mohanty, Teresea de Lauretis, and Bonnie Honig. Yet, despite these criticisms, Young finds a positive notion of home that can be seen constructively as a critical value for feminist ends, one that highlights values of safety, individuality, privacy, and preservation. In a similar project, Alison Weir also finds a positive value of home and continues to extend this critical value by highlighting how home implies connectivity and attentiveness to relationships. Rather than seeing home as a site that cannot ground one's identity, home can be seen as an essential component in identity formation. My analysis emphasizes the positive critical value of home within the transnational context of theorizing; thus I offer a positive role for home to play in transnational feminist solidarity in contrast to Mohanty's critique of the negative implications of home. This analysis will uncover some of the features of a decolonizing methodology when reevaluating the positive critical value of home, which highlight the tension of world-traveling and home-making.

In this chapter, I first examine this notion of home-making within the landscape of intersectionality in feminist theory, then I consider Espiritu's concept of home-making in the context of the lives of Filipino Americans. Finally, I show how Mohanty's transnational feminist theory revives this notion of home, as a process, in its understanding of world-traveling. Home-making, I argue, can also be thought of positively within a transnational context and provide an important contribution to addressing the state of feminist coalitional politics.

INTERSECTIONALITY AND FEMINIST THEORY: SITUATING HOME-MAKING AND WORLD-TRAVELING

Decolonial feminism as articulated by María Lugones can be thought of as a reconfiguration of how we understand concepts such as gender within a coloniality of power, a framework utilized by Anibal Quijano, which "provides us with a historical understanding of the inseparability of racialization and capitalist exploitation."[3] Though the task of a decolonial feminism is to challenge the categorical logic that identifies colonized women as "not women" due to how gender has been constructed within a Eurocentric capitalist ideology, Lugones argues that a decolonial feminist praxical methodology necessarily entails "a lived transformation of the social."[4] In this account, decolonial feminism identifies the need for a resistant epistemic shift in how we understand concepts infused within a colonial framework. Moreover, a decolonial feminist framework emphasizes the importance of the transformation of the social, which enables resistant subjectivities to connect with other culturally differently situated subjectivities within a social realm.

In the following discussion, I draw out the decolonial aspects in the analysis of home-making, world-traveling, and the space-between in feminist theory with three important theorists/activists (Kimberlé Crenshaw, Bernice Johnson Reagon, and Gloria Anzaldúa) who have made significant contributions to developing a theory of intersectionality. In examining these three theorists, I highlight the tension of home animating their discussions of intersectionality and draw out the decolonial feminist commitments in attempting to reconfigure feminist political conceptions of solidarity. This will play an important part in situating my later attempts in reconceiving the positive critical value of home within a transnational context. More specifically, Crenshaw and Reagon wrestle with a notion of home as a place (which can be confining) and offer the negation of home (not at home) as a way of resisting the limitations of home. However, in leaving home, Crenshaw and Reagon envision another kind of home that seeks social transformation and hence does not completely abandon the notion of home. Anzaldúa brings together this tension of home and underscores the process of social transformation in her understanding of the borderlands.

Crenshaw's important contribution in critical race theory includes an analysis of the intersection of race and gender. In "Mapping the Margins: Intersectionality, Identity Politics, and Violence against Women of Color," Crenshaw examines the intersections of race and gender and shows how a singular approach in understanding identity fails to address the complexities of the lives of women of color in the context of violence. While identity politics serves as a way of recognizing the social constructedness of identities, it nonetheless "conflates or ignores intragroup differences."[5] For women of color, this conflation of their multiple race and gender identities resulted in political and social inequities, which rendered situations of domestic violence invisible and unintelligible in a social and political system that was meant precisely to help women in situations of violence. For example, according to Crenshaw, intersectional subordination uniquely manifests for immigrant women who may depend on their spouse for information and are vulnerable to a type of spousal abuse in the form of threats of deportation. In addition, language barriers present an institutional barrier for immigrant women to seek out the necessary support services they may need to escape their situation of violence. Failing to understand how other factors, such as race or citizenship status, have the damaging effect of rendering the experiences of domestic violence among immigrant women as invisible and unintelligible.

Crenshaw understands an intersectional framework also to "mediate the tension between assertions of multiple identity and the ongoing necessity of group politics."[6] An interesting element in Crenshaw's notion of intersectionality is that categories, such as woman or Asian or middle class, need not be stripped of all meaning as they can serve an important function in coalitional politics. While these categories have been created by power and used to marginalize groups, the problem with these categories is not their existence but "the particular values attached to them and the way those values foster and create social hierarchies."[7] Thus, Crenshaw views categories of identity as sites of agency in which subordinated groups "can and do exert in the politics of naming."[8] Rather than eliminate the categories of identities, Crenshaw believes that a source of agency for subordinated groups would "defend a politics of social location."[9]

Her defense for the importance of social location seems curious after she systematically exposes the rigidities of social identities, which leave women of color who occupy multiple social locations vulnerable to structural inequities and violence. So what do group identities amount to, for Crenshaw? Ultimately, Crenshaw views categories of identities as "coalitions, or at least potential coalitions waiting to be formed."[10] Rather than view identities as rigid and fixed, identities are formed as multiple and intersecting social collectives. In the context of anti-racist politics, intersectionality would reconceptualize race as a coalitional concept for both men and women of color rather than as an inert, fixed identity. Understanding identity as a coalitional concept emphasizes that the agency of subordinated groups in determining the meaning of their identities is an *active* process that negotiates the multiple and intersecting aspects of their social identities.

According to Crenshaw, a coalitional identity understands social group identities as "'home' to us, in the name of the parts of us that are not made at home."[11] Here Crenshaw seems to shift between a notion of home as a place that may be confining for those who are marginalized and a notion of home as a coalition that entails a sense of possibility and a process of becoming. The sense of being not "at home" assumes an encounter with differently situated others in a social group. Intersectionality highlights the space-between, which requires "a great deal of energy and arouses much anxiety."[12] It is a social space created at sites where identities intersect or encounter one another. This differs from the notion of home as a place from which one must depart, which assumes that home is a fixed geographic location. In fact, Crenshaw highlights the sense of home as a flexible ideal of belonging, an imaginative space that seeks to make the necessary connections between diverse social actors. Home, in this sense, reveals a sense of liminality, of betweenness, that invites potential coalitions and connections to be made.

Bernice Johnson Reagon, in her speech at the 1981 West Coast Women's Music Festival in Yosemite, takes a more critical approach to the notion of home, as she pares down the notion of home to a "barred room." While the barred room initially is a nurturing place in which one's sense of self is developed in a community, the barred room also functions as an exclusive place. "In fact, in that little barred room where you check everybody at the door, you act out community."[13] Community grounds one's identity through acts of exclusion. The only way in which "coalescing" can be done is to open these barred rooms, allowing those who are different to one's community to enter and mingle within the barred room. At this point, Reagon observes, "And it ain't home no more. It is not a womb no more. And you can't feel comfortable no more."[14] Coalescing is a process that seeks a disruption of home. Those who were "outsiders" to one's community now disrupt the nurturing space of home. The home that served as a ground for one's identity is uprooted and displaced.

However, for Reagon, this sense of displacement, of leaving the womb, is a necessary step in developing coalitions. For Reagon, "Coalition work is not work done in your home."[15] While home may again serve as a limiting concept that prevents the possibility for coalition building, Reagon invites the audience to seek out a liminal space that departs from understanding home as a fixed place in order to develop coalitions. This liminal space that we enter when leaving home is fraught with tension and demands persevering effort. In this sense, commonalities between disparate groups must be created and developed in a social space, rather than intellectually fashioned. The social space is a space of action. The departure from home, from the barred room, need not imply a wholesale rejection of a place of comfort. The departure from home situates the self in between homes, in between identities, in order to form alliances. Thus, leaving home immediately places us in the space-between, which seeks further alliances with others who are culturally and socially different. In this way, Reagon maintains a sense of home as a coalition, as a process that seeks a collective belonging. However, the process of coalition building, of making a home, must be engaged as a place of action.

Coalitions are not fixed centers or closed homes but processes that change the nature of homes. They can serve as "mini-coalitions,"[16] which underscores the tension of belonging that comprises the self's departure from home as well as the need for the self to develop coalitions with others who are differently located. The boundaries of communities represent the space in which belonging is created through effort and where communities are constructed without rigid borders.

In my analysis, I argue that while both Crenshaw and Reagon take a critical stance—in varying degrees—to the notion of home, both their respective approaches to intersectionality and coalition resonate a sense of belonging and a sense of home conceived within a liminal space in between communities and identities. In this space-between, home cannot be conceived as rigid or fixed and hence cannot be wholly viewed as a closed place where one is nurtured and isolated from the social realm. Home motivates our very yearning for belonging. This evokes a reflective process that continually demands one's reinterpretation of the self. The yearning that occurs in the space-between represents the psychological longing for connections between homes in the experience of displacement. I suggest that rather than repress this psychological longing, we embrace it. Gloria Anzaldúa's seminal work *Borderlands/La Frontera: The New Mestiza* offers an embodied experiential account of the space-between in her theory of the borderlands. This theory understands home as both a place of confinement, oppression, and exclusion as well as a place that generates a sense of belonging and establishes temporary homes, open for further interpretations.

Lugones's strategy of world-traveling can be linked to Anzaldúa's theory of border crossing. Opposed to home, travel, according to Lugones, brings us into the realm of the social, the space-between in which the intentionality of the travel places us in direct interaction with culturally different others. In this sense, travel articulates the logic of resistance, an "active subjectivity" that highlights the "traveling of our own against the grain, resistant, oppositional thoughts, movements, gestures among variegated, heterogeneous aggregates of subjects negotiating a life in the tensions of various oppressing-resisting relations."[17] However, home—understood as rigid, fixed, and exclusionary—works against the logic of resistance and is prone to a logic of reification and stability. While Lugones prioritizes the liberating and socially transformative space of travel as opposed to the confining, solid, and permanent space of home, I argue that there are lingering themes of home, which animate Lugones's view of world travel. I establish this perspective through an analysis of home in Anzaldúa's work, which can offer us insight into the movement of Lugones's notion of world-travel.

While Anzaldúa understands borders as a "dividing line" that separates communities, borderlands are a "vague and undetermined place created by the emotional residue of an unnatural boundary."[18] Similar to the experience of being not at home, the inhabitants of the borderlands are "the prohibited and forbidden."[19] The residual emotions of borderlands are fraught with tension and anxiety even as they evoke a sense of yearning for connection. Boundaries viewed within the borderlands appear "unnatural," fictions created by the arrogance of the dominant community's power to name. Borderlands are those physical places that emerge between communities, constantly insisting on an interpretation for their existence.

Nonetheless, the borderlands are homes to those who are multiply oppressed. The "psychic restlessness" that Anzaldúa brings to her audience demands a departure from "the familiar and safe homeground to venture into the unknown and possibly dangerous terrain."[20] Borders may provide a safe haven, much like Reagon's notion of a barred room; however, for those who are multiply oppressed, the displacement is fraught with terror. Anzaldúa dislodges a possible treatment of travel as a touristic act in response to one's banal life. The border crosser is forced to leave home, and this departure reveals the liminal space-between where she lives out of necessity and survival on a "thin edge of barbwire."[21] While borderlands may appear to be antithetical to fixed communities, in my view, borderlands evoke a sense of yearning for connection, which establishes continuities between homes.[22] In viewing the connections of home embedded within the borderlands, the space-between is characterized as a complex relationship of belonging within spaces undergoing constant metamorphic transition. A yearning for stability and home motivates the very desire and/or need to depart and travel. Anzaldúa also describes the borderlands as "in a constant state of transition."[23] This experience manifests in her analysis of *mestizaje*, the process of "continual intermarriage between Mexican and American Indians and Spaniards."[24] This process ultimately created a new race, *la raza nueva.* The process of *mestizaje* formed under conditions of contact and encounter with "gold-hungry conquistadors and soul-hungry missionaries from Mexico," who came along with many mestizos and Indians to the American Southwest. While Anzaldúa highlights the kind of colonial travel enacted by conquistadors and missionaries, she also identifies the return of many Indians to their homeland, Aztlán. This return made Chicanos "secondarily indigenous to the Southwest."[25] The return to the "homeland" is important as it incorporates a mode of travel that maintains a sense of home through seeking to sustain otherwise lost cultural centers. The process of *mestizaje* ensures that the "Indian heritage" remains in Mexico and the U.S. Southwest despite the persistence of colonialism. However, these lost cultural centers are considerably transformed because of this process of interaction. This historical interpretation of colonization and return to the homeland anticipates her theory of the self at the borderlands.

In examining notions of the self at the borderlands, many theorists have commented extensively on Anzaldúa's notion of the self as *Coatlicue*, *la facultad*, *la Llorona*, or *mestiza consciousness*, but to my knowledge, no one has commented on the image of herself as the turtle. In characterizing the movement of resistance, she explains the nature of her departure from "home" as follows:

> I was totally immersed *en lo mexicano*, a rural, peasant isolated *mexicanismo*. To separate from my culture (as from my family) I had to feel competent enough on the outside and secure enough inside to live life on my own. Yet in leaving home I did not lose touch with my origins because *lo mexicano* is in my system. I am a turtle, wherever I go I carry "home" on my back.[26]

The turtle image represents her confidence to rebel and criticize her culture because *lo mexicano* pervades her identity. This embodied commitment to her culture will not disappear simply because she leaves her home. Her notion of travel retains this sense of her culture, which anchors her voyages outside of her culture to a sense of place and community within the borderlands. These anchored voyages establish, on the one hand, continuity between her "home" community and the "outside." On the other hand, carrying her home on her back also characterizes her reflective process as interactive, where she is able to "live life on her own" through skills that involve "being secure" of her identity at "home" as well as having competency in the outside world. The sense of home the turtle represents continually reexamines one's community in the hope of transforming it.

Interestingly, this process of interaction she emphasizes is also characterized by her "fear in going home" because she criticizes her cultural traditions, that is, those that enslave women. However, her criticism of her culture does not mean she is disloyal to her cultural community, since she is able to "defend" her culture from non-Mexicans. Anzaldúa's sense of home connotes an embodied dimension in the fact that home, her commitments to community, are something she can never easily dispense with. Her travels are not characterized as autonomous, individual acts of movement but as being anchored to her community. This prevents her from fully identifying with culturally different others because "every sinew and cartilage" of her body is permeated by "home."[27] Her criticism of her culture is spatially represented at the margins of home, which requires her "leaving home" in attempting to ultimately transform her cultural home.

Anzaldúa's use of the turtle reminds the audience of home as a nurturing place that can also breed oppression, demanding an inevitable departure.

However, the departure also represents the possibility that homes can be transformed by recognizing the borderlands as an interactive place, which invite unknown and possibly dangerous encounters with differently situated others. These perilous spaces establish a sense of continuity between communities and enable social transformation to take place. Anzaldúa represents this temporary psychic state of connection in the following way:[28]

> It passes through my body and comes out of the other side. I collapse into myself—a delicious caving into myself—imploding, the walls like matchsticks softly folding inward in slow motion. . . . Not the heterosexual white man's or the colored man's or the state's or the culture's or the religion's or the parents'—just ours, mine.[29]

The self is multiply harmonizing into a pluralistic rhythm, slowly engaging the various supports of the encounter at the borderlands. The transformation is characterized initially as a sense of the self being blocked by the confining forces of home as a place. However, Anzaldúa articulates a process that "passes through her body." The "walls" of her identity cave in as a new self is formed. There is a sense in which the experience of transformation entails that selves are separated and fractured, and yet these chasms are overcome by a creation of a new identity that harmonizes the various aspects of the self. Coalition emerges as a new identity that involves a transformation of the self. It does not dispense with a notion of home but seeks a vital transformation of it: "And suddenly I feel everything rushing to a center, a nucleus. All the lost pieces of myself come flying from the deserts and mountains and the valleys, magnetized toward that center. *Completa*."[30] Anzaldúa seeks to bring together the various aspects of her experiences. This sense of a center, a nucleus, or a home perhaps exists in the space between homes. It represents not just a place but an unrepressible psychic space created by the yearning for a sense of belonging, for a new interpretation between communities. It is the felt presence of the space-between that animates the condition for the possibility of conceiving larger communities.[31]

Crenshaw, Reagon, and Anzaldúa recognize the importance of home despite the inevitable departures from it. Both Crenshaw and Reagon identify the notion of home as confining and hence a place from which to depart. While it may appear as a place of nurturance, home, as a place, cannot ground coalitions. Hence the notion of "not at home" becomes a place in which coalitions may be constructed. However, "not at home" implies another sense of home as a process of becoming, a possible future where coalitions are formed. Anzaldúa identifies the phenomenological experience that captures the notion of home not only as a limiting condition but also as a process that envisions the formation of new identities within a social collective. It is not fixed or closed but conceived as a reflective process that establishes "mini-coalitions" or "transitory homes" that enable the possibility for multiple communities to remain connected. Instances of travel indicate possibilities for new connections, new relationships, and thus serve as a way of thinking about transnational communities.

WORLD-TRAVELING AND THE PROCESS OF HOME-MAKING

Given the importance of home in thinking about coalitions, I seek to highlight the element of "home-making" in an examination of "world-traveling." In my view, underscoring the notion of home-making reveals how the project of world-traveling has become an important theoretical resource in thinking about feminist coalitional politics. Since Lugones's important paper calling for feminists to "playfully world-travel" in order to bridge the social and cultural differences between women, many feminists have incorporated this concept in projects addressing pluralism.

The project of world-traveling, as Lugones understands it, pays attention to the social.[32] The social assumes that knowledge is partial and that meaning emerges within a shared encounter with others rather than assuming that isolated individual experiences have a more reliable access to knowledge. Standards of meaning must be mutually cultivated. It seems almost impossible to develop a notion of world-traveling prior to any encounter with culturally different others. Moreover, Lugones understands her notion of travel within the experiences of those who are subordinated, in which they practice world-traveling every day. This does not assume a mere perceptual shift in individual states of consciousness to distant cultures or to distant social experiences. These perceptual shifts are predicated on actual experiences of engaging with culturally different others within a space-between that occupies multiply located subjectivities. The partiality of knowledge assumes that individual experiences only reveal a limited view of the social interaction. This recognition of a lack of knowledge should guide inquiry into the ontological space-between, which demands that one actually engages with differently situated others and mutually constitutes meaning.

In extending our notions of world-travel within the space of migration and diasporic identities, Falguni Sheth frames the space of migration within notions of intersectionality through a method of interstitiality.[33] For Sheth, interstitiality considers the transnational political context that is comprised of political and legal exclusions, histories of colonization and intra group identity formation. In this sense, interstiality examines how the self fluidly navigates multiple axes of oppression and thus consequently constructs conceptions of resistance. Understanding the space-between informed by an interstitial methodology reveals the complex relationships migrants may have to notions of home. Moreover, understanding the transnational space as a material expression of the coloniality of power is essential in reconfiguring the tenuous relationships that occur for many migrant subjectivities caught in between the maze of colonial laws, state regulations of the host country, as well as the generational customs of one's homeland, which also has been historically conceived by colonial histories.

In this sense, Yen Li Espiritu's work with Filipino American communities discloses a nuanced sense of the ontological space-between. Situating her notion of home within a transnation, interstitial, and decolonial framework, Espiritu challenges Americanist narratives of immigration, which articulate migratory impulses and patterns through a unidirectional and linear process of assimilation culminating in citizenship. By contrast, Espiritu highlights global relationships of the nation-state through migration, and critically reminds us of the history of the U.S. colonization in the Philippines that has informed the national identities of the Philippines and the United States. Many of the Filipino Americans Espiritu has interviewed "regardless of their regional or class origins, have kept ties with family, friends, and colleagues in the Philippines through occasional visits, telephone calls, remittances, and medical and other humanitarian missions. In doing so, they have created and maintained fluid and multiple identities that link them simultaneously to both cultures."[34] In this way, her account of the space-between is animated by a complex appreciation of being "homebound"—an imaginative process in which Filipinos are "bound for home, and they are also bound to and by home."[35] Being "homebound," in this dual sense, centers one's imaginative mental world-traveling to actual commitments one may have to one's country of origin or sense of home. Espiritu understands the immigrants' notion of home as "not only a physical place that immigrants return to for temporary and intermittent visits but also a concept and a desire—a place that immigrants visit through the imagination."[36] Hence, there is a literal (in the sense of material interactions through travel and communication) and a symbolic (in the sense of self-identification) aspect in thinking about the process of migration that defines the kind of transnational framework informing Espiritu's research.[37] It should be noted that Espiritu links her transnationalism to a critique of the history of U.S. imperialism in the Philippines.

The Filipino American experience of the space-between understands Asian American identity, particularly Filipino American identity, as one of exclusion.[38] However, Espiritu sees Filipino American identity constituted largely by what she terms as *differential inclusion*. Filipinos were understood as U.S. nationals, however, not as citizens. They were allowed to enlist in the Navy or to work in the United States as cheap labor, but they could not vote. Unlike with other Asian immigrants, such as the Chinese, the U.S. hostile takeover of the Philippines created an atmosphere in which Filipinos were not alien, but were, nonetheless, excluded from the benefits of U.S. citizenship. Because of this history, Filipinos were already actively engaged in making the United States a home for them to "return" to. Seeing how the processes of U.S. colonization actually constitute this identity is important in understanding how Filipino Americans have envisioned the home-making process in America.

The experience of Filipino immigrants has been described as transnational, not only because U.S. empire building initiated this transnational link but also because Filipino Americans seem persistently to "carry their home on their backs." To return home or to leave home can be a literal or physical act, as well as one that takes place in one's imagination. Home functions like a geographical point of analysis insofar as a sense of place becomes an important feature in the process of making a home. This becomes an interesting image given the complicated nature of home. Home can be exclusionary, especially if one is a Filipino daughter living in America with conservative Filipino parents or if one is homosexual. For many Filipino American families, a resistant identity is formed in opposition to an American racist culture. In reasserting their cultural identity in resistance to a hegemonic host culture, many Filipino American families reinscribe patriarchal values within the family home.[39] Nonetheless, as Espiritu argues, the notion of home is a site of tension and conflict between the desire for belonging (and not necessarily linked to origin) and the dangers that risk the consummation of this desire. It is interesting that Espiritu does not resolve this conflict but accepts this tension and seeks a curative path for one to "make a home" in relationship to the "departure from home." By doing this, she underscores a continuity between leaving and creating a new space, a space in between, for creative social relationships and communities to emerge.

Moreover, rather than understanding Filipino displacement in terms of "enforced homelessness," Espiritu seeks to reassert a notion of home that many Filipinos have articulated "by memorializing the homeland and by building on familial and communal ties."[40] Quoting Rosemary George, Espiritu argues, "imagining a home is as political an act as is imagining a nation."[41] The commemoration of home signifies a process that defines one's identity and builds communities despite geographical distances. Espiritu argues: "Memory of place is significant because it helps to locate the individual in a community, to bind family members together, and to shape personal identity."[42] According to Espiritu, ties to the homeland through memory are important not only because they serve as a "lifeline" for many immigrants, which form the basis of their group identity, but they also serve as a source that guides the ways in which they build communities and stake their political commitments in their host country.[43] In this sense, Espiritu conceives Filipino American identities within a tension of home, "between the necessity and inevitability of a desire for 'home' and the accompanying dangers of that desire."[44]

Home-making places the subject within a process of social interaction as immigrants carefully create a home in their host country, while remaining insistently homebound in their country of origin. Rather than view home as an unproblematic geographic location, Espiritu seeks to politicize geography by underscoring the realities that "belonging and origin"[45] are not always the same thing. This kind of imaginative journey to distant countries is not abstract but part of the lived experience of those who live in-between nations. Home-making as a concept in social and political life underscores the ways in which the social is realized when one "world-travels."

"WORLD-TRAVELING" AND "HOME-MAKING": THE POLITICS OF BELONGING IN FEMINIST COALITIONAL COMMUNITIES

My analysis in the previous section should not suggest that world-traveling (or home-making) is a skill that is available to only immigrants and other subordinated, less privileged groups. In fact, Lugones makes it clear that white, privileged feminists should practice world-traveling in order to address what Maríana Ortega identifies as their "loving, knowing ignorance."[46] According to Ortega, the "loving, knowing ignorance" attempts to theorize "about women of color without checking and questioning about their actual lives, without actively trying to participate in their actual lives, without knowing any flesh-and-blood women of color, or without practical engagement with them."[47] Ortega reminds privileged feminists of their fear of "plurality that emerges when encountering women of color."[48] This fear of plurality can also be understood as a fear of home-making. In this sense, privileged feminists ignore the messiness of home-making that is corollary to world-traveling. This involves staking one's political and social commitments in pluralistic encounters with culturally different others. This might entail critically examining one's location of privilege. According to Ortega, feminism becomes an imagined homeland for many women of color because white feminists have guarded the doors of feminism.[49] In this sense, the felt and actual displacement guides the criticisms of women of color, such as Ortega's, to encourage white, privileged feminists to actually engage, not just theoretically include, the concerns of women of color. This situates privileged feminist subjectivities in the space-between, the pluralistic encounters, which places their own theoretical homes in actual encounters with women of color. The yearning, which animates the feminist homeland of Ortega, is conceived as one in process, constantly being remade by differently situated feminist subjectivities.

In this sense, world-traveling is not just a shift in individual states of minds to distant cultures or social experiences but also a method that produces heterogeneity or a plurality of selves, in which to resist the traditional notion of the self as an underlying "I." The boundaries that define the traditional notion of a substantial "I" is rigid and fixed and thus incapable of seeing the possibility of travel as a self-transformative endeavor. In contrast, world-traveling can also be seen as a method of appealing to a "togetherness or continuity"[50] of the self, as Ortega suggests. The world-traveler self need not assume a "driver," a "conductor," or a substantial unified "I" systematizing one's experience. This sense of togetherness manifests when Lugones recognizes that in the process of world-traveling, the "I" in one world is different than the "I" in another world. This recognition of difference need not assume a fractured sense of the self. The recognition of difference stimulates a critical reflective process in understanding the continuity of the "I" that similarly is recognized in both worlds. Ortega views the world-traveler self as one that falls between a traditional model of subjectivity, which posits a unified knower as well as a radically fractured subject, lacking any kind of cohesive subjectivity. This sense of the world-traveler self possesses a sense of home-making that has more to do with a process of becoming, seeking unity within cross-cultural encounters rather than assuming antecedent to the interaction shared traits or social experiences. The world-traveler self's sense of unity is lived and practiced. Given the experience of heterogeneity and plurality, the self's reinterpretation requires located and situated instances of travel in the process of home-making. It is in this practical sense that world-traveling offers a path to solidarity.

I have argued that world-traveling and the particular sense of home articulated by Yen Li Espiritu open up new avenues for feminist coalitional politics and solidarity. This is important as I further examine the positive critical value of home within a transnational and decolonial context. Iris Marion Young and Alison Weir consider the notion of home as a metaphor for feminist politics. While feminist theorists have previously thought about home as a site of exclusion and oppression for marginalized subjects, both Young and Weir advocate for a positive critical value of home that is able to ground one's identity and become a source of social criticism. I also advocate for a positive critical value of home. I extend this analysis of home within a transnational context. I emphasize a "return to home" in order to characterize the tension of belonging that emerges from feminist critics who view home as a limiting condition of one's freedom.

Young argues that "home carries a core positive meaning as the material anchor for a sense of agency and shifting and fluid identity."[51] Home identifies more than an abstract ideal but the lived experience of being at home, which involves the concrete materiality of one's belongings. Though

Young agrees that homes can be exclusionary, she refers to hooks's notion of "homeplace" as a site of resistance for oppressed subjects. Hence, Young argues that while homes may be considered markers of privilege and exclusion, the proper response should not reject home but "extend its positive values to everyone."[52] She identifies four positive critical values of home as (1) safety, (2) individuation, (3) privacy, and (4) preservation. In this sense, Young understands home as a mode of belonging while critically asserting one's agency within relations of power.

Weir attempts to destabilize dichotomies of home/not home in thinking about the metaphor of home in feminist politics. She extends Young's critical values of home and articulates complementary values of (1) sustaining connection through conflict, (2) relational identities mutually constituted through relations of power and love and flourishing, (3) relational autonomy through the tension of being in relationships and seeking self-expansion, and (4) connection to past and future through a reinterpretive preservation and transformative identification. Weir first understands safety as experienced by a risk of connection with others. Encounters with others are fraught with conflict, struggle, and tension. However, according to Weir, "an ideal of home as the space where we risk connection might help us set clear limits on conflict and risk, so that these do not develop into violence."[53] Weir also highlights that home emphasizes personal relationships and connection to others rather than individual or collective ownership of property.[54] Drawing on Willet's work on Fredrick Douglass, Weir highlights the alternative notion of freedom ensconced within Douglass's "childhood home, he shared with his grandmother, a source of a social and ethical force he calls 'spirit.' "[55]

Weir further continues developing a relational account of home by extending Young's conception of preservation beyond just individual and collective preservation of histories. Weir argues that Young's retelling of her mother's story in order to preserve her memory and her critique of "the social values of motherhood, orderly housework, and PTA [Parent Teacher Association] motherhood oppress women, especially single mothers"[56] participates in affirmations of preservation that "connects her to her mother, and holds herself together in a way that is redemptive."[57] Weir's analysis of home attempts to "combine the conscious assumption of oppression that [has] shaped us with the affirmation of belonging, and the transformation of the future."[58] For Weir then, preservation is about transforming existing relationships toward better future ones. This involves a process of transformative identification: "Through reinterpretive preservation we transform ourselves, and hold ourselves together, through struggle, and without denying any of the suffering and tragedy this entails."[59] Weir ultimately grounds home ontologically within a "space between" in her understanding of home as one constituted relationally, emphasizing connectivity and personal relationships.

In drawing out the positive values of home within a transnational context, I extend Young's and Weir's analysis that the positive critical value of home can also be conceived within this complex appreciation of being homebound, which involves the notion of a "return to home." As Young points out, "In giving up the idea of home, feminism is consistently postcolonial, exposing the illusion of a coherent stable self or a unified movement of women."[60] Interpreting Bonnie Honig, Young notes, to long for a home means a retreat to a solid unified identity.[61] Espiritu, too, is concerned about a problematic nostalgia of a "home country," that "elides exclusion, power relations, and difference or when it elicits a desire to replicate these inequities as a means to buttress lost status and identities in the adopted country."[62] The implication of this argument is that home can never be understood as a positive critical value in order to advance decolonial and feminist aims. Postcolonial feminism tends to be concerned of the very longing for home, which emphasizes a rigidly idealized notion of the self and consequently risks the repression of identities that are marginalized or threaten the stability of home. Moreover, diasporic identities in navigating the series of exclusions of their adopted country may project a desire for home, which may reify exclusions and oppressive practices of one's home in order to reassert his or her resistance against a hostile host country.[63] Hence, as Young points out as well, many feminist theorists focus on displacement and decentered identities rather than finding home as a liberatory value. Though I agree that the risk of home in postcolonial and diasporic contexts of migration can be experienced as dangerous and potentially reify homogenous and fixed identities, I do think there is a positive critical value of home that can advance the aims of transnational and postcolonial feminism. Following Weir's suggestion of moving beyond the dichotomies of home/not home, I argue that home within a transnational context can be interpreted as a critical value of fluidity, change, and process, whose ontological status is based within an ontology of the space-between.

My reading of Mohanty's conception of home varies from Young's and Weir's interpretation of Mohanty's work. Young understands Mohanty's and Martin's work as rejecting home, though I agree with Weir that this interpretation of Mohanty's work does not seem wholly accurate. According to Weir, Mohanty and Martin do not reject home but emphasize the need "to live in tension between home and not home, identity and nonidentity, safety and risk, oscillating back and forth between the two."[64] However, Weir argues that Mohanty and Martin do in fact reduce home to "the maintenance of exclusion and oppression."[65] Weir further argues that while Mohanty and Martin do not reject home, they do not give it a positive characterization since any attempts to desire for home "must be repeatedly undercut by the recognition that the yearned-for safety is illusory, a protection bought at the price of exclusion of others."[66] In this sense, home does not carry a positive critical meaning since it is constantly undermined by the necessity of exclusion and oppression of others in order to maintain its meaning.

While I do think Weir is right that neither Mohanty nor Martin give a concrete characterization of home, I believe that both Mohanty and Martin gesture toward a sense of a "return to home." As I will show, this is especially true in Mohanty's larger work. In thinking about the transnational context of home, it is important to see the positive critical value of the "return to home." Prior to looking at Mohanty's larger work, which I will argue animates a positive notion of home, I want to highlight what a "return to home" means within a transnational context through Espritu's analysis of the return to home and the dual sense of being homebound.

Although Weir recognizes the oscillating back and forth from home/not home theorized by Mohanty and Martin as not a rejection of home, this oscillation, nonetheless, does not adequately characterize a positive critical value of home. However, I argue that the positive critical value of this oscillation is in the "return to home." Espiritu identifies the space-between occupied by Filipino American immigrants as a productive space: "Living between the old and the new, between homes, and between languages, immigrants do not merely insert or incorporate themselves into existing spaces in the United States; they also transform these spaces and create new ones, such as the space-between."[67] Though oscillation occurs between homes, the characterization of home is not constituted by the risk of exclusion and subordination of others. In fact, one of the responses to home that many Filipino Americans tend to enact is a process of home-making, which is "the processes by which diverse subjects imagine and make themselves at home in various geographic locations."[68] Espiritu further comments that "because home making is most often a way of establishing difference and a means of jostling power, homes are much about inclusions and open doors as they are about exclusions and closed doors."[69] From Espiritu's perspective, the space-between can be a productive space in which immigrants are able to insert themselves within a community in the host country. Living in between need not wholly be defined as exclusionary, though the risk is constantly present. Espiritu focuses on the space of encounter across geographical locations and this space of encounter is defined by the process of home-making; the ability to make oneself at home through imaginative connections to the homeland.

Furthermore, although Young acknowledges that while homes may be problematic on many levels, the extension of the critical values of home should be accessible to all. Within a transnational context, Espirtu argues that "all immigrants—regardless of class—can and do return home through the imagination."[70] This statement should recall the turtle image, insistently carrying one's home on her back that represents Anzaldúa's sense of self. The positive critical value of home that all immigrants enact is the return to home. Home is not a concept one dispenses with but one that seeks an active revitalization of it by invoking imaginative reinterpretations of the self through one's connection back to the home, the homeland. In this sense, Espiritu highlights the complex appreciation of being homebound—experienced not only as exclusionary through the maze of laws of the host country and rigid patriarchal norms of the family but also productively in the sense that one is able to make a home by anchoring one's identity to their cultural roots, while also making new homes in the host country. In fact, home-making can be understood as a way for many Filipino American immigrants to survive in the United States as it acts as a lifeline and support in a racist U.S. culture. Hence, one never really leaves home since the anchor that sets one's identity will ensure its eventual return.

Espiritu's argument of the positive value of the return to home, home-making, and homeboundedness that comprises the lives of Filipino Americans resonates well with Young's and Weir's analysis of home, particularly Young's argument about how home is a material connection to one's identity formation and can offer a space by which social criticism can take place. Espiritu makes a strong case of how a return to home can be used to reinvent the status of Filipino Americans or can be used as an assertion of resistance to a U.S. capitalistic and racist culture. *Balikbayan* remittances (home supplies, clothes, food, health care supplies, and monetary support), which make up the bulk of the Philippine's economy, serve as the material belongings that are constantly being exchanged across borders and further express one's condition of identity. Remittances condition the identity of many Filipino Americans ensuring that families in the Philippines are cared for as well as sharing cultural items from their host country. It becomes a site of social criticism and encourages cross-cultural reflection. Moreover, Weir's notion of home as one identifying relationality and connectivity complements Espiritu's notion of being homebound as immigrants carefully negotiate the personal relationships of families, friends, and colleagues in the Philippines through intermittent visits and *balakbayan* remittances. Reinterpretive preservation of one's affirmation of belonging goes beyond a nation-state narrative and is reimagined through narratives of arrival and survival in a new host country. In recognizing this positive critical value of home in Espiritu's work, I draw out the positive inflections of home that animate Chandra Mohanty's work.

CONCLUSION

Locating agency within situated historical places and interactions characterizes Mohanty's sense of the self as "transnational." Similar to Ortega's concern that Western/white feminists engage in "loving, knowing ignorance," Mohanty seeks to challenge the traditional idea that Third world feminism and white feminism are merely situated knowledges, consisting of the "add and stir" method of inclusion. Mohanty agrees with Sylvia Walby's insight that saw her work as a project of solidarity and shared values, one that views feminism as a process of engagement between Western/white feminism and Third World/women of color feminism in defining feminist communities.[71] According to Mohanty, communities are defined as:

> the product of work, of struggle; it is inherently unstable, contextual; it has to be constantly reevaluated in relation to critical political priorities; and it is the product of interpretation, interpretation based on an attention to history, to the concrete.[72]

By understanding experience in the realm of action and engagement as well as place, Mohanty understands the local as an important insight in thinking about the global. Understanding the local and the global in this way does not assume any universal notions of sisterhood or an "experiential 'unity' among women across cultures."[73] This process of relation is what I have been highlighting in this chapter as a process of home-making.

Home-making, for Mohanty, engages in a logic of the space-between in her examination of the state of feminist politics and solidarity. Rather than employing a categorical logic of sameness and stability, a logic of the space-between can be characterized as a logic that recognizes difference and relationality, much like the logic represented in Anzaldúa's *mestiza* consciousness. A recognition that a third or a middle point emerges among divergent entities and a refusal to accept the law of noncontradiction and thus embraces a tolerance of ambiguity characterizes the elements of a logic of the space-between.[74] This particular logic emerges among feminists theorizing about the space-between, the interstitial, and the transnational. The logic of the space-between assumes knowers as actors engaged in the world, rather than knowers independent and merely describing the world. I highlight the logic because it is important to recognize the pattern of rationality as a distinct epistemological vantage point rather than render this type of thinking as irrational or illogical based on the standards of Western rationality. Women of color theorizing in the space-between employ a particular logic that resonates with their complex experiences and is often misunderstood by dominant white feminist theorists. Hence, the logic of the space-between is often concealed within a relationship of epistemic hierarchies that privilege Western modes of rationality.

The process of home-making that is implicit in Mohanty's work operates in the space-between, in the intersections of global, racial, sexual, and capitalistic inequities. Locating the self engaged within these struggles is an act of choice. One chooses to engage in shared struggles with others. Similar to Espiritu, politicizing geography entails that one's home, understood as a sense of belonging, is as much a political act as making a home in a host country. While one's travel or one's place of birth may not be of one's own choosing, placing oneself within relationships of struggle fundamentally centers a sense of belonging and provides a sense of unity of the self despite its fluid foundations. One's subjectivity is understood as cultivating a sense of belonging, which highlights the unity of the subject as anchored within a social collective.

Mohanty's view of the transnational feminist community recognizes that disparate identities are always connected in between our ethical and political mappings of boundaries. In the chapter with Biddy Martin "What's Home Got to Do with It?" in her book *Feminism without Borders*, Mohanty seeks to challenge the notion that homes are absolutely separate, "based on absolute divisions between various sexual, racial or ethnic identities."[75] Reflecting on Minnie Bruce Pratt's essay on the subject of home, Mohanty writes:

> The historical grounding of shifts and changes allows for an emphasis on the pleasures and terrors of interminable boundary confusions, but insists, at the same time, on our responsibility for remapping boundaries and renegotiating connections. These are partial in at least two senses of the word: politically partial, and without claim to wholeness or finality.[76]

According to Mohanty, theorizing experience places theory within the realm of action. The space-between is conceived as acts of choice in which the claims of ethics and politics move the subject to establish connections and remap boundaries. The insistence of the self as an actor creating her location within situated histories and places provides the possibility in which distinct entities will become connected. Understanding choice within a particular location ensures that boundaries will be remapped in a way that establishes connections. Moreover, this sense of connection is partial, never claiming wholeness, finality, and substantiality of the self, mostly because there are infinite ways in which connections and mappings are established. There can be a sense of unity but no claim of a final interpretation for connections, since the middle point insistently emerges between settled identities.

This sense of unity that lacks finality positions Mohanty's transnational subject of feminist coalitional politics as one ascribing to a sense of hope that is cultivated to ensure the possibility for future connections to be remade. The transnational feminist subject provides a more concrete account of the development of the world-traveling self. Through a commitment to home, the transnational feminist subjectivity anchors discussions of the world-traveling self to actual commitments to her community. In in another chapter from *Feminism without Borders*, "Sisterhood, Coalition, and the Politics of Experience," Mohanty commends Reagon's attention to "our strategic locations and positionings."[77] This strategy locates experience within the ethical and political remappings between disparate entities. Mohanty understands the "old-age perspective" Reagon uses as a prescription for coalitional politics as a transnational or cross-cultural perspective.[78] The "old-age" perspective rejects universal abstractions of unity but is "forged on the memories and counternarratives"[79] on the basis of a politics of engagement that opens up the possibility of self-transformation with culturally different others. This demands the skill of humility, "the gradual chipping away of our assumed, often ethnocentric centers of self/other identifications."[80] Mohanty feels this transnational perspective criticizes totalizing "homes" by "going beyond ourselves."[81] Reagon's call of "throwing yourself into the next century,"[82] for Mohanty, is a strategy that demands that selves must go "beyond ourselves" if one is to take up the task of self-knowledge seriously. Understanding difference through this epistemological dislocation does not result in divisions but seeks an interpretation, a remapping of boundaries, that demands the skill of humility, "a disruption of ethnocentric centers of identities."[83]

The practical necessity of an insistent middle that connects disparate entities and the hope, a commitment for the future that connections are maintained, reveals the process of agency, the complex processes of belonging, within the struggles of a social collective. Mohanty writes, "But location, for feminists, necessarily implies self—as well as collective definition, since meanings of the self are inextricably bound up with our understanding of collectives as social agents."[84] She also suggests that the fragmented nature of the self, the world traveler displaced from her home, "must be historicized before it can be generalized into a collective vision."[85] In this way, it makes no sense to understand world-traveling as simply a solo individual activity that is enacted by privileged world-travelers; a corollary concept of home-making must be incorporated in order to highlight how self-definitions are collectively created. Feminist solidarity and struggle must be accompanied by acts of world-travel as well as home-making in order to guide one's act of choice within a politics of location and geography.

Since there is no final destination or place involved in world-traveling and home-making, Mohanty understands the self as a "temporality of struggle," in which the self must move on and ultimately remap further boundaries and connections. Her notion of the self is a continual process of "re-territorialization through struggle that allows me a paradoxical continuity of self, mapping and transforming my political location."[86] Home-making is a process that pays particular attention to the rootedness of the struggle and engagement with multiple commitments in which acts of choice emerge as a process of creation within the space-between. The sense of political agency generated by this concept enables a more grounded interpretation of coalitional communities within the dominant society. Beginning with these specific struggles in mind "anchors" Mohanty's "belief in the future and in the efficacy of struggles for social change."[87]

It is important to understand feminist politics avoiding fancied flights to the worlds of other women relying on natural or sociological universals[88] to sustain solidarity. World-traveling is ultimately an act of home-making in the sense that a return to home should be viewed as politics of engagement and transformation, essential in one's travels. Mohanty's experiences of travel and border-crossing "always provoke reflections of home, identity, and politics."[89] While conceptions of home may foster exclusion and reify colonial and oppressive practices within postcolonial and transnational feminist theorizing thereby motivating an emphasis of travel, disruption and hybridity, a positive critical value of home animates Mohanty's work by understanding the framework of home-making as a reflective process that involves a "return to home." Espiritu's work on home-making presents a positive critical value of home within a transnational context, which emphasizes connections and relationships and envisions the possibility of hope to transform communities. "Throwing yourself in the next century" demands that concerns are not wholly bound up within present differences. Maintaining connections is an act of hope that guides future actions in order to sustain communities.

NOTES

1. Patricia Hill Collins, *Black Feminist Thought: Knowledge, Consciousness, and the Politics of Empowerment* (New York: Routlege Press, 2009), 21.

2. See Suzanne Jaeger, "World-Traveling as a Clinical Methodology for Psychiatric Care," *Philosophy, Psychiatry and Psychology* (2003): 227–31; Sonia Kruks, *Retrieving Experience: Subjectivity and Recognition in Feminist Politics* (Ithaca and London: Cornell University Press, 2001), 153–76; and Christine Sylvester, "African and Western Feminisms: World-Traveling the Tendencies and Possibilities," *Signs* 20 (4) (1995): 941–69.

3. María Lugones, "Toward a Decolonial Feminism," *Hypatia: A Journal of Feminist Philosophy* 25 (2010): 745.

4. Lugones, "Toward a Decolonial Feminism," 76.

5. Kimberlé Williams Crenshaw, "Mapping the Margins: Intersectionality, Identity Politics, and Violence against Women of Color," in *Critical Race Theory: The Key Writings that Formed the Movement*, eds. Kimberlé Crenshaw, Neil Gotanda, Gary Peller, and Kendall Thomas (New York: The New Press, 1995), 357.

6. Crenshaw, "Mapping the Margins," 375.

7. Crenshaw, "Mapping the Margins," 375.

8. Crenshaw, "Mapping the Margins," 375.

9. Crenshaw, "Mapping the Margins," 375.
10. Crenshaw, "Mapping the Margins," 377.
11. Crenshaw, "Mapping the Margins," 377.
12. Crenshaw, "Mapping the Margins," 377.
13. Bernice Johnson Reagon, "Coalition Politics: Turning the Century," in *Home Girls: A Black Feminist Anthology*, ed. Barbara Smith (New York: Kitchen Table: Women of Color Press, 1983), 358.
14. Reagon, "Coalition Politics," 359.
15. Reagon, "Coalition Politics," 359.
16. Rosemary Marangoly George, *The Politics of Home: Postcolonial Relocations and Twentieth-Century Fiction* (Cambridge, UK: Cambridge University Press, 1996), 33.
17. María Lugones, *Pilgrimages/Peregrinajes: Theorizing Coalition against Multiple Oppressions* (Lanham, MD: Rowman and Littlefield, 2003), 7.
18. Gloria Anzaldúa, *Borderlands/La Frontera: The New Mestiza* (San Francisco: Aunt Lute Books, 1999), 25.
19. Anzaldúa, *Borderlands/La Frontera*, 25.
20. Anzaldúa, *Borderlands/La Frontera*, 35.
21. Anzaldúa, *Borderlands/La Frontera*, 35.
22. In Lugones's essay, "On Borderlands/La Frontera: An Interpretive Essay," she is concerned with a reading of Anzaldúa's sense of crossing-over as a solitary act. However, she argues, "If rebellion and creation are understood as processes rather than as acts, then each act of solitary rebellion and creation is anchored in and responsive to a collective, even if disorganized, process of resistance." See Lugones, "On Borderlands/La Frontera: An Interpretive Essay," *Hypatia: A Journal for Feminist Philosophy* 7 (1992): 36. I view this dual response of resistance and creation as a process of home-making, which highlights the continuity of the self who border crosses through a process of interpreting and revising communities.
23. Anzaldúa, *Borderlands/La Frontera*, 25.
24. Anzaldúa, *Borderlands/La Frontera*, 27.
25. Anzaldúa, *Borderlands/La Frontera*, 27.
26. Anzaldúa, *Borderlands/La Frontera*, 43.
27. Anzaldúa, *Borderlands/La frontera*, 43.
28. I thank Maríana Ortega for pointing this out to me at the First Annual Latina Feminism Roundtable held at John Carroll University, April 2004.
29. Anzaldúa, *Borderlands/La Frontera*, 73.
30. Anzaldúa, *Borderlands/La Frontera*, 73.
31. In articulating the activity of traveling, Lugones acknowledges a sense of home, such as a turtle, but one that does not submit to reification or permanency. "The 'carrying media' for their traveling are by no means permanently and solidly in place. Rather, they are always metamorphosing and in need of attention, the kind of attention that enables us to see deeply into the social. 'They' cannot be reified" (Lugones, *Pilgrimages/Peregrinajes*, 7).
32. Lugones, *Pilgrimages/Peregrinajes*, 20.

33. Falguni Sheth, "Interstitiality: Making Space for Migration, Diaspora and Racial Complexity." *Hypatia: A Journal for Feminist Philosophy* 29 (2014): 75–93.

34. Yen Li Espiritu, *Home Bound: Filipino American Lives across Cultures, Communities, and Countries* (Berkeley: University of California Press, 2003), 10.

35. Espiritu, *Home Bound*, 22.

36. Espiritu, *Home Bound*, 10.

37. Espiritu, *Home Bound*, 11.

38. Lisa Lowe, *Immigrant Acts: On Asian American Cultural Politics* (Durham, NC: Duke University Press, 1999).

39. It is not clear whether Espiritu understands the development of these patriarchal family value norms emerging from the Philippines due to U.S. colonization, but she clearly links these patriarchal family value norms to the model minority immigrant myth in the United States. Filipinas can express better values of femininity and hence are better models of women—even better than the white women—because their gendered cultural values of collectivism, rather than individualism, expect Filipina women to be more chaste, self-effacing, and subservient to male dominance. However, according to Espiritu, the immigrant resistance in this case produces a paradox in which placing heavy restrictions on Filipina immigrant daughters tends to "reinforce patriarchal power and gendered oppression by hinging ethnic and racial pride on the performance of female subordination" (Espiritu, *Home Bound*, 216).

40. Espiritu, *Home Bound*, 14.

41. Espiritu, *Home Bound*, 14.

42. Espiritu, *Home Bound*, 14.

43. Espiritu, *Home Bound*, 14.

44. Espiritu, *Home Bound*, 15.

45. Espiritu, *Home Bound*, 15.

46. Maríana Ortega, "Being Lovingly, Knowingly Ignorant: White Feminism and Women of Color," *Hypatia: A Journal for Feminist Philosophy* 21 (2006): 68.

47. Ortega, "Being Lovingly, Knowingly Ignorant," 68.

48. Ortega, "Being Lovingly, Knowingly Ignorant," 68.

49. Ortega, "Being Lovingly, Knowingly Ignorant," 71.

50. Maríana Ortega, "'New Mestizas,' 'World-Travelers,' and '*Dasein*': Phenomenology and the Multi-voiced, Multi-cultural Self," *Hypatia: A Journal for Feminist Philosophy* 16 (2001): 16.

51. Iris Marion Young, *On Female Body Experience: "Throwing Like a Girl" and Other Essays* (New York: Oxford University Press, 2005), 149.

52. Young, *On Female Body Experience*, 149.

53. Alison Weir, *Identities and Freedom: Feminist Theory between Power and Connection* (New York: Oxford University Press, 2013), 49.

54. Weir, *Identities and Freedom*, 57.

55. Weir, *Identities and Freedom*, 57.

56. Weir, *Identities and Freedom*, 60.

57. Weir, *Identities and Freedom*, 60.

58. Weir, *Identities and Freedom*, 60.

59. Weir, *Identities and Freedom*, 60.
60. Young, *On Female Body Experience*, 148.
61. Young, *On Female Body Experience*, 148.
62. Espiritu, *Home Bound*, 15.
63. See note 40 for further discussion of Filipino parents placing restrictions on their daughters.
64. Chandra Mohanty, *Feminism without Borders: Decolonizing Theory, Practicing Solidarity* (Durham: Duke University Press, 2003), 47–48.
65. Mohanty, *Feminism without Borders*, 48.
66. Mohanty, *Feminism without Borders*, 48.
67. Espiritu, *Home Bound*, 10.
68. Espiritu, *Home Bound*, 2.
69. Espiritu, *Home Bound*, 2.
70. Espiritu, *Home Bound*, 11.
71. Mohanty, *Feminism without Borders*, 224.
72. Mohanty, *Feminism without Borders*, 104.
73. Mohanty, *Feminism without Borders*, 120.
74. Anzaldua, *Borderlands/La Frontera*, 99–113.
75. Mohanty, *Feminism without Borders*, 86.
76. Mohanty, *Feminism without Borders*, 87.
77. Mohanty, *Feminism without Borders*, 118.
78. Mohanty, *Feminism without Borders*, 119.
79. Mohanty, *Feminism without Borders*, 119.
80. Mohanty, *Feminism without Borders*, 119.
81. Mohanty, *Feminism without Borders*, 119.
82. Reagon, "Coalition Politics," 365.
83. Mohanty, *Feminism without Borders*, 119.
84. Mohanty, *Feminism without Borders*, 122.
85. Mohanty, *Feminism without Borders*, 122.
86. Mohanty, *Feminism without Borders*, 122.
87. Mohanty, *Feminism without Borders*, 123.
88. Mohanty sees sociological universals in the same way as natural universals. According to Mohanty, "secondary sociological universals" bind "women together in an ahistorical notion of the sameness of their oppression and, consequently, the sameness of struggles" (Mohanty, *Feminism without Borders*, 112).
89. Mohanty, *Feminism without Borders*, 135.

BIBLIOGRAPHY

Anzaldúa, Gloria. *Borderlands/La frontera: The New Mestiza*. San Francisco: Aunt Lute Books, 1999.

Collins, Patricia Hill. *Black Feminist Thought: Knowledge, Consciousness, and the Politics of Empowerment*. New York: Routledge Press, 2008.

Crenshaw, Kimberlé William. "Mapping the Margins: Intersectionality, Identity Politics, and Violence against Women of Color." In *Critical Race Theory: The Key*

Writings that Formed the Movement, eds. Kimberlé Crenshaw, Neil Gotanda, Gary Peller, and Kendall Thomas, 357–83. New York: The New Press, 1995.

Espiritu, Yen Li. *Home Bound: Filipino American Lives across Cultures, Communities, and Countries*. Berkeley: University of California Press, 2003.

George, Rosemary Marangoly. *The Politics of Home: Postcolonial Relocations and Twentieth-Century Fiction*. Cambridge, UK: Cambridge University Press, 1996.

hooks, bell. *Outlaw Culture: Resisting Representations*. New York: Routledge Press, 1994.

Lowe, Lisa. *Immigrant Acts: On Asian American Cultural Politics*. Durham, NC: Duke University Press, 1999.

Lugones, María. "On Borderlands/La Frontera: An Interpretive Essay." *Hypatia: A Journal for Feminist Philosophy* 7 (1992): 31–37.

———. *Pilgrimages/Peregrinajes: Theorizing Coalition against Multiple Oppressions*. Lanham, MD: Rowman and Littlefield, 2003.

———. "Toward a Decolonial Feminism." *Hypatia: A Journal of Feminist Philosophy* 25 (2010): 742–59.

Mohanty, Chandra. *Feminism without Borders: Decolonizing Theory, Practicing Solidarity*. Durham: Duke University Press, 2003.

Ortega, Maríana. "'New Mestizas,' 'World-travelers,' and '*Dasein*': Phenomenology and the Multi-voiced, Multi-cultural Self." *Hypatia: A Journal for Feminist Philosophy* 16 (2001): 1–29.

———. "Being Lovingly, Knowingly Ignorant: White Feminism and Women of Color." *Hypatia: A Journal for Feminist Philosophy* 21 (2006): 56–74.

Reagon, Bernice Johnson. "Coalition Politics: Turning the Century." In *Home Girls: A Black Feminist Anthology*, ed. Barbara Smith, 343–56. New York: Kitchen Table: Women of Color Press, 1983.

Sheth, Falguni. "Interstitiality: Making Space for Migration, Diaspora and Racial Complexity." *Hypatia: A Journal for Feminist Philosophy* 29 (2014): 75–93.

Weir, Alison. *Identities and Freedom: Feminist Theory between Power and Connection*. New York: Oxford University Press, 2013.

Young, Iris Marion. *On Female Body Experience: "Throwing Like a Girl" and Other Essays*. New York: Oxford University Press, 2005.

Chapter 7

The Special Plight of Women Refugees

Kelly Oliver

Feminism is a contested space. Because different people using the term have varying interests, the meaning, focus, and aims of feminism are context dependent. Challenges from women of color to mainstream white, middle-class feminism developed first out of the women's suffrage movement and then out of the civil rights movement in the United States and the United Kingdom have made it clear that not all women share the same problems, solutions, and goals. More recently, attention to issues of intersectionality, global feminisms, and Indigenous women's voices has further complicated feminism. Feminism has become feminisms, and universal or essentialist notions of woman have given way to the necessity of attending to the particular material, historical, cultural, and geographical situations of different groups of women.

In addition to these crucial challenges and alternatives to a certain feminism that claimed to be universal—in particular, feminism based on liberal notions of universal rights for autonomous individuals—conservative politicians have coopted feminism as justification for war. In the name of liberating "women of cover," former President George W. Bush sent troops to Afghanistan and Iraq. As Gayatri Spivak argues, "saving brown women from brown men" has long been a rallying cry of colonialism. The U.S. "occupation" of Iraq was part of a long tradition of colonization in the name of feminism. The irony and tragedy of this perverted form of feminism are that women in Afghanistan and Iraq were much worse off as a result of U.S. intervention. In fact, until the civil war in Syria (in large part a result of U.S. military operations in the region) caused massive exodus of asylum seekers fleeing the violent conflict, most of the refugees arriving in Europe were from Iraq and Afghanistan as a result of both civil wars, again in large part the result of the U.S. invasions. Instead of helping women in these regions, the United States created a steady stream of refugee women escaping violence at home only to encounter more violence en route to a supposed safe haven elsewhere. Overcrowded refugee camps filled with Iraqi and Afghan women and children, who continued to be victims of violence, especially sexual assault. Additionally, they suffered the violence and indignity of inadequate food, water, shelter, and medical care.

In this context, what would it mean to decolonize feminism? In the contemporary literature, the decolonization of feminism is primarily associated with Indigenous feminist movements and Indigenous feminist voices that challenge the hegemony of "whitestream" feminism.[1] Within these discussions, decolonizing feminism is a question of not speaking on behalf of others but listening to others speaking for themselves.[2] For example, in their research in psychology on decolonizing feminism, Tuğçe Kurtis and Glenn Adams conclude: "Although conceived as a universal theory and practice of liberation, scholars across diverse sites have suggested that feminism—perhaps especially as it manifests in psychological science—is not always compatible with and at times even contradictory to global struggles for decolonization."[3] They argue that universal concepts are ill-fitting, even counterproductive, in various contexts; and, moreover, universalist or mainstream "Western, educated, industrialized, rich, democratic" feminists often see women in other parts of the world as powerless victims in need of rescue. Today, we see this rescue politics at work in the refugee crisis in Europe, where refugees that don't die at sea are literally rescued by the coast guard or navy of European countries, and the only answer to the crisis seems to be throwing more humanitarian aid at the problem.[4]

In general, decolonial feminists have argued against abstract generalized notions of feminism and gender identity or women's issues, and for attention to the particular material and social conditions of specific groups of women.[5] Some of the problems become apparent when trying to define decolonial feminism itself, given that the impetus behind attempts to decolonize feminism are driven by resistance to definitions and generalizations. Decolonial feminisms must walk a fine line between a form of identity politics that acknowledges that cultural, historical, social, and material conditions bind certain groups of women together as a political group, on the one hand, and still acknowledge the fluidity of group identity to avoid essentializing it, on the other. This is why decolonizing feminism involves intersectionality as an insistence that every feminism must address not only gender but also race, class, ability, and other social issues that affect the lives of women, and yet do so in a way that acknowledges the fluidity of all of these categories.

In her compelling essay in *Feral Feminisms*, Rita Kaur Dhamoon names three productive tensions within feminism that may open onto the possibility of decolonization:

> in responding to colonial manifestations of anti-racism, feminists must wrestle with three specific anxieties: 1) the tension among feminists between the nation as a site of liberation or conversely as a site of oppression; 2) how to navigate differentials of power within various interconnected forms of heteropatriarchal and neoliberal racisms and colonialisms; and 3) the simultaneity of being a member of an oppressed group and being structurally implicated in Othering. . . . One way to do this is for feminists to revisit three organizing concepts to comprehend our contradictory roles in settler-colonial projects so that the latter can be dismantled: transnationalism, intersectionality, and settler colonialism.[6]

While I cannot speak as an Indigenous woman, or as a refugee, my focus on refugees, particularly women refugees, is part of a decolonizing project insofar as it both challenges the nation-state as the site of women's liberation and insists on a radical transnationalist approach to feminism. This transnationalism is born out of the material realities of refugees, women refugees in particular, insofar as their existence challenges any notion of nation-state. Nationalism is an outdated by-product of colonialism and imperialism and cannot address either the magnitude of the refugee crisis or the fundamental problem of the refugee today, which is, in large part, the existence of national borders. In other words, national borders create refugees by dividing people into two basic groups: citizens and aliens. By setting up borders, and policing the movements of populations, the nation-state creates refugees who become dependent upon humanitarian aid organizations and the so-called hospitality of their host countries. Nationalism creates the group identity *refugee*, and then renders that group fungible, even disposable, as they are bartered back and forth between nation-states.

One foci of decolonizing feminism has been a discussion of the ways in which transnational feminism challenges the notion that nation-states and national sovereignty serve women's interests. This challenge is aimed at both the conceptual and material levels, insofar as women's interests are always context dependent. Focusing on women refugees as a group with shared interests, and yet acknowledging vast differences in cultural, social, historical, and material conditions among the world's refugee women, demonstrates the need for transnational feminisms that go beyond national sovereignty, beyond universal human rights discourse, and perhaps even beyond feminism itself. The plight of refugee women across the globe is dire; and yet rescue politics is part of the problem and not the solution. While feminist struggles must be fought in every country on earth, and all corners of the globe—at the top and the bottom of every social and political hierarchy—refugee women have the fewest resources for initiating those struggles. Most of them are struggling for their very survival. While gender-based violence is a problem across the globe, women refugees are uprooted from support systems, personal and institutional, and their transitory life provides very few opportunities for organized resistance.[7] Focusing on the plight of refugee women forces us to take a transnational perspective, which gives us a different sense of what both feminism and decolonizing feminism might mean. Most acutely, the focus on refugee women demonstrates the fluidity, and in some cases, counter productivity, of insisting on the opposition between categories of Indigenous and settler.

THE SILENT WAR ON WOMEN

Worldwide, women and girls are more vulnerable to natural disasters, gang violence and extortion, sexual violence, domestic violence, and the dangers of rape, disease, and death when fleeing warzones. For example, 80 percent of those who died in the 2004 tsunami were women and girls. The Women's Refugee Commission explains this staggering discrepancy: "Discrimination before a crisis undermines women's economic and social status, which limits their survival skills and their ability to receive warnings and stay out of harm's way."[8] During emergencies of all sorts, whether natural disasters or wars and civil unrest, women face significantly greater danger of sexual assault, rape, exploitation, and human trafficking.[9] For others, survival sex becomes the last option open to them. The Women's Refugee Commission concludes, "The experiences of women and girls during flight, in exile and post-conflict are significantly different from those of men. Displaced women and girls hold their families together under the most difficult and inhumane circumstances and do so while at increased risk to their safety and well-being—risks that include rape, beatings, torture, hunger and abandonment."[10]

According to United Nations Human Rights Commissions, "Refugee women are more affected by violence against women than any other women's population in the world."[11] The Refugee Council reports, "All refugee women are at risk of rape or other forms of sexual violence." Yet, the number of women refugees affected by sexual and gender-based violence is impossible to access for several reasons, including: many refugee women are escaping war zones without facilities for addressing rape, many refugee women do not report sexual assault or gender-based violence, and some refugee women are shunned for admitting sexual assault or gender-based violence. Many refugee women come from countries where the shame associated with rape is even greater than it is in the United States, and the repercussions for reporting may be grave. The Refugee Council's Vulnerable Women's Project report concludes, "Some women, including many of those claiming asylum on the basis of gender-specific persecution, come from countries where sexual violence by security forces has been institutionalized. Women coming from conflict zones will be especially affected: 'war rape' has reached epidemic proportions. . . . Rape has been used strategically, as a weapon of war in attempts to destroy the opposing culture."[12]

Women refugees fleeing violence at home are at a far greater risk than men of encountering violence, especially sexual assault and rape, en route to their host countries, and while in refugee camps. They risk assault at the hands of human traffickers, smugglers who insist on sex in exchange for help or food, fellow refugees, and even police and soldiers along the way or guarding camps. In general, the journey to safety is perilous for men and women, but women and girls face unique challenges both on the road and in the camps. Inadequate food and medical care disproportionately affect women, especially pregnant women who lack access to prenatal care, adequate nutrition, and midwives or hospital facilities. In addition, lack of feminine hygiene products, birth control, and ob-gyn services present unique problems for girls and women. Furthermore, insofar as women are seen as primarily responsible for children, their burden on the road and in camps is wrenching. And, because of their close connection with children, often the effects of disease and death among their children takes a physical and psychological toll on them that goes unaddressed in overcrowded refugee camps lacking basic food, water, medical supplies, adequate shelter, or medical personnel and supplies.

TODAY'S REFUGEES

Last year, global forced displacement reached an all-time high, with at least 65.3 million people (at a rate of 24 people every minute), displaced from their homes by conflict and persecution.[13] Of the entire world's population, one in every 113 people is a refugee or asylum seeker, and of those roughly half are women and girls, with 51 percent under eighteen years old.[14] More than a million people fled to Europe seeking asylum, primarily from Syria, Afghanistan, and Iraq. The vast majority of them arrived by sea, making a perilous journey that has cost thousands of lives. At least 3,700 people died crossing the Mediterranean Sea; given that thousands more go missing or are unaccounted for, it is impossible to determine how many people have actually died.[15] Given that migrants are forced to attempt illegal border crossings, and therefore avoid detection by authorities, until their dead bodies wash ashore, many more are not counted in statistics of missing or dead.[16] And, statistics coming in for 2016 are significantly higher.[17] For example, in just the first six weeks of this year, crossings increased tenfold, and so have deaths.[18]

Of the refugees escaping from Syria, at least one million women were of childbearing age, and at least 70,000 of them were pregnant when they fled.[19] Their children born in refugee camps are stateless, not just because their mothers fled their country of origin but also and moreover because most Middle Eastern countries base citizenship on soil rather than on the citizenship of parents, whereas most host countries base citizenship on the citizenship of parents rather than soil and thus do not recognize refugees born on their soil as citizens. This means that an entire generation of Syria refugees will be without papers, stateless peoples.[20] The director of the United Nations Population Fund says, "We are dealing with a lost generation of children who have not gone to school, who are not registered, who are stateless."[21]

In Africa, there are more than three million refugees, 12.5 million internally displaced people, and another 700,000 stateless people.[22] The United Nations High Commissioner for Refugees (UNHCR) reports that "of the estimated 529,000 maternal deaths that occur globally every year, 48% are in Africa. And, refugee women and newborns are particularly vulnerable. For each maternal death, at least 30 more suffer from infection, injury and short or long term disability."[23] As with other women and girls, African refugees are at a very high risk of sexual violence, first in areas of civil conflict, then on the road to escape, then in refugee camps and outside camps when searching for firewood, and from the authorities within the camps. Liz Miller reports:

> According to Amnesty International, individuals who commit rape and other violence against women and girls often enjoy near total impunity. Some of the barriers to justice for these crimes include: inability of victims to identify their attackers; lack of will by authorities to investigate; threats and intimidation techniques to prevent victims from testifying; weaknesses in the legal framework; and the use of traditional customs of conflict resolution that do not discourage perpetrators from negative behavior.[24]

The number of refugees worldwide is mind-boggling; and, statistics on violence against women refugees, although woefully inadequate, are astounding. More troubling, the problems of camps seem interminable in that most refugees end up living in camps for decades before resettlement. Unlike refugees from World War II, who were resettled by 1952, many of today's refugees spend substantial portions of their lives in a permanent state of temporary living. For example, the largest refugee camp in the world, Kenya's Dadaab, is twenty-five years old this year. It was built for 90,000 refugees but now "holds more than 420,000. . . . Currently, the number of years a refugee lives in a refugee camp is, on average, 12."[25] Furthermore, conditions in most refugee camps are dangerous and unhealthy, where people are forced to live in overcrowded makeshift tent compounds without adequate basic necessities like bathrooms, clothes, and food. For example, in Dunkirk camp in France, over 3,000 refugees live in rat-infested tents pitched in ankle deep mud and human waste with only two water facets; one resident says, "this place is for animals, not for human beings."[26]

Unfortunately, Dunkirk is not an isolated example. Calais, another camp in France near the Channel Tunnel, known as the "Jungle," housed over 6,000 at its peak last summer, most "living in squalor. Doctors working there describing conditions as 'worse than a war zone' people sleeping in tents surrounded by raw sewage, stagnant water and mud."[27] One resident told a reporter, "We are humans, not animals."[28] Violent protests and clashes with police throwing tear gas have resulted from the French government bulldozing a large section of the camp last March, further displacing already displaced people.[29] At least 129 children have gone missing since the camp was raised.[30] Recently, the Greek interior minister Panagiotis Kouroublis called the Idomeni camp on Greece's border with Macedonia "a modern-day Dachau, a result of the logic of closed borders. Despite being planned for just 2,500 people, the camp hosts around 12,000 refugees—many from Syria and Iraq—in wet, cold and muddy conditions, which Red Cross officials warn are rife for the spread of disease.[31] These refugees "feel like we are dying slowly."[32] And, since the route to Greece from Syria has been effectively closed now, refugees flee through Libya, making an even more dangerous crossing of the Mediterranean Sea into Italy—one that led to over 1,000 people dying, and another 4,000 being rescued, in a matter of days, in what a spokesperson for Save the Children called "a massacre."[33]

Thousands of miles away, in the United States (which so far has taken only 2,500 of the promised 10,000 Syrian refugees), refugees live in detention centers that look like, and are run like, prisons, with locked cells, jumpsuits, and all. And, processing refugees takes months.[34] The United States operates the world's largest immigration detention system, and most centers provide substandard health care.[35] As in other prisons, conditions in detention centers are often poor, with inadequate health care, lack of facilities and personnel, and preventable deaths, including suicide.[36] A recent investigation into subpar health care in detention centers confirmed the lack of health care contributed to several deaths: "system-wide problems remain, including a failure to prevent or fix substandard medical care that literally kills people," and that isolation is improperly used to confine people suffering from mental health issues.[37] Human Rights First reports: "Since 2002, the number of immigrants detained each year has more than doubled—with an increase from 202,000 in 2002 to an estimated population of over 440,000 in 2009. The average daily-detained population has grown from 20,662 in 2002 to 33,400 in 2009. As this network has grown, problems of poor conditions, inadequate medical care, difficulty accessing legal counsel, or receiving religious services have also worsened. Of the hundreds of thousands of immigrants annually who find themselves caught up in this system—all for civil immigration violations—a few thousand are asylum seekers, individuals who come here to ask for protection from persecution."[38] In addition, immigrants and asylum seekers have been denied due process and locked up without legal recourse. According to Human Rights Watch, "Most of the hundreds of thousands of people held in this system each year are subject to harsh mandatory detention laws, which do not allow for an individualized review of the decision to detain them during their immigration proceedings."[39] Many asylum seekers suffer in detention centers for months before their cases are resolved.

Although Syrian refugees arriving in Europe are getting the most media attention, there is another refugee crisis taking place in its shadows involving primarily women and children, refugees fleeing Central America for Mexico and the United States. Tens of thousands of women and children are fleeing violence in El Salvador, Honduras, Guatemala, and parts of Mexico. El Salvador, Honduras, and Guatemala rank first, third, and seventh for rates of homicides of women.[40] The UNHCR reports, "a nearly fivefold increase in asylum-seekers arriving to the United States from the Northern Triangle region of El Salvador, Guatemala, and Honduras" and a "thirteenfold increase in the number of requests for asylum from within Central America and Mexico—a staggering indicator of the surging violence shaking the region."[41] Most of the refugees are women escaping repeated rape, assault, and extortion, threatened by armed criminal gangs, watching their children being recruited into gangs or killed, watching other family members murdered or disappeared, while authorities do nothing. Often, they reach a breaking point when their lives are in imminent danger unless they flee immediately. But escaping presents its own dangers as women are forced to pay exorbitant fees to "coyotes" and then suffer more rape, beating, and sometimes murder by these human traffickers.[42] If they reach Mexico or the United States, they face detention, lack of adequate health care, and lengthy interrogations, which too often exacerbate their psychological trauma. One recent UNHCR report about women on the run from Central America concludes:

> Some [women] felt detention exacerbated traumas suffered at home and in flight. As Alexa from El Salvador put it: "They should help facilitate the asylum process so that one doesn't suffer in detention centers. They shouldn't be causing more harm." One Mexican woman described experiencing severe anxiety each time the officers closed and locked the doors to her cell. She said, "It is better to be free and to die by a bullet than to suffer and die slowly in a cage." . . . Women interviewed for this report emphasized that the experience of being detained remains with them far beyond release. "The things I lived through in detention have marked me for life," said a Salvadoran woman who recently was granted asylum. "Please remember that we are human beings. I didn't want to come here, but for me it was a question of life and death."[43]

CARCERAL HUMANITARIANISM AND "RESCUE POLITICS"

Contemporary detention centers and refugee camps are part and parcel of carceral humanitarianism that turns refugees into criminals and charity cases simultaneously, and which, in turn, becomes the troubling justification for locking them up or locking them in, increasingly in dangerous, disease-ridden, sorely inadequate conditions.[44] Refugees and asylum seekers become targets of the new humanitarian military—in the case of Syrian refugees, navies and coast guards operating in the Mediterranean Sea. Their rescue at sea becomes a way of containing their unauthorized movement. Once rescued, migrants are sorted, contained within fences and checkpoints, and monitored. Their freedom of movement is severely limited, and they are often forced to live in deplorable conditions. As Martina Tazzioli argues, migrants escaping wars and famine become shipwrecked people to be rescued in a problematic rescue politics that is as much about statistics as it is quality of life: "the government of migration is grounded on a politics of numbers that sorts people into 'risk' categories," where very few are eventually granted permanent asylum and allowed to legally enter the host country.[45]

With contemporary rescue politics, the military approach that treats refugees like prisoners of war, terrorist threats, or criminals is fused with the humanitarian approach that treats refugees as charity cases to be rescued and saved. Military and humanitarian organizations operate in tandem, and often in coordinated efforts, to both save and contain refugees. It is well known that humanitarian aid organizations advertise to raise money by using photographs of women (especially mothers) and children.[46] The effectiveness of rescue politics relies on compassion for those being rescued; and within the Western imaginary, women and children have always been in need of rescue and protection by men. Spivak's observation that "saving brown women from brown men" has been a rallying cry for military action applies equally well to humanitarian action. And, in today's rescue politics, humanitarian operations and military operations go hand in hand.

Although the United Nations insists that seeking asylum is a lawfully protected act, in practice, the international laws governing refugee status require illegal entry on the part of asylum seekers; and in turn, this illegal entry authorizes the host country to detain and interrogate asylum seekers. Indeed, the rights granted to asylum seekers by international law are very similar to rights granted to criminals, with the significant exception of lack of due process or access to legal counsel. In the name of Homeland Security in the United States, and security against terrorist threats across the globe, in actuality, regardless of international law, asylum seekers have very few rights. The fact that refugee status requires the applicant to make it to a host country, and then prove his or her persecution at home means that those fleeing war and famine must have a means of escape (which costs money), make it out of their home countries, make an illegal border crossing (unless they have proper passports and visas, which are extremely difficult, if not impossible, to obtain in regions fraught with war and violence), and then prove persecution (which is also difficult for those fleeing war or famine). First, the refugee suffers violence and trauma at home, then she makes the perilous escape, leaving behind home and belongings, to make the dangerous journey to seek asylum elsewhere. She suffers violence and trauma, leaves everything behind, becomes homeless, and then becomes a criminal, and suffers further trauma because of her status as refugee.

National borders and international conventions governing asylum seekers create the refugee. Moreover, they create her as destitute, criminal, and mentally ill. Insofar as she must leave her home country, she becomes homeless and dependent upon others for basic needs; insofar as national and international law requires that she leave her home country and make her request for asylum on foreign soil, and usually do so as an illegal alien, she is made criminal; and the trauma she has suffered at home, the trauma that justifies and legitimates her status as refugee and asylum seeker, creates her as mentally ill. For, in order to legitimately gain refugee status, and be accepted into her host country, she must convincingly testify to the *trauma* of violence and *fear* of persecution. She must convince authorities that she is afraid for her life; that she has been traumatized; in effect, that she has suffered mentally as well as physically.

IMPOSSIBLE TESTIMONY

And yet, as the UNHCR guidelines for interviewing asylum seekers make clear, cultural differences and translation problems are significant dangers in the determination of refugee status. The guidelines give a striking example of the danger of mistranslation: There is a striking example given as a warning in the guidelines: "A Turkish asylum-seeker, applying for refugee status in Switzerland, stated that he had escaped arrest by hiding in the mountains near his home town. The application was rejected. Among the reasons given was the fact that the town was situated amid hills. For the Swiss interviewer there were no mountains in the region and thus the applicant was considered to be not credible. However, in Turkish, the term "mountain" also applies to hilly regions." As the guidelines warn: "Notions of time, of truth and falsehood can also vary from culture to culture and give rise to misunderstandings that put the asylum-seekers' credibility in doubt."[47] And yet, in spite of the monumental risk of misinterpretation and mistranslation, every day, interviews determine the fate of asylum seekers based on this faulty process.

The difficulties of testifying to trauma are compounded when it involves sexual assault and rape. Many women are extremely reluctant to talk about sexual assault or rape. In the United States, where there is marked improvement in blame-the-victim standards and shame over being sexually assaulted, rates of reporting rape continue to be shockingly low; and when women do report, their testimony continues to be dismissed or ignored; and, most women report feeling ashamed or being shamed, even further traumatized, by the process of reporting.[48] In cultures where blame-the-victim is the norm and women face ostracism and retribution for reporting rape, rates of reporting sexual assault are even lower, there are fewer resources for reporting, and the negative consequences of reporting are greater.[49] For example, in her overview of literature on African women refugees, Liz Miller concludes, "The most difficult element of 'rape culture' for advocates to overcome within refugee populations is the cultural perception of rape. First of all, sexual violence is a difficult and painful topic for victims to discuss because sex is a taboo topic, and to report rape feels like an invasion of privacy. Moreover, in many communities the act is seen as an embarrassment to the community and to the victim's family."[50]

Refugee women have the added difficulty that they are on the move, away from whatever social or institutional support systems they may have had at home, which makes reporting sexual assault even more difficult in purely logistical terms. To whom do they report? And when they do, the perpetrator is rarely found or prosecuted. Sometimes, the police themselves are the perpetrators.[51] In some cases, border guards, aid workers, so-called peacekeepers, and community leaders—the very people who are supposed to be helping them—have sexually exploited refugee women.[52] Furthermore, asylum seekers formally testifying to sexual violence and assault at hearings often encounter what legal scholars Baillot, Cowan, and Munro call, "a tendency amongst some asylum professionals to marginalise, trivialise or ignore accounts of rape; a tendency that, we argue, both occludes the narratives of asylum-seeking women who have suffered sexual violence, and poses substantial obstacles to securing justice."[53] In an earlier study, they concluded that refugee women face even more difficulties than other women when reporting sexual assault, and even poorer treatment by legal professionals in the criminal justice system. Refugee women are not able to "tell the story" in their own words because most interviews are conducted through interpreters, whose very presence adds yet another witness in front of whom refugee women who are victims of sexual assault must testify.

While the UNHCR guidelines on interviewing asylum seekers includes several sections on addressing and navigating trauma in order to determine the truth of the applicant's testimony, and points out that people suffering from trauma may give inconsistent testimony, be unable to testify, or even become aggressive when questioned as a result of trauma, Baillot, Cowan, and Munro have found that refugee women traumatized by sexual violence are least likely to be "heard" and believed.[54] The guidelines also insist on verification of the truth of the testimony and resolving inconsistencies through confrontation techniques. While the UNHCR convention clearly states that an asylum seeker must fear returning to her country, and must fear persecution based on belonging to a certain group in particular, in this case women, the interview guidelines admit that fear may adversely affect the interview process. The guidelines specially address sexual violence, indicating: "In the context of seeking asylum, the female victim of sexual violence may be hesitant or unable to speak about such events. Moreover, a female victim of sexual violence may be shunned by her family and alienated from members of her community. The interviewer will therefore have to use a variety of gender-sensitive techniques to obtain information from women during the interview process." These techniques include providing all female interviewers and interpreters, and in extreme cases, allowing written instead of oral testimony. As several studies make clear, however, these guidelines are not necessarily, or even usually, followed.[55]

Even if the guidelines were followed to the letter, testimony to trauma, especially sexual trauma, is vexed, particularly in the context of asylum seekers, and even more so when the legitimacy of their claim to asylum rests on claims of trauma resulting from sexual violence. In general, we might ask: How does she testify to fear in a way that is convincing? The guidelines warn against rehearsed scripted testimony and against retraumatizing applicants. So, how does an interviewer determine the veracity of claims to fear? How can fear be quantified and accessed? Assuming that fear is an emotional or mental state, what formula can interviewers use to assess the legitimacy of fear insofar as it corresponds to actual events? Indeed, within trauma theory and psychoanalytic theory, trauma is often considered an experience that cannot be put into words, an experience that falls outside of linear time and rational comprehension. Furthermore, what does it mean to testify to the trauma of persecution? And, what does it mean to *prove* trauma, especially the mental or psychological trauma of sexual violence? Finally, how much trauma is enough to justify asylum? And, how does one convince administrators and interviewers that one's trauma is real?

The UNHCR requires a "reasonable fear under the circumstances" that the claims to this fear are "well-founded." An application for refugee status must demonstrate persecution that entails serious harm and their home country's refusal or inability to protect them.[56] The United States accepts the UNHCR's interpretation of "well-founded" as a "reasonable possibility," but some countries require a higher "probability" standard. Refugee status is also dependent upon demonstrating membership in a protected group and that the persecution is based on that membership. In other words, until recently at least, women were considered not a protected group under international law, so they also had to show that their persecution was based on something other than their gender alone. Protected grounds include race, religion, and political opinion, and until 2002, applicants needed to demonstrate "a causal link between well-founded fear of persecution and one of more Convention grounds."[57]

The UNHCR defines "a particular social group" as persons who share a common characteristic other than their risk of being persecuted; and historically, those common characteristics will be "innate, unchangeable, or otherwise fundamental to the identity, conscience, or exercise of one's human rights."[58] In the United States, the requirement that the characteristic be immutable has been reinterpreted to acknowledge the fluidity of gender identity. Indeed, in order to skirt the issue of the mutability of gender, the UNHRC considers gender identity immutable, even if the choice of gender is mutable: "The proper analysis of immutability with transgender individuals is not based on the immutability of gender (transgender persons generally believe it is mutable), but based on gender *identity* as a characteristic that is immutable and fundamental to identity."[59]

Unless there are obvious reasons of race or religion for women's persecution, the UNHCR interprets "political opinion" broadly enough to include tacit opinions that a woman should not be beaten or raped; and a woman's escape from a situation where sexual violence is the norm can be interpreted as a "political opinion" at odds with the prevailing political opinion of her state.[60] In 2002, the UNHCR adopted "Gender Guidelines" and "Social Group Guidelines," which address women as a social group, although the definition of "social group" is still being debated and revised. The Gender Guidelines state: "Women are a clear example of a social subset defined by innate and immutable characteristics . . . and who are frequently treated differently than men."[61] In the United States, recent jurisprudence acknowledges that "women hold a significantly different position in many societies than men" and "women may suffer harm solely because of their gender."[62] Recently, domestic violence has become the basis for international protection under refugee laws, and abused women can claim refugee protection based on a gender defined as "particular social group."[63] The UNHCR reports: "Much of the US jurisprudence on this issue involves Central American women. In 2014, in a case involving Guatemalan victims of domestic violence, the federal Board of Immigration Appeals clarified previous rulings and explicitly held that domestic violence could be the basis for refugee protection."[64]

Even though recent jurisprudence is opening up the possibility of refuge for gender-based violence, in practice, state workers continue to discount women's testimony.[65] In many countries, women's persecution is considered a cultural norm rather than a reason to grant asylum.[66] As we have seen, women refugees face even more challenges than other women when it comes to reporting, and testifying to, sexual violence.[67] We could go further and claim that current international policy and practices governing the treatment and status of refugees require testimony to trauma that puts the refugee into an impossible subject position with regard to his or her own experience.[68] Refugees are required to both prove suffering and trauma in their home countries, while also demonstrating that they did everything in their power to overcome those obstacles before fleeing. This is to say, they must testify to both their helplessness and their own resilience in escape. They must prove both their radical victimization and their own sovereignty. Being accepted as a legitimate refugee requires documentable and verifiable fear and trauma. Yet, this position as "shipwrecked" person to be saved or rescued undermines agency and self-sovereignty and creates an aporetic subject position impossible to maintain. Asylum seekers are expected to take matters into their own hands, actively flee violence, but in doing so, they become helpless passive victims to be rescued—victims of rescue politics. Today, rescue politics and carceral humanitarianism produce the helpless, homeless refugees as charity cases and criminals in order to justify detaining, monitoring, controlling, and containing them. More often than not, the women are seen as charity cases, while the men are perceived as criminals.

WOMEN'S RIGHTS VERSUS HUMAN RIGHTS

Recently, Zygmunt Bauman called the refugee crisis "humanity's crisis," arguing for "the solidarity of humans" capable of mutual love rather than hate or indifference beyond the boundaries of national sovereignty. Yet, philosophers Hannah Arendt, Giorgio Agamben, Jacques Derrida, and others, have challenged the abstract concepts of *the human* or *humanity* as apolitical, and therefore are unable to ground political rights for refugees.[69] Taking up the rally cry for humanity and the human does not mean we are necessarily equipped to ward off violence, inside the camps or outside. The abstract category of human rights, founded in the Enlightenment notion of cosmopolitanism, can even become an alibi for genocide.

In 2002, speaking of the way human rights discourse was used as an alibi in North Atlantic Treaty Organization's response to violence in Serbia, Jacques

Derrida questioned the separation of humanitarian missions from government interests:

> precisely where one claims to be acting in the name of humanitarian and human rights principles that are superior to the sovereignty of states, precisely where one grants oneself the right of intervention in the name of human rights, where one judges or intends to judge the authors of war crimes or crimes against humanity, it would be easy to show that this humanitarianism, which cares little about so many other examples of "ethnic cleansing" going on in the world, still remains, and brutally so, in the service of state interests of all kinds (economic or strategic), whether they are interests shared by the NATO allies, or even in dispute between them (for example between the United States and Europe).[70]

There are, of course, so many examples of this disparate caring. For just one case, take disparities between Western media reactions to refugees arriving in Europe, and the deaths of refugees at sea on their way to Greece or Italy contrasted with the lack of Western media coverage of refugees fleeing civil war in Africa and the recent announcement of plans to close the largest refugee camp in the world, Dadaab, which "houses" over 300,000 people on Kenya's border. Another example, mentioned earlier, is the exodus of women refugees from Central America, seeking asylum in Mexico and the United States. In a world where the lives of some matter more than the lives of others, genocidal logics are always on the horizon.

Humanitarian aid is the good face of state sovereignty, and an alibi for the lack of a political solution in the war on terror, a war without an easily identifiable enemy. In terms of refugees, this translates into the unhappy choice identified by Arendt of treating those fleeing violence as either threats to be contained in detention centers or charity cases to be saved in camps, where the difference between the carceral model and the charity model is ever more difficult to discern when refugee camps are surrounded by barbed wire fences and checkpoints, and military personnel deliver medical supplies and food to the very people they've just bombed.

Over sixty years ago, following her own escape from Nazi Germany, Hannah Arendt identified what she called the paradox of "inalienable human rights" that reduce the person to an " 'abstract' human being who seemed to exist nowhere," and "independent of all governments." As stateless, there is "no authority, or basis on which to protect" refugees. Specifically, in the case of Jews fleeing the Holocaust, she says, "Abstract nakedness of being nothing but human was their greatest danger."[71] Arendt argues that rights are political and therefore a matter of enforceable laws, not abstract conceptions of some supposedly innate quality such as humanity. Nearly a decade earlier, already living in exile in 1943, Arendt wrote an essay entitled, "We Refugees," first published in a small Jewish magazine called *The Menorah Journal*. There,

Arendt argues that prior to the war, refugees were people who committed acts or held political opinions making them enemies of one state, thus seeking refuge in another. But, Jews and others escaping the Nazis had done nothing to challenge their nation-state; they were so-called voluntary exiles with the supposed "choice" (individual sovereignty) to leave and live or stay and die. These World War II refugees, in response to whom the 1951 United Nations Refugee Convention protocol was ratified, are akin to contemporary refugees from Syria in that they are not necessarily enemies of the state, and they supposedly flee voluntarily. Yet, unlike refugees from the 1950s, today's refugees are not necessarily fleeing "owing to well-found fear of being persecuted for reasons of race, religion, nationality, membership of a particular social group or political opinion," demanded by the 1951 refugee protocol and its 1967 amendments. Instead, they are caught in a warzone in an undeclared war between the Syrian military, ISIS, Russia, the United States, France, the United Kingdom, and others committed to the "war on terror." At the very least, these refugees are collateral damage in the war on terror, if not also climate refugees from an increasingly draught and famine-wrought region.

Arendt argues for a political solution that takes us beyond human rights. And certainly much of what she had to say about her own situation and that of other refugees fleeing Nazi Germany applies to refugees today. For example, she identifies the problematic binary of treating refugees as either threats to be detained (even worse off than criminals in that they are imprisoned without a trial), or charity cases to be saved, often through so-called voluntary internment: "Apparently nobody wants to know that contemporary history has created a new kind of human beings—the kind that are put in concentration camps by their foes and in internment camps by their friends."[72] And when they aren't interned, refuges are paradoxically considered both "pariahs and parvenus (social climbers)."[73]

Closely following Arendt, fifty years later, Giorgio Agamben transforms her notion of abstract nakedness into what he calls "bare life," and argues there is no place in politics for the concept of the human or rights based on this abstract concept. Like Arendt, he insists only citizens have rights, and even those rights are linked to this problematic apolitical notion of the human. Proposing to take us beyond human rights, and beyond nation-states, Agamben claims the refugee is the central figure for contemporary political philosophy, the figure upon which we can build a new community of those who don't belong, beyond borders and frontiers. He says, "It is even possible that, if we want to be equal to the absolutely new tasks ahead, we will have to abandon decidedly, without reservation, the fundamental concepts through which we have so far represented the subjects of the political (Man, the Citizen and its rights, but also the sovereign people, the worker, and so forth) and build our political philosophy anew starting from the one and only figure of the refugee."[74]

Yet, neither Arendt nor Agamben considers the gender of refugees when criticizing human rights discourse. And, the figure of the refugee that Agamben imagines as the starting point for a new political philosophy is either without gender or assumed to be male. For women refugees, formal equality without attention to gender differences, whether in detention centers or camps, leads to increased gender-based violence, along with lack of medical care and hygiene needs specific to women, which affects women's access to other resources as well (e.g., education, work). In their study of the relation of gender to humanitarian aid, Hilde van Dijkhorst and Suzette Vonhof found, "A lack of gender awareness in humanitarian aid can lead to many unwanted, even unsafe, situations for women. There is clear evidence that for instance poor thought-out infrastructure of refugee camps can lead to an increased risk of gender-based violence."[75]

Wendy Brown discusses the paradox of women's rights as either basing rights on characteristics specific to feminine or female identity, and thereby reinforcing a subordinated, or abject identity, on the one hand, or basing rights on universal characteristics associated with masculine and male identity and thereby continuing to devalue femininity and female identity, on the other. She contends, "The paradox, then, is that rights that entail some specification of our suffering, injury, or inequality lock us into the identity defined by our subordination, and rights that eschew this specificity not only sustain the invisibility of our subordination but potentially even enhance it."[76] This danger is a result of the universal and abstract nature of discussions of rights—and moral principles more generally—that discount the significance of social and historical conditions and contexts. The liberal rights discourse assumes that rights must be recognized as something universally true throughout history, without regard for gender, or the context or social institutions governing gender norms. This ahistorical approach risks reinscribing the subordination and denigration it hopes to eliminate by addressing the symptoms, but not the structures of oppression, including material and economic structures, but particularly linguistic, conceptual, and cultural structures and institutions that take us beyond universal human rights and beyond universal women's rights.

CONCLUSION

The special plight of women refugees across the globe presents various challenges to any universal concept of human rights or access to rights, along with challenges to any concept of universal feminism or essentialist notion of gender identity. Even the United Nations has been forced to finesse the issue of innate, immutable characteristics as the basis for refugee status. There are vast cultural differences between women refugees from different cultures and contexts. For example, the women fleeing organized crime in Guatemala and the women escaping ISIS in Syria may not share race or religion, or notions of femininity, or the same conceptions of family values, and yet, they are all running for their lives to escape violence, primarily at the hands of men, whether it is warring gangs, military operations, or domestic violence. Women on the run, fleeing for their lives, often with children in tow, rarely have the personal and institutional resources or authority for organized resistance to gender-based violence, or organized demands for adequate health care, food, water, and shelter.

Furthermore, women refugees are neither Indigenous nor settlers, at least not as they are discussed in decolonial feminism. Although class is certainly a factor in their experience, even intersectionality cannot begin to address the special plight of women refugees who leave their homes with nothing but what they can carry, and often that means their children, and then only for as long as their strength holds out. And in terms of transnational feminism, women refugees challenge the very notion of national sovereignty assumed by the idea of transnational. Refugees challenge the conception of the nation-state at the heart of liberal political theory, and along with it the notion of the liberal autonomous individual with innate human rights universal to all human beings. As we have seen, a repeated refrain in refugee camps and detention centers from France to the United States is "we are human beings, too."

Yet, as Hannah Arendt points out, being human is not enough. Human beings are not born with rights. They are not born equal. Rights and equality are bestowed by political agencies, by governments, by nation-states. In a world where one's freedom of movement, and access to basic resources is governed, if not determined, by political rights granted to some and not others, based on race, class, gender, ability, and sexuality, refugees more acutely experience the breach of these rights because in addition to being women or people of color or Indigenous or disabled, and so forth, they are also stateless. Whatever the problems with rights discourse, and there are many, the right to have rights, as Arendt says, is denied to refugees, insofar as they are locked up and locked in without basic resources such as food, water, medical and hygiene care, without dignity or freedom of movement, without protection from violence, especially sexual and gender-based violence. The rescue politics that requires women to suffer violence, trauma, fear, poverty, homelessness, detention, and interrogation before they are even considered eligible for asylum is not only inhumane and a breach of human rights but also a perpetuation of the very violence and trauma refugees seek to escape.

NOTES

1. See for example, Maile Arvin, Eve Tuck, and Angie Morrill, "Decolonizing Feminism: Challenging Connections between Settler Colonialism and Heteropatriarchy," *Feminist Formations* 25, no. 1 (2013): 8–34.

2. See for example, Tug?çe Kurtis, and Glenn Adams, "Decolonizing Liberation: Toward a Transnational Feminist Psychology," *Journal of Social and Political Psychology* 3, no. 1 (2015): 2.

3. Kurtis and Adams, "Decolonizing Liberation," 2.

4. For criticisms of humanitarian aid as the flip side of humanitarian war, see Kelly Oliver, *Carceral Humanitarianism: The Logic of Refugee Detention*. Minnesota: University of Minnesota, 2017.

5. Ariadna Estévez López, "Taking the Human Rights of Migrants Seriously: Towards a Decolonised Global Justice," *The International Journal of Human Rights* 14, no. 5 (2010): 658–77. Here López argues against general human rights and for particular rights for international migrants.

6. Rita Kaur Dhamoon, "A Feminist Approach to Decolonizing Antiracism: Rethinking Transnationalism, Intersectionality, and Settler Colonialism," *Feral Feminisms* 4 (2015): 20.

7. Zinthiya Ganeshpanchan, "Domestic and Gender Based Violence among Refugees and Internally Displaced Women," *Human Dignity and Humiliation Studies* (2005); Cf. Liz Miller, "The Irony of Refuge: Gender-Based Violence against Female Refugees in Africa," *Human Rights & Human Welfare* (2009): 77–90, http://www.du.edu/korbel/hrhw/researchdigest/minority/Africa.pdf.

8. Diana Quick, "Women, Children, Persons with Disabilities Most Vulnerable to Typhoon Haiyan," *Women's Refugee Commission*, November 14, 2013, https://www.womensrefugeecommission.org/blog/1763-typhoon-haiyan-women-children-disabilities.

9. Ibid.

10. Women's Refugee Commission, "Displaced Women and Girls at Risk," June 2015, https://www.womensrefugeecommission.org/resources/document/516-displaced-women-and-girls-at-risk-identifying-risk-factors-and-taking-steps-to-prevent-abuse.

11. UNHCR deputy high commissioner L. Craig Johnstone reported in Leo Dobbs, "UNHCR Backs 16 Days of Opposition to Violence against Women," *UNHCR*, November 25, 2008, http://www.unhcr.org/en-us/news/latest/2008/11/492c1eb74/unhcr-backs-16-days-opposition-violence-against-women.html; Refugee Council, *The Vulnerable Women's Project: Refugee and Asylum Seeking Women Affected by Rape or Sexual Violence—Literature Review*. London: Refugee Council, 2009.

12. Refugee Council, *The Vulnerable Women's Project*, Executive Summary, 4–7.

13. Adrian Edwards, "Global Forced Displacement Hits Record High," *UNHCR*, June 20, 2016, http://www.unhcr.org/en-us/news/latest/2016/6/5763b65a4/global-forced-displacement-hits-record-high.html.

14. Ibid.

15. "Migrant Crisis: Migration to Europe Explained in Seven Charts," *BBC News*, March 4, 2016, http://www.bbc.com/news/world-europe-34131911.

16. Martina Tazzioli, "The Politics of Counting and the Scene of Rescue," *Radical Philosophy* (2015), https://www.radicalphilosophy.com/commentary/the-politics-of-counting-and-the-scene-of-rescue.

17. Melissa Fleming, "Crossings of Mediterranean Sea Exceed 300,000," *UNHCR*, August 28, 2015, http://www.unhcr.org/en-us/news/latest/2015/8/55e06a5b6/

crossings-mediterranean-sea-exceed-300000-including-200000-greece.html. The UNHCR reports that in the first eight months of 2015, over 300,000 refugees and migrants crossed the Mediterranean Sea seeking asylum in Europe. Over 2,500 died in those months, and in 2014, 3,500 died. See Tazzioli, "The Politics of Counting," for a discussion of the unaccounted for dead.

18. "Hundreds of Refugees Died on Way to Europe This Year," *Al Jazeera*, February 9, 2016, http://www.aljazeera.com/news/2016/02/400-refugees-die-europe-2016-160209133941502.html.

19. "Women and Girls in the Syria Crisis," *UNFPA*, March, 2015, https://www.unfpa.org/sites/default/files/resource-pdf/UNFPA-FACTSANDFIGURES-5%5B4%5D.pdf.

20. Richard Spencer, "Nearly Half a Million Pregnant Women among Displaced and Refugee Syrians," *The Telegraph*, February 3, 2016, http://www.telegraph.co.uk/news/worldnews/middleeast/syria/12139358/Nearly-half-a-million-pregnant-women-among-displaced-and-refugee-Syrians.html.

21. Ibid.

22. Sulaiman Momodu, "Refugees Turn to Ethiopia for Safety and Asylum: Country Now Hosts the Largest Number of Refugees in Africa," *Africa Renewal*, April 2015, http://www.un.org/africarenewal/magazine/april-2015/refugees-turn-ethiopia-safety-and-asylum#sthash.DnTD4QY5.dpuf.

23. "Safe Motherhood in Refugee Camps," *UNHCR*, accessed online on July 18, 2016 at http://www.unhcr.org/456c56ea2.pdf.

24. Liz Miller, "The Irony of Refuge." This essay includes an excellent annotated bibliography of literature on women refugees.

25. Mac McClelland, "How to Build a Perfect Refugee Camp," *New York Times*, February 13, 2014, http://www.nytimes.com/2014/02/16/magazine/how-to-build-a-perfect-refugee-camp.html.

26. "A Closer Look at 'Europe's Worst' Refugee Camp," *Sputnik International*, January 24, 2016, http://sputniknews.com/europe/20160124/1033644952/dunkirk-france-refugee-camp.html.

27. "Death of the Jungle," *Daily Mail*, March 28, 2016, http://www.dailymail.co.uk/news/article-3511855/Death-Jungle-Incredible-aerial-images-reveal-Calais-slum-just-bare-earth-makeshift-homes-flattened-bulldozers-eviction-thousands-refugees.html#ixzz49ytihWY7.

28. Amelia Gentleman, "The Horror of the Calias Refugee Camp," *The Guardian*, November 3, 2015, http://www.theguardian.com/world/2015/nov/03/refugees-horror-calais-jungle-refugee-camp-feel-like-dying-slowly.

29. "Migrants at Calais Camp Given Dignity in Death," *The Local Fr*, May 23, 2016, http://www.thelocal.fr/20160523/migrants-at-calais-camp-given-dignity-in-death.

30. "Almost 130 Refugee Kids Vanish after 'Calais Jungle' Demolition—Charity," *RT Online*, April 3, 2016, https://www.rt.com/news/338217-129-kids-missing-in-calais/.

31. Will Worley and Lizzie Dearden, "Greek Refugee Camp Is 'as Bad as a Nazi Concentration Camp', says minister," *The Independent*, March 18, 2016, http://www.independent.co.uk/news/world/europe/idomeni-refugee-dachau-nazi-concentration-camp-greek-minister-a6938826.html.

32. Gentleman, "The Horror of the Calias Refugee Camp."

33. Jim Yardley and Gaia Pianigiani, "Three Days, 700 Deaths on Mediterranean as Migrant Crisis Flares," *The New York Times*, May 29, 2016.

34. Devon Cone, "The Process for Interviewing, Vetting, and Resettling Syrian Refugees in America Is Incredibly Long and Thorough," *Foreign Policy*, November 30, 2015, http://foreignpolicy.com/2015/11/30/the-process-for-interviewing-vetting-and-resettling-syrian-refugees-in-america-is-incredibly-long-and-thorough/. Thanks to Jennifer Newman for bringing this to my attention.

35. Janet Golden, "What Will Today's Immigration Detention Centers Look Like to Future Americans?" *Philadelphia Inquirer*, June 22, 2016, http://www.philly.com/philly/blogs/public_health/What-will-todays-immigration-detention-centers-look-like-to-future-Americans-.html.

36. Megan Granski, Allen Keller, and Homer Venters, "Death Rates among Detained Immigrants in the United States," *International Journal of Environmental Research and Public Health* 12 (2015).

37. "US: Deaths in Immigration Detention—Newly Released Records Suggest Dangerous Lapses in Medical Care," *Human Rights Watch*, July 7, 2016, https://www.hrw.org/news/2016/07/06/us-deaths-immigration-detention.

38. "Will the Immigration Detention System Finally Get the Reforms It Desperately Needs?" *Human Rights First*, August 7, 2009, http://www.humanrightsfirst.org/2009/08/07/will-the-immigration-detention-system-finally-get-the-reforms-it-desperately-needs.

39. "US: Deaths in Immigration Detention," *Human Rights Watch*.

40. "Women on the Run," *UNHCR*, 2015, http://www.unhcr.org/en-us/publications/operations/5630f24c6/women-run.html.

41. Ibid.

42. Ibid.

43. Ibid., 47.

44. Tazzioli, "The Politics of Counting"; see Oliver, *Carceral Humanitarianism, 2017.*

45. Ibid.

46. See Denis Kennedy, "Selling the Distant Other," *The Journal of Humanitarian Assistance* (2009); also see Michael Barnett, *Empire of Humanity*.

47. "Interviewing Applicants for Refugee Status (Rld 4)," *UNHCR*, 1995, http://www.unhcr.org/4d9485a69.pdf. Thanks to Jennifer Newman for bringing these guidelines to my attention.

48. I discuss sexual assault and rape in the United States, and U.S. rape culture in *Hunting Girls: Sexual Violence from The Hunger Games to Campus Rape* (New York: Columbia University Press, 2016).

49. In her short overview and literature review, Liz Miller discusses various studies that indicate that sexual violence is a fact of life for refugee women, and reporting rates are very low. In addition, when rapes are reported, they rarely find or prosecute the perpetrators. See Miller, "The Irony of Refuge"; see also Baillot, Cowan, and Munro, "'Hearing the Right Gaps: Enabling and Responding to Disclosures of Sexual Violence within the UK Asylum Process." *Social & Legal Studies* 21, no. 3 (2012): 269–96.

50. Miller, "The Irony of Refuge," 78.

51. See "Women on the Run," *UNHCR*.

52. Elizabeth G. Ferris, “Abuse of Power: Sexual Exploitation of Refugee Women and girls.” *Signs* 32, no. 3 (2007): 584–591.

53. Baillot, Cowan, and Munro, “ ‘Hearing the Right Gaps.’ ”

54. Baillot, Cowan, and Munro, “Seen But Not Heard? Parallels and Dissonances in the Treatment of Rape Narratives across the Asylum and Criminal Justice Contexts,” *Journal of Law and Society* 36, no. 2 (2009): 195–219; Baillot, Cowan, and Munro, “Second-hand Emotion? Exploring the Contagion and Impact of Trauma and Distress in the Asylum Law Context,” *Journal of Law and Society* 40, no. 4 (2013): 509–40.

55. Ibid.

56. “Women on the Run,” *UNHCR*, 34.

57. Ibid.

58. Ibid., 38.

59. Ibid.

60. For a discussion of how racism affects refugee women as they seek asylum, see Pittaway and Bartolomei, “Refugees, Race, and Gender.”.

61. “Women on the Run,” *UNHCR*, 35.

62. Ibid.

63. Ibid.

64. Ibid.

65. For a study of women seeking refuge in Australia and the difficulties of doing so based on sexual violence, see Udara Jayasinghe, “Women as ‘Members of a Particular Social Group’: Some Flexible Judicial Developments,” *Alternative Law Journal* 31, no. 2 (2006): 79.

66. Karen Musalo and Stephen Knight, “Unequal Protection,” *Bulletin of the Atomic Scientists* 58, no. 6 (2002): 57–61.

67. See for example, Baillot, Cowan, and Munro, “Seen But Not Heard?”; Baillot, Cowan, and Munro, “Second-hand Emotion?”; Ferris, “Abuse of Power”; Ganeshpanchan, “Domestic and Gender Based Violence”; Michelle Hynes and Barbara Lopes Cardozo, “Observations from the CDC: Sexual Violence against Refugee Women,” *Journal of Women’s Health & Gender-Based Medicine* 9, no. 8 (2000): 819–23.

68. For a sustained discussion of the paradox of testifying to your own trauma and oppressions, see Kelly Oliver, *Witnessing: Beyond Recognition* (Minneapolis: University of Minnesota Press, 2001).

69. See for example, Wendy Brown and Janet Halley, *Left Legalism/Left Critique*, (Durham: Duke University Press, 2002), 432–33; See also Henry Rosemont Jr., “Rights-Bearing Individual and Role-Bearing Persons,” *Rules, Rituals, and Responsibility: Essays Dedicated to Herbert Fingarette*, ed. Mary Bockover (Chicago: Open Court, 1991), 71–101; Duncan Kennedy, “The Critique of Rights in Legal Studies”; and Duncan Kennedy, “Legal Education and the Reproduction of Hierarchy”. On refugee rights in particular, see Omri Boehm, “Can Refugees Have Rights?” *New York Times*, October 19, 2015.

70. Jacques Derrida, “Unconditionality or Sovereignty: The University at the Frontiers of Europe,” *Oxford Literary Review* 31, no. 2 (2009): 125–26. doi: http://dx.doi.org/10.3366/E0305149809000467.

71. Hannah Arendt, “Decline of the Nation State; End of the Rights of Man,” in *The Origins of Totalitarianism* (New York: Harcourt, Inc., 1975), 291–92, 300;

Hannah Arendt, "We Refugees," in *Altogether Elsewhere: Writers in Exile*, ed. Marc Robinson (Boston: Faber & Faber, 1994), 118.

72. Arendt, "We Refugees," 110.

73. Ibid., 119.

74. Giorgio Agamben, "Beyond Human Rights," *Social Engineering* 15 (2008): 90.

75. Hilde van Dijkhorst and Suzette Vonhof, "Gender and Humanitarian Aid: A Literature Review of Policy and Practice," *Wageningen Disaster Studies*, December 2005.

76. Wendy Brown, "Suffering the Paradoxes of Rights," *Left Legalism/Left Critique* (Durham: Duke University Press, 2002), 423.

BIBLIOGRAPHY

Agamben, Giorgio. "Beyond Human Rights." *Social Engineering* 15 (2008): 90–95.

Arendt, Hannah. "The Decline of the Nation-State and the End of the Rights of Man." In *The Origins of Totalitarianism*, 267–302. New York: Harcourt, Inc., 1975.

———. "We Refugees." In *Altogether Elsewhere: Writers in Exile*, edited by Marc Robinson, 110–19. Boston: Faber & Faber, 1994.

Baillot, Helen, Sharon Cowan, and Vanessa E. Munro. "Seen But Not Heard? Parallels and Dissonances in the Treatment of Rape Narratives across the Asylum and Criminal Justice Contexts." *Journal of Law and Society* 36, no. 2 (2009): 195–219.

———. "'Hearing the Right Gaps': Enabling and Responding to Disclosures of Sexual Violence within the UK Asylum Process." *Social & Legal Studies* 21, no. 3 (2012): 269–96.

———. "Second-Hand Emotion? Exploring the Contagion and Impact of Trauma and Distress in the Asylum Law Context." *Journal of Law and Society* 40, no. 4 (2013): 509–40.

Barnett, Michael. *Empire of Humanity: A History of Humanitarianism*. Ithaca: Cornell University Press, 2013.

Brown, Wendy. "Suffering the Paradoxes of Rights." In *Left Legalism/Left Critique*, edited by Wendy Brown and Janet Halley, 420–34. Durham, NC: Duke University Press, 2002.

Derrida, Jacques. "Unconditionality or Sovereignty: The University at the Frontiers of Europe." *Oxford Literary Review* 31, no. 2 (2009): 115–31. doi: http://dx.doi.org/10.3366/E0305149809000467.

Dhamoon, Rita Kaur. "A Feminist Approach to Decolonizing Antiracism: Rethinking Transnationalism, Intersectionality, and Settler Colonialism." *Feral Feminisms* 4 (2015): 20–38.

Ferris, Elizabeth G. "Abuse of Power: Sexual Exploitation of Refugee Women and Girls." *Signs* 32, no. 3 (2007): 584–91.

Ganeshpanchan, Zinthiya. "Domestic and Gender Based Violence among Refugees and Internally Displaced Women." *Human Dignity and Humiliation Studies*, 2005. Available online. http://www.humiliationstudies.org/intervention/parents.php.

Keefe, Andrew, and Elena Hage. *Vulnerable Women's Project Good Practice Guide: Assisting Refugee and Asylum Seeking Women Affected by Rape or Sexual Violence*. London: Refugee Council, 2009.

Kennedy, Duncan. *Legal Education and the Reproduction of Hierarchy*. New York: New York University Press, 2004.

Kennedy, Duncan. "The Critique of Rights in Critical Legal Studies." In *Left Legalism/Left Critique*, edited by Wendy Brown and Janet Halley. Durham, NC: Duke University Press, 2002.

Kurtiş, Tuğçe, and Glenn Adams. "Decolonizing Liberation: Toward a Transnational Feminist Psychology." *Journal of Social and Political Psychology* 3, no. 1 (2015): 388–413.

López, Ariadna Estévez. "Taking the Human Rights of Migrants Seriously: Towards a Decolonised Global Justice." *The International Journal of Human Rights* 14, no. 5 (2010): 658–77.

Miller, Liz. "The Irony of Refuge: Gender-Based Violence against Female Refugees in Africa." *Human Rights & Human Welfare* (2009): 77–90, http://www.du.edu/korbel/hrhw/researchdigest/minority/Africa.pdf.

Musalo, Karen, and Stephen Knight. "Unequal Protection." *Bulletin of the Atomic Scientists* 58, no. 6 (2002): 57–61.

Pittaway, Eileen and Linda Bartolomei. "Refugees, Race, and Gender: The Multiple Discrimination against Refugee Women." *Refugee: Canada's Journal on Refugees* 19, no. 6 (2001): 21–32.

Quick, Diana. "Women, Children, Persons with Disabilities Most Vulnerable to Typhoon Haiyan." *Women's Refugee Commission*, November 14, 2013, https://www.womensrefugeecommission.org/blog/1763-typhoon-haiyan-women-children-disabilities.

Tazzioli, Martina. "The Politics of Counting and the Scene of Rescue." *Radical Philosophy* 192 (July/August 2015), https://www.radicalphilosophy.com/commentary/the-politics-of-counting-and-the-scene-of-rescue.

van Dijkhorst, Hilde, and Suzette Vonhof. "Gender and Humanitarian Aid: A Literature Review of Policy and Practice." *Wageningen Disaster Studies*, December 2005.

"Women and Girls in the Syria Crisis." *UNFPA*, March 2015, https://www.unfpa.org/sites/default/files/resource-pdf/UNFPA-FACTSANDFIGURES-5%5B4%5D.pdf.

"Women on the Run." *UNHCR*, 2015, http://www.unhcr.org/en-us/publications/operations/5630f24c6/women-run.html.

Women's Refugee Commission. "Displaced Women and Girls at Risk," June 2015, https://www.womensrefugeecommission.org/resources/document/516-displaced-women-and-girls-at-risk-identifying-risk-factors-and-taking-steps-to-prevent-abuse.

Part 4

DECOLONIZING DIALOGUE, SOLIDARITY, AND FREEDOM

Chapter 8

The Dynamics of Transnational Feminist Dialogue

Barbara Fultner

Transnational feminists[1] have argued that there is an increasing need for meaningful dialogue across borders and boundaries while simultaneously highlighting the difficulties of true dialogue across differences. However, they have not developed theoretical accounts of transnational dialogue per se. From the perspective of feminist political practice, the goal of such dialogue ought to be not only transformation of the dialogue partners but also solidarity among them. Building transnational solidarity requires articulating and preserving differences without silencing any of the interlocutors. This chapter examines what constitutes meaningful, transformative, feminist, and decolonized dialogue and the conditions under which it can be realized.

In what follows, I first revisit arguments for the need for dialogue. Second, I argue that the way is paved for establishing such dialogue by showing that cultures are open systems. This allows, third, for a critique of what I call *culturalistic* explanations of difference that have been rightly criticized by feminist scholars but are remarkably persistent in public discourse. Fourth, if we conceive of cultures as open systems, it becomes reasonable to ask not simply how different cultures or communities *vary* in their concepts and beliefs, but *how* concepts travel and are appropriated or *transformed*, how meanings change as they cross borders. Tracing how concepts and theories cross borders creates "languages of perspicuous contrast," to borrow a phrase from Charles Taylor, that allow us to preserve differences between interlocutors while creating a third perspective that unites them.[2] Fifth, I use Allison Weir's conception of identity as identification to conceptualize dialogue as transformative practice. Finally, sixth, I outline the dialogical norms that may emerge from considerations of transnational feminist dialogue with a specific focus on accountability. It is commonplace to say that dialogue occurs against a shared background understanding and has consensus as its end. I argue that feminist dialogical practice demonstrates that dialogue does not require complete agreement in background understanding as either a precondition or a result, especially if the goals are political action and solidarity. Rather, as transformative practice, dialogue transforms interlocutors and their differences and thus can be a dynamic means for bringing about political change.

THE NEED FOR DIALOGUE AND FEMINIST SOLIDARITY

In *Feminism without Borders*, Chandra Talpade Mohanty writes that "one of the greatest challenges we (feminists) face is [the] task of recognizing and undoing the ways in which we colonize and objectify our different histories and cultures, thus colluding with hegemonic processes of domination and rule. Dialogue across differences is thus fraught with tension, competitiveness, and pain . . . multicultural feminism cannot assume the existence of a dialogue among feminists from different communities without *specifying a just and ethical basis* for such a dialogue."[3] Mohanty thus presents feminists with a challenge:

> Undoing ingrained racial and sexual mythologies within feminist communities requires . . . [becoming] fluent in each other's histories, . . . seeking "unlikely coalitions" . . . [and] clarifying the ethics and meaning of dialogue. *What are the conditions, the knowledges, and the attitudes that make a noncolonized dialogue possible?* How can we craft a dialogue anchored in equality, respect, and dignity for all peoples? [O]ne of the most crucial challenges for a critical multicultural feminism is working out how to engage in *ethical and caring dialogues* (and revolutionary struggles) across the divisions, conflicts and individualist identity formations that interweave feminist communities in the United States. Defining genealogies is one crucial element in creating such a dialogue.[4]

Yet although Mohanty asks what the conditions of possibility are for noncolonized, ethical, and caring dialogue with a just and ethical basis, she does not probe available philosophical accounts of dialogue for an answer to this question. Instead, she urges interlocutors to become familiar with each other's histories and genealogies. From a Gadamerian hermeneutic perspective, successful dialogue is only possible against a "shared horizon" or background understanding (a point I address in the following). So one might read Mohanty as asking how we can create a sufficiently shared background in order to make dialogue possible. Yet as we shall see, though a necessary first step, "learning one another's histories and genealogies" is insufficient to ensure the desired kind of dialogue.

Mohanty regards feminist solidarity as a political and ethical goal and defines it "in terms of mutuality, accountability, and the recognition of common interests as the basis of relationships among diverse communities."[5] She writes, "Rather than assuming an enforced commonality of oppression, the practice of solidarity foregrounds communities of people who have chosen to work and fight together."[6] Yet what constitutes feminist solidarity and how is it attained? Is it simply "choosing to work and fight together"? What enables people to do that? Do we perhaps need a more developed account of joint agency?[7]

It is no longer news, though it certainly still bears repeating, that feminists of color have experienced discrimination or oppression in the form of racism, classism, imperialism, and colonialism in putatively feminist contexts and at the hands of white feminists—be it by dismissing the concerns of women of color as irrelevant or silencing and excluding them or by misrepresenting the experiences of women of color and universalizing their own white, middle-class experience. Such occurrences clearly constitute failures of solidarity as well as failures of dialogue. In the context of feminist theorizing, Mohanty's "Under Western Eyes"[8] is an early, but not the only, documentation of ways in which women of color have been constructed as passive objects by white feminist scholars. Furthermore, transnational feminists have argued that women's issues and interests vary from one geopolitical location to another. Uma Narayan, for instance, has pointed out the very different needs and priorities of feminist advocates against domestic violence in India from those of activists in the United States.[9] Peggy Antrobus has noted that some Nigerian women are not interested in equality with men but do want to affirm their reproductive and property rights and understand themselves as feminists in that regard.[10] These examples, together with a widespread endorsement by Western feminist theorists of social constructivism,[11] may lead one to infer that the recognition, assertion, and celebration of difference commits feminists to cultural relativism. Yet transnational and decolonial feminism in fact constitutes a rejection of at least strong forms of cultural relativism.

For transnational feminists have made us aware that women's plights in one place are often deeply connected to women's situations elsewhere. Indeed, this insight is perhaps *the* defining feature of transnational feminist theory. Thus, Alison Jaggar asks white, Western feminists outraged at the ill treatment of Amina Lawal to consider their own—if mediated—role in the oppression of Nigerian women.[12] Rhacel Parreñas highlights the childcare crisis in the Philippines that has resulted from mothers taking on childcare jobs abroad and is thus connected to the needs—and power—of mothers elsewhere.[13] Leila Ahmed juxtaposes Muslim women in the West wearing a veil with non-Muslim women wearing makeup or skimpy clothing, and asks us to reflect on which is more liberating and which is more oppressive.[14] I will address in the following the question of how *concepts* themselves travel. First, however, I shall argue that the insights of transnational feminism either preclude an endorsement of radical cultural relativism or sideline questions of culture altogether, focusing instead on socioeconomic relations, global politics, and power relations. All three of the previous examples undertake cultural comparisons, but they also point out ways in which women, whose situations may appear to be quite distinct if viewed in cultural terms, are nonetheless deeply connected by the global and transnational flows of today's world.

CULTURES AS OPEN SYSTEMS

This chapter is not an intervention in the debate over philosophical relativism and universalism. I raise no objections to the idea that an individual's or a group's beliefs and values may be particular to their cultural context and background. What I reject is the idea that such beliefs and values are in principle accessible *only* from that culture and therefore inaccessible and unintelligible to another. That is, I reject the idea that cultures are closed (or, for that matter, homogeneous) systems—a view that I think underlies at least some forms of cultural relativism and that continues to pervade mainstream understandings of culture. Rejecting this view is a precondition for the possibility of cross-cultural and transnational dialogue.

Intercultural dialogue is often seen as impeded by cultural relativism, the thesis that knowledge and values are relative to one's culture. However, this view is implicitly based on a misconception of cultures as closed systems. If we think of cultures as closed systems, it is easy to view other cultures as monolithic and opaque, as unintelligible. This, in turn, facilitates what I call culturalistic explanations of—and refusals to engage with—difference.

What often seems to underlie cultural relativism is some distinction between conceptual schemes and the content they organize. For the idea seems to be not only that other cultures have different beliefs and customs than we do but also that they view the world differently. Donald Davidson has argued persuasively against the scheme-content distinction and championed "the principle of charity" as an interpretive maxim that maximizes agreement among interlocutors. In response to this argument, one might worry that this principle leads interpreters to falsely project their own beliefs onto others[15]—a worry that is clearly relevant to transnational feminist dialogue. As I have argued elsewhere, the Gadamerian notion of *horizon* offers a better way to theorize cultures as (discursively constituted) worlds that are in principle expansive and, to quote Gadamer, "available to others."[16] A horizon does not have rigid boundaries, but is a "boundless space"[17] that "moves with one."[18] On this view, cultures are *open systems*. This means that they can enter into conversation with each other. For Gadamer,

> just as the individual is never simply an individual because he [*sic*] is always in understanding with others, so too the closed horizon that is supposed to enclose a culture is an abstraction.[19]

The relativism and incommensurability theses rest precisely on this kind of abstraction—and *reification*—of a culture or conceptual scheme. By contrast, the openness and fluidity of horizons make their fusion possible, and that is how Gadamer conceptualizes reaching mutual understanding among interlocutors.[20] Importantly, the notion of horizon—unlike that of conceptual scheme or web—implies a particular standpoint, a location, whence visibility is always limited, but which can change. "Understanding the other," Gadamer claims, "is the most difficult of human tasks."[21] The fusion of horizons, though it may go "beyond what is alien," must both preserve and at the same time transform the voice of the other (and of self). Hence the goal of genuine conversation is not simply to place oneself in the other's position but to develop a *shared* position with her, for in a true conversation we seek to reach agreement about something with someone. A *real* conversation "is a process of coming to an understanding" and of opening oneself to the other.[22] Dialogue thus incorporates the notion of difference—since interlocutors engage one another *as other*—as well as the possibility of overcoming difference—by reaching a shared understanding. If we converse with another simply in order to find out "where she is coming from," Gadamer tells us, we may acknowledge her otherness, but in a way that effectively silences her by our "fundamental suspension of [her] claim to truth."[23] Such an articulation of difference is insufficient, yet may ring true with regard to many inter- or transcultural exchanges. Mohanty's injunction to learn about each other's histories therefore can only be a starting point.

The goal of Gadamerian dialogue is not merely mutual or reciprocal but *shared* understanding. According to Gadamer,

> Every conversation presupposes a common language, or better, creates a common language . . . to reach an understanding in a dialogue is not merely a matter of putting oneself forward and successfully asserting one's own point of view, but being transformed into a communion in which we do not remain what we were.[24]

Dialogue transforms both interlocutors and creates something new that is shared between them. The sharing itself is transformative. The resulting language will rise "to a higher universality that overcomes not only our own particularity but also that of the other."[25] This will be a "language of perspicuous contrast." Dialogue is thus *not* translation. I do not translate what you say into my language. Rather, I have to be open to creating a new language we both share. This can be achieved neither by mere empathy for the other nor by imposing one's own standards on her, but rather requires the application of "the true productivity of language" whereby we seek to attain "real solidarity" (Gadamer's term) in the midst of a manifold of linguistic cultures and traditions.[26] For Gadamer, it is the very nature of language to make it possible for us to reach mutual understanding and solidarity. From a feminist perspective, there are at least two points to be made. First, Gadamer associates solidarity with consensus and unity. Yet much recent feminist scholarship suggests that we should rethink such a tight link between consensus and solidarity, largely because the second-wave ideal of sisterhood turned out to be not only mistaken, projecting a false notion of women's identity as homogeneous, but often also pernicious. As a result, feminists have struggled with the question of how to do justice to differences among women while preserving the idea of a global women's movement. Second, opening oneself to the other implies great vulnerability and therefore risk. Entering into dialogue is risky since we do not know how it may transform us. In the next section, I argue that culturalistic explanations fail to acknowledge this vulnerability and refuse to take this risk.

AGAINST CULTURALISTIC EXPLANATIONS

It has been almost twenty years since the publication of Uma Narayan's *Dislocating Cultures*, where, among other things, she argues persuasively against culturalistic explanations of gender oppression. Narayan argues that culturalistic explanations usually fail to elucidate the culture in question or the phenomenon to be explained. Thus, dowry murders, which are quite frequent in India, have been routinely read as a cultural phenomenon in the West and conflated with the ancient and outlawed practice of *sati*, thus mystifying and exoticizing Indian culture. Dowry murders are directly connected to domestic violence and greed—a point that, according to Narayan, has been lost in (culturalistic) translation that fails to take national context into account and ties the killings to religious practice.[27] Moreover, the reason women are often burned is that kerosene is readily available as it is a cooking fuel—not because fire has a cultural or religious significance. Narayan brilliantly juxtaposes dowry murders by fire with the fact that domestic violence against women resulting in murder in the United States is committed with guns.[28] Yet, she suggests, it would strike U.S. feminists as odd to present this as a *cultural* phenomenon rather than having to do with gun laws, say. That is, we regard the causes of gun violence as complex and as involving multiple types of factors in ways that Narayan argues are not applied to the Indian case. Thus, one of the things Narayan highlights about culturalistic explanations is that "culture" seems to be something that *others* have, but not "*we*" (white Westerners). These explanations thus foreshorten our ability to understand not only the other but ourselves as well.

Nonetheless, culturalistic explanations or approaches to social problems have not gone away; if anything, they seem to be on the rise, even as "other cultures" are becoming more closely enmeshed with "ours" as a result of migration. Yet grumblings—or worse—about the threat to "European" or "German" or any other culture from "letting in" too many migrants "from such a radically different culture" homogenize the cultures of the immigrants. Even if all refugees from Syria, Afghanistan, and Somalia all were Muslim, why should we think that they are *culturally* any more alike than Christians from Great Britain, Italy, Indonesia, Venezuela, India, and Syria? Gender once more provides a case in point of the persistence of culturalistic explanation. *The New York Times* reported in December 2015 on a Norwegian cultural education program for migrant men to help them avoid committing sexual violence by "offering coaching in European sexual norms and social codes."[29] While it may seem reasonable from a cultural perspective to teach immigrants about social signals (colleges do this, too), the idea that the "simple rule that all asylum seekers need to learn and follow [, that] to force someone into sex is not permitted in Norway, even when you are married to that person" (ibid.) is a *local norm* that seems highly problematic.[30] First, (at least some form of) rape is illegal in most of the countries the migrants come from. This is not to say that the laws, not to mention their application, are adequate for the protection of victims of sexual or domestic violence, but many argue that this applies to the law in the West as well.[31] This means that if one wants to claim that migrants from "more conservative societies" come from a rape culture, it behooves one to acknowledge Western rape culture and to examine beliefs about gender relations in both cultures more carefully. Second, rape appears to have been relatively rare in Syria, for example, prior to the war, suggesting that sexual violence is more closely linked to other forms of violence and militarism than to culture.[32] In these cases, culturalistic explanation seems to vilify the other in a particularly insidious way, flattening migrant men into monstrous cultural dopes without actually explaining their behavior. Finally, there seem to be *no* statistics regarding rape or other types of sexual assault, particularly compared to nonmigrant men.[33]

None of these considerations, to be sure, is intended to excuse sexual assault or to minimize the importance of culture or cultural explanation. Rather, they are meant to highlight the importance of assessing *when* cultural explanations are appropriate and when it is appropriate to draw on other factors (which may require placing the phenomenon in a global context). With regard to *culturalistic* explanation, unless we are offered fairly specific reasons and description of why someone's cultural background explains his or her behavior, skepticism regarding the validity of the explanation is warranted—particularly if the appeal to culture is presented not as an invitation to but as a foreclosure of further dialogue. This is relevant to Mohanty's call to learn about one another's histories and genealogies. Yes, we must absolutely learn about one another's *cultural* backgrounds, customs, and habits. Knowing this background helps us to understand how our interlocutors are liable to interpret situations they encounter and what implicit knowledge and beliefs they might bring to the table. By the same token, agents in interaction also have expectations with regard to how *social* relations, such as those between women and men, are institutionally regulated within society. Lastly, speaking and acting subjects have "competencies that enable them to assert their identities" and whereby they are socialized. Thus, *culture*, *society*, and *personality* are implicated, in the course of everyday communicative interactions, in cultural reproduction, societal integration, and individual socialization.[34] Transnational dialogue, however, presents a distinct scenario inasmuch as it explicitly involves communication *across* differences in culture, society, and personality among interlocutors. At issue, then, is the establishment of *new* practices, precisely practices of solidarity that acknowledge these differences.

CONCEPTS ACROSS BORDERS

In the 2013 essay, "Transnational Feminist Crossings: On Neoliberalism and Radical Critique," Mohanty addresses the limitations, if not dangers, of postmodern, postfeminist, post-identity theories and politics and their (unintended) cooptation by, and hence collusion with, neoliberalism in the academy. She worries that "theory—feminist and/or antiracist—is trafficked as a commodity disconnected from its activist moorings and social justice commitments" and race and gender commitments are "recoded" as a mere "politics of presence."[35] She asserts that her previous work has been misread as rejecting all universalism, whereas she defends systemic analysis and a "differentiated universalism" against postmodernism.[36] Mohanty also traces the ways in which her own scholarship has been taken up in different contexts and by different scholars and activists, specifically, in Sweden, Mexico, and Palestine.

Reflecting on the "cross-border dialogues" she takes her own work to have prompted and recognizing that "[her] intention as an author, however, cannot control how [her] works are read,"[37] she rejects misreadings of her work as "essentialist and reductive" and writes:

> The uses and translations of my work as it is embodied in particular sites, communities, and feminist projects illustrate both the productive adaptations of decolonizing antiracist feminist thought and the pitfalls of the convergence of postmodernist feminism and neoliberal logics in the academy. . . . The circulation of ["Under Western Eyes" and "Under Western Eyes Revisited"] in various geopolitical locales reveals feminist complicity in imperial and capitalist/neoliberal projects and points to the limitations of knowledge-making projects in academia.[38]

In Sweden and Mexico, she holds, her work has been misread by hegemonic white or well-established academic feminists who have continued "doing whiteness as usual." In contrast, it has been useful for feminists of color and Indigenous women in all three contexts for "deconstructing hegemonic discourse": "Within privileged circles, my critique of the power of hegemonic feminism from the epistemological space of marginalized communities of women is misread as a representational politics focused primarily on differences within academic feminism."[39] She reports that in South America, her work has been used to critique the colonial effect of the victimization of Indigenous women and to decolonize the Guatemalan academy.[40] Although Mohanty writes that "analytical categories have different rationalities depending on place" and allows for the "potential untranslatability of concepts like women of color,"[41] she does not elaborate on *how* her conceptual framework might be inflected by the different contexts in which it has been used. The mere fact that her work has been "lost in translation" need not in and of itself signify untranslatability—just bad translation or *mis*appropriation, and she seems to allow for that by distinguishing between "faithful translations" and "distorting appropriations."[42] However, she does not elaborate on any of these points. It is therefore unclear how to reconcile her critique of postmodernism and of postmodernist readings of her work with her allowing for the possibility of untranslatability. Indeed, the latter suggests that Mohanty subscribes to some kind of scheme-content dualism. If so, that would push her in the direction of conceiving cultures as closed systems, and that might undermine the possibility of solidarity and dialogue she aims for, if my earlier argument holds.[43]

There are other examples of how concepts travel (or don't). In addition to Narayan's work on domestic violence in India versus the United States discussed earlier, Lata Mani has commented on the very different reception of her work on *sati* in Indian and U.S. contexts; whereas it was received as a historical project in India, it was seen as a postcolonial project relevant to contemporary gender oppression in the United States.[44] Another excellent example is Lisa Tessman and Bat-Ami Bar On's "The Other Colors of Whiteness: a Travelogue," a dialogue between an Israeli and a U.S. woman, both Jewish, about what it means to be white in their respective sociocultural locations—and how dislocating it can be to change from one to another. Importantly, they each have a different understanding of race and whiteness based on their backgrounds and each of their understandings is transformed as a result of their dialogue, but they don't necessarily have the *same* understanding at the end of it. Dialogue, in other words, is transformative but need not lead to consensus. At best, consensus is always only partial.

DIALOGUE AS TRANSFORMATIVE PRAXIS

In *Identities and Freedom*, Allison Weir defends a "transformative identity politics" in an effort to move beyond what she calls the "paradox" of identity politics, according to which we are both subjugated and constrained and enabled by our identities.[45] She argues that "identities can be understood as complex webs of interactions among diverse relations of power and diverse relations of meaning, love, and solidarity."[46] She draws on the work of Charles Taylor and Michel Foucault. The latter, on her account, conceives identity as a source of oppressive constraint and as constituted by "webs of power."[47] The former sees it as a "source of individual and collective meaning" and constituted by "webs of interlocution." Weir's own view is that we must understand identities as constituted *both* by relations of power and relations of intersubjective connections, that is, relations of "mutuality, flourishing, and love."[48] For Weir, women's identity is partly "constituted or constructed by feminists oriented toward solidarity."[49] Feminism itself has *changed* and transformed women's identity. (This, incidentally, applies even to women who do *not* identify as feminists.) Identity is thus not simply a (metaphysical) category but has to do with connections or "identifications." The latter require "an active process of getting to know the other, through an imaginative and empathic engagement that goes beyond recognizing how we are the same, and beyond 'putting oneself in the other's place,' without change to the self. . . . Through identification with the other, we transform ourselves, and we construct a new 'we': a new identity."[50] Thus the collective identity of women (or feminists) is not something that is given or that we can presuppose but something that is actively created. This is not always—or ever—an easy process.

An important theoretical commitment underlying Weir's account throughout is that the self is understood as relational. If the self is constituted by its relations to others, it follows that it is transformed when those relations and the others with whom it interacts change. Weir notes that "many theorists have retreated altogether from thinking about collective identities to a focus on individual identities—as if it's impossible to talk about a collective identity, a 'we.' . . . Is it really the case that individual identities are any less complex and conflictual than collective identities?"[51] I agree with Weir that there is a peculiar gap in feminist theory with regard to collective identity and *action*.[52] (This is why I think that there is interesting work to be done at the intersection between feminist theory and social ontology and especially on joint intentionality.)

The upshot of Weir's argument is that "identity politics is about an active historical, political process of identification with, shaping, and creating a 'we,' "[53] where the identity of this "we" is

> constituted historically and relationally; and . . . is internally complex, differentiated, and conflictual. . . . We develop our collective identities . . . through our associations, our relations to each other, and to meanings, worlds, ideals that might be shared. Through identifications that hold us together. . . . I am arguing that there must be an orientation to solidarity, emerging out of identifications with each other, with a "we," and with feminist ideals, to motivate and to sustain any struggle for unity.[54]

Identity, according to Weir, should be understood "as a site for the risk of connection, of sustaining relationship through conflict."[55] Women who become feminists, she maintains, "come to recognize a position shared with other women *very different from themselves* only through an orientation to solidarity that is facilitated by [an identification—with other women (colonized vs. colonizers)]."[56] Identity thus does not mean sameness for Weir. She illustrates identification with the example of childcare. An American career woman, an immigrant Filipina nanny, and a homeless woman may all share the issue of childcare, but, as Weir interestingly puts it, "it is shared in very different ways." First, their material conditions are very different. The career woman may be looking for after-school care for her children, whereas the homeless woman may have no one to look after her children while, say, she looks for work and may lack the financial resources to care for them altogether. Weir rightly points out that the three women are "related through global care chains in which some of us must take responsibility for the exploitation and oppression of others."[57] The career woman's solution to finding childcare by hiring a Filipina nanny *creates* the latter's childcare problem: to take the job, she needs to find someone to take care of her children while she is halfway around the globe.

Acknowledging global care chains implies recognizing responsibility in a way that goes beyond Mohanty's injunction to learn about each other's histories and genealogies. To see all the various childcare issues as well as other related issues, such as access to contraception and health care, we have to learn about the very different life issues faced by women in different situations. "And we are able to do that," says Weir, "*only* because we approach these issues and each other with an orientation to solidarity, through which we construct and interpret our shared interests, through an interpretive framework that is feminist."[58] Though Weir does not elaborate on the connection, the orientation to solidarity is linked to responsibility.

The exact relationship between identification and solidarity is not always clear in Weir. In some passages identification facilitates solidarity, while in others solidarity is said to facilitate identification. And in her threefold characterization of identifications—with feminist values and ideals of social justice; with ourselves as a (resistant) "we"; and with particular others in relationships of love, empathy, admiration, etc.—the orientation to solidarity seems to *be* an identification. We might say that we need an orientation to solidarity to engage in identifications that then yield solidarity, but Weir also says that the orientation itself emerges from identifications. These apparent inconsistencies can be addressed by keeping in mind the hermeneutic point that communication always proceeds against a background of shared understanding. Applied to transnational dialogue, such a shared background is liable to be quite minimal, but there must be enough to at least motivate engaging in dialogue with the other at all—thus yielding an orientation to solidarity—to get the interaction started.

The solidarity toward which we are orienting ourselves presumably no longer refers to unity as such, since this would again raise the problem of identity, that is, sameness versus difference. An alternative way to understand it is as acting in concert. Weir endorses Amy Allen's definition of solidarity as "the ability of a collectivity to act together for the agreed-upon end of challenging, subverting, and ultimately, overturning a system of domination. She further asserts "the need to affirm feminist solidarity as a collective resistance to oppression, sustained by interactions characterized by reciprocity and mutuality."[59] Thus solidarity here seems to be conceived more as a form of united—and resistant—or *joint action* than as a form of identity.

Perhaps we need to return to Weir's earlier phrase of "sharing in different ways" from a slightly different angle. What does it mean to share something? If we share a cake, it means you and I both get a piece of it. But sharing "meanings, worlds, ideals" or experiences isn't like that. It is more like sharing a perspective or point of view. And here, perhaps, we need to return to questions of dialogue and language. To share a point of view, using the earlier Gadamerian analysis, is to move into the same horizon. Nonetheless, if we share the same point of view, this does *not* necessarily mean that we *see* the same things (i.e., we share differently). Because of my history and genealogy, I may notice different things than my dialogue partner—even if she stands in the same place as I do. My history and genealogy will include both my cultural and sociohistorical background—that is, features that I share with others—*and* my own idiosyncratic personal history—that is, features that are specific to me as an individual. Furthermore, in sharing a conversation, in engaging in dialogue together, participants are not each doing and saying the same thing. Rather, each makes different contributions. This is a characteristic feature of joint actions in general, which constitutes a sense of sharing differently. What binds the agents together is not their identity but their shared goal or purpose and the fact that they are each contributing to that goal.

Weir's framework is useful for conceptualizing transnational feminist dialogue, not only because identity and identification do not mean sameness for her but also because identifications require work and involve risks. Transnational feminist dialogue should not only be sensitive to interlocutors' backgrounds (i.e. their histories and genealogies) but also articulate how these differ from or interlink with one's own (i.e. develop a language of perspicuous contrast). Thus it should be transformative—not only of individual identities but of collective ones as well. Indeed, it can constitute them. It is also a joint activity; it is shared. At the same time, it does not (necessarily) aim at consensus or agreement but at solidarity.

SOLIDARITY AND ACCOUNTABILITY

Let me return to Mohanty's claim that white or privileged feminists have misread her, whereas women of color have used her work productively. This claim should give white, Western, variously privileged feminists pause. It suggests that we need to be especially careful not merely to refer to her work and continue "doing whiteness as usual." Mohanty attributes the misreading of her work, sometimes more implicitly than explicitly, to an unmooring of academic feminist theory from political activist contexts, from "struggles on the ground." She therefore asks:

> What would it mean to be attentive to the politics of activist feminist communities in different sites in the global South and North as they imagine and create cross-border feminist solidarities anchored in struggles on the ground? How would academic feminist projects be changed *if we were accountable to activist/academic communities* like ones [in Sweden, Mexico, and Palestine]? I believe we need to return to the radical feminist politics of the contextual as both local and structural and to the collectivity that is being defined out of existence by privatization projects.[60]

Accountability is what will keep us/me from using the work of feminists of color appropriatively —or, as I prefer to put it—from *misappropriating* it. (For appropriating it, making it my own, presumably is or can be part of the transformation dialogue may bring about.) Accountability is underemphasized in Weir's account, although it is not entirely absent. Recall that she points out the need for some to take responsibility for the exploitation and oppression of others in global care chains.

A Habermasian model of communication lends itself well for a transformative model of dialogue centering on accountability. According to the formal pragmatics at the heart of the theory of communicative action, we raise validity claims in every utterance. In making validity claims, we take on a warrant to make good on, that is, to justify these claims with reasons. That is, making validity claims is inherently connected to accountability. In addition, there are also the discursive norms governing the ideal speech situation (that everyone is presumed to be speaking truthfully, no one is excluded from contributing to the discussion, etc.). These are, to be sure, regulative ideals; that is, they may not ever be fully realized. However, precisely *because* they are regulative ideals, they can be invoked as a way of holding interlocutors accountable. But transnational feminist dialogue calls for inflecting the Habermasian account in certain ways. Accountability needs to be articulated not merely in terms of reasons in reference to the objective world of states of affairs (truth), the social world of interpersonal and ethical relations (normative rightness), and the subjective world of personal authenticity (sincerity). Rather, its parameters need to be expanded to include epistemic responsibility, vulnerability, power and privilege, embodiment, and solidarity. With this expansion of the theory of communicative action, transnational feminist dialogue can emerge as a tool of decolonization.

If I—as a white woman academic, living in global North/West and fully employed—am to engage in transnational feminist dialogue, what are my responsibilities as an interlocutor? To whom am I accountable, and for what? I believe (at least) five aspects of accountability can be identified.

1. *Epistemic responsibility and cultural explanation:* I am responsible not only for listening openly to my interlocutor as she explains her particular positionality and concerns but also for gathering information about that positionality on my own. We might call this part of my epistemic responsibility as an interlocutor.[61] Any number of non-Western feminists and feminists of color have said they are tired of having to explain to white feminists "what it's like." In other words, if I believe that there may be significant disparities in the background understanding we bring to our dialogue, I have the responsibility to find out about what my interlocutor might be bringing to the table, where she is coming from. The dialogue between Bar On and Tessman illustrates this nicely inasmuch as they listen to each other's histories and accounts of race relations in the United

States and Israel. Remember that we know from Gadamer that this is only a starting point. That said, it is here that *cultural*, not culturalistic, explanation surely has a role. That is, it is here that I need to learn about my interlocutor's cultural background, practices, and assumptions. These may explain why she holds a particular view. As indicated earlier, cultural explanations are distinct from culturalistic ones in that the former help us understand our interlocutor and make her actions and beliefs *more* intelligible, whereas the latter flatten our view of her, making her more one-dimensional, less complex, yet, at the same time, *less* intelligible. Cultural explanation is also where any number of differences between interlocutors are liable to emerge. Things we thought were shared may turn out not to be. In such cases, we have the responsibility not to gloss over these differences but to grapple with them.[62] It may not always be clear what to do with the differences once we have articulated them. We may need to revise or altogether reject our previous beliefs—or we may need to figure out how to continue talking and acting collectively despite our differences.

2. *Fallibilism, corrigibility, and vulnerability:* Therefore, I have to be a fallibilist about my own views; listening openly to my interlocutor entails that I have to be open to revising my own views—about who I am and who my interlocutor is. (Weir talks about this in terms of the risk of connection, and because it is tied to our identities, this is not an easy kind of openness.) This aspect is crucial for the transformative role of dialogue insofar as my beliefs are coconstitutive of who I (or we) are and thus changing beliefs is a form of self- (or group) transformation. This also means I have to be open to new claims for inclusion (which may take the form of charges of exclusion) and transformation (perspective shifts). And that requires sensitivity to and vigilance for the effects of power relations.
3. *Power and privilege:* I am responsible for knowing my privileges, ways in which I may be implicated in another's oppression, and power relations that may be shaping the dialogue. What are my privileges? How do they facilitate or impede my interactions? Do they stand in the way of open dialogue, and, if so, how? Mere acknowledgement, however, is not enough. How can I mitigate these effects? This seems to be one element lacking in those whom Mohanty takes to misinterpret her work.
4. *Affect and embodiment:*[63] Taking account of the dynamics of power and privilege requires awareness of oneself as an embodied interlocutor. I am responsible for my emotional responses to what is said. If I feel angry or offended, why? Have I been offended—am I feeling offended because my privilege has been pointed out to me? An important element that is often forgotten in hermeneutic as well as critical theoretical accounts of dialogue is that interlocutors are always embodied. According to Diana Coole, "It is through its corporeal performances that the body achieves

(or suffers) many of its effects within dialogical situations."[64] We are often quite unaware of how we use bodies in communication. Moreover, our embodiment extends beyond the immediate boundaries of our bodies into our environment. How does the physical location of where the dialogue takes place affect it? Is the space being colonized by any of the interlocutors? Who is sitting at the head of the table? Who speaks how frequently? In what language are we conversing? (If it is English, which is likely not a native language for many participants, how should I account for that?)[65]

5. *Solidarity and collective action:* What is the goal of dialogue? What am I as interlocutor seeking to accomplish? If the preceding arguments regarding identity hold, the goal of transnational feminist dialogue need not be consensus. Reaching agreement is certainly one form of transformation. A better understanding of the other and of oneself is another. But political action, coalition, and change are possible goals as well. And these require solidarity—which, presumably, is why for both Mohanty and Weir, *solidarity* is a dialogical goal. A recent conversation among six feminists about the Boycott, Divestment and Sanctions (BDS) movement demonstrates this well. Simona Sharoni, Rabab Abdulhadi, Nadje Al-Ali, Felicia Eaves, Ronit Lentin, and Dina Siddiqi come to the issue from different backgrounds and geographical locations, and while they agree on a transnational feminist framework, their focus is on building solidarity—which in this case means taking collective action in the form of BDS.[66] How does our understanding of dialogue change when we think of solidarity, and specifically feminist solidarity, as its goal? How do our ways of talking with one another change if we are aiming at collective resistance to oppression?

All five of these dimensions place demanding conditions on transnational feminist dialogue. While they derive from a conception of the ideal speech situation and its ensuant discursive norms, they are tailored to the transnational context in which we must be especially mindful of potential disagreements and communicative distortions. By explicitly requiring interlocutors to be epistemically responsible and to take account of the dimensions of power and privilege, transnational feminist dialogue decenters the white, global North subject. This highlights ways in which actual dialogues may be marked by various asymmetries and, by redressing them, is therefore one way of decolonizing feminism. Transnational feminists interested in decolonization do not want to speak *for* others, but rather to give them space to speak themselves.[67] This is why dialogue is key to decolonizing feminism.

CONCLUSION

I have argued that transnational feminism relies on conceiving cultures as open, porous rather than closed systems and have used Gadamerian hermeneutics to support my claim. To view cultures as porous is not to deny the importance of context—historical, economic, political, social, *and* cultural—for understanding any given issue. On the contrary, transnational feminism teaches us that taking such contexts into account matters and that we need to think of cultures not as independent but as intimately connected to local and global economic systems and governance structures. For transnational feminism shows that, in a globalized world, the problems people face in one country are connected in complex, intersecting ways to what is happening elsewhere and to what has happened in the past. This means that we can understand neither cultural difference nor economic or political interests in a vacuum but only as interconnected in particular sociohistorical contexts. I have suggested that there is a normative dimension of accountability connected to this recognition. Moreover, feminist theorists and activists alike borrow concepts, theories, and strategies where they can. Tracing how concepts and theories cross borders can create languages of perspicuous contrast that allow us to preserve differences between interlocutors while creating a third perspective that links them. More such work is required, not only in the form of comparative analysis but also in the form of cross-cultural, transnational dialogue. This approach not only shows the limits of culturalistic explanations of difference, but can also serve to decolonize feminism. In the wake of reconceptions of identity such as that proposed by Weir, more work also needs to be done on solidarity, understood not as unity but as collective agency.

Perhaps the kind of dialogue envisioned here will be regarded as too idealistic, especially in the context of Mohanty's worry that radical critique is impeded by the neoliberal conditions of knowledge production that currently pervade the academy.[68] Yet against this background, characterizing conditions for meaningful transnational dialogue seems all the more important. It is helpful to remember the *liberatory potential* of language. With reference to Adorno, Martin Seel writes that "the potential of an uncoerced [*zwanglos*] interaction with others and with difference is inherent in linguistic practices even and especially where their de facto execution distorts this possibility."[69] Feminists, given their critiques of male domination and power, ought to be well positioned to recognize and be sensitive to the many possible factors of distortion. I have emphasized that dialogue across borders is not an easy process but involves risks and many potential pitfalls. It is thus worth keeping in mind that, just as there is an emancipatory potential, there is a potential for restraint, limitation, and abuse: the fact that we can tell the truth may be but the flipside of our ability to tell lies. Although theorists like Habermas regard the communicative pathologies as contingent aberrations and as identifiable and corrigible relative to an idealizing account of communication, others hold that the possibility of (systematic) distortion is *also* inherent in language. The dynamics of transnational dialogue require interlocutors to keep hold of both these possibilities. Decolonizing feminism depends on the possibility of such transnational and cross-cultural dialogue as a source of new forms of solidarity.[70]

NOTES

1. See, for example, Chandra Talpade Mohanty, *Feminism without Borders: Decolonizing Theory, Practicing Solidarity* (Durham: Duke University Press, 2003); Jacqui Alexander, *The Pedagogies of Crossing* (Durham: Duke University Press, 2005); and Leila Abu-Lughod, "Do Muslim Women Really Need Saving?" *American Anthropologist* 104, no. 3 (2002): 783–90.

2. Charles Taylor, "Understanding and Ethnocentrism," in *Philosophy and the Human Sciences, Philosophical Papers II* (Cambridge: Cambridge University Press, 1985).

3. Mohanty, *Feminism without Borders*, 124, italics added.

4. Mohanty, *Feminism without Borders*, 124–36, italics added. While she refers specifically to feminism in the United States here, the same applies transnationally.

5. Mohanty, *Feminism without Borders*, 3, 7.

6. Mohanty, *Feminism without Borders*, 7.

7. If what constitutes feminist solidarity is indeed "choosing to work and fight together," it sounds somewhat like Margaret Gilbert's account of joint agency, which is based on joint commitment. Is simply saying "we" enough? See Margaret Gilbert, *Joint Commitment: How We Make the Social World* (New York: Oxford University Press, 2013). http://0-www.oxfordscholarship.com.dewey2.library.denison.edu/view/10.1093/acprof:oso/9780199970148.001.0001/acprof-9780199970148.

8. Chandra Mohanty, "Under Western Eyes: Feminist Scholarship and Colonial Discourse," *Boundary 2* 12, no. 3 (1984): 333–58.

9. Uma Narayan, *Dislocating Cultures* (New York: Routledge, 1997).

10. Interview with Obiageli Nwankwo, quoted by Peggy Antrobus, "The Global Women's Movement," in *Women's Lives: Multicultural Perspectives*, eds. Gwyn Kirk and Margo Okazawa-Rey (New York: McGraw-Hill, 2013), 609. This is not currently a universally shared view among Nigerian women. In March 2016, a Gender and Equal Opportunity Bill failed to pass the Nigerian Senate on religious grounds and too much criticism from women's rights activists. See Bridget Chiedu Onochie, "Nigerian Society and the Gender Equality Debate," *The Guardian,* March 20, 2016 (http://guardian.ng/sunday-magazine/newsfeature/nigerian-society-and-the-gender-equality-debate/).

11. While, to be sure, there are different conceptions of the social construction of gender and other categories, thinkers as diverse as Judith Butler, Sally Haslanger,

Linda Alcoff, María Lugones, and even Catherine MacKinnon accept some version of social constructivism. Needless to say that a category is socially constructed does not make it any less real.

12. Alison Jaggar, "'Saving Amina': Global Justice for Women and Intercultural Dialogue," *Ethics and International Affairs* 19, no. 3 (2005): 55–75. Amina Lawal was accused and convicted of adultery and sentenced to death by stoning. The case spawned an international uproar, and the sentence was eventually overturned on technical grounds. Jaggar criticizes a number of assumptions she attributes to Western feminist critics of this and other such cases. First, that there is "injustice by culture; second, that cultures are autonomous; third, that "West is best" for women; and fourth, that it is Western theorists' job to expose injustices against women by local cultures (which is where the Amina campaign fits in). She argues that poverty and abuse of women cannot be understood in cultural terms alone but must be understood in its "global geopolitical and geoeconomic context." Furthermore, cultures are not independent of one another or of politics and economics; and by supporting certain conservative governments (e.g., Saudi Arabia), Western regimes are also supporting their cultures. Jaggar therefore asks Western feminists to consider the ways in which we are connected to poor and victimized women around the globe and cautions against proselytizing Western values in intercultural dialogue rather than inquiring into the effects of Western policies and how they affect poor women. On her account, then, to blame violence and injustice against poor non-Western women on culture *depoliticizes* social problems.

13. Rhacel Parreñas, "The Care Crisis in the Philippines," in *Global Woman*, eds. Barbara Ehrenreich and Arlie Hochschild (New York: Palgrave MacMillan, 2002).

14. Leila Ahmed, "The Veil Debate Again: A View from America in the Early Twenty-first Century," in *On Shifting Ground: Muslim Women in the Global Era*, ed. Fereshteh Nourale-Simone (New York: Feminist Press at the City University of New York, 2005). See also Judith Mahoney Pasternak's letter to the editor of *The New York Times* (http://www.nytimes.com/2016/05/02/opinion/other-pressures-on-women.html?smprod=nytcore-ipad&smid=nytcore-ipad-share) and the article to which it responds, Sylvie Kaufmann's "What's a European Liberal to Do?", *The New York Times,* April 13, 2016 (http://www.nytimes.com/2016/04/13/opinion/international/whats-a-european-liberal-to-do.html). Kaufmann writes, "In a book last year, *Des voix derrière le voile* (*Voices Behind the Veil*), the journalist Faïza Zerouala drew portraits of 10 young Frenchwomen who voluntarily wear the head scarf. 'Some people feel uncomfortable in the company of a veiled woman, but what makes *her* uncomfortable are naked women on billboards,' she said. 'And what feminist would argue that such ads are liberating?'" What the debate often seems to overlook is the possibility that *both* headscarfs *and* skimpy clothes may function in oppressive *and* liberating ways; wearing either may make one complicit in the objectification and subjection of women in sexist and patriarchal societies, yet one may also use them to assert one's agency.

15. See Charles Taylor, "Understanding the Other," in *Philosophical Arguments* (Cambridge, MA: Harvard University Press, 1995), 291–92.

16. Hans-Georg Gadamer, *Truth and Method*, 2nd edition, trans. Joel Weinsheimer and Donald G. Marshall (New York: Continuum, 1994), 447. See Barbara Fultner,

"Incommensurability in Davidson and Gadamer," in *Dialogues with Davidson*, ed. Jeff Malpas (Cambridge, MA: MIT Press, 2011), 219–40.

17. Hans-Georg Gadamer, "Die Vielfalt der Sprachen," in *Gesammelte Werke*, vol. 8 (Tübingen: Mohr Siebeck, 1999), 345. The essay was originally published in 1988.

18. Gadamer, *Truth and Method*, 245.

19. Gadamer, "Vielfalt der Sprachen," 304.

20. There may be important differences between communication between interlocutors belonging to the same culture and interlocutors from different cultures.

21. Gadamer, "Vielfalt der Sprachen," 346.

22. Gadamer, "Vielfalt der Sprachen," 385.

23. Gadamer, "Vielfalt der Sprachen," 303. For a critique of Gadamer's account of otherness, see Marie Fleming, "Gadamer's Conversation: Does the Other Have a Say?" in *Feminist Interpretations of Gadamer*, ed. Lorraine Code (University Park: Pennsylvania State University Press, 2003), 109–32.

24. Gadamer, "Vielfalt der Sprachen," 378–79.

25. Gadamer, *Truth and Method*, 305.

26. Gadamer, "Vielfalt der Sprachen," 346.

27. Narayan compares the national contexts in which feminist agendas have developed in India and the United States, noting important differences in priorities and emphasis. Dowry deaths remain a significant threat to large numbers of women in India; see "24,771 Dowry Deaths Reported in Last 3 Years," *India Express,* July 31, 2015 (http://indianexpress.com/article/india/india-others/24771-dowry-deaths-reported-in-last-3-years-govt/). What is more, the culturalistic explanations Narayan criticized also persist; see for example, Jason Koutsoukis, "India Burning Brides and Ancient Practice Is on the Rise," *The Sydney Morning Herald,* January 31, 2015 (http://www.smh.com.au/world/india-burning-brides-and-ancient-practice-is-on-the-rise-20150115-12r4j1.html). Other pieces refer to the rise of dowry deaths "despite modernization," describing the crimes as an "age-old social ill" (Carol J. Williams, "India 'Dowry Deaths' Still Rising despite Modernization," *LA Times,* September 5, 2013, http://articles.latimes.com/2013/sep/05/world/la-fg-wn-india-dowry-deaths-20130904), as if modernization were an antidote to greed and even though a 2007 *LA Times* piece clearly casts the harassment and murders as the result of greed and avarice—made *worse* by rising affluence.

28. This, too, alas, has not changed since 1997. See "Guns and Violence against Women," *Everytownresearch,* June 16, 2014 (https://everytownresearch.org/reports/guns-and-violence-against-women/).

29. Andrew Higgins, "Norway Offers Migrants a Lesson in How to Treat Women," *New York Times*, December 19, 2015 (http://www.nytimes.com/2015/12/20/world/europe/norway-offers-migrants-a-lesson-in-how-to-treat-women.html). Particularly striking are the comments of Per Isdal, one of the creators of the education program, and of the police chief of one of the towns where it was implemented: "Many refugees 'come from cultures that are not gender equal and where women are the property of men,' Mr. Isdal said. 'We have to help them adapt to their new culture.' The first such program to teach immigrants about local norms and how to avoid misreading social

signals was initiated in Stavanger, the center of Norway's oil industry and a magnet for migrants, after a series of rapes from 2009 to 2011. Henry Ove Berg, who was Stavanger's police chief during the spike in rape cases, said he supported providing migrants sex education because 'people from some parts of the world have never seen a girl in a miniskirt, only in a burqa.' When they get to Norway, he added, 'something happens in their heads.'" The article made the rounds of a number of conservative blogs, though I cannot go into their various problematic interpretations here. The Norwegian case needs to be further placed in the context of widely circulated statistics claiming that 90 percent of sexual assaults (rapes) in Oslo in 2010 were committed by immigrants of (broadly speaking) Arab origin. For a debunking of these manufactured sexual assault statistics, see Farha Khaled, "Gil Ronen's Fabricated Statistics about Oslo Rapists Being All Muslim," *Loonwatch,* December 23, 2011 (http://www.loonwatch.com/2011/12/gil-ronens-fabricated-statistics-about-oslo-rapists-being-all-muslim/, accessed May 17, 2016). By contrast, a 2014 report on rape statistics in Norway indicates extremely low reporting rates, with 9.1 percent of women saying they have been raped, most by people they knew (see "Rape Statistics Surprised Researchers, *News in English,* February 26, 2014, [http://www.newsinenglish.no/2014/02/26/rape-statistics-surprised-researchers/, accessed May 17, 2016]).

30. Nina Machibya, manager of a center offering the course, describes the goal of the course as teaching participants to "know the difference between right and wrong."

31. A full transnational analysis of sexual assault law is obviously beyond the scope of this chapter. For some indication of various legal contexts, see Amnesty International, "Sexual Violence in Algeria, Tunisia, and Morocco," September 2, 2014 (https://www.amnesty.org.uk/sexual-violence-algeria-tunisia-and-morocco), Philip Ross, "Algeria Domestic Violence Law: Violence against Women Illegal But Human Rights Group Remains Skeptical" (http://www.ibtimes.com/algeria-domestic-violence-law-violence-against-women-illegal-human-rights-group-1837942), and Manizha Naderi, "A Law That Would Permit Afghan Men to Hurt and Rape Female Relatives, *The Guardian*, February 6, 2014 (https://www.theguardian.com/commentisfree/2014/feb/06/law-afghan-men-hurt-rape-female-relatives-karzai, accessed June 25, 2016). A key issue is marital rape, which is often exempted from legal prosecution. It is worth noting that marital rape is illegal in Germany only since 1997 and in the United States only since 1993 and that legal loopholes remain (See Bryan Patrick Byrne, "These 13 States Still Make Exceptions for Marital Rape, *Vocativ,* July 28, 2015, [http://www.vocativ.com/215942/these-13-states-still-make-exceptions-for-marital-rape/]).

32. For statistics, see http://www.nationmaster.com/country-info/profiles/Syria/Crime. The connection between sexual violence and militarism was originally made by Cynthia Enloe in *Bananas, Beaches, and Bases* (Berkeley: University of California Press, 1990). Much has also been written on the specific use of sexual violence in war. For a very recent manifestation, see Diana Tietjens Meyers, "Caring about Human Rights: The case of ISIS and Yazidi Women," (http://blog.oup.com/2016/05/human-rights-isis-yazidi-women/, accessed June 10, 2016). The resemblance between the rhetoric and strategy here and in the Balkan wars is stunning. The rhetoric also seems to appear in the discourse surrounding Indian partition and its

violence (women jumping into a well to commit suicide lest they be raped and their cultural purity violated!). Another side of the problem with culturalistic explanations in a globalized environment becomes evident when we learn that, for example, U.S. marines are instructed to be complicit in sexual violence in Afghanistan by "respecting" local culture (See Shane Harris, "Marines Trained That Rape in Afghanistan Is a 'Cultural Issue,'" *Daily Beast*, September 23, 2015 (http://www.thedailybeast.com/articles/2015/09/23/marines-taught-to-look-the-other-way-when-afghans-rape-children.html, accessed May 17, 2016)). Here, culturalistic explanation seems to simply stand in the service of persisting oppression of women by men—no matter what the culture. Marieme Helie Lucas, founder of Women Living Under Muslim Laws, reads the 2015 New Year's Eve attacks in Germany as a coordinated effort of radical fundamentalist Islamic right to exclude (all) women from public spaces. She draws connections between these attacks and the curtailment of women's involvement in Tunis, Tahrir, and first Pan African festival in Algiers in 1969. Noting the shift of description from North African/Arab to Muslim, she writes, "This show of force may meet with success, as was to a large extent the enforcement on women of the 'Islamic veil.' The kind of advice given by some German authorities to the attacked women in Cologne attest to it: adjust to the new situation, stay away from men ('at arm's length'), don't go out on your own, etc. . . . In short, submit or pay the price for it. If anything happens to you, it will be your fault, you have been warned. . . . An advice that brings back to memory what used to be said in court, not so long ago, to women who were raped: why were you in such a place? At such a time? In such a dress? An advice that Muslim fundamentalist preachers will definitely not disavow. That the primary concern was to protect perpetrators and not to defend the victims is a variation on the usual defense of men's violence against women. To what extent is it a defense of patriarchy, or a defense of migrants, of ethnic or religious minorities? When the interests of patriarchy (that the Left does not dare defend officially anymore) merge with the noble defense of the 'oppressed' (their prestige, even on the Left, was somewhat damaged after the November attacks in Paris), it suits many people." See Marieme Helie Lucas, "Eurocentrism as a Fig-leaf and the Art of Conjuring in Politics, *Women Living under Muslim Laws,* January 5, 2016 (http://www.wluml.org/media/euro-centrism-fig-leaf-and-art-conjuring-politics and http://www.siawi.org/article10593.html, accessed June 10, 2016).

33. Some sources stress the fact that crime in general is no more and possibly *less* prevalent among the migrant/refugee population than among the natives. Rape statistics are notoriously difficult to come by (a problem exacerbated by the widespread underreporting of sexual assault) and even more difficult to interpret and compare across national boundaries. Thus, for example, high percentages of sexual violence may be interpreted to reflect a higher willingness of women to report sexual violence or different understandings of what constitutes various forms of sexual violence: "The [2014 report by EU Agency for Fundamental Rights] ranks countries in order depending on the responses to the survey. In three countries often praised for their gender equality, for example, high numbers of women report suffering violence since the age of 15: in Denmark 52%, Finland 47%, and Sweden 46% of women say they have suffered physical or sexual violence. The UK reports the joint fifth highest

incidence of physical and sexual violence (44%), whereas women in Poland report the lowest—19%. However, campaigners to end violence against women advised caution in reporting country-wide differences, given different levels of awareness of what constitutes abuse." See Jane Martinson, "Report Reveals 'Extensive' Violence against Women in EU," *The Guardian,* March 4, 2014 (https://www.theguardian.com/world/2014/mar/05/violence-against-women-eu, accessed June 10, 2016).

34. I am here following Jürgen Habermas's tripartite structuring of the lifeworld, according to which culture, society, and personality provide the substantive content of the lifeworld. See Jürgen Habermas, *A Theory of Communicative Action*, vol. 2 (Boston: Beacon Press, 1987), 138–45. According to Habermas, it is society whereby group membership is established and solidarity is secured (138). For him, at least at this stage, solidarity is measured by group cohesion and integration. As we shall see in the following section "Dialogue as Transformative Praxis," this is unlikely to be an adequate conception of solidarity for transnational feminist interactions. That said, processes of socialization will remain relevant with regard to the transformative dimension of transnational feminist dialogue.

35. Chandra Mohanty, "Transnational Feminist Crossings: On Neoliberalism and Radical Critique," *Signs* 38 no. 4 (2013): 972. One might wonder whether Mohanty underestimates the power of numbers. It seems that some institutions at least, having increased the number of minority students and faculty, are now finding that "living together" is calling for further, more fundamental or structural changes. Presence, in short, has an effect, and difference may make its own demands despite efforts to flatten it.

36. Mohanty, "Transnational Feminist Crossings," 969.

37. Mohanty, "Transnational Feminist Crossings," 977.

38. Mohanty, "Transnational Feminist Crossings," 975.

39. Chandra Mohanty, "Transnational Feminist Crossings," 984.

40. With regard to the Swedish situation, Mohanty cites Diana Mulinari, Suvi Keskinen, Sari Irni, and Salla Tuori, "Introduction: Postcolonialism and the Nordic Models of Welfare and Gender," in *Complying with Colonialism: Gender, Race and Ethnicity in the Nordic Region*, eds. Suvi Keskinen, Salla Tuori, Sari Irni, and Diana Mulinari (Burlington, VT: Ashgate, 2009), 1–16; and Mulinari, Diana, and Nora Räthzel, "Politicizing Biographies: The Forming of Transnational Subjectivities as Insiders Outside," *Feminist Review*, no. 86 (2007): 89–112. For Mexico, see R. Aída Hernández Castillo, "Indigenous Law and Identity Politics in Mexico: Indigenous Men's and Women's Struggles for a Multicultural Nation," *PoLAR* 25, no. 1 (2002): 90–109; and R. Aída Hernández Castillo, "Indigeneity as a Field of Power: Multiculturalism and Indigenous Identities in Political Struggle," in *The Sage Handbook of Identities*, eds. Margaret Wetherell and Chandra Talpade Mohanty (London: Sage, 2010), 379–451. For Palestine, see Islah Jad, "NGOs: Between Buzzwords and Social Movements." *Development in Practice* 17, no. 4–5 (2007): 622–29; and Islah Jad, "The Politics of Group Weddings in Palestine: Political and Gender Tensions," *Journal of Middle East Women's Studies* 5, no. 3 (2009): 36–53.

41. Mohanty, "Transnational Feminist Crossings," 978, 981.

42. Mohanty, "Transnational Feminist Crossings," 982.

43. Costa herself presents translation issues as far more complex and suggests that feminism is itself a process of translation. "Feminist Theories, Transnational Translations, and Cultural Mediations," in *Translocalities/Translocalidades* (Durham, NC: Duke University Press, e-Duke Books, 2014).

44. Lata Mani, "Multiple Mediations: Feminist Scholarship in the Age of Multinational Reception," *Feminist Review* 35 (Summer 1990): 24–41.

45. Allison Weir, *Identities and Freedom: Feminist Theory between Power and Connection* (New York: Oxford University Press, 2013), 3.

46. Ibid.

47. Ibid., 29.

48. Ibid., 53. She goes beyond Foucault and Taylor in arguing that "We can't simply accept our collective identities as given, but we also can't assume that collective identities are always fixed and normalizing categories. Resistant identities are often the *result* of a recognition and critique of oppression, and these identities often emerge out of solidarity, out of a desire for association and relationship, rather than the other way around" (p. 31).

49. Ibid., 63.

50. Ibid., 78.

51. Ibid., 71.

52. Judith Butler's *Toward a Performative Theory of Assembly* (Boston: Harvard University Press 2015) is one recent attempt to fill this gap.

53. Weir, *Identities and Freedom*, 71.

54. Ibid., 72–73.

55. Ibid., 42, 49.

56. Taking up the notion of "positional identity," Weir rejects a thin reading of position as a category ("women" as opposed to "men," say) and prefers a thick reading of position as a location or place "from which values are interpreted and constructed" (p. 67, referring to Alcoff). She quotes Linda Alcoff: "When colonized subjects begin to be critical of the formerly imitative attitude they had toward colonists, what is happening is that they begin to *identify with* the colonized rather than the colonizers." Linda Alcoff, *Visible Identities: Race, Gender, and the Self* (New York: Oxford University Press, 2006), 148; quoted in Weir, *Identities and Freedom*, 67, italics Weir's.

57. Weir, *Identities and Freedom*, 67.

58. Weir, *Identities and Freedom*, 67–68.

59. Weir, *Identities and Freedom*, 113.

60. Mohanty, "Transnational Feminist Crossings," 987, italics added.

61. See José Medina, *The Epistemology of Resistance: Gender and Racial Oppression, Epistemic Injustice, and the Social Imagination* (Oxford University Press: Oxford, 2012).

62. Philip Hogh attributes to Adorno the view that feigning agreement in order to avoid conflict is demeaning not only to one's subject matter but also one's interlocutor. Philip Hogh, "Nicht Alles und Nicht Nichts: Kommunikation bei Adorno und Habermas," in *Sprache und Kritische Theorie*, eds. Philip Hogh and Stefan Deines (Frankfurt: Campus, 2015). For examples of such negotiations, see Elora Halim Chowdhury and Liz Philipose, eds., *Dissident Friendships: Feminism, Imperialism, and Transnational Solidarity* (Urbana: University of Illinois Press, 2016).

63. For discussion of how our embodiment orients our epistemic "habits of attention," see Gaile Polhaus's "Knowing without Borders and the Work of Epistemic Gathering" in this volume. I also take her concept of "nontransactional epistemic responsibility," which requires responsiveness to others, to be consonant with the notion of dialogical accountability I am developing here.

64. Diana Coole, "Gender, Gesture and Garments: Encountering Embodied Interlocutors," in *Dialogue, Politics, and Gender*, ed. Jude Browne (Cambridge University Press: Cambridge, 2013), 173–97. Coole suggests that feminist critics of Habermas have sometimes been "unnecessarily fixated on the more formal, procedural aspects of his thinking" and refers to his earlier work to show that he is alert to the contingencies of everyday communication and does pay some heed to "the phenomenology of emergent communicative circumstances and capacities." By the same token, she adds that feminist critics have not paid sufficient attention to how the lack of attention paid to body language may have blinded Habermas to recognize certain effects of power in dialogue. She describes the body as "communicative prosthesis" and a "means of corporeal capital."

65. For an excellent discussion of the pragmatic challenges of transnational feminist dialogue, see Ellen-Rae Cachola, Gwyn Kirk, and Lisa Natividad, and María Reinat Pumarejo, "Women Working across Borders for Peace and Genuine Security," *Peace Review: A Journal of Social Justice* 22, no. 2 (2010): 164–70.

66. Simona Sharoni et al., "Transnational Feminist Solidarity in Times of Crisis," *International Feminist Journal of Politics* 17, no. 4 (2015): 654–70.

67. Sharoni et al., "Transnational Feminist Solidarity," 663.

68. Interestingly, this is in line with Adorno's view that the possibility of genuine communication that is unafraid of disagreement and challenging the other's views is threatened under conditions of late capitalism. See Hogh, "Nicht Alles und Nicht Nichts," 231.

69. Martin Seel, "Das Potential der Sprache: Adorno—Habermas—Brandom," in *Sprache und Kritische Theorie*, eds. Stefan Deines and Philip Hogh (Frankfurt: Campus, 2016), 279, my translation.

70. I am grateful to Denison University for supporting this research with an R.C. Good Fellowship and to the Cluster of Excellence on the Formation of Normative Orders at Goethe Universität in Frankfurt, where I spent my 2015–2016 sabbatical. Thanks to Jonathan Maskit, Chris Zurn, Rainer Forst, Margaret McLaren, members of the political theory colloquium in Frankfurt, and the audience at the Critical Theory Conference in Prague, where I presented earlier versions of this essay, for their helpful comments.

BIBLIOGRAPHY

Abu-Lughod, Lila. 2002. "Do Muslim Women Really Need Saving?" *American Anthropologist* 104, no. 3, 783–90.

Ahmed, Leila. 2005. "The Veil Debate Again: A View from America in the Early Twenty-first Century." In *On Shifting Ground: Muslim Women in the Global Era*, ed. Fereshteh Nourale-Simone. New York: Feminist Press at the City University of New York.

Alexander, Jacqui. 2005. *Pedagogies of Crossing*. Durham: Duke University Press.

Amnesty International. 2014. "Sexual Violence in Algeria, Tunisia, and Morocco." September 2, 2014, https://www.amnesty.org.uk/sexual-violence-algeria-tunisia-and-morocco.

Antrobus, Peggy. 2013. "The Global Women's Movement." In *Women's Lives: Multicultural Perspectives*, eds. Gwyn Kirk and Margo Okazawa-Rey. New York: McGraw-Hill, 2013, 608–15.

Butler, Judith. 2015 Toward A Performative Theory of Assembly. Boston: Harvard University Press.

Byrne, Bryan Patrick. 2015. "These 13 States Still Make Exceptions for Marital Rape." *Vocativ,* July 28, http://www.vocativ.com/215942/these-13-states-still-make-exceptions-for-marital-rape/.

Cachola, Ellen-Rae, Gwyn Kirk, Lisa Natividad, and María Reinat Pumarejo. 2010. "Women Working across Borders for Peace and Genuine Security." *Peace Review: A Journal of Social Justice* 22, no. 2: 164–70.

Chambers, Clare, and P. Parvin. "What Kind of Dialogue Do We Need? Gender, Deliberative Democracy, and Comprehensive Values. In *Dialogue, Politics and Gender*, ed. Jude Browne. Cambridge: Cambridge University Press.

Chiedu Onochie, Bridget. 2016. "Nigerian Society and the Gender Equality Debate, *The Guardian,* March 20, http://guardian.ng/sunday-magazine/newsfeature/nigerian-society-and-the-gender-equality-debate/.

Chowdhury, Elora Halim, and Liz Philipose. 2016. Eds. *Dissident Friendships: Feminism, Imperialism, and Transnational Solidarity*. Urbana: University of Illinois Press.

Enloe, Cynthia. 1990. *Bananas, Beaches, and Bases*. Berkeley: University of California Press.

Everytownresearch. 2014. "Guns and Violence against Women." *Everytownresearch,* June 16, https://everytownresearch.org/reports/guns-and-violence-against-women/.

Fultner, Barbara. 2011. "Incommensurability in Davidson and Gadamer." In *Dialogues with Davidson*, ed. Jeff Malpas. Cambridge, MA: MIT Press, 219–40.

———. 2013. "Gender, Discourse, and Non-Essentialism." In *Dialogue, Politics and Gender*, ed. Jude Browne. Cambridge: Cambridge University Press.

Gadamer, Hans Georg. 1994. *Truth and Method*, trans. Joel Weinsheimer and Donald G. Marshall. New York: Continuum.

———. 1999. "Die Vielfalt der Sprachen." In *Gesammelte Werke*, vol. 8 (Tübingen: Mohr Siebeck).

Habermas, Jürgen. 1984/1987. *A Theory of Communicative Action*, 2 vols. trans. Thomas McCarthy, Boston: Beacon Press.

Higgins, Andrew. 2015. "Norway Offers Migrants a Lesson in How to Treat Women." *New York Times*, December 19, http://www.nytimes.com/2015/12/20/world/europe/norway-offers-migrants-a-lesson-in-how-to-treat-women.html.

Jaeggi, Rahel, S. Hark, I. Kerner, H. Meißner, and M. Saar. 2015. "Das umkämpfte Allgemeine und das neue Gemeinsame. Solidarität ohne Identität." *Feministische Studien, Zeitschrift für interdisziplinäre Frauen- und Geschlechterforschung*, no. 1, 99–103.

Jaggar, Alison. 2005. "'Saving Amina': Global Justice for Women and Intercultural Dialogue." *Ethics and International Affairs* 19, no. 3: 55–75.

Kaufmann, Sylvie. 2016. "What's a European Liberal to Do?", *The New York Times,* April 1, http://www.nytimes.com/2016/04/13/opinion/international/whats-a-european-liberal-to-do.html.

Khaled, Farha. 2011. "Gil Ronen's Fabricated Statistics about Oslo Rapists being All Muslim," *Loonwatch,* December 23, http://www.loonwatch.com/2011/12/gil-ronens-fabricated-statistics-about-oslo-rapists-being-all-muslim/.

Koutsoukis, Jason. 2015. "India Burning Brides and Ancient Practice Is on the Rise." *The Sydney Morning Herald,* January 31, http://www.smh.com.au/world/india-burning-brides-and-ancient-practice-is-on-the-rise-20150115-12r4j1.html.

Mani, Lata. 1990. "Multiple Mediations: Feminist Scholarship in the Age of Multinational Reception." *Feminist Review* 35 (Summer): 24–41.

Mohanty, Chandra Talpade. 1984. "Under Western Eyes: Feminist Scholarship and Colonial Discourse." *Boundary 2* 12, no. 3: 333–58.

———. 2003. *Feminism without Borders: Decolonizing Theory, Practicing Solidarity*. Durham: Duke University Press.

———. 2013. "Transnational Feminist Crossings: On Neoliberalism and Radical Critique." *Signs* 38, no. 4: 967–991.

Naderi, Manizha. 2014. "A Law That Would Permit Afghan Men to Hurt and Rape Female Relatives." *The Guardian*, February 6, https://www.theguardian.com/commentisfree/2014/feb/06/law-afghan-men-hurt-rape-female-relatives-karzai.

Parreñas, Rhacel. 2002. "The Care Crisis in the Philippines: Children and Transnational Families in the New Global Economy." In *Global Woman: Nannies, Maids, and Sex Workers in the New Economy*, eds. Barbara Ehrenreich and Arlie Hochschild. New York: Palgrave MacMillan.

Pasternak, Judith Mahoney. 2016. "Other Pressures on Women," Letter to the Editor, *The New York Times,* May 2, http://www.nytimes.com/2016/05/02/opinion/other-pressures-on-women.html?smprod=nytcore-ipad&smid=nytcore-ipad-share.

Ross, Philip. 2015. "Algeria Domestic Violence Law: Violence against Women Illegal, But Human Rights Group Remains Skeptical." *International Business Times*, May 3, http://www.ibtimes.com/algeria-domestic-violence-law-violence-against-women-illegal-human-rights-group-1837942.

Seel, Martin. 2016. "Das Potential der Sprache: Adorno, Habermas, Brandom." In *Sprache und Kritische Theorie*, eds. Stefan Deines and Philip Hogh. Frankfurt: Campus, 275–96.

Sharoni, Simona, Rabab Abdulhadi, Nadje Al-Ali, Felicia Eaves, Ronit Lentin, and Dina Siddiqi. 2015. "Transnational Feminist Solidarity in Times of Crisis." *International Feminist Journal of Politics* 17, no. 4: 654–70.

Taylor, Charles. 1985a. "Language and Human Nature." In *Human Agency and Language, Philosophical Papers I*. Cambridge: Cambridge University Press, 215–47.

———. 1985b. "Understanding and Ethnocentrism." In *Philosophy and the Human Sciences, Philosophical Papers II*. Cambridge: Cambridge University Press.

———. 2002. "Understanding the Other: A Gadamerian View of Conceptual Schemes." In *Gadamer's Century: Essays in Honor of Hans-Georg Gadamer*, ed. Jeff Malpas, Ulrich Arnswald, and Jens Kertscher. Cambridge, MA: MIT Press.

———. 2014. "Rape Statistics Surprised Researchers, *News in English,* February 26, http://www.newsinenglish.no/2014/02/26/rape-statistics-surprised-researchers/.

Weir, Allison. 2013. *Identities and Freedom: Feminist Theory between Power and Connection. Studies in Feminist Philosophy*. New York: Oxford University.

Williams, Carol J. 2013. "India 'Dowry Deaths' Still Rising despite Modernization." *LA Times,* September 5. http://articles.latimes.com/2013/sep/05/world/la-fg-wn-india-dowry-deaths-20130904.

Chapter 9

Building Transnational Feminist Solidarity Networks

Sergio A. Gallegos

Chandra Mohanty has advocated for the development of an inclusive feminism that, avoiding the biases and limitations of traditional Western feminist approaches and methodologies, would be decolonizing, anti-capitalist, and allow for solidarity among women across different countries.[1] Now, one of the key questions that this project raises is the following one: how can feminists create networks of solidarity across borders (particularly, across existing borders between nations in the global South and the nations in global North)? My chapter takes up the key issue of feminist solidarity across borders, specifically solidarity between feminists located in the global South and the global North. Feminists have generally advocated two opposing approaches to the issues of transnational solidarity. I argue here that these approaches are not opposed but in fact complementary and mutually reinforcing.

Let me be more specific. Though numerous scholars such Caren Kaplan, Valentine Moghadam, Pascale Dufour, Sonia Álvarez, and Janet Conway maintain that the creation and maintenance of transnational feminist networks depends crucially on strategies that promote solidarity between women, there is a disagreement between them on what these strategies should be. This disagreement is reflected on the different characterizations of transnational feminist networks they offer. For instance, while Valentine Moghadam describes transnational feminist networks as entities that are very closely related with (though ultimately different from) transnational social movements since the former may "identify themselves with social movements, such as the feminist, environmentalist, human rights, or peace justice movements, and thus may be oriented towards social change,"[2] Kaplan has highlighted that transnational feminist networks are best understood through the lens of what she calls a "politics of location" that "identifies the grounds for historically specific differences and similarities between women in diverse and asymmetrical relations, creating alternative histories, identities and possibilities for alliances."[3] Thus, as we can see, it is a matter of debate whether the creation and the maintenance of transnational feminist networks depend on strategies that are primarily goal dependent (as Moghadam suggests) or identity based (as Kaplan suggests).

My goal in this chapter is to offer a detailed analysis of two cases that illustrate the development and the effective maintenance of transnational feminist solidarity networks to address this question. On the basis of these two cases, I argue that, to create and maintain transnational feminist solidarity networks (particularly, in the context of the struggle against labor exploitation), both the existence of common goals (such as the struggle for labor rights) and the development of shared identities by feminists across borders must be recognized as central elements that are complementary and mutually reinforcing. Indeed, as I show here through a detailed discussion of the case studies selected, on one hand transnational identities among groups of feminists often emerge as a consequence of the articulation and the pursuit of certain goals in response to certain shared experiences. And, on the other hand, the explicit articulation as well as the effective pursuit of some of the goals that transnational feminist networks have often depends on the development of a common identity between different groups of women in different geographic and social locations.[4] If what I argue for here is correct, one of the upshots of my work is the following one: in order to develop and maintain effective transnational feminist solidarity networks, feminists must recognize that their creation and maintenance rest both on the creation of a common transnational identity and on the articulation and pursuit of certain goals, since both processes are complementary and mutually reinforcing. In virtue of this, activists that are involved in transnational feminist networks should engage in careful reflection when shifts of goals are suggested, since this may result in changes to the social identities that they share. To address this, I explore very briefly how the notion of transversal politics, which was developed by Nira Yuval-Davis, can be of assistance to transnational feminists seeking to create solidarity networks.

I proceed in the following fashion. I offer in the section "Transnational Feminist Solidarity: Identity-Based or Goal-Based?" a brief review of some of the work previously done on transnational feminist networks, focusing on the contributions made by Moghadam, Conway, Thayer, and Álvarez. In particular, I show that though these scholars agree on issues such as the nature of transnational feminist networks and the period in which they have emerged, they disagree on how they are developed and maintained insofar as some hold that the key process that gives rise to them is the establishment of common goals, whereas others claim that the key process is the creation of a collective social identity. I also put forth the central claim of this chapter, which is that both positions are not opposed but in fact complementary and mutually reinforcing, as the establishment and the pursuit of certain goals by transnational feminist activists shape the development of a shared social identity (and vice versa). To show this, I consider in the section "The First Case Study: The Network of Indigenous Women inside the FIOB" the case of the development of a transnational feminist network created by Indigenous Mexican women within the framework of the *Frente Indígena de Organizaciones Binacionales* (FIOB). Using as a basis the works of Centolia Maldonado and Patricia Artía, Laura Velasco Ortiz, and Maylei Blackwell, I show that the transnational feminist network that Indigenous Mexican women have created (which spans from Oaxaca to California) relies crucially on the interdependence between a transnational identity that is created on the basis of a collective consciousness based on shared experiences and certain specific goals that are articulated by the women in the network. In the section "The Second Case Study: The REMTE Network," I consider the case of the *Red Latinoamericana de Mujeres transformando la Economia* (REMTE), a Latin American transnational feminist network. Building on the work of Carmen Leticia Díaz Alba, Almudena Cabezas, and Nicole Bidegain Ponte, I show that REMTE also relies on the mutual dependence between a collective identity created on the basis of shared experiences and some specific goals that the members of the network have. Finally, in the "Conclusion" section, I offer some brief concluding remarks.

TRANSNATIONAL FEMINIST SOLIDARITY: IDENTITY BASED OR GOAL BASED?

Here I lay out the main claims and common assumptions of the two main competing positions for understanding transnational feminist solidarity. For instance, Pascale Dufour, Dominique Masson, and Dominique Caouette point out that, though international feminist solidarity movements have a very long history that stretches back to the nineteenth century,[5] the development of transnational feminist networks is usually taken by scholars to be a recent phenomenon.[6] In particular, Moghadam maintains that the development of transnational feminist networks must be understood as a phenomenon that emerged in the 1980s in the context of the process of globalization.[7] To be more specific, she argues in her recent work that the current process of globalization must be understood as being crucially underpinned by two simultaneous but also opposed trends (one of which incorporates the development of transnational feminist networks): "One is the expansion of neo-liberal economic policies, including integrated financial markets . . . and a transnational capitalist class. . . . The other trend is transnational activism in response to, and rejection of, neo-liberalism. In particular, transnational feminist activism is one of the distinguishing features of globalization from below, which has challenged the masculinized hegemony of business and political elites."[8] Moreover, Conway also agrees that the creation of transnational feminist networks is a relatively recent phenomenon that has been motivated by two main forces: (1) a series of UN-sponsored international women's conferences spanning from 1975 to 1995 that brought women's movements from all over the world together and (2) a series of parallel conferences and encounters (such as the World Social Forum) that are mostly organized by NGOs and as well as independent groups and grassroots movements (such as the MST [Movimento dos Trabalhadores Sem Terra] in Brazil).[9] Thus, the creation of transnational feminist networks is something that several scholars such as Moghadam and Conway agree upon as being a relatively recent phenomenon.

In addition, feminist scholars such as Richa Nagar and Amanda Swarr stress an important terminological assumption, which is connected to the abovementioned temporal claim. As Nagar and Swarr observe, Moghadam and others defend *transnational* feminism rather than *international* or *global* feminism because "international feminisms are seen as rigidly adhering to nation-states borders and paying inadequate attention to the forces of globalization [and] global feminisms have been subjected to critical scrutiny for prioritizing northern feminist agendas and for homogenizing women's struggles for sociopolitical justice, especially in colonial and neocolonial contexts."[10] In particular, this terminological choice (along with the associated distinction) stems from Mohanty's influential critique of Western first- and second-wave feminisms. Indeed, as she acutely pointed out, when Western feminists sought to analyze the oppression that women are subject to, they assumed that all women could be treated as a uniform group, and thus failed to understand that "the application of the notion of women as a homogenous category to women in the Third World colonizes and appropriates the pluralities of the simultaneous location of different groups of women, in social class and ethnic frameworks."[11] Now, in order to defend the importance of clearly distinguishing the historical and the geographical situatedness of the struggles of different groups of women (in particular, of women of color in colonial or neocolonial contexts), Mohanty subsequently made the following argument: given that the main homogenizing force behind first- and second-wave feminism is capitalism, which she describes as a system that "depends on and exacerbates racist, patriarchal and heterosexist relations of rule,"[12] feminists should then adopt what she dubbed "an anti-capitalist transnational practice."[13] Thus, it is in virtue of recognizing that the limitations of Western feminism were in good part due to the noxious influence of capitalism that Mohanty and many others in her footsteps have advocated the need to develop a transnational feminist activism, where the term *transnational* connotes taking an anti-capitalist stance (in contrast with "international" or "global"). Once we appreciate this, we can understand why many scholars hold that the emergence of transnational feminist networks is a relatively recent phenomenon. Indeed, since the expansion of neoliberal economic policies and the development of integrated financial markets at a global level, which Moghadam mentions began to take place also in the 1980s, it is not surprising that the emergence of transnational feminist networks (which is a response to this trend) is considered to coincide temporally with this phenomenon.

Now, just as there is some agreement on the fact that the emergence of transnational feminist networks is relatively recent, there is also a certain level of agreement on what transnational feminist networks are, even though there are some discrepancies regarding how they should be defined or characterized precisely. To wit, authors such as Moghadam characterize transnational feminist networks as feminist mobilizations based in more than one country or region that "advocate for women's participation and rights while also engaging critically with policy and legal issues and with states, international organizations and institutions of global governance."[14] Others, such as Dufour, Masson, and Caouette put forth an inductive approach to characterize transnational feminist networks, which involves examining "the daily convergence of interests and identities among activists who have multiple territorial and organizational affiliations."[15] In virtue of this, they hold that transnational feminist networks cannot be defined *a priori*, but they have to be theorized in terms of a series of different activities performed by individuals or groups (which include, for instance, organizing to gain recognition, protesting oppressive structures and practices, or educating others about various alternatives, etc.) "not only by which solidarities travel beyond well established borders, but also by which they are deepened among women or among feminists." Following Dufour, Masson, and Caouette partially, Millie Thayer characterizes transnational feminist networks as a type of "counterpublics," and she specifies that a "counterpublic" is "an oppositional space in which networks, organizations and individuals who share certain values or identities engage with one another around a certain theme."[16] As we can appreciate by considering in detail these three different characterizations, though scholars differ on how transnational feminist networks should be precisely defined, they all seem to agree on the fact (and this is of crucial relevance for a point that I argue in the following sections) that they are social entities the members of which are feminists[17] unified or coalesced despite occupying different social or geographic locations (in particular, geographic locations separated by state borders). In addition, these characterizations show that the views of scholars mainly diverge on what unifies transnational feminist networks: whereas some (e.g., Moghadam) maintain that it is the existence of common goals pursued by their members, others (e.g., Thayer) suggest that it is rather the sharing or convergence of individual identities into a larger collective identity.

This difference on what precisely unifies transnational feminist networks is reflected in the two main positions that authors take in the literature vis-à-vis the question of how these networks are created and maintained. For instance, Devaki Jain appears to adopt Moghadam's position when she writes that "networks are thus a necessary but not a sufficient condition by themselves of bringing women's collective strength together to bear on society and on the state. They need a political premise and purpose, even a mass base to be able to effectively transform."[18] In a similar fashion, when Geraldine Pratt reflects on her work with *Ugnayan ng Kabataang Pilipino sa Canada* (the Filipino-Canadian Youth Alliance), focusing in particular on the fact that when she collaborated with the organization it promoted simultaneously both anti-racist campaigns in Canada and the ousting of President Joseph Estrada, she maintains that "it became apparent that, for Ugnayan, transnationalism is a political achievement, and a destination as much as an origin,"[19] thus echoing the basic tenet of Moghadam's goal-dependent position.

In contrast to this position (which underscores the central role of goals for the creation and functioning of transnational feminist networks), other scholars have taken another position, which reflects the identity-based view that Kaplan puts forth. For instance, in her analysis of how a transnational feminist network focuses on women's health and reproductive issues, Sylvia Estrada-Claudio points out that the International Women and Health Meeting (IWHM) has managed to survive and thrive despite tensions between its members, and she argues that "the success of the IWHM lies in the negotiation and the recognition of various political identities of feminist activists."[20] Also, in a parallel way, when Álvarez analyses the development and the functioning of Latin American feminist networks, she points out the following about their members:

> [they] view themselves as an integral part of a larger women's movement that encompasses other feminists (in other types of organizations and *sueltas* or independents) as well as the poor working-class women for or on behalf of whom they profess to work. . . . This double or hybrid identity led most professionalized feminist institutions to build horizontal linkages to a wide variety of organized expressions of the larger women's movements—from women in trade unions and urban community organizations to Church-linked mother's clubs—while constructing vertical links to global and local policy-making arenas. And it had been this two-way political articulation that arguably fueled feminist NGO's success in advancing a progressive gender policy agenda.[21]

Thus, as these passages make clear, despite the great influence of the goal-dependent position endorsed by Moghadam, several scholars endorse the identity-based position that Kaplan proposed since they maintain that the creation and the success of transnational feminist networks depend on the recognition of different identities of its participants and on the creation of new collective identities. Now, even though these positions are clearly different, I do not believe that they are opposed to each other, and I also think that each one captures an important aspect of the truth about the emergence and maintenance of transnational feminist networks. But how can the goal-dependent position be reconciled or merged with the identity-based position? To address this question, let me first consider another related question: in the case of a single individual, how are her specific goals or ends in life typically related with her identity? At this stage, Gloria Anzaldúa's discussion in *Borderlands/La Frontera* of the emergence of what she dubs "mestiza consciousness" provides us with a tentative solution to this question. Indeed, Anzaldúa mentions that, in virtue of being torn throughout her early years between contradictory demands imposed on her by different social groups in virtue of her sexual orientation, her gender, and her mixed-race origins, she developed a "mestiza consciousness," which she characterizes in the following terms: "the new mestiza copes by developing a tolerance for contradictions, for ambiguity. . . . She learns to juggle cultures. . . . Not only does she sustain contradictions, she turns the ambivalence into something else."[22]

As this passage shows, one of Anzaldúa's main goals through the development of a "mestiza consciousness" consisted in being able to reconcile contradictory demands. Now, as she becomes able to reconcile these contradictory demands, she develops a particular social identity, as she clearly indicates further down: "I am an act of kneading, of uniting and joining that not only has produced both a creature of darkness and a creature of light, but also a creature that questions the meanings of light and dark and gives them new meanings."[23] And, as her new identity emerges, it shapes in turn a new goal: "The mestizo and the queer exist at this time and point on the evolutionary continuum for a purpose. We are a blending that proves that all blood is intricately woven together, and that we are spawned out of similar souls."[24] As the process through which the mestiza consciousness arises shows, there is a connection that goes both ways between pursuing certain goals and embracing certain social identities in the case of individuals. In a similar way, I contend here that the same sort of connection holds at the level of groups or collectives. To be more specific, my general contention is that when individuals establish and pursue certain goals together, this usually leads to the development and the embrace of a certain social identity that is shared by these individuals, and that the adoption of this social identity is something that in turn shapes the goals that these individuals have, both as individuals and as members of a certain collective. This claim is important as it bears on the question concerning whether the creation and the success of transnational feminist networks is goal-dependent or identity-based. In a sense, both answers are correct since the establishment and pursuit of certain goals by transnational feminists influence the creation of certain shared social identities, and the establishment of these identities in turn shapes the goals that these feminists pursue and how they pursue them. Thus, the creation and the flourishing of transnational feminist networks are processes that are goal-dependent and identity based all at once. In order to appreciate this more clearly, in the next two sections I turn to the detailed analysis of two concrete case studies that illustrate how the development and the successful functioning of transnational feminist networks rest both on the establishment and the pursuit of common goals by feminists and on the creation of shared social identities.

THE FIRST CASE STUDY: THE NETWORK OF INDIGENOUS WOMEN INSIDE THE FIOB

In order to understand how Indigenous Mexican women have managed to create as well as maintain a transnational feminist network that extends from Oaxaca in southern Mexico to California (while encompassing also other locations in Sinaloa and Baja California), it is important to bear in mind several facts about the history of Indigenous peoples in southern Mexico as well as the various economic, social, and political forces to which they have been subject to throughout time. Given limitations of space, I want to stress here just some of these facts. The first fact is the relatively isolated and peripheral status of the region in southern Mexico from which the founders of the FIOB (who were mostly Mixtecs and Zapotecs) stem. Since this region (which overlaps mountainous areas in the states of Oaxaca and Guerrero that are difficult to access) has traditionally been isolated from Mexico City, it has been less exposed than other parts of Mexico to the homogenizing influences of the Spanish colonial government and, subsequently, of the Mexican state. As a result of this, there is a large proportion of the inhabitants of this region (as well as their diaspora in other places) that still speak Indigenous languages and whose lives have been shaped by systematic experiences of oppression in many domains of life (political, economic, cultural, etc.) as well as by attempts to develop resistance strategies to keep reproducing their forms of life.[25]

The second fact that I want to highlight here is that, given the isolation and poverty that Indigenous populations had been traditionally subject to, many Mixtecs and Zapotecs in rural Oaxaca and Guerrero began progressively to seek work outside their homelands. While the desperation to find employment initially pushed many to migrate to Mexico City and other urban areas in the 1940s and 1950s, the commercialization of crops such as tomatoes led them to migrate north in 1970s to look for work, first in the valleys of Sinaloa and Baja California (particularly, around San Quintín and Tijuana), and then subsequently in California. While men constituted the bulk of migrants during the early period, women also began gradually to join the ranks of those who left their hometowns in Oaxaca and Guerrero to look for work in other places. This process led to a gradual challenge to traditional gender roles within Indigenous groups both in their places of origin and in their communities in northern Mexico and the United States. Indeed, insofar as Indigenous migrant women began to take little by little a more active role as workers in different fields (not only in agriculture but also in the garment industry on both sides of the United States-Mexico border), they began to contest the roles as caregivers and homemakers that they had been traditionally assigned in the division of labor. In addition, for the Indigenous women who stayed in their hometowns, the absence of husbands and fathers also led them to challenge gradually gender roles insofar as they took a more active role in their communities to address administrative issues as well as political problems.

Finally, the third fact that I want to underscore is that despite radical changes brought to Indigenous communities by migration (both in southern Mexico as well as in their new homes) and the emergence of new challenges (such as maintaining a sense of belonging between communities in different locations that are separated by state borders), these communities have been able to achieve a remarkable success in defending their interests against attempts by outsiders (in particular, by the Mexican federal government or by local politicians) to oppress them by pooling their strengths and creating solidarities that traverse borders. For instance, in June 2006 the state police in Oaxaca brutally repressed a teachers' strike following the orders of the then governor Ulises Ruiz Ortiz. In response to this event, several Indigenous groups formed a social movement named *Asamblea Popular de Pueblos de Oaxaca* (APPO) to protest and resist the repression. And, as Lynn Stephen recounts, since many members of the APPO had relatives or friends living in California (mostly in Los Angeles), different Indigenous communities in Los Angeles (mostly Zapotecs, Mixtecs, and Triquis) swiftly organized street demonstrations in front of the Mexican Consulate to pressure the governor to resign and to express their solidarity with their sister communities in Mexico.[26]

Having provided background information on the FIOB, let me now turn to how it was created, and how Indigenous women have developed within FIOB a transnational feminist network that supports FIOB's goals as well as their own agenda (which have become to a great extent intertwined). As one of its founders, Rufino Domínguez Santos, points out, the FIOB was preceded by another organization, the Mixteco-Zapoteco Binational Front

(*Frente Mixteco-Zapoteco Binacional*; FMZB) that was founded in 1992 by Mixtec and Zapotec immigrants in California to protest the celebration of the "discovery" of the Americas.[27] However, as the efforts of the FMZB to incorporate individuals from other Indigenous groups (in particular, Triquis and Mixes) were successful, the organization grew in size and changed its name to *Frente Indígena Oaxaqueño Binacional* in 1994 to reflect its wider base.[28] Indeed, the first organizers and leaders of the FMZB (and later, of the FIOB) realized that their respective communities of origin in Mexico were often in conflict with each other despite facing the same structural problems (i.e., lack of land access, discrimination by *mestizo* government officials, repression or incarceration of Indigenous leaders) and that their communities in northern Mexico and the United States, despite being divided by language and culture, also faced the same types of problems (e.g., wage theft, labor exploitation, lack of legal assistance as undocumented immigrants). As they became aware of this, the members of the FIOB sought to organize different Indigenous groups on both sides of the United States-Mexico border to collectively defend their rights. This process has been characterized as follows by Kearney:

> the Mixtec associations in California are now intentionally elaborating this Pan-Mixtec identity, which has the advantage of encompassing all the fragmented identities into which post-Conquest history has shattered the "Mixtec." Now another cultural innovation of these organizations is to define their purpose. . . . This general purpose is attained in large part by the additive effect of the combined purposes of the three kinds of organizations that are all brought together in the California associations under one general rubric, and this is the rubric of human rights. The point here is that such grassroots defense of human rights is of necessity predicated on a co-existing sense of ethnicity.[29]

As this passage makes clear, since the founders of the FIOB realized that the many goals of the Indigenous communities to which they belonged could be better pursued by subsuming them under a single common goal (i.e., the defense of their human rights), and since they realized this could only be achieved by developing a pan-Indigenous social identity, one of their goals was to create a social identity that could serve to defend the rights of all those who would share it.[30] In virtue of this, the birth of the FIOB illustrates that goals influence the creation of identity and vice versa. Indeed, this case shows clearly that the development of a transnational solidarity network based on a pan-Indigenous identity that was explicitly built as an instrument to resist oppression (both in Mexico and the United States) is intimately connected (as Kearney observes) with the establishment of a general objective that the members of this particular transnational network pursue.

This joint process of common identity construction and of establishment and pursuit of commons goals is even more visible in the case of Indigenous women, who have not only played a key role in the construction of the pan-Indigenous identity that underpins FIOB and in the achievement of some of the goals of the organization but also used the experience of participating in the struggles of the FIOB (and of other groups) to articulate their own specific goals and to construct a specific shared identity. As several authors have pointed out, although the participation of Indigenous women in community assemblies to address common problems was rather sporadic in the 1970s and the early 1980s, they began to take a more active role in the late 1980s and the early 1990s, which is the period when the first Indigenous hometown associations that preceded the FIOB began to flourish in California and when the groundwork of the pan-Indigenous identity that Kearney mentions was laid down. In fact, Laura Velasco Ortiz has argued that migrant Indigenous women in the border region played a crucial role in the articulation of this pan-Indigenous identity through the following process in the early 1990s:

> The women interviewed stated that they had arrived in Tijuana with a family member and little by little become established on their own, which made adaptation easier. Once established on the border with the United States, they become hosts for migrants who come and go, share information, and send news with great speed across the networks. The women's function as hosts is situated in the economic and cultural terrain whose social action allows for the collective reproduction of a migratory chain for the indigenous group. This process generates cohesion and reinforces ethnic identity.[31]

However, even though women have played a key role in the construction of the pan-Indigenous identity that allowed the development of the FIOB, they have experienced at different stages various obstacles and difficulties to engage in certain forms of political participation. In particular, as Centolia Maldonado (an Indigenous Mixtec woman who was a long-time activist within the FIOB) has pointed out in her joint work with Patricia Artía, women began to participate in the early 1990s in FIOB as activists engaged in protests and street demonstrations, first against the corruption and negligence of the government of Oaxaca, and then subsequently against many forms of oppression that their communities in northern Mexico and the United States were subject to.[32] But their efforts to engage in different forms of political activism were often met with resistance by men from their own communities who resisted their attempts to challenge traditional gender roles. In particular, in her analysis of three case studies involving Mixtec women from migrant communities in northern Mexico and California, Velasco Ortiz has shown that one of the most important hindrances to the political engagement of these women has been a form of gender subordination that manifests itself through the need to obtain "permits" from their husbands before engaging in certain activities.[33] And, in the case of women who have remained in the Oaxacan homelands but whose husbands or partners have migrated to northern Mexico or the United States, the involvement in different forms of political activity has been hindered by the fact that, as Maldonado and Artía point out, these women are expected to accomplish the tasks that were traditionally performed by men (e.g., the *tequio*)[34] while still continuing to fulfill the tasks traditionally assigned to them (childcare, cooking, etc.).[35]

In response to these different manifestations of gendered oppression within their own communities, Indigenous women have sought through different strategies to subvert the traditional gender hierarchies. For instance, considering that men have traditionally held decision power in households as the main breadwinners, Indigenous women have created savings clubs that enable them to put money aside in order to create wealth that can be used to set up small businesses or better their material conditions. Now, in addition to challenging the male-dominated economic hierarchy through the accumulation of small amounts of capital that are controlled by women, these savings clubs have empowered Indigenous women in a different respect since they have produced, as Maldonado and Artía emphasize, a form of "cultural capital" to the extent that "as they take on responsibilities in the clubs, the women acquire an increased knowledge of official documents and gain the skills to manage and administer their accounts."[36] Another strategy that Indigenous women have pursued has consisted in adopting an "anchoring" role with respect to migrant men. Indeed, as María Cristina Velásquez has shown in her analysis of certain Mixtec communities in Oaxaca (in particular, of the community of San Martín Huamelulpan), since the massive migration of men from Huamelulpan led to a systematic absence of men to participate in debates concerning community matters, women successfully lobbied to obtain the right to actively participate in the assembly to defend the interests of their husbands or partners.[37] In doing this, Indigenous women have partially subverted their traditional subordination to men since they made patent that it is primarily through their continuous actions that the men who have migrated can preserve their links to their home communities.

The pursuit of these strategies to resist gender subordination within the framework of the political activities undertaken by FIOB and inside their specific communities has led Indigenous women to develop a particular kind of shared identity. This common identity is characterized by a hybrid or ambiguous status, which Verónica Vázquez García characterizes as follows: "They are not 'insiders' nor[*sic*] 'outsiders' of a particular culture, but rather 'in/outsiders.' Being at the 'borderland' of their own culture gives them a position from which to analyze reality, raise new themes and make new questions visible."[38] This characterization is also echoed by Maylei Blackwell, who writes that the common identity of these Indigenous women is based on the development and use of "nepantla strategies [that] include differential modes of consciousness, hybrid political discourses and the ability to move and shift between sites of struggle and to traffic meanings and knowledge from one context to another to create new cultural narratives of gender and empowerment."[39] To be more specific, as Blackwell points out in a more recent work, Indigenous women have developed a specific feminist identity that stands in contradistinction with traditional feminist identities that involve the exclusion of men.[40] In contrast with those, the feminist identity developed by Indigenous women is one in which Indigenous men are considered as partners and allies (and not as adversaries) in the struggle to end the subordination of women. Indeed, as Blackwell further elaborates, Indigenous women view their social identity as decisively shaped by their struggles to resist the oppression that they are subject to as *Indigenous* and as *women* to the extent that these struggles are intimately connected to each other as one Indigenous activist named Tomasa Sandoval that she interviewed stressed:

> [Tomasa Sandoval] suggested that without a consideration for women, the political and cultural project of indigenous autonomy would not be "a complete autonomy because women's right to land and equality with men is not recognized." This idea, echoed in many other forums, is a key feature of the political vision emerging from indigenous women's organizing. It builds on the idea that indigenous women's rights are inalienable and inextricably linked to indigenous people's rights and to women's rights.[41]

In virtue of this, it seems then clear that Indigenous women have adopted what Gloria Anzaldúa calls "nepantla strategies," which consist in actions aimed at creating an "in-between" space where identities are developed, mixed, and sometimes reshaped. And, as a result of the creation of this "in-between" space that enables them to reshape themselves, women belonging to the FIOB have developed a common social identity as *Indigenous feminists* in which *indigeneity* and *feminism* are considered as different but complementary tools that enable them to resist simultaneously different forms of oppression (in particular, racial and gendered ones) that are enacted by the capitalist system. This particular social identity, which is part of the pan-Indigenous identity that underpins FIOB, has enabled Indigenous women to articulate and pursue certain specific feminist goals within the framework of the general goals of the FIOB. To appreciate this, let me consider a particular instance of how some specific feminist goals became part of the overall agenda of the FIOB. As Odilia Romero Hernández, Centolia Maldonado Vásquez, Rufino Domínguez Santos, Maylei Blackwell, and Laura Velasco Ortiz recount, the FIOB organized a series of workshops throughout 2006 and 2007 in California, Baja California, and Oaxaca with the help of certain academics in the context of the project *Otros Saberes* to reflect upon the challenges that the organization faced to develop more equitable forms of participation (particularly, vis-à-vis women and young people) and to identify barriers that prevented a more effective participation in the FIOB of community members.[42] One of the results of these workshops consisted in the realization that, even if women were heavily involved in the FIOB, their activities were usually circumscribed to community matters (such as the organization of cultural events like the Guelaguetza festival) since there was a systematic lack of women in political leadership positions.

Now, in order to address this problem, the participants in the *Otros Saberes* project made recommendations to the FIOB, one of which was to establish women's leadership development programs in order to diversify their leadership and promote the participation of women in the political activities of FIOB. Following this proposal, the FIOB decided to create, in partnership with some other organizations, the program *Mujeres Indígenas en Liderazgo* (MIEL). In her study of the impact of MIEL, Blackwell has shown that, although the program was created in 2010 (and is, consequently, still rather recent), it has already had some modest results given that a few women who participated in the training offered have been recruited to occupy leadership positions in the FIOB.[43] Moreover, Blackwell has also pointed out that another consequence of the MIEL program (in addition to the training of women leaders) is the development of an awareness among Indigenous women of a common identity based on their shared experiences:

> MIEL was not only about developing leaders in the FIOB but also about developing consciousness about the social geographies of cultural dislocation of the immigrant experience and the dual discrimination of being Mexican and indigenous. . . . MIEL addresses the limited civic and political access for indigenous migrant women caused by these geographies of exclusion and institutional barriers.[44]

As this passage makes clear, the goal of training and recruiting women leaders within the framework of the FIOB, which was pursued through the establishment of the MIEL program, also helped to establish and reinforce a shared social identity among Indigenous women based on their common experiences. In virtue of this, we can appreciate that this first case study supports my thesis that the creation and the maintenance of transnational feminist networks is a process that is both goal dependent and identity based because the pursuit of certain goals goes hand in hand with the development of certain specific social identities. Let me now turn to the examination of the second case study.

THE SECOND CASE STUDY: THE REMTE NETWORK

As Díaz Alba maintains in her seminal study of the network, the REMTE was created in 1997 by the convergence of several women's organizations that were based on different Latin American countries.[45] These different organizations were concerned about the proliferation throughout the 1990s of free trade agreements such as the NAFTA [North American Free Trade Agreement] in 1992 and the Bolivia-MERCOSUR agreement in 1996, since these various agreements were often justified by a discourse that promised better economic conditions for all women after their signing and implementation. Now, given that many women belonging to different national organizations throughout Latin America were concerned about the impact on women's lives of the structural readjustment programs that were demanded by the free trade agreements, they created REMTE, as Díaz Alba stresses, to be "a space of analysis and action that aims to contribute to the critical appropriation of the economy by women through the development of ideas, debates, actions and political initiatives."[46] More specifically, given the women's misgivings about the consequences of the free trade agreements spearheaded by several governments in the region, one of the central objectives of REMTE when it was created was to oppose the implementation of this neoliberal free trade agenda. In taking this central (and explicit) position against the expansion of free trade, REMTE stood apart from other feminist movements in the region, since those had been more concerned traditionally with political rights and reproductive issues than with economic concerns.

In addition to differentiating itself from many other feminist movements by focusing primarily on economical matters generated by the drive to implement a free trade agenda, REMTE has also distinguished itself by opposing free trade in some very specific ways. Rather than attempting to lobby governments and other institutional agents involved in free trade discussions, REMTE has focused its efforts, as Díaz Alba states, on "the empowerment of women at the grassroots level and the creation of feminist knowledge regarding macro-economic issues."[47] There are three main reasons that REMTE has pursued this strategy to oppose the implementation of the free trade agenda. First, as Díaz Alba maintains, most of the women that compose REMTE are not economists or free trade "experts" versed in the technical jargon employed by academics or by high-level government employees working to justify and implement the free trade agenda. In virtue of this, the members of REMTE sought to develop an understanding of how free trade agreements would impact women's lives on issues such as labor rights.[48] Second, as Bidegain Ponte underscores, REMTE decided from its very inception to oppose frontally the free trade agenda through social mobilizations and street demonstrations rather than by attempting to participate in the discussions between Latin American governments and other institutions because, for REMTE members, "capitalism is considered an anthropocentric and androcentric system based on sexual, racial and international division of work."[49] In taking this anti-capitalistic stance, REMTE members showed that they were well aware of a central insight that has been articulated by Aníbal Quijano, which is that "the racist distribution of new social identities was combined . . . with a racist distribution of labor and the forms of exploitation of colonial capitalism."[50] Thus, in light of this, any attempt to participate in the free trade discussions to influence governments would have been considered as tantamount to a tacit acceptance of the capitalist system and of the racial and gender hierarchies that underlie it. Third, as Cabezas shows, since the founders of REMTE were deeply influenced by the experiences of previous social movements in Latin America during 1960s and 1970s (and since these movements tended to have explicit leftist political orientations and also emphasized direct action to enact social change), REMTE has chosen to "emphasize the distributive and national side."[51]

As a consequence of their radical opposition to the free trade agenda (and of the ways in which they have carried this opposition), the members of REMTE have developed a particular social identity. In the words of Díaz Alba, "REMTE has contributed also to the development of a collective identity of feminists who denounce the logic of free trade."[52] To be more specific, a key component of this identity is the realization that, insofar as the logic of free trade is one in which everything is turned into a commodity that can be traded, the commodification and the exploitation of women's bodies go hand in hand with the commodification and exploitation of nature, as Bidegain Ponte makes clear when she writes that, for REMTE, "the logic of overexploitation of nature as if it were an inexhaustible resource is the same as [the logic of] overexploitation of women's bodies and work."[53] Thus, while other feminist organizations have constructed collective identities around programs that involve fighting against the subordination of women primarily in the political domain and/or in sexual and reproductive matters, REMTE's collective identity has been built, as Cabezas holds, "around a sisterhood of women in economic solidarity."[54] Moreover, it is also important to notice here that, insofar as Latin American countries have historically been treated in colonial or quasi-colonial ways by the United States in accordance with the Roosevelt corollary to the Monroe Doctrine, REMTE has chosen to emphasize since its foundation its regional identity as a Latin American network since one of its goals is to oppose free trade through the empowerment of women's movements in the South. Thus, even though REMTE has some strong links with certain women's organizations in the United States and Canada, the network stresses its Latin American character because, in the words of one its founders that are reported by Cabezas, "it would be only Latin American to strengthen the capacities of women's organizations from the South."[55] In pursuing this strategy, REMTE members appear to follow a suggestion made by Quijano, which consists in the fact that, to avoid succumbing to defeat by capitalist forces, they need to "learn to free [themselves] from the Eurocentric mirror where [their] image is always, necessarily, distorted."[56]

As the previous discussion has illustrated, the main goal of REMTE (i.e., the struggle by women against the free trade agenda imposed in Latin America), as well as the various ways in which this goal has been pursued since REMTE's creation (i.e., the empowerment of women's movements at the grassroots level, the mass mobilization of women to put pressure on governments that are favorable to the free trade agenda, and the production of feminist knowledge about macroeconomic issues), has been key in the development of a certain collective identity that is shared by REMTE members. Indeed, they view themselves as *anti-capitalist Latin American feminists* insofar as they consider their struggles against the subordination of women in Latin America and against the economic exploitation of nature and of vulnerable groups as two sides of the same coin. Embracing this particular collective identity has had important consequences for REMTE insofar as it has enabled the network to pursue and attain certain specific goals such as weaving feminist concerns into the agenda of broader social movements. For instance, as Bidegain Ponte remarks, the participation of Bolivian REMTE members in the People's Summit in Rio de Janeiro in 2012 was particularly important because of the following:

> The Bolivian members stated that the transformation of colonial structures of society must include the questioning of patriarchal structures and relations. "Decolonization" must be accompanied by a process of "depatriarchization" of the state and society. The notion of depatriarchization of the state was incorporated into the discourse of REMTE's Brazilian focal point when assessing gender aspects of public policies in Latin America.[57]

By stressing this demand, the Bolivian Indigenous members of REMTE made clear that they considered the patriarchal structures of domination in the state and the society as instruments of a colonial system that had to be dismantled to fully achieve decolonization. Their actions are quite significant since they show that Bolivian REMTE members grasped well a key idea that has been articulated by María Lugones, which is that "the imposition of this gender system was as constitutive of the coloniality of power as the coloniality of power was constitutive of it. The logic of the relation between them is of mutual constitution."[58] In other terms, since REMTE Bolivian members came to realize that the racial oppression that they were subject to (which is a product of what Quijano calls "the coloniality of power") was reinforced by the gender subordination they also faced, they also realized that they had to dismantle the patriarchal structures in order to achieve a full decolonization of society.

Thus, considering the above-mentioned evidence, an analysis of the history, as well as the actions of REMTE, supports the thesis that I put forth in the section "Transnational Feminist Solidarity: Identity-Based or Goal-Based?," which is that the building and maintenance of transnational feminist networks are processes that are both goal dependent and identity based since the establishment and the pursuit of certain goals by transnational feminists networks shape their collective identities, and these collective identities influence in turn the goals that the networks have. As the case of REMTE shows, the main goal of its members (as well as the ways in which this goal has been pursued) has led them to adopt a collective identity as *anti-capitalist Latin American feminists*, and this collective identity has helped them articulate and pursue other goals, such as the need to depatriachize the state since they have come to acknowledge, as Lugones has persuasively argued, that patriarchal structures and relations reinforce the capitalist system.

CONCLUSION

Let me recap. I have argued here, through the analysis of two case studies, that the two traditional positions regarding the creation and maintenance of transnational feminist networks (namely, the goal-dependent position and the identity-based position) are not really opposed or competing, but rather complementary and mutually reinforcing because the articulation and the pursuit of certain goals by feminists shape a collective identity, which in turn influences the pursuit of certain goals. Now, if it is indeed the case that both processes are complementary, what lessons should feminists draw? Let me just focus on one issue. In order to have a larger impact in an increasingly complex world where different actors compete for public support, several transnational feminist networks recently have engaged in a process of alliance-building with other movements through the "stretching" of solidarities. However, such a process, as Estrada-Claudio warns, faces a potential challenge, which is that alliance-building often involves adopting rather simple political positions that obscure differences, and this "runs contrary to the complexity of the emergent feminist politics."[59] Now, though this is indeed a genuine concern, I believe that the study of the two cases that I have presented earlier in this chapter suggests a way in which this pitfall may be avoided. If we keep in mind that the women involved in the FIOB and in REMTE have developed an awareness of the fact that they are subject to different forms of oppression and that these different forms of oppression are deeply intertwined within the framework of a system that oppresses and marginalizes the most vulnerable groups (women, of course, but also Indigenous communities, disabled individuals, LGBT groups, etc.), they have the tools to develop effective alliances with other movements (in particular, with other social movements that emphasize other priorities) in virtue of being committed to the ideal of a transversal politics, which Yuval-Davis has characterized as being based upon three main elements: the adoption of a standpoint epistemology, the encompassment of difference by equality and a conceptual differentiation between positioning, identity, and values.[60] Indeed, an analysis of their actions shows that they embrace a form of transversal politics. For instance, as Cabezas observes, though the primary focus of REMTE has been (and still remains) the struggle against the free trade agenda in Latin America, its members have also engaged with the LGBT organization South-South Dialogue, which is "an international coalition aimed to strengthen the full citizenship of people who face discrimination due to their sexual orientation."[61] In addition, even if the main focus of the FIOB's efforts remains the defense of the rights of Indigenous Mexicans on both sides of the United States-Mexico border, the FIOB leaders have engaged other groups such as U.S. unions that share some of their concerns (e.g., demands for better working conditions and higher wages) in order to build alliances.[62] In virtue of this, the practice of a form of transversal politics can be potentially used as an effective decolonizing tool. Indeed, given that colonial systems of domination typically relied on the creation of caste divisions that pitted different groups against one another, engaging in transversal politics can help create solidarities among different groups by showcasing how individuals in different social locations can nevertheless share the same values and pursue common goals. Thus, to conclude, I would like to suggest that building and maintaining effective transnational feminist networks capable of building effective alliances with other groups require that the members of these networks be committed to transversal politics.[63]

NOTES

1. Chandra T. Mohanty, "'Under Western Eyes' Revisited: Feminist Solidarities through Anti-Capitalist Struggles." *Signs* 28 (2003): 499–535.

2. Valentine Moghadam, *Globalization and Social Movements. Islam, Feminism and the Global Justice Movement*, 2nd ed. (Lanham: Rowman and Littlefield, 2013), 7.

3. Caren Kaplan, "The Politics of Location as Transnational Feminist Critical Practice." In *Scattered Hegemonies: Postmodernity and Transnational Feminist Practices* (Minneapolis: University of Minnesota Press, 1994), 139.

4. Sonia Álvarez distinguishes two logics that, according to her, have guided the formation and the action of transnational feminist movements: an identity-solidarity

logic and an IGO-advocacy logic. My thesis is that these two logics are not really opposed, but rather complementary and mutually reinforcing. See Sonia Álvarez, "Translating the Global: Effects of Transnational Organizing on Local Feminist Discourses and Practices in Latin America." *Meridians* 1 (2000): 31.

5. For a detailed study of the emergence of the International Women's movement at the end of the nineteenth century, see Leila Rupp, *Worlds of Women: The Making of an International Women's Movement* (Princeton: Princeton University Press, 1997).

6. Pascale Dufour, Dominique Masson, and Dominique Caouette, "Introduction." in *Solidarities Beyond Borders*, edited by Pascale Dufour, Dominique Masson, and Dominique Caouette (Vancouver: UBC Press, 2010), 1.

7. Valentine Moghadam, *Globalizing Women: Transnational Feminist Networks* (Baltimore: John Hopkins University Press, 2005), 5–7.

8. Valentine Moghadam, "Transnational Feminist Activism and Movement Building." In *The Oxford Handbook of Transnational Feminist Movements*, edited by Rawida Baksh and Wendy Harcourt (New York: Oxford University Press, 2015), 53.

9. Janet Conway, "Transnational Feminisms Building Anti-Globalization Solidarities." *Globalizations* 9, no. 3 (2012): 380–81.

10. Richa Nagar, and Amanda L. Swarr, "Introduction." In *Critical Transnational Feminist Praxis*, edited by Richa Nagar and Amanda L. Swarr (Albany: SUNY Press, 2010), 4.

11. Chandra. T. Mohanty, "Under Western Eyes: Feminist Scholarship and Colonial Discourses." *Feminist Review* 30 (1988): 79.

12. Mohanty, "'Under Western Eyes' Revisited," 510.

13. Ibid., 509.

14. Moghadam, *Globalization and Social Movements*, 134.

15. Dufour et al., "Introduction," 3.

16. Millie Thayer. *Making Transnational Feminism* (Routledge: New York, 2010), 26.

17. The notion of feminist that I use here (and throughout the rest of the article) stems from the characterization of feminism that Myra Marx Ferree provides in the following passage: "Activism for the purpose of challenging and changing women's subordination to men is what defines 'feminism'. Feminism is a goal, a target for social change, a purpose informing activism, not a constituency or a strategy." See Ferree, "Globalization and Feminism: Opportunities and Obstacles for Activism in the Global Arena." In *Global Feminism*, edited by Myra Marx Ferree and Aili Mari Tripp (New York: New York University Press, 2006), 6.

18. Devaki Jain, "Feminist Networks, People's Movements and Alliances: Learning from the Ground." In *Feminist Politics, Activism and Vision*, edited by Luciana Ricciutelli, Angela Miles, and Margaret McFadden (London: Zed Books, 2004), 64.

19. Geraldine Pratt, the Philippine Women Centre of BC, and the Filipino-Canadian Youth Alliance, "Seeing beyond the State: Toward Transnational Feminist Organizing." In *Critical Transnational Feminist Praxis*, edited by Richa Nagar and Amanda L. Swarr (Albany: SUNY Press, 2010), 80.

20. Sylvia Estrada-Claudio, "The International Women and Health Meetings: Deploying Multiple Identities for Political Sustainability." In *Solidarities Beyond*

Borders, edited by Pascale Dufour, Dominique Masson, and Dominique Caouette (Vancouver: UBC Press, 2010), 114.

21. Sonia Álvarez, "Advocating Feminism: The Latin American Feminist NGO 'Boom.'" In *Feminist Politics, Activism and Vision*, edited by Luciana Ricciutelli, Angela Miles, and Margaret McFadden (London: Zed Books, 2004), 124.

22. Gloria Anzaldúa, *Boderlands/La Frontera* (Aunt Lute Books: San Francisco, 1987), 79.

23. Ibid., 81.

24. Ibid., 85.

25. Michael Kearney has clearly appreciated this, as the following passage shows: "The cultural and legal status of Mixtecs and Zapotecs has long been problematic for the Mexican government, which in the twentieth century has sought to incorporate them into mainstream mestizo Mexican society and culture. The dynamics of Mixtec and Zapotec transnational culture and politics . . . have . . . lent new energies to grassroots indigenous projects that seek forms of political and cultural autonomy that challenge the hegemony of the nation-state and its assimilative project." See Michael Kearney, "Transnational Oaxacan Indigenous Identity: The Case of Mixtecs and Zapotecs." *Identities* 7, no. 2 (2000): 175.

26. Lynn Stephen, *We Are the Face of Oaxaca: Testimony and Social Movements*, (Durham: Duke University Press, 2013), 258–59.

27. Rufino Domínguez-Santos, "The FIOB Experience: Internal Crisis and Future Challenges." In *Indigenous Mexican Migrants in the United States*, edited by Jonathan Fox and Gaspar Rivera-Salgado (La Jolla: University of California, San Diego, 2014), 71–72.

28. The name was subsequently changed to *Frente Indigena de Organizaciones Binacionales* to reflect a further enlargement.

29. Kearney, "Transnational Oaxacan Indigenous Identity," 187.

30. Echoing Kearney's remarks about the emergence of a pan-Indigenous identity in the 1990s, Laura Velasco Ortiz (2005, 187) maintains that one of the key indicators of the emergence of the FIOB as a cohesive movement that advocates effectively for the rights of its members consists in the fact that "the boundary between Mixtecos and Zapotecos becomes less sharp in view of a shared identity as Oaxacan Indigenous people."

31. Laura Velasco Ortiz, "Women, Migration and Household Survival Strategies: Mixtec Women in Tijuana." In *Women and Migration in the US-Mexico Borderlands*, edited by Denise A. Segura and Patricia Zavella (Durham: Duke University Press, 2007), 356–57.

32. Centolia Maldonado and Patricia Artía. "'Now We Are Awake': Women's Political Participation in the Oaxacan Indigenous Binational Front." In *Indigenous Mexican Migrants in the United States*, edited by Jonathan Fox and Gaspar Rivera-Salgado (La Jolla: University of California, San Diego, 2000), 498.

32. Laura Velasco Ortiz. *Mixtec Transnational Identity* (Tucson: University of Arizona Press, 2005), 169–76.

33. James Robson and Raymond Wiest characterize the *tequio* as follows: "The tequio is community service—the contribution of voluntary (unpaid) labor to community projects that require the participation of large numbers of people including

the maintenance and improvement of the community basic infrastructure (sewerage, roads) and the conservation of territorial resources." See James Robson and Raymond Wiest, "Transnational Migration, Customary Governance and the Future of Community: A Case Study from Oaxaca, Mexico." *Latin American Perspectives* 41, no. 3 (2014): 106.

35. Maldonado and Artía, " 'Now We Are Awake,' " 500.

36. Ibid., 501.

37. María C. Velásquez, "Eslabones entre el migrante y su pueblo: las mujeres en la nueva institucionalidad comunitaria indígena de la Mixteca Oaxaqueña." In *Ilusiones, Sacrificios y Resultados. El Escenario Real de las Remesas de Emigrantes a Estados Unidos*, edited by Blanca Suárez and Emma Zapata Martelo (México, DF: GIMTRAP, 2007), 286.

38. Verónica Vázquez García, "Gender, Ethnicity and Indigenous Self-Government in Oaxaca, Mexico." *International Feminist Journal of Politics* 15, no. 3 (2012): 317.

39. Maylei Blackwell, "Lideres Campesinas: Nepantla strategies and Grassroots Organizing at the Intersections of Globalization." *Aztlán: A journal of Chicano Studies* 35, no. 1 (2010): 15.

40. Maylei Blackwell, "The Practice of Autonomy in the Age of Neoliberalism: Strategies from Indigenous Women's Organizing in Mexico." *Journal of Latin American Studies* 44, no. 4 (2012): 721–22.

41. Ibid., 723.

42. Odilia Romero Hernández, Centolia Maldonado Vásquez, Rufino Domínguez Santos, Maylei Blackwell, and Laura Velasco Ortiz, "Género, generación y equidad: los retos del liderazgo indígena binacional entre México y Estados Unidos en la experiencia del Frente Indígena de Organizaciones Binacionales." In *Collaborative Research on Indigenous and Afro-Descendant Cultural Politics*, edited by Charles R. Hale and Lynn Stephen (Santa Fe, NM: School for Advanced Research Press, 2013), 75–100.

43. Maylei Blackwell, "Geographies of Difference: Transborder Organizing and Indigenous Women's Activism." *Social Justice* 42 (2015): 146.

44. Ibid., 149.

45. Carmen L. Díaz Alba, "Building Transnational Feminist Solidarity in the Americas." In *Solidarities beyond Borders*, edited by Pascale Dufour, Dominique Masson, and Dominique Caouette (Vancouver: UBC Press, 2010), 199–222.

46. Carmen L. Díaz Alba, "La Red Latinoamericana de Mujeres Transformando la Economía: Construir Puentes entre la Justicia Económica y la Equidad de Género." *La Ventana* 26 (2007): 74.

47. Díaz Alba, "Building Transnational Feminist Solidarity in the Americas," 210.

48. Díaz Alba, "La Red Latinoamericana de Mujeres Transformando la Economía," 79.

49. Nicole Bidegain Ponte, "Gender, Economic, and Ecological Justice Demands in Latin America: Toward an Interlinked Frame for Collective Action." *Latin American Policy* 5, no 2 (2014): 324.

50. Aníbal Quijano, "Coloniality of Power, Eurocentrism and Latin America," *Nepantla: Views from the South* 1, no. 3 (2000): 537.

51. Almudena Cabezas, "Transnational Feminist Networks Building Regions in Latin America." *Latin American Policy* 5, no. 2 (2014): 214.

52. Díaz Alba, "La Red Latinoamericana de Mujeres Transformando la Economía," 89.

53. Bidegain Ponte, "Gender, Economic, and Ecological Justice Demands in Latin America," 324.

54. Cabezas, "Transnational Feminist Networks Building Regions in Latin America," 214.

55. Ibid., 216.

56. Quijano, "Coloniality of Power, Eurocentrism and Latin America," 574.

57. Bidegain Ponte, "Gender, Economic, and Ecological Justice Demands in Latin America," 324–25.

58. María Lugones, "Colonialidad y género." *Tabula Rasa* 9 (2008): 93.

59. Estrada-Claudio, "The International Women and Health Meetings," 123–24.

60. Nira Yuval-Davis, "What Is 'Transversal Politics'?" *Soundings* 12: 94–95.

61. Cabezas, "Transnational Feminist Networks Building Regions in Latin America," 219.

62. Eduardo Stanley, "El Retorno del Sindicato de Campesinos," *UITA-Secretaría Regional Latinoamericana*, March 31, 2009, accessed January 20, 2017, http://www6.rel-uita.org/internacional/retorno_sindicato_de_campesinos.htm.

63. I am grateful to the American Association of Mexican Philosophers for allowing me to present a previous version of this essay at their 2016 conference at Syracuse University. Thanks in particular to my commentator Itzel Mayans Hermida, Roberta Liliana Flores Angeles, Carla Merino Rajme, Teresa Bruno Nino, Adriana Renero, Manuel Vargas, Enrique Chávez Arvizo, Arturo Javier Castellanos, and Matías Bulnes for their helpful questions and suggestions. Last, but not least, I thank Margaret McLaren for her generous and insightful feedback at various stages.

BIBLIOGRAPHY

Álvarez, Sonia. "Translating the Global: Effects of Transnational Organizing on Local Feminist Discourses and Practices in Latin America." *Meridians* 1, no 1 (2000): 29–67.

———. "Advocating Feminism: The Latin American Feminist NGO 'Boom.'" In *Feminist Politics, Activism and Vision*, edited by Luciana Ricciutelli, Angela Miles, and Margaret McFadden, 122–48. London: Zed Books, 2004.

Anzaldúa, Gloria. *Borderlands/La Frontera*. San Francisco: Aunt Lute Books, 1987.

Bidegain Ponte, Nicole. "Gender, Economic, and Ecological Justice Demands in Latin America: Toward an Interlinked Frame for Collective Action." *Latin American Policy* 5, no 2 (2014): 319–30.

Blackwell, Maylei. "Lideres Campesinas: Nepantla Strategies and Grassroots Organizing at the Intersections of Globalization." *Aztlán: A journal of Chicano Studies* 35, no. 1 (2010): 13–48.

———. "The Practice of Autonomy in the Age of Neoliberalism: Strategies from Indigenous Women's Organizing in Mexico." *Journal of Latin American Studies* 44, no. 4 (2012): 703–32.

———. "Geographies of Difference: Transborder Organizing and Indigenous Women's Activism." *Social Justice* 42 (2015): 137–54.

Cabezas, Almudena. "Transnational Feminist Networks Building Regions in Latin America." *Latin American Policy* 5, no. 2 (2014): 207–20.

Conway, Janet. "Transnational Feminisms Building Anti-Globalization Solidarities." *Globalizations* 9, no. 3 (2012): 379–93.

Díaz Alba, Carmen L., "La Red Latinoamericana de Mujeres Transformando la Economía: Construir Puentes entre la Justicia Económica y la Equidad de Género." *La Ventana* 26 (2007): 70–100.

———. "Building Transnational Feminist Solidarity in the Americas." In *Solidarities beyond borders*, edited by Pascale Dufour, Dominique Masson, and Dominique Caouette (Vancouver: UBC Press, 2010), 199–222.

Domínguez Santos, Rufino. "The FIOB Experience: Internal Crisis and Future Challenges." In *Indigenous Mexican Migrants in the United States*, edited by Jonathan Fox and Gaspar Rivera-Salgado (La Jolla: University of California, San Diego, 2014), 69–80.

Dufour, Pascale, Dominique Masson, and Dominique Caouette. "Introduction." In *Solidarities beyond Borders*, edited by Pascale Dufour, Dominique Masson, and Dominique Caouette (Vancouver: UBC Press, 2012), 1–31.

Estrada-Claudio, Sylvia. "The International Women and Health Meetings: Deploying Multiple Identities for Political Sustainability." In *Solidarities beyond Borders*, edited by Pascale Dufour, Dominique Masson, and Dominique Caouette (Vancouver: UBC Press, 2010), 108–26.

Ferree, Myra M. "Globalization and Feminism: Opportunities and Obstacles for Activism in the Global Arena." In *Global Feminism*, edited by Myra Marx Ferree and Aili Mari Tripp (New York: New York University Press, 2006), 3–23.

Jain, Devaki. "Feminist Networks, People's Movements and Alliances: Learning from the Ground." In *Feminist Politics, Activism and Vision*, edited by Luciana Ricciutelli, Angela Miles, and Margaret McFadden (London: Zed Books, 2004), 64–75.

Kaplan, Caren. "The Politics of Location as Transnational Feminist Critical Practice." In *Scattered Hegemonies: Postmodernity and Transnational Feminist Practices*, edited by Inderpal Grewal and Caren Kaplan (Minneapolis: University of Minnesota Press, 1994), 137–52.

Kearney, Michael. "Transnational Oaxacan Indigenous Identity: The Case of Mixtecs and Zapotecs." *Identities* 7, no. 2 (2000): 173–95.

Lugones, María. "Colonialidad y género." *Tabula Rasa* 9 (2008): 73–101.

Maldonado, Centolia, and Patricia Artía. " 'Now We Are Awake': Women's Political. Participation in the Oaxacan Indigenous Binational Front." In *Indigenous Mexican Migrants in the United States*, edited by Jonathan Fox and Gaspar Rivera-Salgado (La Jolla: University of California, San Diego, 2000), 495–510.

Moghadam, Valentine M. *Globalizing Women: Transnational Feminist Networks*. Baltimore: John Hopkins University Press, 2005.

———. *Globalization and Social Movements. Islam, Feminism and the Global Justice Movement*, 2nd ed. Lanham: Rowman and Littlefield, 2013.
———. "Transnational Feminist Activism and Movement Building." In *The Oxford Handbook of Transnational Feminist Movements*, edited by Rawida Baksh and Wendy Harcourt (New York: Oxford University Press, 2015), 53–81.
Mohanty, Chandra. T. "Under Western Eyes: Feminist Scholarship and Colonial Discourses." *Feminist Review* 30: 61–88.
———. "'Under Western Eyes' Revisited: Feminist Solidarities through Anti-Capitalist Struggles." *Signs* 28 (2003): 499–535.
Nagar, Richa, and Amanda L. Swarr. "Introduction." In *Critical Transnational Feminist Praxis*, edited by Richa Nagar and Amanda L. Swarr (Albany: SUNY Press, 2010), 1–20.
Pratt, Geraldine, the Philippine Women Centre of BC, and the Filipino-Canadian Youth Alliance. "Seeing beyond the State: Toward Transnational Feminist Organizing." In *Critical Transnational Feminist Praxis*, edited by Richa Nagar and Amanda L. Swarr (Albany: SUNY Press, 2010), 65–86.
Quijano, Aníbal. "Coloniality of Power, Eurocentrism and Latin America." *Nepantla: Views from the South* 1, no. 3 (2000): 533–80.
Robson, James P., and Raymond Wiest. "Transnational Migration, Customary Governance and the Future of Community: A Case Study from Oaxaca, Mexico." *Latin American Perspectives* 41, no. 3 (2014): 103–17.
Romero-Hernández, Odilia, Centolia Maldonado Vásquez, Rufino Domínguez Santos, Maylei Blackwell, and Laura Velasco Ortiz. "Género, generación y equidad: los retos del liderazgo indígena binacional entre México y Estados Unidos en la experiencia del Frente Indígena de Organizaciones Binacionales." In *Collaborative Research on Indigenous and Afro-Descendant Cultural Politics*, edited by Charles R. Hale and Lynn Stephen (Santa Fe, NM: School for Advanced Research Press, 2013), 75–100.
Rupp, Leila J. *Worlds of Women: The Making of an International Women's Movement*. Princeton: Princeton University Press, 1997.
Stanley, Eduardo. "El Retorno del Sindicato de Campesinos," *UITA-Secretaría Regional Latinoamericana*, March 31, 2009, accessed January 10, 2017, http://www6.rel-uita.org/internacional/retorno_sindicato_de_campesinos.htm.
Stephen, Lynn. *We Are the Face of Oaxaca: Testimony and Social Movements*. Durham: Duke University Press, 2013.
Thayer, Millie. *Making Transnational Feminism*. Routledge: New York, 2010.
Vázquez García, Verónica. "Gender, Ethnicity and Indigenous Self-Government in Oaxaca, Mexico." *International Feminist Journal of Politics* 15, no. 3 (2012): 314–32.
Velasco Ortiz. Laura. *Mixtec Transnational Identity*. Tucson: University of Arizona Press, 2005.
———. "Women, Migration and Household Survival Strategies: Mixtec Women in Tijuana." In *Women and Migration in the US-Mexico Borderlands*, edited by Denise A. Segura and Patricia Zavella (Durham: Duke University Press, 2007), 341–59.

Velásquez, María C. "Eslabones entre el migrante y su pueblo: las mujeres en la nueva institucionalidad comunitaria indígena de la Mixteca Oaxaqueña." In *Ilusiones, Sacrificios y Resultados. El Escenario Real de las Remesas de Emigrantes a Estados Unidos*, edited by Blanca Suárez and Emma Zapata Martelo (México, DF: GIMTRAP, 2007), 259–300.

Yuval-Davis, Nira. "What Is 'transversal politics'?" *Soundings* 12: 94–98.

Chapter 10

Decolonizing Feminist Freedom: Indigenous Relationalities

Allison Weir

In this chapter I argue that decolonizing feminist theory requires that we foreground Indigenous struggles for freedom from settler colonization, and hence that we foreground relations to land and to sovereignty in our theories.[1] Attending to Indigenous feminist ontology, epistemology, ethics, and politics can transform Western secular feminist theory, including our understandings of the self, and our politics of freedom. Foregrounding Indigenous women's critical interventions into feminist theory requires that we expand feminist models of intersectionality to include the dimension of relationship to land and sovereignty, and the dimension of secularity/spirituality/religiosity. This in turn requires that we challenge binaries of essentialism/anti-essentialism, secular/religious, and colonizer/colonized. Understanding the specificity of Indigenous relation to land requires understanding the philosophy and practice of Indigenous relationalities. And that means challenging Western secular ontologies, epistemologies, and understandings of freedom.

I begin by taking up Aileen Moreton-Robinson's argument for an Australian Indigenous women's standpoint theory, from the perspective of a white secular settler feminist. I consider the implications of Indigenous relational ontology, epistemology, and axiology, and respond to the challenges these concepts pose for Western secular feminist philosophy and political theory, arguing that these concepts point to a radically relational understanding of freedom.

Finally, I argue that feminist critiques of essentialism often rely on particular, provincial, Western secular conceptions of what freedom is. Thus they *misread* Indigenous relationality and Indigenous relational freedom. I argue that this misreading, and the reliance on this conception of freedom, leads to misreadings of Indigenous political struggles: of feminist struggles within Indigenous communities and of Indigenous struggles for sovereignty.

I argue that Indigenous philosophy offers a conception of relational freedom that includes heterogeneity and change while maintaining rootedness in relation to land. Indigenous philosophy calls all of us to open up to a radically relational theory and practice of freedom, reframing questions of individual freedom and politics of sovereignty within a theory and politics of relationality.

As a settler feminist theorist, I am engaging here in a politics of listening. Many contemporary Indigenous thinkers have called for a shift in Indigenous politics, from a politics of seeking recognition to a politics of resurgence. Rather than waiting for recognition from settler colonial states, a politics of resurgence involves asserting Indigenous forms of sovereignty; revaluing and renewing Indigenous knowledge, law, philosophies, and practices; and building Indigenous communities and political solidarity.[2]

I would argue that in response, settler colonial academics, activists, governments, and societies need to work on a politics of listening: to engage in a politics of self-transformation through listening, to become capable of a politics of mutual recognition. Linda Tuhiwai Smith quotes Gayatri Spivak: "For me, the question 'Who should speak?' is less crucial than 'Who will listen?' "[3]

Here we can learn from Miriam-Rose Ungunmerr-Baumann, an artist, educator, and elder of the Ngangikurungkurr tribe in Nauiyu (Northern Territory, Australia). She writes that the name of her tribe, *Ngangikurungkurr*, means "Deep Water Sounds" or "Sounds of the Deep." And in her language, the practice of tapping into the deep spring within us is called *Dadirri*: this is a practice of "inner, deep listening and quiet, still awareness." This practice of listening—*Dadirri*—she writes "is perhaps the greatest gift we can give to our fellow Australians. Dadirri recognises the deep spring that is inside us. We call on it and it calls to us. This is the gift that Australia is thirsting for. It is something like what you call 'contemplation.' " And she adds: "It's not 'Aboriginal spirituality.' Everybody's got it. It's just that they haven't found it."[4]

In our practices of listening, we need to beware of the dangers not only of ignorance and denial but also of romanticism of the Other, and of appropriating and instrumentalizing Indigenous knowledge and philosophy. While it is crucial that settler colonials learn from this knowledge, we need to remember that for Indigenous peoples, "what is more important than what alternatives Indigenous peoples offer the world is what alternatives Indigenous peoples offer each other."[5]

A note on terminology and scope: in this paper, I generally use the term *Indigenous* but also follow Indigenous scholars' uses of the terms *Native*,

Aboriginal, and *Indian* to refer to First Nations peoples, philosophies, and practices. While all of these terms are problematic generalizations, I follow Indigenous scholars' usages of the terms and their own generalizations about indigeneity. I am drawing on a range of scholarship in Indigenous studies, including work by philosophers, political theorists, and cultural and social theorists in Australia, New Zealand, Canada, and the United States.[6] While the name *Indigenous* is taken on by diverse groups with diverse practices, and while any generalizations are subject to controversy and contestation, these scholars argue that relationality is a distinctive and generalizable Indigenous philosophy. I return to these questions later in the chapter.

INDIGENOUS RELATIONALITY AND INDIGENOUS WOMEN'S STANDPOINT: CHALLENGES TO SECULAR FEMINISMS

Aileen Moreton-Robinson argues that Indigenous women's standpoint theory can both draw from and extend feminist standpoint theory. "Indigenous and feminist scholars share an understanding that their respective production of knowledge is a site of constant struggle against normative dominant patriarchal frameworks."[7] An Indigenous women's standpoint is produced through inheritance and achieved through struggle:

> It is constituted by our sovereignty and constitutive of the interconnectedness of our ontology (our way of being); our epistemology (our way of knowing) and our axiology (our way of doing). It generates its problematics through Indigenous women's knowledges and experiences, acknowledging that intersecting oppressions will situate us in different power relations and affect our different individual experiences under social, political, historical and material conditions that we share either consciously or unconsciously. These conditions and the sets of complex relations that discursively shape us in the everyday are also complicated by our respective cultural, sexual, racialised, abled and class differences. Thus our cultural and social positioning informs how, when, where and why we conduct research as well as our disciplinary knowledges and training as Indigenous women academics. Our lives are always shaped by the omnipresence of patriarchal white sovereignty and its continual denial of our sovereignty. In our everyday existence we deploy a "*tactical subjectivity* with the capacity to recentre depending upon the kinds of oppression to be confronted" within and outside our communities.[8]

While Moreton-Robinson draws from the standpoint theories of feminists of color, in particular Patricia Hill-Collins's theory of subjugated knowledges, she argues that feminist standpoint theories are typically predicated on a body/earth split and do not address their privileged relationship to the nation's sovereignty. Moreton-Robinson draws on the work of Karen Martin, Shawn Wilson, Linda Tuhiwai Smith, and others, to argue that the constitutive elements of Indigenous social research paradigms in New Zealand, Canada, and Australia are a specific ontology, epistemology, and axiology (ways of being, knowing, and doing) "rooted in our embodied connection to our respective countries, all living entities and our ancestors; our sovereignty" conceptualized as "relationality."[9] Thus the three tenets of Indigenous women's standpoint theory are:

> *Ontology (Way of Being):* "Indigenous women's ontology is derived from our relations to country." According to Moreton-Robinson, in Australia, Indigenous people's belonging can be traced to the origin time when ancestral creator beings created the land and all living things tied to particular tracts of land. The creator beings metamorphosed as stones and other aspects of the natural world including humans, changing form and gender; thus all beings share a common life force. "The ontological relationship occurs through the inter-substantiation of ancestral creator beings, humans and country; it is a form of embodiment based on blood line to country. As such Indigenous women's bodies signify our sovereignty."[10]
>
> *Epistemology (Way of Knowing):* "As an Indigenous woman my ontological relation to country informs my epistemology. My coming to know and knowing is constituted through what I have termed relationality. One is connected by descent, country, place and shared experiences where one experiences *the self as part of others and others as part of the self* [my italics]; this is learnt through reciprocity, obligation, shared experiences, co-existence, co-operation and social memory." According to Indigenous epistemology, "I am worth no more or no less than other living things: the world I inhabit has been created by ancestral creator beings and it is organic and alive with spirits and signs which inform my way of knowing. Thus respect and caution frame my approach to knowledge production; the more that I know the less that I know because *there are other forms of knowledge that exist beyond us as humans* [my italics].One cannot know everything and everything cannot be known."[11]
>
> Moreton-Robinson writes that Indigenous women's ways of knowing are informed by shared knowledge and experiences, conscious and unconscious, shaped by social positioning, and achieved through struggle. "Such a standpoint does not deny the diversity of Indigenous women's individual concrete experiences. Rather it is where our shared knowledges and experiences within hierarchical relations of ruling and power converge and are operationalised."[12]
>
> *Axiology (way of doing):* "Indigenous women's ways of doing things within the academy are informed by our ontology and epistemology and are an extension of our communal responsibilities and sovereignties. . . . We do things on the basis of our relationality."[13]

Moreton-Robinson argues that Indigenous women's standpoint differs from feminist standpoint theories in two ways. Feminist standpoint theorists, she writes, "do not address their privileged relationship to the nation's sovereignty." And feminist standpoint theories are typically "predicated on a body/earth split, discursively positioning women as female humans above other non-human living things."[14] I shall address each of these claims in turn.

In response to the charge that they do not address their privileged relationship to the nation's sovereignty, feminist standpoint theorists might point out that many of them have criticized patriarchal and racialized understandings of the individual and private property; of the nature/culture division; and of nationalism, capitalism, and imperialism, and have developed complex theories of relationality and interconnectedness. But decolonizing feminism would require that we frame all of these critiques within an explicit analysis of the legacy and continuing politics of colonization: Western concepts of the individual, rights, and sovereignty have all been predicated on the assumption of property rights entrenched through the theory and practice of colonization.[15] For instance, John Locke's understanding of rights to property, and to the self as property, was developed in part through an explicit justification of the invasion and theft of land in the Americas, on the grounds that the settlers earned these rights by mixing their labor with the land in a way that was productive, whereas the original peoples were savages who did not. (He was, of course, mistaken on every point.)[16]

Moreover, decolonizing feminism would involve thematizing questions of sovereignty. Many Indigenous theorists argue that the legitimacy of nation-state sovereignty is rarely questioned by political theorists, who fail to question its history and future: to acknowledge that settler states are founded not just on liberal and democratic principles but on genocide, and to question the assumption that nation-states will persist into the future.[17]

This requires, as Moreton-Robinson has argued in *Talkin' Up to the White Woman*, acknowledgement and reflection on settler colonial women's privilege and agency in the oppression of Aboriginal women. Larissa Behrendt has argued that the white women's movement in Australia has failed Aboriginal women. White women gained the right to vote in all federal and state elections in 1903, but Aboriginal women were not recognized as citizens and did not have voting rights until 1967. Moreover, "issues high on the political agenda for Aboriginal women are not issues of concern for white women."[18] Such issues include sovereignty rights, land claims, protection and communication of culture, protection of women's sacred sites, maintaining social relations in their communities, the high levels of incarceration and abuse of Indigenous adults and children, destructive government intervention into communities and removal of essential infrastructure, and the continuing practice of removal of children from families and communities. Obviously any feminist movement that claims to represent women would have to prioritize these and other issues of priority to Aboriginal women. It would also not assume the right to intervene in Aboriginal communities on behalf of Aboriginal women, or to include Aboriginal women in universalizing claims about women's issues.[19]

It is also, however, important to question the unity of the category of "settlers," and the unity of a privileged relation to the nation's sovereignty, when we foreground relations to land. An intersectional analysis of settler states will recognize multiple waves of immigration of settlers who are very differently positioned on the land. So, we need to recognize the different positions of governments, corporations, property owners (and there are obviously various types of property ownership and power), renters, squatters, privileged cosmopolitans, mestizas, refugees, asylum seekers, homeless peoples, slaves and descendants of slaves, racialized groups, groups identified as white, groups that have struggled to be classified as white, oppressed and displaced nations within states, peasant farmers, landless workers, formerly colonized peoples, citizens of formerly colonized and still racialized "Third World" states, along with diverse Indigenous peoples, who occupy very different positions in systems of ownership of and responsibility for land. In Australia many of the original settlers were convicts: desperately poor people charged with petty crimes in Britain and sent to a prison colony on an island on the other side of the world, as an alternative to execution. Many new prospective settlers are asylum seekers detained in prison camps on a barren island off the coast of Australia. Such an analysis complicates any simple binary of colonizers and colonized, settlers and Indigenous peoples. Yet we need to recognize the *specificity* of the history and continuing colonization of Indigenous peoples, of Indigenous relations to land, and of Indigenous struggles for decolonization.

Moreton-Robinson's second argument is that in contrast to non-Indigenous feminist standpoint theory, "Indigenous research paradigms are founded on a construction of humanness that is predicated on the body's connectedness to our respective countries, human ancestors, creative beings and all living things."[20] For Indigenous peoples, relation to land includes all of these relationships.

Feminist theorists have analyzed the complex relations between constructions of gender, racialized femininity, and "nature," the mind-body split, and the links between patriarchal and racist domination and the domination of nature. Ecofeminists have long argued for ethical relations with the nonhuman world, and a growing number of Western feminist philosophers are working on animal ethics and interspecies ethics.[21] Still, feminist theories do tend to be human focused. In Indigenous relational ontologies there is no primacy of humans as agents or ends, or as knowers. Indigenous *relation to land* refers to the relationality of all beings and the specific connection of each being to specific areas of country.

INDIGENOUS RELATIONAL ONTOLOGY AND EPISTEMOLOGY

A central and powerful concept in some Indigenous metaphysics is the understanding of breath. Anne Waters writes:

> In Diné (Navajo) thought, for example, because the breath of life (air) is constantly being exchanged in the universe, from the cosmos and to the earth, breath plays a central role in complementary metaphysical thought. . . . smoke, as manifesting aspects of breath, operates as the medium for air to reach the sky, the cosmos, as do words when spoken or sung. The exchange of breath is important because all things in the universe are related through air, and all are made of the same basic elements. Just as we take in air to breathe, so also we let out breath, giving back to that from which we take. . . . spirit (energy) infuses everything.[22]

Waters argues that the centrality of the breath that passes through skin and connects rather than separates expresses an Indigenous nonbinary metaphysics, focused on connections rather than on separate and opposed entities and individuals. The breath (energy, spirit) circulates among all elements in the universe.[23]

Some Western feminist theorists have drawn on such worldviews to theorize feminist process metaphysics.[24] And some have theorized the relational human self in ways that echo the Indigenous conception of connecting breath. Against the assumption that the self is essentially separate and bounded, that it is simply self-evident that the body is a container that separates us from others and from the world, Catherine Keller argues that the human skin is a permeable boundary: "Our skin does not separate—it connects us to the world through a wondrous network of sensory awareness. . . . Through my senses I go into the world, and the world comes into me."[25]

The focus on breath in Indigenous ontology is also central to Indigenous theories of knowledge. As Miriam-Rose Ungunmerr-Baumann tells us:

To know me is to breathe with me.

She connects this understanding of knowledge with the practice of deep listening:

To breathe with me is to listen deeply.
To listen deeply is to connect.

Knowledge, then, could be described as a practice of *being with* and *knowing with*—very different from the subject-object model of knowledge, which involves a distanced subject who learns by testing objects, asking sceptical questions, and manipulating variables. Research is done *with*, not *on*, other beings in relationships. Relational knowing involves a practice of attentiveness and attunement, listening, watching and waiting for signs, attending with all the senses over long periods of time, remembering, and reflecting. And knowledge is conveyed through narrative, in the form of stories, rather than through the assertion of truth claims. As Thomas King writes: "The truth about stories is that that's all we are."[26]

In Indigenous philosophy, "knowing with" means that knowledge is not universal but is dispersed among diverse knowers. Even more radically, knowledge is not restricted to humans, because humans are not the only ones who know. Moreton-Robinson, along with many other Indigenous thinkers, argues that in Indigenous thought humans do not assume their knowledge to be primary or superior to the knowledge of rocks, trees, animals, spirits, and ancestors. Thus, relational knowing means not prioritizing human knowledge: listening to the knowledge of rivers and trees, recognizing those other beings as co-knowers, collaborators, and sometimes recognizing their knowledge as primary, and superior to ours. For some Indigenous thinkers, it is self-evident that stones have the most knowledge, because they have been there for the longest time.

That means that any view that assumes that humans take primacy as knowers *fails* to situate the knower in a web of relations with all beings. And any knowledge of the world or any part of it that does not include these relations is incomplete and inadequate knowledge. But it's worse than inadequate. This kind of knowledge is directly linked to the relations of domination that characterize colonization. The arrogance of assuming that humans are the only ones who know, and the failure to listen to the knowledge of animals, and of rivers and trees, lead to the understanding of the land as property, to the perception of land and all elements of the earth as raw material to be transformed into commodities. José Medina has argued that blindness to social relationality is an epistemic vice.[27] I think that if we take Indigenous relational epistemology seriously, then we will see that blindness to the radical cosmic relationality of an entirely animate world is an epistemic vice of even greater magnitude.

The idea that knowledge is dispersed among multiple knowers in an entirely animate universe is of course very difficult for Western secular academics to comprehend, let alone accept. What does it mean to say that a stone or a river has knowledge? The impulse is to see these ideas as primitive and prescientific, or, if we are more generous, romantic and beautiful but not real: not accurate representations of reality. It may be possible to see this as "Indigenous knowledge," but it's much more difficult to accept it as *knowledge*.

But this may be changing. For example, in the science of forest ecology, in the past twenty years there has been "a burst of careful scientific research occurring worldwide that is uncovering all manner of ways that trees communicate with each other above and below ground."[28] Forest ecologist Suzanne Simard has found that trees in forests communicate with each other through what she terms the *wood wide web*, and argues that "mother trees recognize and talk with their kin, shaping future generations." Thus trees are being seen as active and knowing agents. Moreover, they are being seen as social beings. Simard writes: "These discoveries have transformed our understanding of trees from competitive crusaders of the self to members of a connected, relating, communicating system."[29] In *The Hidden Life of Trees*, Peter Wohlleben describes the ways in which trees know how to interact with each other and with other beings in the natural world. With Wohlleben, Tim Flannery writes that trees are clearly sharing information, and that they appear to be in relations of care for each other.[30] It appears that Western science is just discovering what Indigenous scientists have known for many thousands of years. In the words of Murrumu Walubara Yidindji: "When you look at a tree, you see a tree. When I look at a tree, I see the tree and all of its friends."[31]

Some scientists are now pursuing connections between Indigenous knowledges and Western science, and processes of sharing knowledge.[32]

But the idea that trees are knowers is of course controversial. Can communication among trees be recognized as knowledge? Or is this "knowledge" really just an automatic response to stimuli? (Of course, some scientists believe that human knowledge too can be explained mechanistically.) As feminist epistemologist Elizabeth Potter has written, empirical facts can be open to diverse and competing interpretations that explain the findings equally well. The choice of explanatory frames is influenced, in part, by our politics.[33] In this case, our understandings of the relationships among trees are influenced by the political and ethical commitments that shape very different worldviews, or systems of knowledge. Is the communication of trees a form of knowledge among sentient beings, or is it just a mechanistic processing of electronic impulses? Are trees competitors in a universe of selfish individuals, or social beings in relations of not only power but also cooperation and love? I am suggesting that feminist theorists, especially those of us with commitments to relational ethics and relational knowledge, have very good ethical and political reasons to take Indigenous scientific knowledge seriously, and to pursue collaborations between Indigenous and Western science.

As the example of the knowledge of trees indicates, expanding our understanding of *who knows* requires expanding our understanding of *what knowledge is*. Does knowledge require consciousness and reflection? Is knowledge necessarily universal or are there diverse knowledges? Feminist standpoint theorists do recognize diverse knowledges among human knowers, who are situated in diverse positions and relations of power, producing dominant and subjugated knowledges. Can Western feminist theorists recognize the diverse knowledges of trees and even rocks?

These questions of knowledge raise questions of relativism and universalism. Is the knowledge of trees (and the Indigenous knowledge of that knowledge) something all of us could and should learn? Or should these knowledges be recognized as specific and local knowledges? Indigenous theorists argue that both are true. There are knowledges that are not meant for all of us. And there are specific knowledges that can transform universals. Many Indigenous peoples recognize diverse knowledges, connected to responsibilities for specific areas of land, and to specific roles and kin relations.[34] Recognizing the diversity of knowledge would in itself transform our general knowledge, and our understandings of objectivity and universality. A decolonized feminist theory of knowledge would need not only to recognize some Indigenous knowledge as "Indigenous knowledge" but to recognize it as *knowledge*—and, in many cases, as *better* knowledge. As Moreton-Robinson argues, Indigenous knowledge, learned through thousands of years of study, can provide a basis for what Sandra Harding calls "strong objectivity."[35]

Decolonizing feminist knowledge would require practices of self-transformation to enable a fusion of horizons. It would also require transforming our practices of knowledge. And this is where Indigenous epistemology and Indigenous axiology meet, in the practices of knowledge.

INDIGENOUS RELATIONAL AXIOLOGY: PRACTICES OF KNOWLEDGE

The relationship between knowledge and doing in Indigenous philosophy presents a further challenge to Western secular feminists. Many Indigenous theorists argue that Indigenous knowledges are misused by non-Indigenous researchers. Anishnabe scholar Deborah McGregor identifies "the fundamental dichotomy at the heart of current controversy in the field of Traditional Ecological Knowledge (TEK) in Canada: namely, the vast and ongoing separation between the academic "experts" who study TEK and TEK issues, and the Aboriginal people who actually live according to TEK teachings."[36] As McGregor points out, Indigenous knowledge is inseparable from doing. Knowledge is meant to be *lived.* Anishnabe philosopher Winona Laduke describes the Aboriginal concept of "Minobimaatisiiwin," meaning "the good life" or lifeway.[37] "From an Aboriginal perspective, if you are not living the good life, then you are not doing TEK."[38]

At a minimum, this means not using Indigenous people and knowledge as objects of research and not stealing Indigenous knowledge for profit. Linda Tuhiwai Smith writes that "research" is a dirty word among Indigenous peoples, who have been researched to death. Pharmaceutical corporations routinely steal Indigenous knowledge of plants to produce medicines, cosmetics, and "natural" supplements. Vandana Shiva has written and worked extensively against the practice of biopiracy: the corporate theft of seeds, water, and other forms of natural life, and the Indigenous knowledges of these forms of life.[39]

Here, I shall focus on only one aspect of the practice of knowledge as an ethical practice, and will consider its implications for conceptions of freedom. Indigenous philosophies criticize not only the assumption that knowledge is necessarily universalizable but also the assumption that knowledge is best practiced through (individualized) sceptical critique. Brian Yazzie Burkhart argues that in many Indigenous philosophies there is *a limit to what should be questioned.* Unlike modern Western philosophy and science, which depend on unending question-asking and testing, Indigenous philosophy is based on patient observation and contemplation. To formulate questions to test the earth, "to see if it conformed best to this pattern or that" is "to not really observe, to not really listen."[40] Knowledge involves listening, both to everything around us and to the stories that have been passed down to us. Knowledge then is relational.

Thus while it involves contemplation, this knowledge is also different from the ancient Greek contemplation of an objective world separate from the subject. "Unlike Thales and Plato, American Indian philosophers see the act of displacing oneself from the world in order to do philosophy not only as unnecessary but as highly problematic, since in doing so one is only guessing whether what one is striving after is really knowledge at all and whether the questions one has formulated are even really questions."[41] This means that there are things that should not be questioned, and questions that should not be asked. An example of such a question is the response that Western people will often give to a certain Indigenous account of creation.

> In this account, the earth rests on the back of a turtle. The Western response to this account is simply the question, "What holds the turtle?" One elder storyteller responded to this question by saying simply, "Well, then there must be turtles all the way down." The storyteller had no patience with this way of thinking. It seemed to her that asking such a question was like asking for proof that she had a mother or for proof that plants grow in the earth and nourish the people—questions, in her mind, that only someone extremely confused would ask.[42]

The "turtles all the way down" story seems to be common to many Indigenous as well as East Indian cultures (it was encountered by Jesuits in India in the sixteenth century) and has been used in both Indian and Western philosophy to illustrate the problem of infinite regress. In the Western stories the turtle view of the world is typically attributed to an "Oriental," or an old woman. In response, the Western man of knowledge scoffs, pointing out that such a view is incoherent. But what if it's the Western man of knowledge who doesn't get it? What if the story of the earth resting on the back of a turtle, who stands on the backs of more turtles, is a different form of knowledge: a story of interdependence and responsibility, in a nonmechanistic, animate universe held together not by truth claims but by stories, not by inanimate materials but by active agents?

The response to such a story is not to question its truth claims, but to appreciate the connectedness of all of creation, and the responsibilities entailed by that interdependence. Is it an accurate representation of the mechanics of the universe? No. But it does seem to have guided Indigenous communities to develop very detailed and accurate knowledge of land, water, and weather patterns, and plant and animal life, along with ways of cultivating and sustaining country. If the point of knowledge is to appreciate our place in the universe and to guide our actions, to guide us in our interactions with each other and with the world, then this kind of knowledge has served very well.

Western models of knowledge derived through sceptical questioning and critique are linked to a very specific understanding of *freedom*: the subject is free from ties to the object, and is free to test and manipulate the object.

Freedom allows, even requires, that we criticize, question, and test; these are the actions of the free thinker. We typically regard the absence of this capacity to engage in sceptical critique as an absence of individual freedom. But what if Indigenous knowledge is linked to a *different conception of freedom*: if the self is part of others and others are part of the self, then knowledge is developed with others, in our intimate relations with others, and freedom is situated in these relations. We are not free to subject others to interrogation or manipulation, because our freedom is relational freedom: we are free only in and through our relations with others, including all creatures in an animate universe.[43]

Of course Indigenous knowledge and knowledge practices include capacities for critique, and provide a basis for very strong political critiques of colonization. But these are not distanced and sceptical critiques. These are critiques of domination from within a relational perspective: critiques of distorted and broken relations, and critiques of colonizers' contempt for relations.[44]

The practices of knowledge oriented toward stories rather than truth claims, toward deep listening and *being with* rather than distanced observation, testing, and sceptical questioning, are rooted in Indigenous spirituality. As the image of breath as spirit suggests, Indigenous relationality includes more than the natural world. It also includes relations to ancestors and spirits, and can, as Moreton-Robinson notes, include relations to creator gods. This means that ancestors and spirits must also be recognized as knowers, and human knowledge will be practiced in relation with these knowers. In this animate and enspirited world, relations to all elements of creation are sacralized, and the spirits of ancestors who have passed on are still present. So we come to the difficult question of the relation between the secular and the spiritual. What is the status of forms of knowledge that McPherson and Rabb describe as "higher states of consciousness," such as the vision quest in North American communities and the dreaming in Australian Aboriginal communities? How can Western secular feminist philosophy respond to the belief that sustaining relations in a sacralized world means considering when questioning is appropriate?

Linda Tuhiwai Smith writes:

> The arguments of different Indigenous peoples based on spiritual relationships to the universe, to the landscape and to stones, rocks, insects and other things, seen and unseen, have been difficult arguments for Western systems of knowledge to deal with or accept. . . . Concepts of spirituality which Christianity attempted to destroy, then to appropriate, and then to claim, are critical sites of resistance for Indigenous peoples. The values, attitudes, concepts and language embedded in beliefs about spirituality represent, in many cases, the clearest contrast and mark of difference between Indigenous peoples and the West. It is one of the few parts of ourselves which the West cannot decipher, cannot understand and cannot control . . . yet.[45]

The spiritualities central to Indigenous ontology and epistemology present a challenge for secular Western feminism. But a practice of decolonizing feminism requires that we ask just how secular Western feminist theory actually is. The modern Western faith in the primacy of the individual is bound up with a Christian heritage: this is a culture organized around the idea that a human individual (and only a human individual) is the incarnation of a transcendent and omniscient God on earth. From this perspective, the Western feminist faith in women's individual rights and autonomy, and in a conception of individual freedom characterized by a capacity for distanced questioning, in a quest for universal truths, appears somewhat less than secular.

For Vine Deloria Jr., Christianity is the foundation of Western secular thought. In *God is Red: A Native View of Religion*, he argued that the Christian belief that the (white) human being is not a part of nature but a transcendent species has been central to the domination of Indigenous peoples. The Christian faith in the hierarchical ordering of beings justified and organized, through missions in support of settler states, the domination of Indigenous people classed as lesser beings. Moreover, Deloria argues that Christian proselytizing is rooted in the disconnection of truth from land: whereas Indigenous knowledge is relative to particular land areas and the inhabitants of those lands, the claim to a single universal truth that should be recognized by all, and the attempt to convert all to that truth, has been central to Christian missions and imperialist regimes.[46]

Talal Asad argues that while it is certainly connected to Christianity, liberal secularism has its own distinctive myths—or is in itself a myth—distinct from Christianity.[47] Deloria and Asad agree, however, that the faith in the primacy of the individual and in the individualist model of distanced and sceptical critique without limits is central to this myth. And both argue that from nonsecular perspectives, this kind of critique can be seen and experienced as a transgression of relationship. Here I want to emphasize that the Western secular understanding of individual *freedom* involves a very particular myth: that the individual has not only the right but also the duty to question and criticize without limits. Ironically, this is a certainty that we tend to accept without question. It is rooted in the secular myth that question-asking will lead us to the Truth, which is in turn linked to a particular conception of progress.

While we may believe that we can sever the practice of sceptical questioning from its roots in seeking the Truth, from an Indigenous perspective, this practice becomes not only destructive but irrational: we keep asking questions without knowing why we are doing it, in the name of a freedom that is practically meaningless.

RELATIONAL INDIVIDUAL FREEDOM

None of this should be taken to imply that Indigenous knowledges do not include individual questioning and independent thought and action. Dennis McPherson and Douglas Rabb write that individual autonomy and independent thought are highly valued and nurtured in Indigenous communities.[48] In contrast to European and settler societies in which child-rearing and education require the imposition of rules and structure, and many years of direct instruction, Indigenous child rearing has traditionally avoided any kind of coercion or punishment. McPherson and Rabb draw a striking contrast between Kantian and Indigenous understandings of the development of autonomy. While both Kantian and Indigenous models value autonomy, for Kant, children learn to be autonomous only by undergoing a long period of heteronomy: children learn to impose laws upon themselves only by learning to obey the laws imposed by parents and teachers. In contrast, Indigenous children are considered to be autonomous persons from a very young age. They are not constantly watched and controlled; they are free to explore their environments, and are expected to be independent and to take responsibility for their actions and choices. From the Indigenous perspective, the Kantian model is contradictory: what kind of strange society expects people to learn to be autonomous by being controlled?[49]

According to McPherson and Rabb, Indigenous children are taught, but they are taught not through direct instruction (which is considered a disrespectful imposition) but through narratives and rituals, through examples set by elders, and through the direct experience of a way of life. This philosophy of education is described by McPherson and Rabb as a narrative ethic: parents and elders teach by telling stories that provide the child with frameworks that help the individual to think about and decide on actions. V.F. Cordova argues that Indigenous child rearing involves pointing out choices, and letting children make their own decisions and experience consequences, so that they learn to accept responsibility. The full status of human is attained when the child comes to recognize that his actions have consequences for all his relations. Thus, autonomy requires "self-initiative combined with a high degree of self-sufficiency," but it also requires "an enhanced perception of the needs and emotions of others as well as a keen perception of where the child was in the world (a sense of place)."[50] This child-rearing practice is consistent with the ethic that guides interactions among adults: "An Aboriginal person does not tell another Aboriginal what to do. The act of directly interfering in someone's life is considered rude. . . . This is not to say that people never interfere, but when they do, it is in an indirect way designed not to offend."[51]

Some Indigenous theorists have argued that these practices reflect an "ethic of noninterference."[52] Shay Welch argues that it is "a full-throttle version of noninterference."[53] But all of these theorists stress that this ethic is situated in the context of a strong communal ethic and a practice of supportive guidance. So this is a conception of noninterference very different from the one described by Hobbes and Isaiah Berlin, who imagined an atomistic individual whose freedom was demarcated in the circumscribed space within which he was unconstrained by others. And it is very different from the image of the primitive Indian wild and alone on the empty frontier, unconstrained by rules or laws. This is a conception of noninterference that presupposes a radically relational self as part of others and others as part of the self.

This means that Indigenous practices of question-asking have not been rooted in a conception of individual freedom that demands that each individual contributes to a quest for universal truth, or that each individual must find her own Truth, or that each individual is free to test and experiment without limits and without connections or responsibilities to what is being tested.

Instead, practices of question asking are rooted in a sense of responsibility to a community, to a land and its inhabitants. And they are rooted in a philosophy of relationality, which emphasizes an experience of being with, rather than in authority, which provokes critique of authority. They are rooted, then, in a conception and practice of freedom in relationship. This is a practice of freedom not based in fear or defense against authority and constraint, not characterized by lonely atomism, and not expressed in the imaginary of doing whatever you want, or unending questioning. This is a freedom and autonomy grounded in the security that you are never alone, and the knowledge that your power comes from all your relations, to whom you are always responsible. And this understanding of individual freedom has arguably been more conducive to democratic governance than the Western conception of freedom as noninterference, which sits in conflict with conceptions of freedom as participation in democracy.

Elsewhere I argue that the Western liberal conception of individual freedom as noninterference was developed through a *misreading* of Indigenous freedom. Here I shall argue that feminist critiques of essentialism in Indigenous thought often rely on particular provincial conceptions of what freedom is. Thus they *misread* Indigenous relationality and Indigenous relational freedom. And I argue that this misreading leads to misreadings of Indigenous political struggles: of feminist struggles within Indigenous communities and of Indigenous struggles for sovereignty. I argue that understanding these struggles requires an understanding of the distinctiveness of Indigenous relational freedom.

QUESTIONS OF ESSENTIALISM: MISREADINGS OF INDIGENOUS RELATIONALITY

Indigenous theorists are frequently told that their invocation of Indigenous perspectives and knowledge, and arguments for Indigenous nationalism and sovereignty, are essentialist. Indigenous researchers do address a number of questions about essentialism. The term *Indigenous* is used to identify vastly different and diverse peoples, and Indigenous researchers certainly do not agree about what kinds of generalizations can be made about Indigenous people. Many argue that no such generalizations can be made. Moreover, essentialized categories have been used by colonizers to classify Indigenous peoples in ways that have been divisive and destructive.[54] Indigenous peoples are forced to provide evidence of authentic Indigenous identity to substantiate land claims and intellectual property claims. Such policies have served to fragment and divide communities and perpetuate racialized discourses as to who counts as a "real Indian" or "real Aboriginal."

Linda Tuhiwai Smith writes that while claiming essential Indigenous characteristics is often strategic, in struggles for Indigenous rights, there is also a spiritual conception of essence that is important to Indigenous worldviews:

> In these views, the essence of a person has a genealogy which can be traced back to an earth parent, usually glossed as an Earth Mother.
>
> A human person does not stand alone, but shares with other animate and, in the Western sense, "inanimate" beings, a relationship based on a shared "essence" of life. The significance of place, of land, of landscape, of other things

> in the universe, in defining the very essence of a people, makes for a very different rendering of the term essentialism as used by Indigenous peoples.[55]

Are these spiritual conceptions of an essence of a people and a shared essence of life even thinkable for Western secular feminism? What would it mean for a decolonized feminism to seriously engage with these ideas?

Here I want to focus on the more practical implications of the claim that relationality, rooted in connection to land, is a distinctive Indigenous worldview. Is this an essentialist claim? Again, the term *essentialism* is used to refer to a diverse array of issues.

Universality

First of all, the argument for the existence of a distinctive Indigenous worldview—connection to land and relationality—does not entail that all Indigenous people embrace this worldview. It is an argument not for universality but for *specificity*: this worldview is specific to many Indigenous peoples. The extent to which a particular worldview is generalizable across diverse Indigenous groups and diverse individuals is of course open to question. At this point we know that the worldview of relationality has been identified by many Indigenous philosophers, researchers, and activists as a distinctive Indigenous worldview.

Exclusivity

Against claims that the identification of indigeneity with relation to land excludes urban dwellers, many Indigenous theorists and activists argue that the experience of relation to land is actually just as strong among urban groups as it is among those living on country. Urban centers have typically been built on Indigenous land, and many urban Indigenous communities continue to cultivate and to sustain the lands on which they live. Renya Ramirez draws on her ethnography of urban Indigenous communities to argue that travelling back and forth between city and country actually strengthens connection to country for urban Indians. She argues that Indigenous people in diverse geographical areas are oriented around "hubs" that organize their relations and roles in community.[56]

Authenticity, Unity of Self, and Tradition

Many Indigenous people identify as Christians, Muslims, Buddhists, and embrace liberal modernity and capitalism. To what extent do they subscribe to an "Indigenous worldview"? In fact, modern individuals generally embrace heterogeneous perspectives and worldviews that do not cohere and may be in conflict. Like other modern individuals, Indigenous individuals are heterogeneous, and negotiate multiple, conflicting, and changing perspectives and worldviews.[57] Indigenous practices and traditions are not fixed but change through history and through various interactions and relations. Indigenous cultures are continuous, not static.

The assertion of a special connection to land does pose certain dangers. Indigenous and non-Indigenous theorists and activists can romanticize the image of the authentic Indian, and do make truth claims about origins and history that are open to question. Indigenous feminist theorists point out that claims of Indigenous tradition often mask patriarchal, homophobic, and racist views and practices.[58] As Andrea Smith writes, Indigenous scholars can draw on postcolonial and queer critiques of origin stories to question these claims, and to ask whether some "Indigenous traditions" are actually *effects* of colonization.[59] As Uma Narayan points out, ideologies of a pure and homogeneous culture and unchanging traditions typically mask not only differences but also power relations internal to "cultures," as well as interpenetrations between and among cultures, which are always changing. What counts as "culture" is produced through historical change and is subject to conflict and contestation.[60]

Moreover, the claim of a special connection to land can pose the danger of exclusive nationalism. Claims to sovereignty may fail to consider the claims of other precarious groups, including non-Indigenous refugees, asylum seekers, immigrants, and racialized groups. As I've already noted, we need to resist a simple binary model of relation to land, to complicate our understandings of settlers and colonized.

While all of these arguments are important, they sometimes obscure the fact that indigeneity and Indigenous sovereignty can be grounded in connections to land without being exclusive, essentialist, or ahistorical. Indigenous theorists do address these issues, and have conceptualized Indigenous relationality and sovereignty in ways that do take account of these issues, while also explicitly criticizing forms of internal oppression.

RESPONDING TO CRITIQUES OF ESSENTIALISM: HETEROGENEOUS RELATIONAL SELVES AND FREEDOMS, AND INDIGENOUS FEMINIST POLITICS

Moreton-Robinson argues that from an Indigenous standpoint, anti-essentialist critiques of the idea of an Indigenous relational self actually rely on an essentialist, specifically Western ideal of the self as "multiple, becoming and unfixed." This is a conception of self in which "humanness is disconnected from the earth," and it is "falsely universalized." Insistence on this ideal of self as a universal "can silence and dismiss non-Western constructions, which do not define the self in the same way."[61] The implication of Moreton-Robinson's argument is that anti-essentialist arguments and assertions of a fluid unfixed self are not just specifically Western and provincial; such arguments are also typical of a colonizing worldview—a view that idealizes the cosmopolitan disconnected self as the model for liberation. Do secular feminists need to ask whether our models of fluid multiple unfixed selves are actually still dependent on ideals of liberal negative freedom?

Feminist theorists, along with postcolonial, socialist, and queer theorists, have long criticized the ideal of the unitary, independent, and self-determining subject bent on mastery and control. Similarly, the ideal of the true and authentic pre-given self has been criticized with the argument that subjects are constituted through relations of power and social relations of meaning. The conception of the subject as fluid, hybrid, plural, in process, and unfixed was developed by many feminist and queer theorists as an alternative to the spectre of the unitary subject.

But Indigenous theorists have argued that theories of fluid and unfixed selves often bear traces of the ideal of the liberal individual. The fluid unfixed self echoes, in some ways, the ideal of the unfixed cosmopolitan liberal individual, which has historically been posited against the Native subject who is fixed in place and tradition. Like the cosmopolitan liberal individual, the fluid subject in process, who is heterogeneous and mobile, who easily crosses borders, is contrasted to a premodern Native subject, who is defined by ties of belonging and connection to land, and thus is locked in place and in history.[62]

Some queer of color theorists have similarly argued that in valorizing a fluid and unfixed self, a "postidentity" politics and "subjectless critique," "freedom from norms" and "tradition-free subject," postcolonial and queer theories tend to retrench white liberal ideals and identities while disavowing them.[63] For example, as Indigenous queer theorist Andrea Smith notes, Michael Warner "marks queer culture as free-floating, unlike race, which is marked by belonging and not-belonging."[64] Smith argues that these understandings of freedom are posited against a background of the fixed and unchanging Native. "The 'Native' serves as the origin story that generates the autonomous present for the white queer subject."[65]

Smith argues that this critique also applies to the feminist/queer of color ideal of the *mestiza*, which is widely embraced in feminist theory as an alternative to a fixed essential identity. Gloria Anzaldúa's *Borderlands*, a foundational text of mestiza theory, "situates Indians and Europeans in a dichotomy that can be healed through mestizaje." In *Borderlands*, "Anzaldúa positions Indian culture as having 'no tolerance for deviance,' a problem that can be healed by the 'tolerance for ambiguity' that those of mixed race 'necessarily possess.' Thus a rigid, unambiguous Indian becomes juxtaposed unfavourably with the mestizo who 'can't hold concepts or ideas in rigid boundaries.'" And thus "Native identity is relegated to a primitive past, a premodern precursor to the more modern, sophisticated mestizo identity."[66] Indigenous claims of connection to land are reformulated as expressions of fixed essences locked in place and time, and serve as a contrast or ground for images of mestiza world traveling, boundary crossing, heterogeneity, fluidity, and multiplicity.

Clearly, feminist critiques of the self-determining unitary subject need to include analyses of the ways in which this subject is posited against the primitive land-bound Native. The alternative is not to affirm the true and authentic noble Native. Indigenous groups and peoples *are* heterogeneous, multiple, and diverse. Many can trace their lineages through relations among diverse groups, including diverse groups of settlers. But this heterogeneity is not opposed to a strong affirmation of identity in relation to land. Indigenous struggles against colonization depend on a conception of self that is rooted in belonging to place *and* is heterogeneous and in process. This affirmation of indigeneity that includes heterogeneity has been particularly important in combatting the divisive tactics of colonizing states. In Australia, for instance, the Half Caste Act of 1886 and the Aboriginal Protection policies that were in effect until 1969 legislated the removal of children of "mixed" parentage from Aboriginal communities, as a means of assimilating them into white society, in an explicit eugenics policy: the aboriginal would be gradually bred out of those with white blood, who could be civilized, while the "full-blooded" Aboriginals would die out. In response to these tactics, Aboriginal Australians resist the label "mixed race" as inherently racist, recognize that most people are of "mixed" descent, and affirm that Aboriginal identity includes any line of descent, along with identification and acceptance as part of an Aboriginal community or kin network. Thus Aboriginal identity explicitly includes heterogeneity.[67]

Against the dualistic opposition of a heterogeneous, unfixed mestiza self and a fixed Native self related to land, the Indigenous relational self is both heterogeneous and rooted in place, connected to land. Against the opposition of movement and fixity, movement is grounded in connection to particular land: many Aboriginal tribes have been nomadic, and many are able to navigate vast distances following "songlines," detailed maps of the land held in songs, which mark the paths of creator beings. The idea of the relational self—the self as part of others and others as part of the self—entails a radical relationality: connection to land includes connection to the living enspirited world, in all of its diversity and processes of change. So this self is not "fixed" but radically heterogeneous through its connections.

As I have argued, this radical relationality produces a unique conception of *freedom*. Individual freedom is not based on an opposition between fixed and unfixed, autonomous and determined, but is found in connection.

Some theorists have pointed to parallels between the Indigenous relational self and feminist theories of the relational self and relational autonomy.[68] While there are commonalities, Indigenous relational individual *freedom* is distinct in that it is situated in relation to land (in the broadest sense), and is deeply connected to struggles for *sovereignty*. For Indigenous women and feminists, ideals of individual freedom, and resistance to patriarchal oppression, are intrinsically connected to struggles for sovereignty.

Feminist theorists of relational autonomy focus on the need to structure relationships to support individual autonomy. For Nedelsky, this is the capacity to discover and to follow one's own will or law.[69] For Iris Young, relational autonomy "entails recognizing that agents are related in many ways that they have not chosen." But it also entails recognizing that in these relationships "agents are able either to thwart one another or support one another. Relational autonomy consists partly, then, in the structuring of relationships so that they support the maximal pursuit of individual ends."[70]

Many Indigenous women and feminist theorists are wary of a philosophy that prioritizes the maximal pursuit of individual ends, even if it is situated in a relational conception of self. For them, Indigenous women's freedom must be connected to Indigenous struggles for sovereignty. Both of these struggles do require the restructuring of relationships, but the focus is on recognizing women's historic and contemporary roles as legitimate participants in governance and as leaders of Indigenous communities.

Freedom from violence and oppression is understood not simply as an individual right but as a quality of ethical relationships. If we do not understand the specificity of Indigenous conceptions of relational selves and relational freedom, we risk misreading Indigenous feminist struggles.

An example of such a misreading is a common interpretation of the historical challenge to the primacy of Indigenous sovereignty mounted by the Native Women's Association of Canada (NWAC). During the debates on constitutional reform in the 1990s, following the establishment of the Canadian Charter of Rights and Freedoms, the NWAC resisted the Assembly of First Nations' call for exemption of Aboriginal self-government from the Charter of Rights and Freedoms. While the NWAC supported the right to aboriginal self-government, they argued that the Canadian Indian Act had structured status, band membership, and governance according to patriarchal laws, such that Indigenous governance and representation were overwhelmingly controlled by men. Thus they argued that Aboriginal self-government should be subject to the rights and freedoms guaranteed by the Charter, to ensure that Indigenous women would have the same rights as other Canadians, including individual rights of citizenship, thought and belief, conscience and religion, assembly, association, press, speech, and especially equality rights.

The debate between the NWAC and the Assembly of First Nations was framed around the opposition between individual and collective rights, and not only by observers. The Assembly of First Nations argued that the NWAC was introducing Eurocentric individual rights against Aboriginal law of collective rights. But the interpretation of this case as an example of the struggle for women's individual rights against Indigenous sovereignty misrepresents the issues. In fact, the NWAC does support Indigenous sovereignty but has asserted the importance of individual rights as protection from patriarchal oppression masked as collective rights. Moreover, the NWAC was arguing for the collective rights of Indigenous women, mounting a court action demanding a seat at the table—a demand that was denied.

The NWAC argued for women's rights as legitimate participants in Indigenous and state governance, noting that women had always exercised considerable power in the governance of Indigenous communities, and they argued for protection under the Charter of Rights and Freedoms from oppression within Indigenous communities and within the Canadian state. They were not opposed to Indigenous sovereignty, they did not argue for individual rights against Indigenous sovereignty, and they were not arguing for the structuring of relations to support the maximal pursuit of individual ends.

Decolonizing feminist theory would require us to ask to what extent our alternatives to liberal feminism—including queer and mestiza feminist theories, and feminist theories of relational autonomy—are still wedded to particular Western liberal ideals of individual freedom. This does not mean that they ask us to reject the ideal of individual freedom. They challenge us to consider the possibility of a different conception of individual freedom in relationship. I have argued that the Indigenous conception of freedom in relationship is distinctive, and that it is essentially related to the freedom and sovereignty of Indigenous peoples. This conception of freedom grounds Indigenous feminist resistance to patriarchal power, as well as other forms of oppression.

CONCLUSION: INDIGENOUS RELATIONAL SOVEREIGNTY

> In these "postcolonial" times, terms such as *sovereignty* and *nation* have gone out of fashion. . . . Nationalism and sovereignty, it is suggested, inevitably lead to xenophobia, intolerance, factionalism, and violence. . . . The assumptions behind some of this analysis are that nations can be equated with nation-states and that the end goal of a national liberation struggle must be the attainment of a state or statelike form of governance.[71]

Indigenous struggles for sovereignty are often misread as struggles for nation-statehood, with all of the forms of oppression and exclusion that have characterized nation-states. In fact, Indigenous legal and political theorists criticize the nation-state model of sovereignty and argue for forms of sovereignty that draw on the history of systems of Indigenous political governance.[72] While the concept of sovereignty is contested and many Indigenous theorists reject the term, many argue that Indigenous sovereignty is not conceived on the model of the nation-state but is conceived in terms of relations of reciprocity. As Maaka and Fleras write, "Indigenous sovereignty rarely invokes a call for independence or noninterference: preference is in cultivating relationships as a way of working through difference in a non-combative manner."[73] As Irene Watson writes, "Aboriginal sovereignty is different from state sovereignty because it embraces diversity, and focuses on inclusivity rather than exclusivity. Aboriginal sovereignty poses a solution to white supremacy in its deflation of power."[74]

Andrea Smith argues that Indigenous women and feminists are at the forefront of Indigenous arguments for alternative relational forms of sovereignty. Indigenous feminists are critical of the heteropatriarchal logic of colonialism, and of the internalization of this logic in some struggles for Native sovereignty. They believe that when Indigenous liberation movements accept the assumption that social hierarchy is natural, assume male domination and heteronormativity, and accept property ownership as the model for land claims, they are internalizing the values of the colonizer. In response, they draw on the histories of Indigenous law and governance and on Indigenous philosophies of relationality to articulate alternative conceptions of sovereignty.

> Native women activists have begun articulating spiritually based visions of nation and sovereignty that are separate from nation-states. Whereas nation-states are governed through domination and coercion, [these visions of] Indigenous sovereignty and nationhood are predicated on interrelatedness and responsibility. In opposition to nation-states, these visions of Indigenous nationhood are based on care and responsibility for land that all can share. These models of sovereignty are not based on a narrow definition of nation that would entail a closely bounded community and ethnic cleansing. So, these articulations pose an alternative to theories that assume that the endpoint to a national struggle is a nation-state and that assume the givenness of the nation-state system.[75]

Indigenous feminists are rejecting hierarchical structures that have too often been replicated in liberation movements, and inventing models of decolonial struggle that are being taken up by contemporary Indigenous movements like Idle No More, along with other resistance movements, including Black Lives Matter. The philosophy of "Taking Power, Making Power" in Indigenous-led social movements in Latin America, as described by Adjoa Jones de Almeida and Paula Rojas in *The Revolution Will Not Be Funded*, involves both opposition to corporate and state power (taking power) and also "creating those structures within our organizations, movements, and communities that model the world we are trying to create" (making power). Recognizing that "not everyone can take up guns and go into the mountains to become revolutionaries," Indigenous feminist activists are developing organizing models that integrate political organizing into everyday lives, involving daily activities such as food preparation, and that emphasize pleasure and the liberation of self in community with others. "How do we build movements that engage our whole selves, and in which we get back as much as we give? What this theorizing of Native feminist activists suggests is that by starting to build the world we want to live in, we create a revolutionary movement that is sustainable over the long term."[76]

While Smith is writing about Indigenous feminist activism, these ideas and practices can be taken up in a politics of decolonizing feminism.

"Native feminisms transform how we understand the project of sovereignty and nation-building. . . . They challenge how we conceptualize the relationship between Indigenous nations and nation-states, how we organize for sovereignty, and how we tie sovereignty to a global struggle for liberation."[77]

NOTES

1. I am grateful to all of the participants in the Decolonizing Feminism seminar led by Kiran Grewal, Linda Martín Alcoff, and myself at the Institute for Social Justice at Australian Catholic University (ACU), Sydney, Australia, in September 2016, as well as participants at the panel on Indigenous Feminisms at the 2015 Feminist Ethics and Social Theory Conference, for responses to parts of this chapter. I especially thank Kiran Grewal, Shay Welch, and Lorraine Mayer for their challenging critiques. And I thank Jennifer Newman and Raewyn Connell for providing direction. My thanks also to Margaret McLaren and Hoyt Edge for their very helpful responses to this chapter.

2. See for example, Alfred, *Peace, Power, Righteousness*; Coulthard, *Red Skin, White Masks*; Simpson, *Dancing on Our Turtle's Back*; and Watson, *Aboriginal Peoples, Colonialism, and International Law*.

3. Gayatri Spivak, 1990. "Questions of Multiculturalism." In S. Harasayam, ed. *The Post-Colonial Critic: Interviews, Strategies, Dialogues* (New York: Routledge). Quoted by Linda Tuhiwai Smith, *Decolonizing Methodologies. Research and Indigenous Peoples*. Second Edition (London: Zed Books, 2012), 74.

4. Miriam Rose Ungunmerr-Bauman, 2015. Miriam Rose Foundation videos. https://www.youtube.com/watch?v=pkY1dGk-LyE, accessed online October 17, 2016.

5. Tuhiwai Smith, *Decolonizing Methodologies*, 109.

6. The primary scholars considered in this chapter are Aileen Moreton-Robinson (Goenpul and Quandamooka) and Larissa Behrendt (Eualeyai and Kamillaroi) in Australia; Linda Tuhiwai Smith (Ngati Ara and Ngati Porou Maori iwi) in New Zealand; Anne Waters (Seminole), Brian Yazzie Burkhart (Cherokee), and Andrea Smith (Cherokee) in the United States; and Dennis McPherson (Ojibwa), Deborah McGregor (Anishnaabe), and Taiaiake Alfred (Mohawk) in Canada.

7. Aileen Moreton-Robinson, "Towards an Australian Indigenous Women's Standpoint Theory: A Methodological Tool." *Australian Feminist Studies* 28 (78) (2013): 331.

8. Ibid., 340. Quoting Chela Sandoval, "U.S. Third World Feminism: The Theory and Method of Differential Oppositional Consciousness." In Sandra Harding, ed. *The Feminist Standpoint Theory Reader* (New York: Routledge, 2004).

9. Moreton-Robinson, "Towards an Australian Indigenous Women's Standpoint Theory," 337. The term *country* is used by Aboriginals in Australia to refer to the land to which they belong. It refers also to the relations of connection of all beings to that land, and the various practices and knowledges of relation to land and to sacred places, including songs, art, and stories.

10. Moreton-Robinson, "Towards an Australian Indigenous Women's Standpoint Theory," 340–41. The truth status of creation stories is of course disputed among Indigenous scholars. But there is wide agreement that these stories are important to Indigenous worldviews.

11. Moreton-Robinson, "Towards an Australian Indigenous Women's Standpoint Theory," 341.

12. Ibid., 342.

13. Ibid., 342.

14. Ibid., 335.

15. See Anibal Quijano, "Coloniality of Power and Eurocentrism," on the organization of global Eurocentric capitalist power, organized around the axes of coloniality and modernity.

16. See Robert Williams and James Tully on Locke. In fact the first invaders to North America did recognize that many tribes were farmers and had formal governments and signed treaties, which recognized some property rights, usually interpreted as rights of use and of course usually contravened by the state. Australian Aborigines were seen as hunters and gatherers, and the land was officially regarded as *terra nullius* prior to British settlement, until the historic Mabo ruling by the High Court of Australia in 1992, which recognized the Meriam people as traditional owners of islands in the Torres Strait. In fact custodial relationships of "care for country" are essential to Australian Aboriginal philosophy and practice. See Bill Gannage on Aboriginal cultivation of land.

17. Andrea Smith, "American Studies without America: Native Feminisms and the Nation-State." *American Quarterly* 60 (2) (2008): 309–15.

18. Larissa Behrendt, "Aboriginal Women and the White Lies of the Feminist Movement: Implications for Aboriginal Women in Rights Discourse." *Australian Feminist Law Journal* 1 (1993): 34.

19. See Moreton-Robinson on the "Huggins-Bell debate" (Moreton-Robinson, *Talkin' Up to the White Woman*, 111–25).

20. Moreton-Robinson, "Towards an Australian Indigenous Women's Standpoint Theory," 335.

21. See for example, Adams and Gruen, *Ecofeminism*; and Willett, *The Soul of Justice*.

22. Anne Waters, "Language Matters: Nondiscrete Nonbinary Dualism." In Anne Waters, ed. *American Indian Thought* (Blackwell, 2004, 103).

23. See Waters, "Language Matters," for the argument that the centrality of breath is indicative of an Indigenous nonbinary metaphysics. This focus on the breath is also found in yoga and the ancient Eastern teaching traditions, which also have their roots in Indigenous knowledges. So it appears that this ontology is common to many Indigenous worldviews.

24. See for example, Irigaray, *This Sex Which Is Not One*.

25. Catherine Keller, *From a Broken Web: Separation, Sexism, and Self* (Boston: Beacon Press, 1986), 234.

26. Thomas King, *The Truth about Stories. The Truth about Stories: A Native Narrative*. Massey Lectures Series (Toronto: Anansi Press, 2003), 2. Dian Million writes that Indigenous stories are theories See Million, "There Is a River in Me."

27. José Medina, *The Epistemology of Resistance* (Oxford University Press, 2013).

28. Suzanne Simard, "Notes from a Forest Ecologist." In Peter Wohlleben, ed. *The Hidden Life of Trees: What They Feel, How They Communicate* (Black Inc., 2016), 249.

29. Ibid., 248–49.

30. Peter Wohlleben, *The Hidden Life of Trees: What They Feel, How They Communicate* (Black Inc., 2016); and Flannery, "Introduction."

31. Murrumu Walubara Yidindji, in discussion with Nikolas Kompridis, during a visit to the Institute for Social Justice at ACU, Australia. Murrumu Walubara is foreign affairs minister of the Sovereign Yidindji Government, on land that has never been ceded to the government of Australia. See also Nerida Blair, *Privileging Australian Indigenous Knowledge* (Champaign, IL: Common Ground Publishing, 2015). We can find echoes of this understanding in feminist theories. For example, see the analysis of the work of Barbara McClintock by Evelyn Fox Keller, which has been hugely influential for feminist epistemology. For McClintock, Keller writes: "In comparison with the ingenuity of nature, our scientific intelligence seems pallid." (Fox Keller, *Reflections on Gender and Science*, 162). McClintock believed that good science required listening with humility and getting to know the plants she was studying: "No two plants are exactly alike. . . . I don't feel I really know the story if I don't watch the plant all the way along. So I know every plant in the field. I know them intimately, and I find it a great pleasure to know them" (p. 164). In her study of chromosomes, she wrote that she felt like she was part of them and they were her friends (p. 165). But "feeling like" that is different from actually believing that one is part of an animate universe.

32. See the annotated bibliography in Carson Vile and Kyle Powys Whyte, 2015, "Traditional Indigenous Knowledge in Climate Change Research," https://michiganstate.academia.edu/KyleWhyte.

33. Elizabeth Potter, "Gender and Epistemic Negotiation." In Linda Alcoff and Elizabeth Potter, eds. *Feminist Epistemologies* (New York: Routledge, 1993).

34. This can include knowledges specific to gender groups: women's knowledge and men's knowledge. This is clearly another difficult issue for feminism, but do not have the space to consider it here.

35. Moreton-Robinson, "Towards an Australian Indigenous Women's Standpoint Theory," 342.

36. Deborah McGregor, "Traditional Ecological Knowledge: An Anishnabe Woman's Perspective." *Atlantis* 29 (2) 2005: 103.

37. Winona Laduke, *All Our Relations: Native Struggles for Land and Life* (Cambridge, MA: South End Press, 1999).

38. McGregor, "Traditional Ecological Knowledge," 104.

39. See Vandana Shiva, *The Vandana Shiva Reader* (University Press of Kentucky, 2014).

40. Brian Yazzie Burkhart, "What Coyote and Thales Can Teach Us: An Outline of American Indian Epistemology." In Anne Waters, ed. *American Indian Thought: Philosophical Essays* (Malden, MA: Blackwell, 2004), 22.

41. Burkhart, "What Coyote and Thales Can Teach Us," 21.

42. Ibid., 20. Note that for many Indigenous people, including the Iroquois and Anishnaabe, the name for North America is Turtle Island.

43. I discuss relational freedom in Weir, *Identities and Freedom*, and in Allison Weir, *Decolonizing Freedom*, in progress.

44. See Cynthia Willett on the philosophy of hubristic contempt for relationship in social domination (Willett, *The Soul of Justice*).

45. Tuhiwai Smith, "*Decolonizing Methodologies*," 78.

46. Vine Deloria Jr., *God Is Red: A Native View of Religion* (Golden, Colorado: North American Press, 1994).

47. Talal Asad, *Formations of the Secular: Christianity, Islam, Modernity* (Stanford University Press, 2003).

48. Dennis McPherson and J. Douglas Rabb, *Indian from the Inside: Native American Philosophy and Cultural Renewal*. Second Edition (Jefferson, NC: McFarland, 2011).

49. My thanks to Shay Welch for bringing this argument to my attention. See Shay Welch, "Radical-cum-Relation: Bridging Feminist Ethics and Native Individual Autonomy." *Philosophical Topics* 41 (2) (2013): 203–22.

50. Viola Cordova, "Ethics: The We and the I." In Anne Waters, ed. *American Indian Thought: Philosophical Essays* (Malden, MA: Blackwell, 2004), 173–81.

51. Lorraine Mayer Brundige, "Continuity of Native Values: Cree and Ojibwa." MA Thesis, Lakehead University, Thunder Bay 1997, 42.

52. Brant 1990, Mayer Brundige, "Continuity of Native Values"; McPherson and Rabb, *Indian from the Inside*; Welch, "Radical-cum-Relation."

53. Welch, "Radical-cum-Relation," 209.

54. In Australia designations of "half-caste" Aboriginals were used to remove children from families and communities and force them into residential schools and indentured servitude, on the grounds that half-castes could gradually "assimilate" with whites. In Canada, according to the Indian Act of 1867, an Indigenous woman lost her Indian status when she married a non-Indigenous man, and was hence not entitled to live on reserves or to access benefits. The act was amended in 1985 to

eliminate this clause, yet discriminatory status designations still remain in effect. (See Suzack, Huhndorf, Perreault, and Barman, *Indigenous Women and Feminism*.)

55. Tuhiwai Smith, *Decolonizing Methodologies*, 77.

56. Renya Ramirez, *Native Hubs: Culture, Community, and Belonging in Silicon Valley and Beyond*. Durham NC: Duke University Press, 2007.

57. See, for example, Vera Palmer's incisive analysis of the preservation of Iroquoian worldviews in the seventeenth century "conversion" to Christianity of Kateri Tekakwitha, who was recently canonized by the Vatican.

58. Andrea Smith and J. Kēhaulani Kauanui, "Native Feminisms Engage American Studies." *American Quarterly* 60 (2) 2008: 309–15.

59. Andrea Smith, "Queer Theory and Native Studies: The Heteronormativity of Settler Colonialism." *GLQ: A Journal of Lesbian and Gay Studies* 16 (1–2) (2010): 41–68.

60. Uma Narayan, *Dislocating Cultures: Identities, Traditions, and Third World Feminism*. New York: Routledge, 1997.

61. Moreton-Robinson," Towards an Australian Indigenous Women's Standpoint Theory," 343.

62. Denise Ferreira da Silva has argued that the liberal ideal of the self-determining subject reflects an anxiety about control and a defensive opposition to the "affectable" raced or Native other (Ferreira da Silva, *Toward a Global Idea of Race*).

63. Puar, *Terrorist Assemblages*; Smith, "Queer Theory and Native Studies."

64. Smith "Queer Theory and Native Studies," 45.

65. Ibid., 48.

66. Ibid., 52.

67. On the other hand, divisive state policies and laws have led to internecine battles among status Indigenous people and those who claim Indigenous descent. See Audra Simpson, *Mohawk Interruptus* (Duke University Press, 2014); and Annette M. Jaimes, "Some Kind of Indian: On Race, Eugenics, and Mixed-Bloods," In Naomi Zack, ed. *American Mixed Race: The Culture of Microdiversity* (Rowman and Littlefield, 1995). Andrea Smith has been attacked for claiming Cherokee status.

68. See Napoleon, "Aboriginal Self-Determination"; and Welch "Radical-cum-Relation."

69. Nedelsky, *Law's Relations*. 2012.

70. Young, *Global Challenges*, 47.

71. Smith, "American Studies without America," 311.

72. Watson, *Aboriginal Peoples, Colonialism, and International Law*; Moreton-Robinson, *Sovereign Subjects*; Alfred, *Wasáse*.

73. Roger Maaka and Augie Fleras, "Engaging with Indigeneity: Tino Rangatiratanga in Aotearoa." In Duncan Ivison, Paul Patton, and Will Sanders, eds. *Political Theory and the Rights of Indigenous Peoples* (Cambridge: Cambridge University Press, 2000), 93.

74. Irene Watson, "Settled and Unsettled Spaces: Are We Free to Roam?" In Aileen Moreton-Robinson, ed. *Sovereign Subjects: Indigenous Sovereignty Matters* (Allen and Unwin, 2007), 20. See also Watson, *Aboriginal Peoples, Colonialism, and International Law*.

75. Smith, "American Studies without America," 312.
76. Smith, "American Studies without America," 313–14.
77. Smith and Kauanui, "Native Feminisms Engage."

BIBLIOGRAPHY

Adams, Carol J., and Gruen, Lori. 2014. *Ecofeminism: Feminist Intersections with Other Animals and the Earth.* London: Bloomsbury.

Alfred, Taiaiake. 1999. *Peace, Power, Righteousness: An Indigenous Manifesto*. New York: Oxford University Press.

———. 2005. *Wasáse: Indigenous Pathways of Action and Freedom*. Peterborough: Broadview Press.

Asad, Talal. 2003. *Formations of the Secular: Christianity, Islam, Modernity*. Stanford Research Park: Stanford University Press.

———. 2009. "Free Speech, Blasphemy, and Secular Criticism." In *Is Critique Secular?* Eds. Talal Asad, Wendy Brown, Judith Butler, and Saba Mahmood. Berkeley: University of California Press.

Behrendt, Larissa. 1993. "Aboriginal Women and the White Lies of the Feminist Movement: Implications for Aboriginal Women in Rights Discourse." *Australian Feminist Law Journal* 1: 27–44.

Blair, Nerida. 2015. *Privileging Australian Indigenous Knowledge*. Champaign, IL: Common Ground Publishing.

Brant, Clare. 1990. "Native Ethics and Rules of Behavior." *Canadian Journal of Psychiatry* 35(6): 535–39.

Burkhart, Brian Yazzie. 2004. "What Coyote and Thales Can Teach Us: An Outline of American Indian Epistemology." In *American Indian Thought: Philosophical Essays*. Ed. Anne Waters. Malden, MA: Blackwell.

Cordova, Viola. 2004. "Ethics: The We and the I." In *American Indian Thought: Philosophical Essays*. Ed. Anne Waters. Malden, MA: Blackwell.

Coulthard, Glen. 2007. "Subjects of Empire: Indigenous Peoples and the 'Politics of Recognition' in Canada." *Contemporary Political Theory* 6: 437–60.

———. 2014. *Red Skin, White Masks: Rejecting the Colonial Politics of Recognition*. Minneapolis University of Minnesota Press.

Deloria, Vine Jr. 1994. *God Is Red: A Native View of Religion*. Golden, CO: North American Press.

Ferreira da Silva, Denise. 2007. *Toward a Global Idea of Race*. Minneapolis University of Minnesota Press.

Flannery, Tim. 2016. "Introduction." In *The Hidden Life of Trees: What They Feel, How They Communicate*. Ed. Peter Wohlleben. Black Inc.

Fox Keller, Evelyn. 1985. *Reflections on Gender and Science*. Yale University Press.

Irigaray, Luce. 1985. *This Sex Which Is Not One*. Trans. Catherine Porter. Ithaca: Cornell University Press.

Keller, Catherine. 1986. *From a Broken Web: Separation, Sexism, and Self.* Boston: Beacon Press.

King, Thomas. 2003. *The Truth about Stories: A Native Narrative*. Massey Lectures Series. Toronto: Anansi Press.

Laduke, Winona. 1999. *All Our Relations: Native Struggles for Land and Life*. Cambridge, MA: South End Press.

Maaka, Roger, and Augie Fleras. 2000. "Engaging with Indigeneity: Tino Rangatiratanga in Aotearoa." In *Political Theory and the Rights of Indigenous Peoples*. Eds. Duncan Ivison, Paul Patton, and Will Sanders. Cambridge: Cambridge University Press.

Martin, Karen. 2008. *Please Knock before You Enter: Aboriginal Regulation of Outsiders and the Implications for Researchers*. Teneriffe, Queensland, Australia: Post Pressed.

Mayer Brundige, Lorraine. 1997. "Continuity of Native Values: Cree and Ojibwa." MA Thesis, Lakehead University, Thunder Bay, 42–46.

McGregor, Deborah. 2005. "Traditional Ecological Knowledge: An Anishnabe Woman's Perspective." *Atlantis* 29 (2): 103–9.

McPherson, Dennis H., and J. Douglas Rabb. 2011. *Indian from the Inside: Native American Philosophy and Cultural Renewal*. Second Edition. Jefferson, NC: McFarland.

Medina, José. 2013. *The Epistemology of Resistance*. New York Oxford University Press.

Million, Dian. 2014. "There Is a River in Me: Theory from Life." In *Theorizing Native Studies*. Eds. Audra Simpson and Andrea Smith. Durham, NC Duke University Press.

Moreton-Robinson, Aileen. 2000. *Talkin' Up to the White Woman: Indigenous Women and Feminism*. Queensland University of Queensland Press.

———. 2007. *Sovereign Subjects: Indigenous Sovereignty Matters*. London Allen and Unwin.

———. 2013. "Towards an Australian Indigenous Women's Standpoint Theory: A Methodological Tool." *Australian Feminist Studies* 28 (78): 331–47.

Napoleon, Val. 2005. "Aboriginal Self-Determination: Individual Self and Collective Selves." *Atlantis* 29 (2): 1–21.

Narayan, Uma. 1997. *Dislocating Cultures: Identities, Traditions, and Third World Feminism*. New York: Routledge.

Nedelsky, Jennifer. 2011. *Law's Relations: A Relational Theory of Self, Autonomy, and Law*. New York Oxford University Press.

Quijano, Anibal. 2000. "Coloniality of Power and Eurocentrism in Latin America." *International Sociology* 15 (2): 215–32.

Potter, Elizabeth. 1993. "Gender and Epistemic Negotiation." In *Feminist Epistemologies*. Eds. Linda Alcoff and Elizabeth Potter. New York: Routledge.

Puar, Jasbir. 2007. *Terrorist Assemblages: Homonationalism in Queer Times*. Durham, NC: Duke University Press.

Ramirez, Renya. 2007. *Native Hubs: Culture, Community, and Belonging in Silicon Valley and Beyond*. Durham, NC: Duke University Press.

Shiva, Vandana. 2014. *The Vandana Shiva Reader*. Lexington University Press of Kentucky.

Simard, Suzanne. 2016. "Notes from a Forest Ecologist." In *The Hidden Life of Trees: What They Feel, How They Communicate*. Ed. Peter Wohlleben. Black Inc.

Simpson, Leanne. 2011. *Dancing on Our Turtle's Back*. Winnipeg, Canada: Arbeiter Ring.

Smith, Andrea. 2008. "American Studies without America: Native Feminisms and the Nation-State." *American Quarterly* 60 (2): 309–15.

———. 2010. "Queer Theory and Native Studies: The Heteronormativity of Settler Colonialism." *GLQ: A Journal of Lesbian and Gay Studies* 16 (1–2): 41–68.

Smith, Andrea, and J. Kēhaulani Kauanui. 2008. "Native Feminisms Engage American Studies." *American Quarterly* 60 (2): 309–15.

Suzack, Cheryl, Shari M. Huhndorf, Jeanne Perreault, and Jean Barman, eds. 2010. *Indigenous Women and Feminism: Politics, Activism, Culture*. Vancouver: University of British Columbia Press.

Tuhiwai Smith, Linda. 2012. *Decolonizing Methodologies: Research and Indigenous Peoples*. Second Edition. London: Zed Books.

Tully, James. 1993. *An Approach to Political Philosophy: Locke in Contexts*. Cambridge: Cambridge University Press.

Ungunmerr-Bauman, Miriam Rose. 2015. Miriam Rose Foundation videos. https://www.youtube.com/watch?v=pkY1dGk-LyE, accessed online October 17, 2016.

Waters, Anne. 2004. "Language Matters: Nondiscrete Nonbinary Dualism." In *American Indian Thought*. Ed. Anne Waters. Oxford Blackwell.

Watson, Irene. 2007. "Settled and Unsettled Spaces: Are We Free to Roam?" In *Sovereign Subjects: Indigenous Sovereignty Matters*. Ed. Aileen Moreton-Robinson. Sydney Allen and Unwin.

———. 2014. *Aboriginal Peoples, Colonialism, and International Law: Raw Law*. London Routledge.

Weir, Allison. 2013. *Identities and Freedom*. New York: Oxford University Press.

Welch, Shay. 2013. "Radical-cum-Relation: Bridging Feminist Ethics and Native Individual Autonomy." *Philosophical Topics* 41 (2): 203–22.

Willett, Cynthia. 2001. *The Soul of Justice: Social Bonds and Racial Hubris*. Ithaca: Cornell University Press.

———. 2014. *Interspecies Ethics*. New York: Columbia University Press.

Williams, Robert A, Jr. 1992. *The American Indian in Western Legal Thought: The Discourses of Conquest*. New York: Oxford University Press.

Wilson, Shawn. 2008. *Research Is Ceremony: Indigenous Research Methods*. Halifax, Canada: Fernwood.

Wohlleben, Peter. 2016. *The Hidden Life of Trees: What They Feel, How They Communicate*. Black Inc.

Young, Iris. 2007. *Global Challenges: War, Self-Determination, and Responsibility for Justice*. Cambridge: Polity Press.

Index

About the Contributors

Professor Linda Martín Alcoff is professor of philosophy at Hunter College and the Graduate School, C.U.N.Y. She is a past president of the American Philosophical Association, Eastern Division. Recent books include *Visible Identities: Race, Gender and the Self* (2006), and *The Future of Whiteness* (2015). Her website is www.alcoff.com.

Dr. Celia T. Bardwell-Jones is an associate professor of philosophy and chair of the Gender and Women's Studies Program at the University of Hawaii in Hilo, United States. Dr. Bardwell-Jones's research interests span the areas of feminist philosophy; American philosophy; and philosophy of race, immigration, and transnational thought. In addition, she is interested in the intersections of nature and Indigenous philosophies.

Dr. Pascha Bueno-Hansen is an associate professor of Women and Gender Studies at the University of Delaware in the United States. She also coordinates the Sexualities and Gender Studies Minor as well as the LGBTQ+ and Racial Justice Activism Living and Learning Community. She earned her doctoral degree in Politics, Feminist Studies, and Latin American and Latino Studies from the University of California, Santa Cruz. Her book *Feminist and Human Rights Struggles in Peru: Decolonizing Transitional Justice* was published in 2015.

Dr. Sylvanna M. Falcón is an associate professor in the Department of Latin American and Latino Studies at the University of California, Santa Cruz in the United States. Her research and teaching interests are in human rights activism, transnational feminism, racism and antiracism, and transitional justice in Peru. She is the author of the award-winning book *Power Interrupted: Antiracist and Feminist Activists inside the United Nations* (2016) and the coeditor of *New Directions in Feminism and Human Rights* (2011). She is a former UN consultant to the UN Special Rapporteur on Violence Against Women. She is also the host of a news and public affairs radio program called *Voces Críticas/Critical Voices* on 88.1FM KZSC (UCSC's radio station).

Dr. Barbara Fultner is professor of philosophy and women's and gender studies at Denison University, United States. Her research interests include intersubjectivity, embodiment, normativity, and social practices. Her current project on feminist social ontology draws on feminist and critical theory, social philosophy, and philosophy of language and mind. She is editor of *Jürgen Habermas: Key Concepts* and translator of Habermas's *Truth and Justification.*

Dr. Sergio A. Gallegos is assistant professor in the Department of Philosophy of Metropolitan State University of Denver, United States. He received his BA in philosophy at the National Autonomous University of Mexico (UNAM) and his PhD in philosophy at the Graduate Center of the City University of New York (GC-CUNY). His works have appeared in *Hypatia*, *Studies in History and Philosophy of Science*, *Axiomathes*, and *Inter-American Journal of Philosophy*.

Dr. Kanchana Mahadevan is professor at the Department of Philosophy, University of Mumbai, India. She researches and publishes in the areas of feminist philosophy, critical theory, and political thought. She has also published in the interdisciplinary fields of aesthetics and film philosophy. Her book *Between Femininity and Feminism: Colonial and Postcolonial Perspectives on Care* (2014) examines the relevance of Western feminist philosophy in the Indian context.

Dr. Margaret A. McLaren is George D. and Harriet W. Cornell chair of philosophy, and coordinator of the Sexuality, Women's and Gender Studies Program, at Rollins College in Winter Park, Florida, United States. Her articles on women and human rights, feminism, cooperatives and economic empowerment, and Foucault have appeared in several journals, including *Social Theory and Practice*, *Journal of Developing Societies*, *Forum on Public Policy*, *Philosophy Today*, and *Hypatia*, as well as in a number of book anthologies. She is the author of *Feminism, Foucault, and Embodied Subjectivity* (2002), and *Women's Activism and Transnational Feminism: From the Local to the Global* (forthcoming).

Professor Chandra Talpade Mohanty is Dean's Professor of the humanities, and distinguished professor in the Department of Women's and Gender Studies at Syracuse University, in Syracuse, New York, United States. She is the coeditor of *Sage Handbook of Identities* (2010); *Feminism and War:*

Confronting U.S. Imperialism (2008); *Feminist Genealogies, Colonial Legacies, Democratic Futures* (1997); and *Third World Women and the Politics of Feminism* (1991); and the author of *Feminism without Borders: Decolonizing Theory, Practicing Solidarity* (2003).

Professor Kelly Oliver is W. Alton Jones Professor of philosophy at Vanderbilt University, in Nashville, Tennessee, United States. She is the author of over 100 articles, over 15 books, and 10 edited volumes. Her authored books include, most recently, *Carceral Humanitarianism: The Logic of Refugee Detention* (2017) *Hunting Girls: Sexual Violence from The Hunger Games to Campus Rape* (2016); *Earth and World: Philosophy after the Apollo Missions* (2015); *Technologies of Life and Death: From Cloning to Capital Punishment* (2013); *Knock Me Up, Knock Me Down: Images of Pregnancy in Hollywood Film* (2012); and *Animal Lessons: How They Teach Us to be Human* (2009); Also, *Women as Weapons of War: Iraq, Sex and the Media* (2007); *The Colonization of Psychic Space: A Psychoanalytic Theory of Oppression* (2004); *Noir Anxiety: Race, Sex, and Maternity in Film Noir* (2002); and perhaps her best-known work, *Witnessing: Beyond Recognition* (2001).

Dr. Gaile Pohlhaus, Jr. is associate professor of philosophy and affiliate of women's, gender, and sexuality studies at Miami University in Oxford, Ohio, United States. Her research interests include feminist epistemology, feminist theory, social epistemology, and the work of the later Wittgenstein. She is coeditor of *The Routledge Handbook of Epistemic Injustice* (2017).

Professor Allison Weir is research professor and director of the Doctoral Program in Social and Political Thought in the Institute for Social Justice at the Australian Catholic University in Sydney, Australia. She is a social and political philosopher, focusing on feminist theory and critical theories. She is the author of *Identities and Freedom* (2013); *Sacrificial Logics: Feminist Theory and the Critique of Identity* (1996); and a book in progress, *Decolonizing Freedom*.